Kodachrome by LEON V. KOFOD

Christian Faith in Action

Commemorative Volume

THE FOUNDING OF THE
NATIONAL COUNCIL OF THE
CHURCHES OF CHRIST IN THE
UNITED STATES OF AMERICA

Published by the

Central Department of Publication and Distribution

NATIONAL COUNCIL OF THE CHURCHES OF CHRIST
IN THE UNITED STATES OF AMERICA

Dr. Luther A. Weigle, Chairman of the Planning Committee and Dean Emeritus of Yale University Divinity School.

"The new Council should be regarded not only as a more effective instrument for common tasks but as something still more significant. It is the outward manifestation of a deepening sense of our spiritual unity in our Lord Jesus Christ as the one Head of the Church. It is a forward movement in the direction of a greater Christian unity while at the same time we preserve the Christian liberty which is our precious heritage."

ℭhis ℕation 𝔘nder 𝔊od

IMPORTANT HISTORY *for the world as well as for the Christian Church was made at Cleveland as the year 1950 drew to a close. The event might have proved to be a bit of superficial pageantry trying to be impressive. It might have been merely another dull routine convention. But it was neither of these. The representative gathering that formally constituted the National Council of the Churches of Christ in the United States of America was a notable achievement in cooperative relationship, and marked the beginning of a new era of coordinated activity. The atmosphere which prevailed augurs well for the future. There was drama, color, feeling. There was also sincerity and depth and very real aspiration and high determination. The Spirit of the Living God seemed to be moving in the hearts of the followers of Jesus Christ, whom they sought to exalt as their divine Lord and Saviour.*

This commemorative volume endeavors to set forth briefly the story of this significant occasion, what led up to it, what took place, and what is expected from the new organization, together with the major addresses, minutes, and other factual material. It is impossible within reasonable limits to extend to all individuals and groups adequate recognition for the parts they have played in the total undertaking. Four individuals, however, must be saluted for their outstanding services. Dean Luther A. Weigle through all the nine years provided an overall vision and a consistently stimulating leadership for this project, among all his many major responsibilities. Dr. Hermann N. Morse as Secretary of the Planning Committee ably supplemented Dr. Weigle, and his clear and creative mind kept order in all the stages of

5

development. Dr. Samuel McCrea Cavert, with a wealth of ability and experience, brought to difficult and delicate problems a sound Christian statesmanship that reconciled varying viewpoints and led to common agreements. Dr. Roy G. Ross with his genius for organization, helped greatly in the formulation of the multitudinous by-laws, and in the devising of a financial structure based on sound budgetary principles. A special word of appreciation is due Dr. Earl Frederick Adams, Executive Secretary of the Planning Committee, and his immediate staff, upon whose energy, patience, and true Christian devotion so much depended during the final two years of labor leading to this happy culmination. To these individuals, and to the many others who have been associated with the Council and related bodies in any capacity, these pages are offered as partial tribute, as well as to provide information, and it is hoped, inspiration, for all the wider fellowship of the cooperating churches.

THE EDITORIAL COMMITTEE

Robbins W. Barstow, *Chairman*

Franklin D. Cogswell   Donald C. Bolles
Luther Wesley Smith   Norman E. Tompkins

TABLE OF CONTENTS

LIST OF PHOTOGRAPHS

8

SECTION I

The Event

This Nation Under God

A NEW DAY DAWNS FOR THE CHURCH IN AMERICA

ROBBINS W. BARSTOW

A SENSE of spiritual expectancy was much in evidence, even though the war clouds were hanging low and menacing over the whole world, as representatives of many Protestant and Orthodox churches of the United States of America gathered in Cleveland to translate into reality what had long been a stirring dream. The tensions originating in Korea, and unresolved at Lake Success, were reflected in many of the addresses, and personal concern echoed through conversations in the auditorium corridors and hotel lobbies and as delegates walked to and from the meetings between piles of grimy snow. But the atmosphere of grave apprehension only deepened and sharpened the emphasis of the Convention upon its primary spiritual objectives—the finding and the following of the will of God for these times, in a forward-looking program of genuine commitment, full cooperation, and common action.

The key-note was sounded in a preliminary statement by the Right Reverend Henry Knox Sherrill, later to be elected the first president of the new organization. "In a day of world crisis and disorder, when men's hearts are failing them for fear, it is a cause of hope that the National Council is to be established. It is a proclamation that God, as revealed in Jesus Christ, lives and reigns, that the primary issues of today are spiritual and that no part of the wide range of life is alien to the application of the Gospel. The Council marks a new and great determination that the American way will be increasingly the Christian way, for such is our heritage. The final answer will be given not simply by a new constitution and organization but in the sacrificial lives, in the spiritual power of the clergy and people of the constituting Churches. The Cleveland Convention signifies a great first step. Together the Churches can move forward to the goal—a Christian America in a Christian world."

At the very outset of the crowded sessions, time was given to special prayer for the United Nations, and a message of confidence and hope was dispatched to Secretary General Trygve Lie. The Convention had received a message of greeting from the President of the United States in which he referred to the Council as a step to "enable the American churches to exert a greater influence in the strengthening of the spiritual foundation of our national life at a time when a materialistic philosophy is rampant." The Convention returned to the White House a special message, emphasizing the spiritual implications of the present crisis, and pledging full support of the principles of freedom and justice and peace. Thus were interwoven throughout the four days, the common concern for the military and political issues of the hour, and the weightier problem of our seeming spiritual inadequacies, and the need for thoroughgoing revaluations and reconsecrations.

Greetings to the Council were received from many church bodies in many parts of the world and fraternal delegates brought messages of good-will and cooperation. Dr. Ralph W. Sockman in his opening sermon on Tuesday evening referred to the Council itself as representing "a spirit of unity which long has been growing, and the seed for a harvest which only God can forecast." But he went on to warn against relying on the machinery of organization and to call for the deeper understandings and commitments without which neither Christ nor our fellows could be loved and served. And the closing sermon on Friday evening, by Dr. Eugene C. Blake of Pasadena, California, on the theme "The Cost of Discipleship," reflected the same necessity for moving forward solidly and realistically and sacrificially toward the "long-range victory of the whole family of God."

A WIDELY REPRESENTATIVE GATHERING

The abnormal snowfall which almost paralyzed Ohio and neighboring states for several days kept many from attending, and gave early arrivals an unexpected touch of pioneering as they plodded with their bags through unploughed and taxiless streets. But despite the war and the weather, a very substantial company of nearly four thousand persons filled the front part of the great Public Auditorium for the opening session on Tuesday evening and the attendance remained at about that figure for all the plenary sessions up through Friday evening. The official enrollment figures for the week are as follows:

Voting delegates present 475
Alternate delegates present 193
Consultants 611
Student delegates, staff, etc. 80

Total 1359

Visiting Delegates and
Single Session Registrations 3485
(This last figure includes some duplications but there were at least 4000 individuals present at one or more of the sessions.)

12

There were also many who registered but could not be present:

Voting delegates.................. 62
Alternate delegates............... 52
Consultants...................156
Visiting delegates................866
                                    ———
Total................1136

This makes a grand total of more than 5000 individuals who were directly concerned as actual or intended participants in the Constituting Convention, and is some indication of the widespread interest in this historic event.

A CONGENIAL SETTING

The physical arrangements had been planned with combined imagination and practicality, all the way from hotel accommodations to the press rooms and the exhibit hall, and of course, the huge auditorium itself. There the vast stage was given a dignified and churchly but colorful and dramatic setting. Above the proscenium in great shining letters was the theme phrase of the Convention and the Council—"THIS NATION UNDER GOD." In the background against the dark curtain was erected a fifteen foot cross, and centered below it was a linen draped altar, flanked by tall candlesticks, and bearing as the focus of attention, between great vases of white flowers, an open Bible. This Bible was a copy of the Bruce Rogers World Bible, called the most beautiful Bible ever published in America, and suitably ranked with the Gutenberg, the original folio King James, the Doves and the Oxford Lectern Bibles.

On either side of the stage were tables for officers and speakers, with two lecterns and several microphones conveniently spotted. Behind these tables to provide symbolic background were massed the flags of all nations. Around the edge of the balcony at intervals were banners bearing the seal of the Council and alternating with them, groups of three flags, the Church flag, the flag of the United States of America, and the flag of the United Nations.

On the main floor were long tables for the convenience of the company. Immediately below the stage, white covered tables formed another great cross. This was flanked by red covered tables. In this section were seated the official representatives of the twenty-nine denominations, each delegation identified by its proper name card. Behind a dividing aisle were other tables covered with blue, to accommodate the many consultants, the staffs of the merging agencies, fraternal guests, and the visiting delegates, many of whom also filled the lower front sections of the balcony. There was even a section especially reserved for photographers—although at times they seemed to be everywhere!

The Convention was favored in having unusually fine music, contributed by many choral groups and the Cleveland Symphony Orchestra, as may be noted in the detailed program appearing on later pages. The congregational singing, both at the plenary sessions and at the special Music Hall sessions for visiting delegates, was ably led by Mrs. Rosa Page Welch of Chicago. With a touch of genius she could blend untrained voices to produce sweet harmonies as they followed her in the spirituals of her race. And notable was her leading of that great company as they closed the Thursday evening session by singing "The Lord's Prayer." Vincent Percy was the Convention organist.

Another very important feature of the Convention embraced the remarkably extensive and helpful exhibits, where in ample booths and sections, many departments of church life and work had informative presentations. The literature of the church and of the Christian faith was attractively evident. There was useful display and demonstration of equipment and materials for churches and church organizations ranging from organs and carillons to office equipment and audio-visual apparatus. Moving pictures were shown almost continuously in a specially curtained section of the great exhibit area. Mr. John B. Ketcham served as chairman of the Exhibits Committee, whose work was rendered particularly difficult because of delays caused by the storm.

It seemed that nothing was overlooked or omitted that might contribute to the comfort and convenience of the guests and the expedition of the business in hand. The ushering and distribution of orders of worship and special documents was well cared for by special student delegates. Mention must be made of the helpfulness of local Boy Scouts who, as messengers, gave more than 500 man hours of service. Thanks are also given to the full auditorium staff for their most willing and hearty cooperation in all respects. In short, special appreciation is due to all, particularly the National Committee on Arrangements headed by Dr. J. Quinter Miller, and the Cleveland Committee under the chairmanship of Mr. Herbert J. Lambacher, President of the Cleveland Church Federation and Dr. Raymond L. Spoerri, its Executive Secretary. These were the groups who planned and carried through with such completeness and smoothness the many infinite details which did so much to maintain the high level of inspiration as well as efficiency.

NOTEWORTHY MESSAGES

There were many highlights of inspiration throughout the week in addition to the opening and closing sermons, and the official message from the Council to the Nation prepared by a committee representing all the member denominations and chaired by Dr. Douglas Horton. This document is far more than an announcement of accomplishment. It is also an interpretation and a summons, as indicated in a few lines from its closing paragraphs. In this time that is "big with peril and with opportunity . . . we are conscious of our own short-comings. Knowing that men too often dream in marble and then build with straw, we whose very human lives are not separate from sin and ignorance can make no boast of past or future excellence. But this we have done: by God's grace we have forged an implement for cooperation such as America has never seen before—to serve the spiritual needs of all the people. Our hope is in Jesus Christ. . . . Let nation and nation, race and race, class and class unite their aims in His broad purposes for man."

A particular guest of honor was Dr. W. A. Visser 'tHooft, of Geneva, General Secretary of the World Council of Churches. He not only brought greetings from that great body, similarly instituted at Amsterdam in 1948, but he challenged the delegates to make of the church once again a fighting organization, battling against odds for the spiritual values which, typified in the developments of the ecumenical movement, "represent the essential, and truly significant history of our time."

On account of the Korean crisis, the Secretary of State, the Honorable Dean Acheson, could not leave Washington, but his address to the Convention was heard in the Auditorium by radio, and carried to the nation on all major networks. He spoke most earnestly of the "grave danger for the peace of the world" brought about by the "shocking aggression" of Communist China. He expressed confidence that "the United Nations cannot be intimidated by this new challenge to its authority into shaking off its responsibilities to the people of Korea." He also referred to the "intelligent and responsible participation" of the constituency of the Christian churches in the consideration of these grave issues of international morality.

The same critical situation prevented Sir Oliver S. Franks, British Ambassador to the United States, from being in Cleveland, and his place on the program was filled by Dr. O. Frederick Nolde, Director of the Joint Commission of the Churches on International Affairs, under the World Council of Churches and the International Missionary Council. Dr. Nolde insisted that "so long as there remains even a marginal possibility of averting total global war, we must utilize every means which will not betray conviction or offend conscience." He then proceeded to outline eight practical steps which he said might help to avert war. This address with its astute analysis, impressive logic, specific recommendations, and deeply moving Christian conviction, called forth from the assembly a spontaneous ovation.

At another session, national and world problems and policies were discussed from the Christian point of view of a layman by President Harold E. Stassen, of the University of Pennsylvania. Still another special feature

15

was a "We the People" broadcast, bringing to the Convention and to the country at large, by short-wave radio, messages from His Grace the Archbishop of York, Dr. Boaz Carmargo of Mexico, and Dr. Visser 'tHooft of the World Council of Churches.

SPECIAL MEETINGS FOR VISITING DELEGATES

The afternoon sessions for visiting delegates, held in the Music Hall, were also noteworthy for both depth and wide range of program content. In fact, many of the official delegates had cause to regret that they were obligated to . end the business sessions, and thus had to miss so much that was stirring and significant.

On Wednesday afternoon, Professor Nevin C. Harner of Lancaster spoke on "Religious Education—Foundation of the National Life" setting forth the thesis that a vital religious life is necessary for the safety of our national life. He was followed by President Howard F. Lowry, of the College of Wooster, whose subject was the place of such an institution as he himself serves with great distinction. Speaking on "The Christian College and the National Life" he plead for greater support for the Church Colleges as the centers that out of all proportion to their size are helping create and maintain the kind of faith and the kind of life the nation needs.

At this same rich session Mr. F. William Barrick, President of the United Christian Youth Movement, announced "A Call to United Christian Youth Action" and Mr. John Deschner of the United Student Christian Council spoke on "Christian Youth and the Nation," outlining the eager search of youth for a sense of certainty and stability as they face a difficult future. The church, he said, must do better in making the Christian faith and way vital and convincing and appealing to youth. Dr. Edwin T. Dahlberg, of St. Louis, then spoke on "The Nation's Dependence on the Local Church." A notably successful pastor himself, Dr. Dahlberg emphasized before that great national gathering, the significance of the individual parish, where faith is nurtured and character is formed.

On Thursday afternoon, another great sequence of addresses was heard, beginning with Dr. Hermann N. Morse, former President of the Home Missions Council, who out of his own rich experience spoke on "The Church in the Nation." Dr. Morse stressed the need for "a revitalization of religious faith and a renewed effort to win our people to a convinced and courageous discipleship" for, he continued, "the spiritual character of America may well have a decisive effect upon the future of the whole world." Next came Miss Sarah Chakko, of Isabella Thoburn College in India, on "The Church in the World." With her penetrating Oriental insight she boldly questioned the material smugness of the Occident, and reminded her hearers of the essentially spiritual function of Christianity.

16

The Convention in Session

The Installation of the Vice-Presidents

Dr. Fry receives from President Stamm of the Federal Council the certificate of affiliation

A part of the processional at the Constituting Service

She even hinted that so-called Western civilization may have failed, and that God may be compelled to use other instruments for the ultimate redemption of the world!

Dr. Albert D. Stauffacher of the Congregational Christian Missions Council followed with an address on "Our Missionary Responsibility in the Nation and the World" in which he discussed the dimensions of the task of the church in bringing into its fellowship as responsible participators in its life all the individuals in all the earth! This session concluded with a stirring address by that dynamic personality, the great little apostle of Japan, Dr. Toyohiko Kagawa. His subject was "God and the Nations" and his burning words set forth the need of the nations to repent and be reunited with God so that they may be united with one another in the redemptive Love of Christ.

The third and final special session for the visiting delegates heard two other memorable presentations. The Honorable Francis B. Sayre, Delegate of the United States to the Trusteeship Council of the United Nations, spoke on "The Christian Witness in our National Life." Decrying the tendency to make of Christianity merely a form of idealistic escapism, he called for more realism in the individual witness. "God," he said, "waits upon us for the doing of His work. Are we in dead earnest? Are we prepared to take the hand of Christ and go forward?" Mrs. Douglas Horton, former President of Wellesley College, former Commander of the WAVES, and one of the Vice Presidents of the National Council, brought these discussions to a close as she spoke on the theme "The Witness of the Church in Public Affairs." She alluded to the fact that the church is itself a public institution and a part of all public affairs. It should consider more seriously its fourfold responsibility to be the teacher of the truth, the voice of judgment, the guardian of moral and spiritual values, and the herald of a better day.

INSPIRATION WIDELY SHARED

A noteworthy feature of the Cleveland Convention was the splendid cooperation of the nation's system of mass communication, which carried the march of events and these messages of challenge and hope to the American people, and to millions in other parts of the world. Upon returning home, the delegates found that their families and friends all knew that something tremendous had taken place, and they shared in the uplift of such a great demonstration of harmonious cooperation. The months of preparation and the work of half a hundred skilled craftsmen on the spot resulted in press, radio and television, news photo services, and magazines, both secular and religious, supplementing one another to make the public aware of a historic moment in religious history.

Virtually every newspaper carried daily stories issuing from the press room where a record breaking corps of 90 newsmen and religious journalists toiled over their clip sheets and typewriters. National, regional, and local radio programs, ranging from mention by news commentators to panel interviews, exceeded 100 in number and totaled some 26½ hours of radio time. There were seven television programs, and one or more embraced the nation's network of 80 stations. The Voice of America and the press associations carried the news to Europe and other continents. Movie houses with 80,000,000 weekly customers showed newsreel shots of the Act of Constitution, through the cooperation of the Motion Picture Association. And weekly magazines with a total circulation of millions—LIFE, NEWSWEEK, and TIME, together with the religious press, gave major attention to the Convention.

These public relations services were arranged by the Planning Committee through its publicity subcommittee headed by Dr. Stanley I. Stuber, Chairman, and Donald C. Bolles, Staff Executive. The operatives were recruited from many interdenominational agencies and denominational offices. Protestant Radio Commission executives Everett Parker and Albert Crews were in charge of radio and television. William Clemes was news editor and Walton W. Rankin produced the convention newspaper.

THE THRILL OF PROPER PAGEANTRY

The most colorful moments, perhaps, were the two sessions, Wednesday morning when the Council was formally constituted, and Friday evening when the officers and staff were installed. In particular, the session which included the Act of Constitution provided a major touch of stirring pageantry such as is seldom found in Protestantism. Without any artificiality or false emphasis on externals, there is a natural emotionalism which need not be relegated entirely to military parades, football games, or the special events of any other fraternal or religious organizations. It seemed to be a wholesome experience for the entire company to share in those moments of solemn celebration distinguished by a touch of triumph and also a deep sense of responsibility and devotion, fused together and lifted up by the strains of music, the masses of color, the orderly movement, the sense of enthusiastic community in a sacred cause.

At the hour appointed for the formal initiation of the Council, heralded by a quartet of trumpets, and with the entire assembly swelling the volume of the hymn "God of our Fathers," the dignified and inspiring processional entered the great auditorium. First came a Crucifer and then the blue and white robed male choir from Christ Church, Shaker Heights, followed by two altar boys bearing the American and the Church flags. Next came the designated representatives of the twenty-nine communions, the ones who would officially sign the scroll. Next followed representatives of the merging agencies, and various officials of the Planning Committee and of the Convention itself. Then came a large Bible, suitably inscribed and a gift of the American Bible Society. This was borne by a Seminary student, Grover Wilson of Yale Divinity School, and following him came the red and white robed choir of Cleveland's Schauffler College. Finally came the voting delegates, each preceded by a standard bearer with a white banner designating in maroon the name of the communion, along with the emblem of the National Council. Most of the delegates, as well as the officials, were in full ecclesiastical or academic vestments, making a memorable picture in its color and variety as well as its magnitude and significance.

The climactic moment came when after the chosen signatories of the denominations had placed their names on the official roll, and the representatives of the merging agencies had placed in the hands of the presiding officer, Dr. Franklin C. Fry, their certifications of accord, the Declaration of Constitution was given, and the whole auditorium rang with the inspiring strains of the Doxology.

Equally impressive in its distinctive way was the final installation service when the officers and staff, also in their vestments, entered in colorful processional, and when called to the stage in their respective groups and categories, responded to their charges of responsibility and were consecrated for their new duties.

Such events take place but seldom, and truly stirred the hearts of all who were present as well as those who had a personal part in these meaningful formalities.

THE BUSINESS IN HAND

But this was a working meeting, not merely one of rich ceremonial and high inspiration. There was much business to be transacted in order that the new organization might be properly set upon its mission of varied service. Resolutions of authorization and incorporation had to be passed, officers elected, committees established, and other necessary details cared for. Although most of the business moved expeditiously as presented, it was not just the clicking of a well oiled machine. Every vote represented the result of long consultations by representative groups of planners, laymen and women and parish ministers as well as denominational officials and staff executives. Here had been true democracy in action, with ample consideration of all the many aspects of each separate issue of organization or policy. The final votes, unanimous in almost all cases, were but the registering of approval of the deliberations and decisions of the competent representatives who had studied the various items in the very complex pattern that was being evolved.

The presiding officers at the business sessions, Dr. Franklin C. Fry, Bishop G. Bromley Oxnam, Dr. L. W. Goebel, and Dr. Marvin O. Sansbury chaired the assemblies with consummate wisdom and tact. The matter which evoked the most discussion from the floor was the question of permanent headquarters. Differing viewpoints were presented and the parliamentary procedures at one time became somewhat involved in the almost equal division of sentiment between those who favored an eastern headquarters, close to the largest concentration of denominational home offices, and those who felt strongly that the location should be nearer to the geographical center of the constituency of the Council. The matter was wisely referred to a special committee to be "widely representative both denominationally and geographically" for further study, and recommendation to the General Board.

FAIT ACCOMPLI

Thus was brought into lively being, a comprehensive organization drawing into active partnership in Christian service twenty-nine denominations reporting a total membership of more than thirty-one millions of American church men and church women. The occasion has been characterized by more than a few competent observers as the most significant religious event in the history of this country. Some have even cited it as the most important since the Protestant Reformation. It must be emphasized again and again that it did not constitute a union or merger of the denominations or communions. Their individual creeds, structure, and polity are not affected. But it did signalize a common desire and determination to share their insights and correlate their efforts more fully in the facing together of the difficult tasks and problems of the modern world. It is a spiritual fellowship bent upon very practical purposes through cooperative ministries. This is what the rank and file in the churches have been longing for and now rejoice to see in fact.

The actual form of organization is set forth fully in the Constitution and By-Laws. Final authority rests with the full General Assembly, numbering between four hundred fifty and five hundred, made up of proportionate representatives of the several member denominations, and meeting biennially. A General Board of sixty-five, chosen from the roster of the Assembly, will meet bimonthly to handle routine and interim matters. Beyond this, in brief, provision is made for the carrying forward of all present undertakings and responsibilities of the merging agencies, as well as new activities that may develop in the future, through four principle Divisions and a number of related Departments. The Division of Home Missions will continue the broader operation of the former Home Missions Council. The Division of Foreign Missions succeeds to the responsibilities of the Foreign Missions Conference. The Division of Christian Education carries on the functions of the International Council of Religious Education. The Division of Christian Life and Work will in general be responsible for much of the activity hitherto carried on by the Federal Council of the Churches of Christ in America.

Supplementing these principal Divisions are a score or more of Departments, some of them definitely within the Divisions, others semi-independent, but closely related to one or more of the Divisions. In this way it is planned to conserve and promote all the particular interests and techniques which have in the past proved to be effective ways of accomplishing Christian service and securing the necessary support. Worthy of special mention are two General Departments, one of United Church Women, succeeding the United Council of Church Women, and the other of United Church Men, a new development designed to provide for laymen a larger participation in church affairs, and to enlist and channel their maximum cooperation. This fuller recruitment of lay leadership in the work of the Council and all the churches was also presaged by the significant activities of a pre-convention National Laymen's Committee under the able chairmanship of Mr. J. Howard Pew.

The financial aspects of this great consolidation are inevitably somewhat complicated. But the vast amount of skillful planning that was devoted to this particular problem by the Budget Committee led by Dr. Roy G. Ross has resulted in a carefully integrated set of figures which, for the first year at least, approximates the combined budgets of the merging agencies. The preliminary recommendations which were adopted at Cleveland cover a Basic Budget of $2,604,682; a New Work Budget of $280,953 for approved projects to be undertaken only when funds can be found; and a Supplementary Budget of $1,549,691 providing for a variety of operations but only within limitations imposed by assured designated income. Thus the potential budget comes to a grand total of $4,435,326 representing but a reasonable challenge to the great combined constituency which has pledged itself in partnership to undertake greater service for Christ and his Church. It is not without real significance that at one session of the convention, as concrete evidence of confidence in and enthusiasm for the new Council, those present in the Auditorium, as individuals, gave more than $4,000 in cash and pledged another $21,000 for 1951, to help get the organization away to a good start.

The election of the Right Reverend Henry Knox Sherrill, Presiding Bishop of the Protestant Episcopal Church, to be the first President of the National Council met with hearty approval, and likewise the election of Dr. Samuel McCrea Cavert to be its first General Secretary and Dr. Roy G. Ross, Associate General Secretary. The Executive Secretaries of the four Divisions are to be as follows: For Christian Life and Work, Dr. Roswell P. Barnes, the experienced Associate General Secretary of the Federal Council of Churches for more than a dozen years; for Christian Education, Dr. Roy G. Ross, who will divide his time between the Division

21

and his responsibilities to the General Administration; for Home Missions, Miss Edith E. Lowry and Dr. I. George Nace; for Foreign Missions, Miss Sue Weddell and Dr. Fred Field Goodsell. These persons, and their associates too numerous to mention, have amply demonstrated their fitness for high posts of leadership in times that are so critical for the whole world, as well as pioneering and formative for the new and greater cooperative life of the churches. The Treasurer is a prominent Baptist layman, Mr. Charles E. Wilson, former President of the General Electric Company and now Chairman of the Defense Mobilization Board. The Vice-Presidents, Division Chairman, and other major staff associates are all men and women who have been active and effective in the life of the churches, and have substantial backgrounds of understanding and experience for their fresh allocations of responsibility.

A TOTAL EXPERIENCE TO REMEMBER

The Council drew to a close under the inspiring words of its new President. Bishop Sherrill lifted the thoughts of the assembly to the loftiest interpretation of what had been accomplished and what must lie ahead. He spoke of "promise of a high hope for the future" in "a time of confusion and discord." It was felt that he expressed the feeling of all when he declared that "the churches here represented are determined without compromise to cooperate wholeheartedly in those great fields of endeavor in which we are essentially one." And then placing the responsibility right where it properly rests, with each church, and each individual member, he concluded: "The real problem which confronts the churches is not the strength of the enemy without, but the quality of the spiritual life within. The Council can be strong only as the churches are strong."

All in all, those who were fortunate enough to get to Cleveland, were more than repaid for any inconveniences of transportation or slushy street crossings, whether their chief interests were in the general sense of spiritual fellowship, the inspirational addresses, the details of organization or the study of latest methods and materials for education and youth activities.

And over the entire convention, kept aware of the approaching Christmas season by the store windows and street decorations of the hospitable host city, brooded a spirit of seriousness, of quiet confidence, of earnest determination. As the purpose of the Council is centered in action and rooted in a common fundamental faith, so the ways are now open for closer integration, stronger mutual support, more effective service, for the good of man and the Glory of God.

SECTION II

The Background

The Decade of Preparation

SAMUEL McCREA CAVERT

BEHIND THE official creation of the National Council of the Churches of Christ in the United States of America lies a decade of discussion and negotiation. Indeed, the roots of the new movement, which unites eight national interdenominational agencies, go much further back than a decade. In many informal ways, and sometimes through joint committees, several of the agencies had been dealing with common concerns almost from the beginning of their life. In this brief sketch only a few of the developments along this line can be cited but they are illustrative of a host of others.

As a result of a conference convened by the President of the International Council of Religious Education in 1933 a permanent intercouncil committee was created for the coordination of the field programs of the national interdenominational agencies and the furthering of local and state councils of churches which would serve the churches of the area in the whole range of their common interests. This committee came to be known, a little later, as the Inter-Council Field Department. Representing seven of the eight interdenominational bodies, it had a continuous influence in drawing them closer together around common responsibilities and functions.

The annual meetings of the Association of Council Secretaries were also a very important factor. Beginning in 1939 they brought together the executives of local and state councils of churches with executives of the several national agencies. These conferences, a week in length, fostered an increasing sense of fellowship across organizational lines and developed common emphasis in cooperative programs across the nation.

The Federal Council's Commission on the Study of Christian Unity, beginning in 1937, gave special attention to a strengthening of cooperation as the most promising next step toward a more united church. In 1938 two overtures came to it from the General Assembly of the Presbyterian Church in the U. S. A., proposing "a fuller unity in Christian service" and especially urging the importance of this in missionary work both at home and abroad. This led the Federal Council to address a communication to the other national interdenominational agencies inviting them to engage in a joint study of their relationships to one another.

25

In 1940 a joint committee was formed representing the Federal Council of Churches, the Foreign Missions Conference, the International Council of Religious Education, the Home Missions Council, the Council of Women for Home Missions (soon to be combined with the Home Missions Council), and the National Council of Church Women (which was later succeeded by the United Council of Church Women). The defined purpose was to make a preliminary survey of the possibility of closer relations among themselves. The survey outlined three possible procedures: (1) an increasing practice of cooperation without any change of organizational structure; (2) a federation of the existing agencies, with certain functions carried out in common; (3) the uniting of the existing agencies in a single new body.

The third procedure made the strongest appeal to the imagination but it seemed doubtful whether it could receive the kind of support that would make it practicable. It was decided, however, to explore the whole subject further and then to hold, during the following year, a conference of official representatives of the interdenominational agencies to receive and consider a report. Three additional interdenominational agencies,—the Missionary Education Movement, the Council of Church Boards of Education (later known as the National Protestant Council on Higher Education) and the United Stewardship Council were invited to participate and agreed to do so.

The new committee was convened on April 18, 1941, and elected Dean Luther A. Weigle as its chairman and Dr. Hermann N. Morse as its secretary. During the following months it made an analysis of the form of organization and program of work of all of the eight participating agencies, with special reference to all points of common interest or activity. One of the impressive items in the Committee's report was a listing of no fewer than twenty-four projects or operations carried on by two or more of the agencies together. The report urged the need for some form of closer relation among all of the agencies on the following grounds:

> "as an essential step in creating an integrated cooperative movement for the service of the churches;

> "as a recognition of the essential interrelatedness of the functions and interests of these agencies;

> "as a practical measure for increased efficiency in operation;

> "as a dramatic and convincing demonstration of the Churches' desire for united action in this time of crisis."

The committee reported its judgment:

> "That the lack of an integrated and coordinated strategy of church work is a limiting and weakening factor in many areas of the churches' service influence;

"That existing interdenominational organizations on every level are limited in their effectiveness, first, because they represent only a part of the churches; second, because they represent only a part of the interest of the churches included in their constituency; third, because in different degrees they are all inadequately supported; fourth, because their interrelations are such that each is not sufficiently reinforced by the strength of all;

"That, in spite of all limitations, the cooperative movement as a whole is a striking demonstration of the growing unity of the church and of the great actual and potential value of united effort."

The report was presented to a Conference convened at Atlantic City, New Jersey, December 9-11, 1941. This Conference consisted of twenty-five persons appointed by each agency together with six persons appointed by the Association of Council Secretaries. Four alternative proposals were submitted: (1) An expanded program of inter-council cooperation; (2) creation of a supplementary inter-council service agency; (3) creation of a single corporate agency to succeed *all* the existing councils; (4) creation of a corporate agency to succeed *some* of the existing councils.

After a thorough discussion the Conference voted to approve in principle the third proposal, viz., the creation of an inclusive cooperative organization which will provide for the continued, expanded, and more effective coordination and integration of our respective Councils. For the continued study of the constitution and program of such an organization and its relation to the denominations, to the existing councils and to the state and local councils, it was recommended that a special committee be set up to report a year later. These recommendations were approved by each of the agencies.

The Committee thus constituted was known as the Committee on Closer Relationships of General Interdenominational Agencies. At its initial meeting on March 23-24, 1942, it organized by electing Dr. Weigle as Chairman and Dr. Morse as Secretary.

Just a year after the Atlantic City Conference it proved possible to hold a joint session of the agencies in Cleveland, Ohio, to receive the report of the Committee, including a preliminary draft of a constitution for a new united Council in which all of the existing interdenominational agencies might merge their activities. At this session, held on December 8, 1942, it was proposed that each of the agencies be now invited to appoint six representatives to serve on a Committee on Further Procedure, which should submit the constitution, after revision, both to the interdenominational agencies and the constituent denominations and boards for official action. All of the agencies agreed to appoint representatives. Three of them, however, were not yet prepared to commit themselves to participation in the

27

proposed united body. Five of the agencies voted to approve the report and its proposals, in substance, and to proceed upon the assumption that they would unite their forces in a new Council.

At the joint meeting in Cleveland it was contemplated that the Churches of Canada might be included with those of the United States in a "North American Council of the Churches of Christ." After further consultation, however, with representatives of the Canadian Churches, it was deemed better for them to form their own Council of Churches to deal with Canadian affairs, with the understanding that their boards would share in the work of various divisions of the Council in the U.S.A.

On April 25, 1944, the revised draft of the Constitution for a united body to be known as the "National Council of the Churches of Christ in the United States of America" was presented to the interdenominational agencies. They, in turn, submitted it to their constituent bodies for their official decision.

By January 1950 all eight of the interdenominational agencies had taken official action approving the formation of the National Council. In the case of two of them a period of nearly six years of study and discussion had been required before a common judgment could be crystallized. It was agreed on all sides, however, that there should be no pressure for action by any narrow majorities. It was felt to be far wiser to take as much time as might be necessary for thorough understanding, general agreement and the development of a common mind.

During the same years, 1944-1950, the denominations, both in their plenary bodies and in the denominational boards, were taking action, one by one, on the proposal. By October, 1950, the last of the denominations which were considering the plan had taken favorable action. Among the American denominations which had been members of the Federal Council there was now unanimous approval, and in addition, four other denominations had voted to become members. Meanwhile, it had become so clear that in all probability the new body could be formed, that the name of the Committee on Further Procedure was changed, early in 1948, to the Planning Committee for the National Council of the Churches of Christ in the United States of America. An office for the Planning Committee was opened in May, 1948, with Dr. Earl F. Adams as the executive secretary.

As the plans for the National Council matured other interdenominational agencies became interested. In addition to the original eight, Church World Service, the Protestant Radio Commission, the Protestant Film Commission and the Interseminary Committee voted to give up their separate identities and to join in the National Council.

In the course of the six years during which the constitution for the National Council was being discussed many minor revisions were proposed,

28

but none which affected the essential genius of the movement. After careful study of scores of suggested revisions, the Planning Committee submitted a series of proposed amendments, and a complete series of By-Laws, both for the Council and its various divisions and departments, three months prior to the scheduled date for the Constituting Convention. During the last two years of its life the Planning Committee or its executive committee met almost every month for sessions usually lasting two days. The amount of time and thought and devotion, given to forming the best possible instrument for united action can hardly be exaggerated.

On the evening of November 28, 1950, a great service of worship was held in the Cleveland Auditorium at which the keynote was thanksgiving for the unity in Christ which makes the National Council possible. On the next morning, November 29, 1950, the official act of constituting the National Council took place. The "decade of preparation" had come to an end. The National Council was now a reality.

Those Who Helped—

Planning Committee for the

NATIONAL COUNCIL OF THE CHURCHES OF CHRIST IN THE UNITED STATES OF AMERICA

April 1948—December 1950

Luther A. Weigle, *Chairman;* Hermann N. Morse, *Secretary*

Earl F. Adams, *Executive Secretary*

FEDERAL COUNCIL OF THE CHURCHES OF CHRIST IN AMERICA: Roswell P. Barnes (*Alternate*), Samuel McCrea Cavert, Frederick L. Fagley, Francis S. Harmon, Ivan Lee Holt, W. H. Jernagin, Ralph Waldo Lloyd, J. Quinter Miller (*Alternate*).

FOREIGN MISSIONS CONFERENCE OF NORTH AMERICA: Raymond A. Dudley, Wynn C. Fairfield, Luther A. Gotwald, Byron S. Lamson, Elizabeth M. Lee, Glenn P. Reed, Sue Weddell (*Alternate*).

HOME MISSIONS COUNCIL OF NORTH AMERICA: G. Pitt Beers, Mrs. J. D. Bragg, Helen M. Brickman, Truman B. Douglass, Edith E. Lowry (*Alternate*), I. George Nace.

INTERNATIONAL COUNCIL OF RELIGIOUS EDUCATION: Arlo Ayres Brown, David Forsyth, Ivan M. Gould, Gerald E. Knoff (*Alternate*), Philip C. Landers (*Alternate*), Paul C. Payne, Roy G. Ross, John Q. Schisler.

MISSIONARY EDUCATION MOVEMENT OF THE UNITED STATES AND CANADA: Franklin D. Cogswell, Gilbert Q. LeSourd, S. Franklin Mack, Mrs. Arthur M. Sherman, Dorothy A. Stevens, Horace W. Williams.

NATIONAL PROTESTANT COUNCIL ON HIGHER EDUCATION: E. Fay Campbell, Robert W. Gibson, Bernard J. Mulder, Harry T. Stock, Gould Wickey.

UNITED COUNCIL OF CHURCH WOMEN: Mrs. Jesse M. Bader, Mabel Head, Mrs. Abram LeGrand (*Alternate*), Mrs. W. Murdoch MacLeod, Mrs. William H. Medlicott, Mrs. Harper Sibley, Mrs. William Sale Terrell.

UNITED STEWARDSHIP COUNCIL: Paul H. Conrad, H. D. Davies, Arthur H. Limouze, Harry S. Myers, John T. Peters, Stanley I. Stuber.

In addition to those who are now members of the Planning Committee, the following persons have served as members of this Committee during the period June 1, 1948 to December 1, 1950: *Bette S. Brittingham, *Ralph E. Diffendorfer, Mrs. R. A. Doane, J. L. Dodds, Mabel E. Emerson, Donald Faulkner, Darby C. Fulton, Fred Field Goodsell, Corliss P. Hargraves, *William E. Lampe, Eric M. North, Edward A. Odell, *William Barrow Pugh, Pearl Rosser, Mrs. O. A. Sardeson, Henry F. Schuh, Amy O. Welcher, Jesse R. Wilson.

*Deceased

The Member Denominations

THE AFRICAN METHODIST EPISCOPAL CHURCH

This body was formed in Philadelphia in April, 1816, by delegates representing the several scattered groups of former members of the Methodist Episcopal Church, mostly from Philadelphia and Baltimore. This church has always felt keenly its responsibility towards the educational and cultural advancement of its constituency, having established in 1856 Wilberforce University, the first Negro college in America and later some fifteen others in the United States, the West Indies, South and West Africa. Although established in the North, this body quickly spread throughout the South and West after the Civil War, and today its membership is well distributed throughout the United States, the West Indies, South and West Africa.

Principal offices in various cities.

THE AFRICAN METHODIST EPISCOPAL ZION CHURCH

This church was organized as an autonomous body out of the John Street Church, New York, in 1796. The first congregation was Mother Zion, the oldest Negro Church in the United States. Similar churches in Long Island and on the Hudson, in 1820, joined with Mother Zion in its first yearly conference. During its development it has emphasized education and its major schools are Livingstone College, North Carolina; Clinton College, South Carolina; Walters Southland College, Arkansas; Lomax Hannon College, Alabama; Dinwiddie Institute, Virginia; and Johnson High School, Mississippi. This church has conferences in Liberia, Nigeria, and two Gold Coast conferences, with a total membership of 70,000. The principal school is at Mt. Coffee in Liberia. It also has foreign conferences in the Virgin Islands and South America.

Principal offices: Washington, D. C., Charlotte, N. C., and other cities.

THE AMERICAN BAPTIST CONVENTION (FORMERLY NORTHERN)

This Convention of Baptist churches was formed in 1907. Preceding this, several great missionary agencies served the churches of the North and

31

were governed by delegates from the churches. The oldest of these was the American Baptist Foreign Mission Society which was organized in 1814. Then followed the American Baptist Publication Society, the American Baptist Home Mission Society, the Woman's American Baptist Foreign Mission Society, and the Woman's American Baptist Home Mission Society. After the Convention was organized the Board of Education and the Ministers and Missionaries Benefit Board were added to the roster of the Societies. Today, there are also 34 State Conventions and 16 City Societies affiliated with the Convention. The basic purpose of the Convention and its Societies is to channel the activity and support of the churches into a great missionary program.

In changing its name to the American Baptist Convention, uniformity in the names of the antecedent organizations was brought about. The resolution reads in part,—" . . . affirming as we adopt the name American Baptist Convention that we hold the name in trust for all Christians of like faith and mind who desire to bear witness to the historic Baptist convictions in a framework of cooperative Protestantism."

Headquarters: 152 Madison Avenue, New York 16, N. Y.

The Augustana Evangelical Luthern Church

This body, whose constituency originally was of Swedish extraction, is a member of the American Lutheran Conference and the Lutheran World Federation, and is also a participating body in the National Lutheran Council. The date of its organization is 1860.

Headquarters: 2445 Park Avenue, Minneapolis 4, Minnesota.

The Church of the Brethren

Founded at Schwarzenau, Germany, under the leadership of Alexander Mack in 1708, this group emigrated to Germantown, Pennsylvania, in 1719, whence its constituency has expanded widely. The Brethren accept the entire New Testament as their only creed, believe in the expression of religion through the good life, uphold the principles of non-violence. They have six colleges and one seminary, have mission work in India, China, Africa and South Africa, and engage in Brethren Service work on every continent.

Headquarters: 22 S. State Street, Elgin, Illinois.

The Colored Methodist Episcopal Church

This independent denomination was organized in Jackson, Tennessee, in 1870, by Bishop Robert Paine, Senior Bishop of the Methodist Episcopal Church, South, upon the authorization of the General Conference of that church.

Headquarters: Jackson, Tennessee.

Platform group at the Constituting Service

THE CONGREGATIONAL CHRISTIAN CHURCHES OF THE UNITED STATES OF AMERICA

Congregational Churches originated in the settlement of the Pilgrims at Plymouth, Massachusetts, in 1620. Accepting the Pilgrim pattern of church government, the Puritans became the largest element numerically in the origin of Congregational Churches. Congregationalism spread with the New England migrations westward. The denominational name became "Congregational Christian" in 1931 with the merger of Congregational and Christian Churches. The latter were an 18th century fruit of the Wesleyan movement. Emphasis is on local church autonomy, democratic church government, pioneer missionary projects, education, intellectual breadth of religious outlook.

Headquarters: 287 Fourth Avenue, New York 10, New York.

THE DANISH EVANGELICAL LUTHERAN CHURCH OF AMERICA

This body was organized in 1872 by missionaries from Denmark under the name Kirkelig Missionsforening. It now has a constituency in 20 states and Canada. It supports Grand View College and Seminary, in Iowa; a Children's Home, two Old People's Homes, Eben-Ezer Mercy Institute, and also 7 home mission congregations and the Santal Mission in India.

Headquarters: Des Moines 16, Iowa.

THE INTERNATIONAL CONVENTION OF DISCIPLES OF CHRIST

The Disciples of Christ movement began in the first decade of the 19th century as a fellowship of Christians calling for the reunion of the divided church. It was agreed by the founders, Thomas and Alexander Campbell and Barton W. Stone, and has been held by their followers, that divisions within the Church of Christ are sinful and that reunion can best be brought about by seeking to restore New Testament practices, names, and fellowship. The Disciples of Christ practice immersion, observe the Lord's Supper weekly, are congregational in government, and state that their only creed is Christ.

Headquarters: 516 K of P Building, Indianapolis 4, Indiana.

THE EVANGELICAL AND REFORMED CHURCH

This body was formed on June 26, 1934, by a union of the Evangelical Synod of North America and the Reformed Church in the United States, at Cleveland, Ohio. In accordance with the liberty of conscience inherent in the Gospel, it permits freedom in the interpretation of the doctrinal standards which is inherited from the Protestant Reformation. However, it adheres to the conviction that the final norm is the Word of God. Its polity

33

is determined equally by traditional and functional considerations. In its relation to other churches it is thoroughly ecumenical.

Principal offices in St. Louis, Philadelphia, and other cities.

The Evangelical United Brethren Church

This body had its origin in Johnstown, Pennsylvania, in 1946, in the consummation of organic union between the Evangelical Church and the Church of the United Brethren in Christ. Both these former communions had their beginning in Pennsylvania in the evangelistic movement of the early 19th century. Jacob Albright was the founder of the Evangelical Church, and Dr. Philip Otterbein was the founder of the United Brethren Church in 1800. In doctrine this Church is Arminian and in government Methodistic.

Headquarters: U. B. Building, Dayton, Ohio.

The Evangelical Unity of the Czech Moravian Brethren in North America

In 1903, congregations established by Czech and Moravian immigrants to Texas, beginning about 1855, formed the Evangelical Union, and later with the accession of other groups of Brethren, became the Evangelical Unity of the Czech Moravian Brethren. This is a bilingual church with presbyterian-congregational polity, being a continuing body of the ancient Unity of the Brethren dating from 1457, the result of the Czech Protestant Reformation fired by Jan Hus and driven underground after 1620. The Unity continues to demand a fully-trained ministry, practices infant baptism and confirmation, serves leavened and unleavened bread at the Lord's Supper with wine.

No established headquarters.

The Five Years Meeting of Friends

Formed in 1902, the Five Years Meeting of Friends now consists of ten Yearly Meetings of Friends in the United States and one in each of the following countries: Canada, Cuba, East Africa and Jamaica. The Five Years Meeting contains both pastoral and non-pastoral Meetings, though chiefly pastoral, whereas several Yearly Meetings outside the Five Years Meeting are non-pastoral. The fourteen Yearly Meetings of the Five Years Meeting hold their quinquennial sessions at headquarters: Richmond, Indiana.

The Religious Society of Friends of Philadelphia and Vicinity

This organization dates back to 1681. The Yearly Meeting, which constitutes the highest governing body of the Society of Friends, is made up of a number of Quarterly Meetings and they in turn of a number of Monthly Meetings. A Book of Faith and Practice, which is revised from time to time, regulates the procedure of meetings. Philadelphia Friends now maintain committees actively engaged in work for Friends' schools, for better interracial relations, for peace, for religious education, for helping the Indians, for temperance, for missions, for advising on family relationships, for church unity, and for an improved social order. In common with other Quaker groups they support the American Friends Service Committee, and the Friends Committee on National Legislation, and through the World Committee for Consultation, they cooperate with Friends throughout the world.

Headquarters: 304 Arch Street, Philadelphia, Pennsylvania.

THE METHODIST CHURCH

The present organization of the Methodist Church began in May, 1939, with the unification of three branches of Methodism—the Methodist Episcopal Church, the Methodist Episcopal Church, South, and the Methodist Protestant Church. All three of the uniting churches were in unbroken historical connection with Methodism in America. The 1948 General Conference adopted a resolution stating that the Christmas Conference of 1784 is regarded as the date on which the organized Methodist Church was founded as an ecclesiastical organization. At this Conference, held in Lovely Lane Chapel, Baltimore, Francis Asbury and Thomas Coke were elected superintendents and a program of expansion was outlined. The Methodist Movement began in England with John and Charles Wesley, leaders of an evangelical revival, and was carried to America in 1760 by Methodist emigrants from Ireland.

Headquarters: 150 Fifth Avenue, New York 11, New York.

THE MORAVIAN CHURCH IN AMERICA

Founded in 1457 at Lititz, Bohemia, by followers of John Hus, the name of this pre-Reformation body was "Unitas Fratrum" or "The Unity of the Brethren." Crushed in the Counter Reformation except for scattered remnants, this Protestant Church was revived at Herrnhut, Germany, in 1722, and spread soon to the Netherlands, the British Isles, Switzerland, Sweden and Denmark. The first permanent settlement in the United States was at Bethlehem, Pennsylvania, in 1740. Moravian Missions were begun in 1732 and now include thirteen separate fields. The Moravian Church is broadly evangelical, liturgical, with an episcopacy as a spiritual office, and in form of government "conferential."

Headquarters: Bethlehem, Pennsylvania.

The National Baptist Convention, U.S.A., Incorporated

The older and parent convention of Negro Baptists, this body is to be distinguished from the National Baptist Convention of America, usually referred to as the "unincorporated body."

Principal offices in various cities.

The National Baptist Convention of America

In 1895 three Baptist bodies merged to form the National Baptist Convention. It is an organization of independent Baptist churches, State Conventions, District and County Associations, in forty states. It has member churches in the Republic of Panama, the Canal Zone, Cuba, the Bahama Islands, Haiti, Jamaica, Canada, Hawaii, and Australia as well as in Liberia, the Gold Coast, and the West Coast of Africa.

Principal offices in Nashville and other cities.

The Presbyterian Church in the United States

This is the branch of the Presbyterian Church which from 1861 to 1865 was known as the Presbyterian Church in the Confederate States of America. Its constituency is located largely in the South, and it is often called the "Southern" Presbyterian Church.

Principal Offices: Atlanta, Nashville, Richmond, and other cities.

The Presbyterian Church in the United States of America

This body, distinguished by its representative form of government and its Calvinistic theology, appeared among the earliest colonists of America. Its first church was established about 1640 and its first presbytery in 1706. The rapid increase in churches and ministers led to the organization, in 1716, of the first Synod. The National General Assembly was organized in 1788. The church now has 265 Presbyteries and 40 Synods under one General Assembly.

Headquarters: 156 Fifth Avenue, New York 10, New York.

The Protestant Episcopal Church

This Church is the American unit of the Anglican Communion. It entered the colonies with the earliest settlers (Jamestown, Virginia, 1607), as the Church of England. Becoming autonomous in 1789, it adopted its name, a constitution, and an American Book of Common Prayer. It comprises 74 Dioceses, 18 American Missionary Districts and 9 overseas Missionary Districts, each with its own Bishop. Its supreme legislative body, the General Convention, comprising the House of Bishops and House of Deputies, meets triennially.

Headquarters: 281 Fourth Avenue, New York 10, New York.

THE REFORMED CHURCH IN AMERICA

The first Reformed Church in this country was organized in New Amsterdam, now New York City, in 1628 by the Classis of Amsterdam, the Netherlands. A hundred years ago colonists of the Reformed faith, driven from Holland by poverty and religious persecution, settled in Holland, Michigan, and Pella, Iowa, from which centers the church spread into surrounding territory. Recently there has been promising growth in California. The denomination promotes a vigorous evangelistic, missionary, and educational program. It is a member of "The Alliance of Reformed Churches throughout the World holding the Presbyterian System."

Headquarters: 156 Fifth Avenue, New York 10, N. Y.

THE ROMANIAN ORTHODOX CHURCH

The Eastern Orthodox Christians of Romanian descent in the United States, Canada, and South America, with their Churches and Parishes, are organized into one diocese, under the name of "The Romanian Orthodox Episcopate of America." This body, while in spiritual and canonical unity with all Orthodox Churches, is an autonomous organization, with the right to legislate and administer all its religious, cultural and financial affairs, and to elect, in special session of its highest legislative body, the Church Congress, the spiritual head of the Episcopate who is the Bishop.

President's office: 6201 Detroit Avenue, Cleveland 2, Ohio.

THE RUSSIAN ORTHODOX GREEK CATHOLIC CHURCH OF NORTH AMERICA

The Russian Orthodox Church established a mission at Kodiak, Aleutian Islands, in 1793 and extended its activities to Alaska. In 1872 the headquarters was transferred to San Francisco. To serve immigrant groups, Orthodox centers were established in Minneapolis, Chicago, Cleveland, Pittsburgh, Wilkes Barre and New York, and in 1905 the mission was elevated to the rank of an Archdiocese and located in New York. After the Russian revolution, the American Church declared itself autonomous and has continued to function as a self-governing group without administrative affiliation with the Mother Church in Russia. The Metropolitanate includes parishes in the United States, Canada, Alaska, and the Aleutian Islands. It maintains seminaries in New York and South Canaan, Pennsylvania. Also, in South Canaan, it maintains an Orphanage and a Monastery.

Headquarters: 59 East 2nd Street, New York 3, New York.

37

The Seventh Day Baptist General Conference

Seventh Day Baptists in America stem from the organization of a church at Newport, Rhode Island, in 1671. Represented now in 21 states, the General Conference participates in cooperative, ecumenical movements. Belief in the efficacy of observing the Biblical Sabbath (the seventh day of the week) as established by Mosaic law, adhered to by the prophets, and observed by Christ and the early Church, gives Seventh Day Baptists reason for maintaining a denomination distinguished from other Baptist churches. Missions are maintained in China, Jamaica, British Guiana, New Zealand, Africa, Germany and Holland.

Headquarters: Plainfield, New Jersey.

The Syrian Antiochian Orthodox Archdiocese of New York and North America

This body is a division of the Orthodox Church which is under the jurisdiction of the Patriarch of Antioch. It is a member of the Federation of Orthodox Greek Catholic Churches in America.

Headquarters: 239 85th Street, Brooklyn 9, New York.

The Ukrainian Orthodox Church of America

This body was organized in America in 1928 when the first convention was held. Its first Bishop was consecrated in 1932, and in 1937 the Most Reverend Archbishop Bohdan was consecrated by the order of the Ecumenical Patriarchate of Constantinople.

Headquarters: 1410 Vyse Avenue, New York 59, New York.

The United Lutheran Church in America

This body dates back to the Ministerium of Pennsylvania, organized in 1748, and beyond that to early colonial days. First Lutheran services were conducted in North America in 1619. It represents the union in 1918 of the General Synod, the General Council, and the United Synod of the South. It includes 33 district synods in the United States and Canada, uses 17 languages, has "affiliated churches" in India, China, Japan, Liberia, Argentina, British Guiana, 14 colleges, 9 theological seminaries and 2 deaconess motherhouses.

Headquarters: 231 Madison Avenue, New York 16, New York.

The United Presbyterian Church of North America

This body, formed in 1858 by the union of the Associate and Associate Reformed Presbyterian churches in this country, goes back to two churches in Scotland which broke away from the Church of Scotland but continued their Presbyterian government and doctrine. The denomination has been noted for its interest in missionary work, and daughter churches in four mission lands report a communicant membership of more than one third that of the American church. Small, and conservative in policy, the church has continued through the years interest in and support of inter-denominational agencies thus expressing its motto, "The Truth of God: Forbearance in Love."

Headquarters: 209 Ninth Street, Pittsburgh, Pennsylvania

SUMMARY LISTING OF DENOMINATIONS WITH COMMUNICANT MEMBERSHIP

African Methodist Episcopal Church...........................1,066,301
The African Methodist Episcopal Zion Church................ 520,175
The American Baptist Convention...........................1,583,360
The Augustana Evangelical Lutheran Church................ 312,326
The Church of the Brethren................................ 185,088
The Colored Methodist Episcopal Church.................... 381,000
The Congregational Christian Churches of the United States
   of America...1,184,661
Danish Evangelical Lutheran Church of America............. 13,931
The International Convention of Disciples of Christ..........1,738,605
The Evangelical and Reformed Church...................... 714,583
The Evangelical United Brethren Church.................... 711,537
The Evangelical Unity of the Czech Moravian Brethren in
   North America.. 5,136
The Five Years Meeting of Friends......................... 69,595
The Religious Society of Friends of Philadelphia and Vicinity... 5,215
The Methodist Church......................................8,792,569
The Moravian Church in America........................... 33,787
The National Baptist Convention, U.S.A., Inc...............4,385,206
The National Baptist Convention of America................2,594,521
The Presbyterian Church in the United States............... 653,594
The Presbyterian Church in the United States of America......2,401,849
The Protestant Episcopal Church...........................1,671,366
The Reformed Church in America........................... 179,085
The Romanian Orthodox Church............................ 50,000
The Russian Orthodox Greek Catholic Church of N.A......... 300,000
The Seventh Day Baptist General Conference............... 6,462
The Syrian Antiochian Orthodox Archdiocese of New York and
   North America.. 20,300
The Ukrainian Orthodox Church of America................. 39,500
The United Lutheran Church in America....................1,349,663
The United Presbyterian Church of North America........... 213,810

(Note: These were the pre-convention figures. The latest statistics will appear shortly in the new Year Book of American Churches.)

The Eight Merging Agencies

THE FEDERAL COUNCIL OF THE CHURCHES OF CHRIST IN AMERICA

A federation of twenty-three Protestant and four Eastern Orthodox national church bodies for cooperative work in evangelism, in social service and in advancing Christian influence in all human relations. Founded in 1908 it has pioneered in the field of interdenominational fellowship and integrated activity. Related to it for more effective Christian witness and service in their respective areas have been more than eight hundred city, county and state councils of churches. In matters of international goodwill, economic justice, race relations, family life, mental health and other challenging problems, the Federal Council through conferences and consultations, pronouncements and study pamphlets, and direct staff action has sought to quicken the conscience, and stir to appropriate action the entire Christian community.

THE FOREIGN MISSIONS CONFERENCE OF NORTH AMERICA

An agency enabling fifty-four denominations with ninety-nine mission boards in the United States and Canada to plan and carry through with common understandings and cooperation, their programs of evangelism, education, medical and industrial services in Africa, Asia, the Near East and Latin America. It has also had consultative relationship with the churches of Europe for devising most effective procedures for interchurch aid and worldwide evangelism. Organized in 1893 it brought into the life of the boards at home the same type of cooperation that had developed in many areas of service overseas. Increasingly of late years it has been recognizing the strength and effectiveness of the so-called "younger churches" and seeking to develop a relationship of full partnership in the spreading of the Christian Gospel.

THE HOME MISSIONS COUNCIL OF NORTH AMERICA

The organization through which thirty-seven home mission boards of twenty-two major denominations exchange information, coordinate their

41

plans and cooperate in their various ministries to special groups or in particular situations. Founded in 1908, the functional cooperation of this body has been focused upon such problems as the physical, economic, and spiritual needs of the share croppers, migrant workers, American Indians and other underprivileged or minority peoples. It has also concerned itself for the provision of church facilities and competent ministries in new housing developments, public works projects, and wherever the strong witness of the cooperative fellowship of the Christian Church is needed.

THE INTERNATIONAL COUNCIL OF RELIGIOUS EDUCATION

A means for closer cooperation among forty denominational boards of Christian Education and thirty-three state councils of churches in such services as leadership education, educational evangelism, and Sunday, week-day and vacation school programs for children, young people, and adults. The outgrowth of the first National Sunday School Convention in 1832, the International Council and its several intermediate forms of organization have given primary attention and strong leadership to the training of youth. The provision of materials, and the setting up of summer conferences have been of service to all denominations, and the emphasis on family life and service activities has been widely influential. It has sponsored the editing and production of the Revised Standard Version of the Bible.

THE MISSIONARY EDUCATION MOVEMENT OF THE UNITED STATES AND CANADA

Since 1902, the agency representing the boards of home and foreign missions, departments of missionary education and boards of Christian Education of twenty-nine denominations. Its significant activities have prevented duplication and wastage and been the means of providing the best possible materials in books, pamphlets, maps and other teaching aids regarding the mission of the churches at home and abroad. It has directed many leadership training programs and has kept abreast of latest developments in audio-visual techniques. It has helped greatly in informing and inspiring both clergy and laity and especially youth regarding the widest implications and responsibilities of the Christian Gospel.

THE NATIONAL PROTESTANT COUNCIL ON HIGHER EDUCATION

A body concerned for maintaining and increasing the influence of religion on our college and university campuses. Organized in 1911 it has represented the Protestant church-related colleges, and also the voluntary work carried on by boards of Christian Education in both publicly and privately supported colleges and universities. It has maintained religious centers on many campuses, cooperated in providing the best possible college preaching, and in setting up conferences, seminars, and study courses for students. It has sought constantly to present in the most positive, creative and compelling ways the claims of the Gospel of Jesus Christ for the young men and women who will be the leaders of tomorrow.

THE UNITED STEWARDSHIP COUNCIL

A voluntary association of twenty-eight communions in the United States and Canada for the promotion of full Christian stewardship of time, abilities and material possessions. Since 1920 this agency has been seeking to supplement the activities of all the churches in enlisting systematic financial support and personal dedication to service. Through research and publication, through the supplying of materials, and through the encouragement of such techniques as the United Church Canvass, the entire subject of personal stewardship has been set before the membership of the cooperating churches with increasing effectiveness and important practical results.

THE UNITED COUNCIL OF CHURCH WOMEN

The wide fellowship of Protestant Christian women, with sixteen hundred state and local councils and twelve thousand World Day of Prayer groups. The youngest of these eight agencies, organized in 1940, it has had a tremendous influence in stimulating interest and activity in all the many primary issues and undertakings of the Christian churches. The World Day of Prayer, in Lent; World Community Day, in November; and May Fellowship Day, are but three particular points of emphasis within a comprehensive program of support for regular church activities and also for special projects.

IN ADDITION *to the original eight agencies which established the Planning Committee, the following agencies subsequently decided to merge their efforts in the program of the National Council of Churches:*

CHURCH WORLD SERVICE

The agency through which 23 Protestant and Orthodox denominations, acting cooperatively, carry out their program of relief, reconstruction and interchurch aid. Created in 1946, it has conducted this work chiefly in Asia, Europe and the Middle East. Thousands of local churches have cooperated in its Contributed Supplies program. Over $50,000,000 in cash and material aid has been contributed through this agency. It has also had the responsibility for the selection, clearance and reception of Displaced Persons. Twenty-seven thousand DP's have been brought over to date, with about thirty to thirty-five thousand scheduled for 1951. It has also kept the churches informed concerning the various areas and varieties of need.

Interseminary Movement

A body consisting of students and faculty members of theological seminaries dedicated to the ecumenical movement within the Christian Church. One hundred twenty-five theological schools participate in this Movement and eight student regional councils are responsible for all student activities. It seeks to encourage students to explore together the issues of Church unity and the Christian mission in the modern world through a series of regional and smaller area conferences, groups meetings on the seminary campuses, visits by special speakers, and a Triennial National Conference of Theological students. It was sponsored in 1949 by the Federal Council of Churches and the National Student Committee of the YMCA, but its beginnings date from 1880.

Protestant Film Commission

An agency composed of nineteen major Protestant denominations and twelve interdenominational organizations to aid in advancing all phases of Christian life and work through the medium of film. Organized in 1947, to be the churches' cooperative agency, it has produced films for non-theatrical release and maintained liaison with the motion picture industry. Its functions are to give strategic leadership in the development of an adequate film program for the churches, to produce professional-quality films for church use. It maintains offices in New York and Hollywood.

Protestant Radio Commission

An agency composed of sixteen major Protestant denominations and nine interdenominational organizations whose most important function is to help make religion a vital force in American life through broadcasting, thereby supporting and strengthening the work of the local church. To carry out this work, last year, it produced 601 network programs. The overall total of broadcasts produced including network, local, television, transcriptions and four television films was 2,128. It sponsors institutes and workshops for the purpose of training local Protestant leaders in the use of radio and television techniques. Since its founding in 1949, it has also acted as a service agency for its members as well as for Protestantism as a whole.

44

SECTION III

The Culmination

The Convention Program*

Organist, MR. VINCENT PERCY
Song Leader, MRS. ROSA PAGE WELCH

Tuesday Evening, November 28, at 8:00
IN THE AUDITORIUM

OPENING SERVICE OF WORSHIP AND THANKSGIVING

ORGAN PRELUDE

1. A Song for the Golden Harvest   *Harvey Gaul*
(Based on an ancient Succoth theme)

2. A Song of Gratitude   *Rossetter Cole*

INTROIT

HYMN OF PRAISE

Praise to the Lord, the Almighty, the King of creation!
O my soul, praise him, for he is thy health and salvation!
All ye who hear, now to his temple draw near;
Join me in glad adoration!

Praise to the Lord, who o'er all things so wondrously reigneth,
Shieldeth thee under his wings, yea, so gently sustaineth!
Hast thou not seen how thy desires e'er have been
Granted in what he ordaineth?

Praise to the Lord, who doth prosper thy work and defend thee;
Surely his goodness and mercy here daily attend thee.
Ponder anew what the Almighty can do,
If with his love he befriend thee.

Tune: Lobe den Herren   *Joachim Neander, 1680*
Translated by Catherine Winkworth, 1863

ACT OF ADORATION

Right Reverend Frank W. Sterrett
Bishop of the Protestant Episcopal Church

Leader: All praise and glory and thanksgiving, more than we can utter, be unto thee, O God; worthy art thou, O God, to receive the glory and the honor and power, for thou didst create all things, and because of thy will they are and were created.

People: Blessing and honor and glory for ever and ever.

Leader: Blessed be thou, O God, who hast given us the light of the knowledge of thy glory in the face of Jesus Christ.

People: Blessing and honor and glory for ever and ever.

Leader: Blessed be thou, O God, who hast made known to us that it is thy will to gather in one all things in Christ, both which are in heaven and which are on earth.

People: Blessing and honor and glory for ever and ever.

* This is the program as prepared. Variations from it are indicated by asterisks.

Leader: Blessed be thou, the God and Father of our Lord Jesus Christ, who in him hast blessed us with all spiritual blessings in heavenly places, and in him hast chosen us that we should be holy and without blame before thee in love.

People: Blessing and honor and glory for ever and ever.

Leader: Blessed be thou, the Father of glory, the Father from whom all fatherhood in heaven and earth is named, who for the great love wherewith thou lovest us, has quickened us together with Christ, that thou mayest show forth the exceeding richness of thy grace.

People: Blessing and honor and glory for ever and ever.

Leader: Now unto him that sitteth on the throne, unto him who maketh all things new, unto him who hath made us meet to be partakers of the inheritance of the saints in light, unto him who hath delivered us from the powers of darkness and translated us into the kingdom of the Son of his love, unto him who is able to do exceeding abundantly above all that we ask or think,

People: Be blessing and honor and glory for ever and ever.

PRAYER

Bishop John A. Gregg
Senior Bishop of the African Methodist Episcopal Church

Almighty God, our Father, who through the years hast dealt bountifully with thy people, we praise thee for thy present loving kindness which has brought us to this hour of fellowship and great promise. We humbly confess that too often our vision has been dull, our Christian relationships limited, and our faith insufficient. Forgive us where we have failed thee; and now send us forth in this new fellowship to large undertakings and worthy achievement. Set thyself constantly before us as the one God and the Father of us all; and grant that fidelity to our one Lord may create a singleness of purpose which shall empower our Christian witness. In his name we pray who is thy Son and our Redeemer. Amen.

ANTHEM

Praise We the Lord   *Freylinghausen*

PRAYERS OF THANKSGIVING

Reverend P. O. Bersell
President of the Augustana Evangelical Lutheran Church

Leader and People: Almighty God, Father of all mercies, we, thine unworthy servants, do give thee most humble and hearty thanks for all thy goodness and loving kindness to us, and to all men. We bless thee for our creation, preservation, and all the blessings of this life; but above all, for thine inestimable love in the redemption of the world by our Lord Jesus Christ; for the means of grace, and for the hope of glory. And, we beseech thee, give us that due sense of all thy mercies, that our hearts may be unfeignedly thankful; and that we show forth thy praise, not only with our lips, but in our lives, by giving up ourselves to thy service, and by walking before thee in holiness and righteousness all our days; through Jesus Christ our Lord, to whom, with thee and the Holy Ghost, be all honor and glory, world without end. Amen.

Leader: For thy beloved Church to which thou hast entrusted the precious Gospel of our Lord and Savior, Jesus Christ,

People: We thank thee, O God.

Leader: For the varied insights and convictions of the branches of thy Church which have enriched her total life,

People: We thank thee, O God.

Leader: For the growing spirit of understanding and comradeship which is bringing deeper unity,

People: We thank thee, O God.

Leader: For the abundance of accomplishment which has marked the years of the organizations uniting in the National Council of Churches,

People: We thank thee, O God.

Leader: For the large possibilities which lie ahead for increasing Christian usefulness and power,

People: We thank thee, O God.

Leader: For the stimulus of troubled times to thought and faith and action,

People: We thank thee, O God.

Leader: For the promise of the Holy Spirit to guide and sustain us in the years ahead,

People: We thank thee, O God.

Leader: Accept, O God, our thanksgivings for thy many mercies; and constantly put a song of praise on our lips. Through Jesus Christ our Lord, Amen.

THE DOXOLOGY

The Choir

SCRIPTURE READING

President Benjamin R. Lacy, Jr.
Moderator of General Assembly of the Presbyterian Church in the U.S.

Ephesians 4: 1-7, 11-16

ANTHEM

God Is a Spirit

Kopyloff

SERMON

Reverend Ralph W. Sockman
Christ Church (Methodist), New York, N. Y.

ANTHEM

Blessed Be Thou, Lord God of Israel

Greenfield

PRAYERS OF INTERCESSION

Reverend Henry A. Vruwink
President of the General Synod of the Reformed Church in America

Almighty God, who art the God and Father of our Lord Jesus Christ, and our God; we pray in gratitude for the leading of thy Spirit which is bringing us together in the new bonds of the National Council of Churches.

Grant that each step of the way may be forward.

Grant that obstacles small and great may be overcome.

Grant that mutual confidence and trust may always prevail.

Grant that this fellowship may enrich our walk with thee.

Grant that it may deepen our usefulness to human kind.

Grant that we all may be glad that we have come together.

In the Name of Jesus Christ, our Lord. Amen.

O God, our Father, we pray for thy Church which is set today amid the perplexities of a changing order, and face to face with new tasks. Baptize her afresh in the life-giving spirit of Jesus. Bestow upon her a greater responsiveness to duty, a swifter

49

compassion with suffering, and an utter loyalty to the will of God. Put upon her lips the ancient gospel of her Lord. Help her to proclaim boldly the coming of the Kingdom of God. Fill her with the prophet's scorn of tyranny, and with a Christ-like tenderness for the heavy-laden and downtrodden. Bid her cease from seeking her own life, lest she lose it. Make her valiant to give up her life to humanity; that like her crucified Master, she may mount by the path of the Cross to a higher glory; through Jesus Christ our Lord. Amen.

O holy and merciful God, who hast given thy Son to be the Savior of the world; hear our prayer as we thy servants meet for this memorable assembly. As day after day we seek thy face, may we grow together in unity of faith, and find peace and concord in obedience to thy will. Grant us so to take counsel together that no fear or prejudice may hinder us; but in quietness and confidence may we be wise to know and strong to fulfil thy whole counsel. Grant us, we beseech thee, such a measure of thy grace that in this privileged companionship the causes of thy kingdom may be furthered and thy people blessed; through Jesus Christ our Lord and Savior. Amen.

HYMN

All hail the power of Jesus' name!
Let angels prostrate fall;
Bring forth the royal diadem,
And crown him, crown him, crown him,
Crown him Lord of all!

Crown him, ye martyrs of your God
Who from his altar call;
Extol the stem of Jesse's rod,
And crown him, crown him, crown him,
Crown him Lord of all!

Sinners, whose love can ne'er forget
The wormwood and the gall,
Go spread your trophies at his feet,
And crown him, crown him, crown him,
Crown him Lord of all!

Let every kindred, every tribe,
On this terrestrial ball,
To him all majesty ascribe,
And crown him, crown him, crown him,
Crown him Lord of all!

O that with yonder sacred throng
We at his feet may fall,
Join in the everlasting song,
And crown him, crown him, crown him,
Crown him Lord of all!

Tune: Miles' Lane   *Edward Perronet, 1785*

BENEDICTION

Reverend Ralph W. Sockman

ORGAN POSTLUDE

Festal Postlude   *Oscar Schminke*

EPWORTH-EUCLID METHODIST CHURCH CHOIR
Cleveland

ELWIN HASKIN, Conductor

ALVINA WOCHELE, Organist

VINCENT H. PERCY, Cleveland, Organist

MRS. J. POWELL JONES, Cleveland, Alternate Organist

MRS. ROSA PAGE WELCH, Chicago, Song Leader

The Act of adoration is from "The Kingdom, the Power, and the Glory," Oxford University Press. Used by permission.

The second prayer of intercession is from "Communion With God." The final prayer of intercession is based on a prayer in "A Book of Public Worship."

Wednesday Morning, November 29, at 9:30
IN THE AUDITORIUM

PLENARY BUSINESS SESSION OF THE GENERAL ASSEMBLY

Presiding, DR. FRANKLIN CLARK FRY, President of the United Lutheran
Church in America

PROCESSION OF OFFICIAL DELEGATES

SCRIPTURE AND PRAYER FOR DIVINE GUIDANCE
led by Bishop John S. Stamm, Evangelical United Brethren Church

REPORT OF THE PLANNING COMMITTEE
Dr. Hermann N. Morse, Secretary and Acting Chairman

Reading of the Call for this Meeting
The Constitution as submitted to the Denominations and Interdenominational
Agencies
Statements of Approval by Denominations and Interdenominational Agencies
Announcement of Chairmen and Recording Secretaries for this Meeting
Statement concerning Registration and Credentials
Reading of Charter and Action thereunder

ACT OF CONSTITUTING THE COUNCIL

HYMN

The Church's One Foundation   *(The people standing)*

The Church's one foundation
Is Jesus Christ her Lord,
She is His new creation
By water and the word:
From heaven He came and sought her
To be His holy bride;
With His own blood He bought her,
And for her life He died.

Elect from every nation,
Yet one o'er all the earth,
Her charter of salvation,
One Lord, one faith, one birth;
One holy Name she blesses,
Partakes one holy food,
And to one hope she presses,
With every grace endued.

'Mid toil and tribulation,
And tumult of her war,
She waits the consummation
Of peace forever more;
Till, with the vision glorious
Her longing eyes are blest,
And the great Church victorious
Shall be the Church at rest.

(The people will be seated)

ROLL CALL OF THE DELEGATIONS

*(The chairman will call upon the denominational delegations
to rise. He will ask them the following question:)*

(Chairman)

Do you, as members of the constituting denominations declare that your communions have approved the formation of the National Council of the Churches
of Christ in the United States of America and have agreed to become members
thereof, and do now authorize your representatives to sign the official documents?

(Delegations will reply in unison:)

We Do.

(The denominational delegations will be seated.)

51

(Chairman)

Consent having been given, and authority having been invested in twenty-nine denominational representatives to affix their names to the official documents, I now call upon each of these duly appointed representatives to come forward and sign such official documents as the name of his communion is announced:

African Methodist Episcopal Church
African Methodist Episcopal Zion Church
American Baptist Convention
Augustana Lutheran Church
Church of the Brethren
Colored Methodist Episcopal Church
Congregational Christian Churches
Danish Evangelical Lutheran Church
Disciples of Christ
Evangelical and Reformed Church
Evangelical United Brethren
Evangelical Unity of Czech Moravian Brethren in N. A.
Friends—Five Years Meeting
Friends of Philadelphia and Vicinity
Methodist Church

Moravian Church (No. and So. Provinces)
National Baptist Convention, USA, Inc.
National Baptist Convention of America
Presbyterian Church in the U. S.
Presbyterian Church in the U.S.A.
Protestant Episcopal Church
Reformed Church in America
Roumanian Orthodox Episcopate of America
Russian Orthodox Church in America
Seventh Day Baptists General Conference
Syrian Antiochian Orthodox Church
Ukrainian Orthodox Church of America
United Lutheran Church in America
United Presbyterian Church of N. A.

(After all have signed the chairman will declare:)

THE ACT OF CONSTITUTION

(Chairman)

The representatives of the communions have now certified their official intent to be members of and to share in the work of the National Council. Therefore, as your presiding officer, I declare that the National Council of the Churches of Christ in the United States of America is officially constituted. Let us now dedicate it to the glory of God and to the service of mankind.

*(The people will stand and join in the following expression
of dedication in unison with the chairman:)*

THE DEDICATION

(All in Unison)

And now, as a fellowship of Christian churches,
In the communion of the saints,
In love and goodwill toward all,
In gratitude for the labors and sacrifices of our fathers,
In loving remembrance of those who have finished their course,
Acknowledging that without us their work is not made perfect,
We invoke the blessing of God upon this National Council of the Churches of
    Christ in the United States of America
And dedicate the Council to His glory and the service of mankind,
In the name of the Father,
    and of the Son
    and of the Holy Spirit.
    Amen.

*(Organ fades in during the dedication and proceeds to a
crescendo leading into the Doxology.)*

DOXOLOGY

Praise God, from whom all blessings flow:
Praise Him, all creatures here below;
Praise Him above, ye heavenly host;
Praise Father, Son, and Holy Ghost.

(The people will be seated.)

DEMONSTRATION OF NEW ALLEGIANCE BY
THE INTERDENOMINATIONAL AGENCIES

*(The chairman will turn to the representatives of the following
interdenominational Agencies and will ask them to stand)*

The Federal Council of the Churches of Christ in America
The Foreign Missions Conference of North America
The Home Missions Council of North America
The International Council of Religious Education
The Missionary Education Movement of the U.S. and Canada
The National Protestant Council on Higher Education
The United Council of Church Women
The United Stewardship Council

(Chairman)

As a demonstration of your relationship within this National Council of Churches,
which has come into being as the result of your joint initiative, and as a visible
sign of the delegation of your responsibilities to the newly formed organization,
will you place in my hands official documents indicating that you are now united
in this new organization of cooperative Christianity?

(Agencies)

We Will.

*(Each representative of the Agencies hands the chairman a document which
he places beside the other official documents. The representatives will be seated.)*

(Chairman)

State, County and City Councils of Churches cooperate with the National Council
in communities throughout the nation. As an expression of their new relationship
to this Council, and of their devotion to the cause of Christian cooperation, their
representative will lead all of us in the prayer of consecration to new tasks.

*(All representatives of State, County and City Councils of
Churches will stand during the prayer.)*

PRAYER

led by the representative of the Councils of Churches.

Almighty God, our heavenly Father, whose wisdom is everlasting and whose
patience is very great, we thank Thee for this hour of achievement and promise.
As we bow before Thee, kindle our imagination that we may more clearly envision
the possibilities which Thou hast set before us, and more quickly think Thy thoughts
after Thee. Inspire us with a holy zeal for the new tasks, and a renewed determination to press on in our high calling in Christ Jesus.

As we go forward together, grant us, most loving Father, new insights into Thy
truth and a deeper understanding of one another. Lead us into new experiences of
unity, new paths of service and new areas of victory. Mindful of Thy steadfastness
beyond our weakness and Thy resources beyond our frailties, may we be strengthened to fulfill Thy expectations for us.

Accept from us, our gracious Father, unworthy though we be, all that we have
and are as an offering upon Thine altar.

This we ask in the name of Jesus Christ our living Saviour and Lord, to whom
with Thee and the Holy Ghost we give adoring praise, world without end. Amen.

(Chairman)

This Act of Constituting the National Council of the Churches of Christ in the
United States of America will close with the singing of the hymn "God of Grace
and God of Glory."

(The people will rise)

HYMN

God of Grace and God of Glory

God of grace and God of glory,
On Thy people pour Thy power;
Crown Thine ancient church's story;
Bring her bud to glorious flower.
Grant us wisdom,
Grant us courage,
For the facing of this hour.

Cure Thy children's warring madness,
Bend our pride to Thy control;
Shame our wanton, selfish gladness,
Rich in things and poor in soul,
Grant us wisdom,
Grant us courage,
Lest we miss Thy kingdom's goal.

Lo! the hosts of evil round us
Scorn Thy Christ, assail His ways!
From the fears that long have bound us
Free our hearts to faith and praise:
Grant us wisdom,
Grant us courage,
For the living of these days.

Set our feet on lofty places:
Gird our lives that they may be
Armored with all Christ-like graces
In the fight to set men free.
Grant us wisdom,
Grant us courage,
That we fail not man nor Thee!

RECESSIONAL

REPORT OF PLANNING COMMITTEE (continued):

Adoption of Agenda and Program

Appointment of Convention Committees: On Registration and Credentials, on Business, on Message, on Resolutions of Courtesy

Recommended Amendments to Constitution

Recommended General By-Laws

Statement concerning Organization of Divisions, General Departments, Joint Departments, Central Departments, Commissions

Legal Matters

Action on Constitution, with Amendments Recommended by Planning Committee

ASSIGNMENT OF MEMBERS OF THE COUNCIL TO SERVE AS MEMBERS OF FOUR DIVISIONS

WELCOME FROM THE CLEVELAND CHURCH FEDERATION
Mr. Herbert J. Lambacher, President

ORDER OF THE DAY AT 12:00 O'CLOCK
*Worship, led by Mrs. Howard G. Colwell,
former President of American Baptist Convention*

Wednesday Afternoon, November 29, at 2:15

A. INITIAL MEETINGS OF THE FOUR DIVISIONS FOR PURPOSES OF ORGANIZATION:

Division of Home Missions: Assembly Room, Hotel Hollenden
Division of Foreign Missions: Ball Room, Hotel Hollenden
Division of Christian Education: Ball Room, Hotel Cleveland
Division of Christian Life and Work: Euclid Ball Room, Hotel Statler

B. FOR VISITING DELEGATES—GENERAL SESSION IN MUSIC HALL

Theme: "This Nation Under God—Our Educational Task"
Presiding: Mrs. Clifford Heinz

54

DEVOTIONAL SERVICE

led by Dr. Desmond W. Bittinger, President of McPherson College

Addresses: "Religious Education—Foundation of the National Life," by *Prof. Nevin C. Harner, Theological Seminary of the Evangelical and Reformed Church, Lancaster, Penna.*

"The Christian College and the National Life," by *President Howard F. Lowry, College of Wooster*

Music by the a cappella choir of Oberlin University

Prof. Robert Fountain, Director

An Announcement: "The Call to United Christian Youth Action," by *F. William Barrick, President of the United Christian Youth Movement*

"Christian Youth and the Nation," by *John Deschner, Executive Secretary, United Student Christian Council*

"The Nation's Dependence on the Local Church," by *Dr. Edwin T. Dahlberg, Minister of Delmar Baptist Church, St. Louis, Mo.*

Wednesday Evening, November 29, at 8:00

IN THE AUDITORIUM

THEME: "THIS NATION UNDER GOD"

Presiding: DR. EDWARD H. PRUDEN, President of the American Baptist Convention

ORGAN PRELUDE

1. Fantasy on a Welsh Tune (Tony-y-Botel)   *T. Tertius Noble*
2. Choral Prelude on the Tune "Walsal"   *T. Tertius Noble*

ORCHESTRA

Overture "Freischnetz"   *Weber*

HYMN

O God beneath thy guiding hand
Our exiled fathers crossed the sea;
And when they trod the wintry strand,
With prayer and psalm they worshiped thee.

Thou heard'st, well pleased, the song, the prayer:
Thy blessing came; and still its power
Shall onward, thro' all ages, bear
The memory of that holy hour.

Tune: Duke Street

Laws, freedom, truth, and faith in God
Came with those exiles o'er the waves;
And where their pilgrim feet have trod,
The God they trusted guards their graves.

And here thy Name, O God of Love,
Their children's children shall adore,
Till these eternal hills remove,
And spring adorns the earth no more.

Leonard Bacon, 1833

INVOCATION

Reverend J. McDowell Richards
President, Columbia Theological Seminary

Almighty God, King of Kings and Lord of Lords, in the memory of thy great goodness to other generations, we bow in humility and gratitude. Our fathers put their trust in thee and were not confounded. Thou didst overcome their enemies and didst put strength and hope and courage in their hearts. They wrought diligently and triumphed gloriously, sustained by thy sufficient grace.

We thank thee that those into whose labors and life we have entered kindled here the fire of freedom and built a nation on justice and mercy. We praise thee that they put their trust in thee, fashioning their common life in faith in Jesus Christ.

Give to us of this present generation the wisdom and the will to hold fast to our heritage of devotion to Jesus Christ, our Lord. Amen.

ORCHESTRA

1. Symphony No. 1—Allegro con brio   *Brahms*
2. Choral Prelude—"A Mighty Fortress Is Our God"   *Bach-Damrosch*

SCRIPTURE READING

Exodus 20:1-17

Matthew 22:34-40

PRAYER FOR THE NATION

Bishop Ivan Lee Holt
The Methodist Church

Almighty God, who hast given us this good land for our heritage; we humbly beseech thee that we may always prove ourselves a people mindful of thy favor and glad to do thy will. Bless our land with honorable industry, sound learning and pure manners. Save us from violence, discord, and confusion; from pride and arrogancy, and from every evil way. Defend our liberties, and fashion into one united people the multitudes brought hither out of many kindreds and tongues. Endue with the spirit of wisdom those to whom in thy Name we entrust the authority of government, that there may be justice and peace at home, and that through obedience to thy law we may show forth thy praise among the nations of the earth. In the time of prosperity, fill our hearts with thankfulness, and in the day of trouble, suffer not our trust in thee to fail; all of which we ask through Jesus Christ our Lord. Amen.

Book of Common Prayer

SOPRANO SOLO

Gretchen Garnett

Aria—"Hear Ye, Israel" (Elijah)   *Mendelssohn*

*MESSAGE FROM THE PRESIDENT OF THE UNITED STATES

THE ADDRESS†

The Honorable Dean Acheson   *Secretary of State*

HYMN

God of our fathers, whose almighty hand
Leads forth in beauty all the starry band
Of shining worlds in splendor through the skies,
Our grateful songs before thy throne arise.

Thy love divine hath led us in the past;
In this free land by thee our lot is cast;
Be thou our Ruler, Guardian, Guide, and Stay;
Thy word our law, thy paths our chosen way.

From war's alarms, from deadly pestilence,
Be thy strong arm our ever sure defense;
Thy true religion in our hearts increase,
Thy bounteous goodness nourish us in peace.

Refresh thy people on their toilsome way,
Lead us from night to never ending day;
Fill all our lives with love and grace divine,
And glory, laud, and praise be ever thine.

Tune: National Hymn   *Daniel C. Roberts, 1876*

PRAYER AND BENEDICTION

* A special message from President Truman was here read to the Convention.

† Being unable to leave Washington by reason of the pressure of his responsibilities, Secretary Acheson delivered his address to the Convention by radio.

ORCHESTRA

Dream Pantomime—"Hansel and Gretel"   *Humperdinck*

ORGAN POSTLUDE

Festival Toccata   *Percy Fletcher*

CLEVELAND PHILHARMONIC ORCHESTRA

F. KARL GROSSMAN, Conductor

VINCENT H. PERCY, Cleveland, Organist

MRS. J. POWELL JONES, Cleveland, Alternate Organist

MRS. ROSA PAGE WELCH, Chicago, Song Leader

Thursday Morning, November 30, at 9:30

IN THE AUDITORIUM

PLENARY BUSINESS SESSION OF THE GENERAL ASSEMBLY

Presiding: BISHOP G. BROMLEY OXNAM, Secretary of the Council of Bishops
of the Methodist Church

PERIOD OF MEDITATION AND PRAYER

led by Errol F. Elliott, Clerk of Five Years Meeting of Friends

REPORT OF BUSINESS COMMITTEE

ACTION ON CONSTITUTION, WITH AMENDMENTS RECOMMENDED BY
PLANNING COMMITTEE (continued)

a. Vote by Assembly

b. Vote by Delegations

Proposed Amendments (if any) to General By-Laws

Address: "Our Christian Responsibility for Men and Women in the Armed Forces"
by *Chaplain Stanton W. Salisbury (U.S.N.), Chairman of the Board of Chaplains*

General Recommendations of Planning Committee for Consideration by National
Council

Reports from Meetings of the Divisions

Report of General Board on Assignment of Members to General Departments,
Joint Departments, Central Departments

Other Business of the Council

ORDER OF THE DAY AT 12:00

Worship, led by Dr. Benjamin E. Mays, President of Morehouse College

Thursday Afternoon, November 30, at 2:15

A. INITIAL MEETINGS OF GENERAL DEPARTMENTS AND JOINT DE-
PARTMENTS FOR PURPOSES OF ORGANIZATION:

General Department of United Church Women, Euclid Ball Room, Hotel Statler

General Department of United Church Men, Assembly Room, Hotel Hollenden

Commission on Christian Higher Education, Rose Room, Hotel Cleveland

Joint Commission on Missionary Education, Red Room, Hotel Cleveland

57

Joint Department of Stewardship, Room 345, Hotel Statler
Joint Department of Evangelism, Ohio Room, Hotel Statler
Joint Department of Religious Liberty, Parlor C, Hotel Statler
Joint Department of Christian Family Life, Private Dining Room 34-36, Hotel Cleveland
Joint Department of American Communities Overseas, Parlor B, Hotel Hollenden

At 4:00 o'clock

Commission on General Christian Education, Ball Room, Hotel Cleveland
Joint Department of Christian Life Service, Empire Room, Hotel Cleveland

Note: For the General Department of United Church Men, since this is a new structure without a previous organizational base, the program will include a discussion as to its purpose and program. MR. J. HOWARD PEW, former President of the Sun Oil Company, will speak as chairman of the group of lay sponsors for the Constituting Convention. MR. CHILTON G. BENNETT, Director of the Board of Lay Activities of the Methodist Church, will speak from the viewpoint of the denominational lay organizations. DR. LUTHER WESLEY SMITH, Executive Secretary of the Baptist Board of Education and Publication, will represent the Planning Committee for the National Council.

B. FOR VISITING DELEGATES—GENERAL SESSION IN MUSIC HALL
Theme: "This Nation Under God—Our Missionary Responsibility"

Presiding: Mrs. Hugh D. Taylor

DEVOTIONAL SERVICE

led by Dr. J. Lowrie Anderson, Moderator of the General Assembly of the United Presbyterian Church of North America

ADDRESS: "The Church in the Nation," by Dr. Hermann N. Morse, General Secretary, Board of National Missions of the Presbyterian Church in the U.S.A.

ADDRESS: "The Church in the World," by Dr. Sarah Chakko, President of Isabella Thoburn College, India; Secretary of the World Council's Commission on the Life and Work of Women in the Church

MUSIC by Baldwin-Wallace College Choir   *Cecil W. Munk, Conductor*

ADDRESS: "Our Missionary Responsibility in the Nation and the World," by Dr. A. D. Stauffacher, Executive Secretary of the Missions Council of the Congregational Christian Churches

ADDRESS: "God and the Nations," by Toyohiko Kagawa, of Japan

Thursday Evening, November 30, at 7:45

IN THE AUDITORIUM

THEME: "THE NATIONS UNDER GOD"

Presiding: DR. HUGH I. EVANS, Moderator of the General Assembly of the Presbyterian Church in the U.S.A.

ORGAN PRELUDE
    1. In Te, Domine, Speravi   *H. Leroy Baumgartner*
    2. The Cathedral at Night   *Frederick Marriott*

HYMN

God of the spirit wind, whose rushing quickened
Men of all nations to faith in thy word,
Waken our courage as theirs was awakened,
Breathe out thy spirit on us, O Lord.

Touch us with cloven flame, forging forgiveness,
Fusing our hearts into fervent accord,
Steeing our wills with the faith that thou livest,
Temper our souls with thy fire, O Lord.

God of the glowing love, making men brothers,
Burn out the dross of belief in the sword;
Fashion one vision more golden than others;
Peace ever more through thy mercy, Lord.

Then shall thy spirit sons, purged of all hatred,
Spurning all envy and martial reward,
Stand a world—nation, united and sacred,
Pledging eternal good-will, O Lord. Amen.

Tune: Russian Hymn

Earl Marlatt, 1944

PRAYER FOR THE NATIONS

Mrs. James D. Wyker
Chairman of the Ohio Council of United Church Women

O God, who sitting on the throne sayest, Behold, I make all things new: fulfil now thy word in the world. Instil a new sense of the brotherhood of the nations. Form them into one great family. Give them new ambitions, not to destroy rivals, but to strengthen brethren; not to dominate the world, but to serve it. Let every nation with new devotion bring its peculiar gifts, its glory and its honor, and lay them at thy feet to be the adornments of thy Kingdom; that we may see fulfilled the saying that is written, "The kingdom of this world is become the Kingdom of our Lord and of his Christ."

Edwin James Palmer

ANTHEM

"Onward, Ye Peoples"

Sibelius
(Arranged by Lefevre)

ADDRESS

Dr. W. A. Visser 't Hooft
General Secretary of the World Council of Churches

"The Church in the World of Nations"

HYMN

Glorious things of thee are spoken,
Zion, city of our God;
He whose word can not be broken
Formed thee for his own abode:
On the Rock of Ages founded,
What can shake thy sure repose?
With salvation's walls surrounded,
Thou mayst smile at all thy foes.

See, the streams of living waters,
Springing from eternal Love,
Well supply thy sons and daughters,
And all fear of want remove:
Who can faint, while such a river
Ever flows their thirst to assuage;
Grace, which, like the Lord the Giver,
Never fails from age to age?

Round each habitation hovering,
See the cloud and fire appear
For a glory and a covering.
Showing that the Lord is near:
Thus deriving from their banner
Light by night and shade by day,
Safe they feed upon the manna
Which he gives them when they pray. Amen.

Tune: Austrian Hymn

John Newton, 1779

ADDRESS*

Sir Oliver S. Franks
Ambassador from Great Britain to the United States of America

* Sir Oliver Franks being unable to leave Washington, his place on the program was taken by Dr. O. Frederick Nolde, Director of the Commission of the Church on International Affairs, who addressed the Convention on "A Christian View of the International Crisis."

59

ANTHEMS

1. "Thanks Be to Thee" *Handel*
   (Arranged by Lefevre)
2. "Let Their Celestial Concerts All Unite," from "Samson" *Handel*
3. "Good News from Heaven" *Bach's Christmas Oratorio*

MESSAGES BROADCAST FROM CHRISTIAN LEADERS ABROAD†

Britain
Germany
Korea
Mexico

HYMN

Jesus shall reign where'er the sun
Does his successive journeys run;
His Kingdom stretch from shore to shore,
Till moons shall wax and wane no more.
For him shall endless prayer be made,
And praises throng to crown his head;
His name, like sweet perfume, shall rise
With every morning sacrifice.

People and realms of every tongue
Dwell on his love with sweetest song;
And infant voices shall proclaim
Their early blessings on his Name.
Blessings abound where'er he reigns;
The prisoner leaps to lose his chains,
The weary find eternal rest,
And all the sons of want are blest.

Let every creature rise and bring
Peculiar honors to our King;
Angels descend with songs again,
And earth repeat the loud Amen! Amen.

Tune: Duke Street

Isaac Watts, 1719

PRAYER AND BENEDICTION

Bishop D. Ward Nichols
African Methodist Episcopal Church

ORGAN POSTLUDE

Festival Postlude on Veni Creator Spiritus *Camil Van Hulse*

THE SINGERS' CLUB, Cleveland
ROBERT M. STOFER, Conductor
LAWRENCE STEVENS, Accompanist
VINCENT H. PERCY, Cleveland, Organist
MRS. J. POWELL JONES, Cleveland, Alternate Organist
MRS. ROSA PAGE WELCH, Chicago, Song Leader

Friday Morning, December 1, at 9:30
IN THE AUDITORIUM

PLENARY BUSINESS SESSION OF THE GENERAL ASSEMBLY
Presiding: Dr. L. W. Goebel, President of Evangelical and Reformed Church

SCRIPTURE AND PRAYER

Bishop J. Arthur Hamlett, Colored Methodist Episcopal Church

† The actual transcriptions heard on this special "We the People" broadcast were by His Grace the Archbishop of York, Dr. Boaz Carmargo of Mexico, and Dr. Visser 't Hooft of the World Council of Churches.

ACTION ON CONSTITUTION AND BY-LAWS (concluded)

REPORTS OF COMMITTEES
On Registration and Credentials, on Resolutions of Courtesy, on Business

REPORT OF GENERAL BOARD ON NOMINATIONS

ELECTION OF OFFICERS
ADDRESS: "The Laity and the National Council" by Dr. Harold E. Stassen, President of the University of Pennsylvania
*

REPORTS from General Departments and Joint Departments and Joint Commissions
STATEMENT concerning Budget for 1951
OTHER BUSINESS OF THE COUNCIL

ORDER OF THE DAY AT 12:00
Worship, with Devotional Address by *Very Rev. Georges Florovsky, Dean of St. Vladimir's Orthodox Seminary*

Friday Afternoon, December 1, 2:00-3:30

A. INITIAL MEETINGS OF CENTRAL DEPARTMENTS:
Broadcasting and Films, Empire Room, Hotel Cleveland
Church World Service, Room 345, Hotel Statler
Ecumenical Relations, Cypress Room, Hotel Hollenden
Field Administration, Parlor C, Hotel Statler
Finance, Assembly A, Hotel Cleveland
Public Relations, Room 341, Hotel Statler
Publication and Distribution, Assembly B, Hotel Cleveland
Research and Survey, Parlor E, Hotel Statler
Church Building and Architecture, Parlor H, Hotel Hollenden
Washington Office, Parlor B, Hotel Hollenden

ALSO INITIAL MEETINGS OF DEPARTMENTS WITHIN DIVISIONS:
Department of Young People's Work, Private Dining Room 34-36, Hotel Cleveland
Department of the Church and Economic Life, Parlor G, Hotel Statler
Department of International Justice and Goodwill, Euclid Ball Room, Hotel Statler
Department of Race Relations, Ohio Room, Hotel Statler
Department of Pastoral Services, Parlor F, Hotel Statler
Department of Social Welfare, Parlor H, Hotel Statler
Department of Worship and the Fine Arts, Parlor A, Hotel Hollenden
Department of Town and Country, Assembly Room, Hotel Hollenden
Department of the Urban Church, Parlor C, Hotel Hollenden

B. FOR VISITING DELEGATES—GENERAL SESSION IN MUSIC HALL
Theme: "This Nation Under God—Our Christian Witness"
Presiding: DR. CHARLES J. TURCK, President of Macalester College

*Mr. J. Howard Pew, Chairman of the Layman's Advisory Committee was here introduced by Dr. Stassen and addressed the Convention.

61

DEVOTIONAL SERVICE

Rev. Elmo F. Randolph, Minister of Seventh Day Baptist Church, Milton, Wis.

ADDRESSES: "The Christian's Witness in Our National Life" by Honorable Francis B. Sayre, Delegate of the U.S. to the Trusteeship Council of the United Nations "The Witness of the Church in Public Affairs" by Mrs. Douglas Horton, former president of Wellesley College and former Commander of the WAVES

Friday Afternoon, December 1, 4:00-5:00
IN THE AUDITORIUM

PLENARY BUSINESS SESSION OF THE GENERAL ASSEMBLY

Presiding: DR. MARVIN O. SANSBURY, President of the International Convention of Disciples of Christ

PRAYER

Dr. Alfred Jensen, President of the Danish Evangelical Lutheran Church of America

Presentation of Program for Simultaneous Emphases in the Denominations
Recommendations to National Council:
   a. From Planning Committee
   b. From Denominational Boards and Agencies
Business of the Council
Presentation of Message to the Churches

Friday Evening, December 1, at 8:00
IN THE AUDITORIUM

SERVICE OF INSTALLATION AND CONSECRATION

ORGAN PRELUDE

1. Caprice Heroique   *Joseph Bonnet*
2. Interludio and Fugue from Sonata in E Minor   *James H. Rogers*

PROCESSIONAL HYMN

We praise thee, O God, our Redeemer, Creator,
In grateful devotion our tribute we bring.
We lay it before thee, we kneel and adore thee,
We bless thy holy name, glad raises we sing'

We worship thee, God of our fathers, we bless thee:
Through life's storm and tempest our Guide hast thou been.
When perils o'er-take us, escape thou wilt make us,
And with thy help, O Lord, life's battles we win.

With voices united our praises we offer,
And gladly our songs of true worship we raise.
Thy strong arm will guide us, our God is beside us,
To thee, our great Redeemer, forever be praise.
Tune: Netherlands Folk Song   *Julia Cady Cory*

ACT OF ADORATION

Reverend Vere Y. Loper
Moderator of the General Council of Congregational Christian Churches

Leader: Glory to thee, O Christ, our ascended and ever present Lord, through whom we have access to the Father.

People: Glory to thee who lovest us and hast loosed us from our sins.

62

Leader: Glory to thee who hast reconciled us all in one body unto God through thy cross, so that we are no more strangers and sojourners, but fellow citizens with the saints in the household of God.

People: Glory to thee who hast led captivity captive, and hast given gifts for the perfecting of thy saints.

Leader: Glory to thee who dost redeem unto God with thy blood men of every title and tongue and people and nation.

People: Glory to thee who art with us always, even unto the end of the world.

Leader: Glory to thee who art in our midst when we are gathered together in thy name.

People: Glory to thee, the author and finisher of our faith. Amen.

INVOCATION

Reverend F. P. Stocker
President of Provincial Elders Conference, Moravian Church

SCRIPTURE LESSON
Romans 12:1-21

Mrs. Harper Sibley
Former President of the United Council of Church Women

PRAYER FOR THE CHURCH

Very Reverend John Trutza
President of the Episcopate's Council, Roumanian Orthodox Church of America

In unison: Almighty and merciful God, our heavenly Father, we confess that we have grievously sinned against thee in thought, and word, and deed. We have come short of thy Glory. We have broken the unity of thy holy Church. We have turned every one of us away from thy way of life. Yet do thou, O most merciful Father, hear us when we call upon thee with penitent hearts. Pardon our sins and grant us thy peace. Confirm us in all goodness, that we may serve thee with a quiet mind, and bring us to the life everlasting: through Jesus Christ our Lord. Amen.

Leader: Remembering in reverent gratitude the great Head of the Church; let us give thanks that in the fullness of time God sent his Son into the world that the world through him might be saved.

Silence for prayer.

Leader: Remembering the age-long life of the Church; let us give thanks that throughout the generations the Church has broken to men the bread of eternal life

Silence for prayer.

Leader: Remembering the tribulations of this present day; let us pray for the Church as it endures suffering and persecution, as it steadfastly holds to the faith, as it binds up the bleeding wounds of humanity, and as it holds aloft in these dark times the light of faith, hope and love.

Silence for prayer.

Leader: Remembering the prayer of our Lord that his disciples might be one; let us pray that the Church may be cleansed of all hatred and prejudice, and whatsoever else may hinder it from godly union and concord, that it may be united in one heart and soul, in one holy bond of truth and peace, of faith and charity, and may with one mind and one mouth glorify God.

Silence for prayer.

Leader: Remembering with gratitude the leading of the Holy Spirit through which in these days Christian believers have been drawn into deeper fellowship; let us pray for the National Council of Churches and all kindred organizations, that they may have in them a brotherly unity, a far-sighted wisdom, a self-sacrificing devotion, and a deep love for Christ and his Kingdom.

Silence for prayer.

In unison: O gracious Father, we humbly beseech thee for thy holy Church; that thou wouldst be pleased to fill it with all truth, in all peace. Where it is corrupt, purify it; where it is in error, direct it; where in anything it is amiss, reform it. Where it is right, establish it; where it is in want, provide for it; where it is divided, reunite it; for the sake of him who died and rose again, and ever liveth to make intercession for us, Jesus Christ, thy Son, our Lord. Amen.

ANTHEMS

1. "And the Glory of the Lord," from the Messiah
2. "Worthy the Lamb," from the Messiah

George Frederick Handel

SERMON

"The Cost of Discipleship"

Reverend Eugene C. Blake
First Presbyterian Church, Pasadena, California

HYMN

I love thy kingdom, Lord,
The house of thine abode,
The Church our blest Redeemer saved
With his own precious blood.

I love thy Church, O God:
Her walls before thee stand,
Dear as the apple of thine eye,
And graven on thy hand.

For her my tears shall fall,
For her my prayers ascend;
To her my cares and toils be given,
Till toils and cares shall end.

Beyond my highest joy
I prize her heavenly ways,
Her sweet communion, solemn vows,
Her hymns of love and praise.

Sure as thy truth shall last,
To Zion shall be given
The brightest glories earth can yield,
And brighter bliss of heaven.

Tune: St. Thomas

Timothy Dwight, 1800

INSTALLATION

OF THE OFFICERS, GENERAL BOARD, AND STAFF OF THE NATIONAL COUNCIL OF THE CHURCHES OF CHRIST IN THE UNITED STATES OF AMERICA.

The members of the Council being assembled, the newly elected Officers, General Board, and Staff shall present themselves before the Acting Chairman of the Planning Committee, Reverend Hermann N. Morse, who shall then say:

"Now therefore ye are no more strangers and foreigners, but fellow citizens with the saints, and of the household of God; and are built upon the foundation of the apostles and prophets, Jesus Christ himself being the chief corner stone; in whom all the building fitly framed together groweth unto a holy temple in the Lord: in whom ye also are builded together for a habitation of God through the Spirit."

Inasmuch as it is the conviction of the Churches of Christ in the United States of America that in the providence of God the time has come when it seems fitting more fully to manifest oneness in Jesus Christ as divine Lord and Savior, by the creation of an inclusive cooperative agency of our Churches;

We therefore, your brethren, representatives of the member churches, have chosen you to lead the activities of the Council, following in the goodly succession of those who formerly carried similar responsibilities.

The installing clergyman shall then address the incoming President as follows:

Do you accept the high office of President of the National Council of the Churches of Christ in the United States of America; and do you faithfully promise to perform its constitutionally prescribed duties, and to exercise the leadership which it implies, as God may give you strength and understanding?

The incoming President shall then reply:

I do.

The installing clergyman shall then address the incoming Vice-Presidents, Secretary, and Treasurer as follows:

Do you accept the high office to which you severally have been elected by the National Council of the Churches of Christ in the United States of America; and do you faithfully promise to perform its constitutionally prescribed duties, and to exercise the leadership which it implies, as God may give you strength and understanding?

The Installation of the General Staff

The Convention Song Leader, Mrs. Rosa Page Welch

The Crucifer leads the processional

Bishop Sherrill and Dr. Vere Loper

Some of the Boy Scouts who were so helpful

The incoming officers shall then reply:
We do.

The installing clergyman shall then address the incoming members of the General Board as follows:
Do you accept your election as overseers of the life and work of this Council committed to your charge by the representatives of the member churches of the National Council of the Churches of Christ in the United States of America; and do you faithfully promise to perform the constitutionally prescribed duties of members of its General Board?

The incoming members of the General Board shall then reply:
We do.

The installing clergyman shall then address the incoming members of the Staff as follows:
Are you now ready to take upon you the ministries and services to which you have been called by the National Council of the Churches of Christ in the United States of America; and will you endeavor to administer your several offices to the glory of God, and the advancement of His Kingdom in constant fidelity to the constitution of this Council?

The incoming members of the Staff shall then reply:
We do.

The installing clergyman shall then address the members of the Council as follows:
Do you the elected representatives of the churches constituting the National Council of the Churches of Christ in the United States of America consent to this induction into office of these leaders as being in accordance with the constitution of the Council and under the guidance of the Spirit of God; and do you pledge to these brethren and those associated with them your prayers that they may be enabled rightly to fulfil their responsibilities, and your support of them in behalf of united Christian service?

The members of the Council shall then reply:
We do.

The installing clergyman shall then say:
The offices and ministries to which you have been elected are committed to you, in the Name of the Father, and of the Son, and of the Holy Ghost. Amen.

May God in the fullness of his grace strengthen us with might by his spirit in the inward man, that Christ may dwell in our hearts by faith; and being rooted and grounded in love, may we be able to comprehend with all saints what is the breadth and length and depth and height, and to know the love of Christ which passeth knowledge.

PRAYER OF CONSECRATION

Bishop William J. Walls
African Methodist Episcopal Zion Church

Most merciful Father, we beseech thee to send down upon these thy servants thy heavenly blessing; and so endue them with thy Holy Spirit that they may fulfil their sacred duties with all faithfulness, diligence and courage. Grant that we in steadfast devotion may go forward with them in ministering in the name of Christ to a bewildered and needy world. Hasten the day when all people shall be blessed in thee, and be led in the way everlasting; through Jesus Christ, our Lord. Amen.

CLOSING STATEMENT
"This Nation under God"
By the President of the National Council of the Churches of Christ in the United States of America

CHORAL AFFIRMATION
"Halleluia," from the Messiah   *George Frederick Handel*

65

BENEDICTION

President of the National Council of the Churches of Christ in the United States of America

Now unto him that is able to do exceeding abundantly above all that we ask or think, according to the power that worketh in us, unto him be glory in the Church by Christ Jesus throughout all ages, world without end. Amen.

RECESSIONAL HYMN

The Church's one foundation
Is Jesus Christ her Lord;
She is his new creation
By water and the word;
From heaven he came and sought her
To be his holy bride,
With his own blood he bought her,
And for her life he died.

Elect from every nation
Yet one o'er all the earth,
Her charter of salvation,
One Lord, one faith, one birth;
One holy Name she blesses,
Partakes one holy food,
And to one hope she presses,
With every grace endued.

Tune: Aurelia

'Mid toil and tribulation
And tumult of her war,
She waits the consummation
Of peace forevermore;
Till with the vision glorious,
Her longing eyes are blest,
And the great Church victorious
Shall be the Church at rest.

Yet she on earth hath union
With God the Three in One,
And mystic sweet communion
With those whose rest is won.
Oh happy ones and holy!
Lord, give us grace that we
Like them, the meek and lowly,
On high may dwell with thee.   Amen.

Samuel J. Stone, 1866

ORGAN POSTLUDE

Allegro from Symphonie VI

Charles Marie Widor

THE MESSIAH CHORUS
Cleveland

T. R. EVANS, Conductor

ANN GRIFFITH, Pianist

JOSEPH HOFRICHTER, Organist

VINCENT H. PERCY, Cleveland, Organist

MRS. J. POWELL JONES, Cleveland, Alternate Organist

MRS. ROSA PAGE WELCH, Chicago, Song Leader

The Act of Adoration is from "The Kingdom, the Power, and the Glory," copyright Oxford University Press. Used by permission.

Saturday, December 2, at 9:30 A.M. and 2:00 P.M.

MEETINGS OF THE GENERAL BOARD

On Sunday, December 3, the first Sunday in the life of the National Council, all churches have been asked to join in nation-wide services of thanksgiving and rededication of the great united task of bringing every area of life under the influence of Christ and His Kingdom.

SOME WHO HELPED

Dr. Earl Frederick Adams
Executive Secretary

Among the members of the Planning Committee of the National Council of the Churches of Christ in the U.S.A. are: (front row) Mrs. William Sale Terrell, Dr. Roy G. Ross, Dr. Luther A. Weigle, Dr. Earl Frederick Adams, Dr. Wynn C. Fairfield, Mrs. W. H. Medlicott; (second row) Mrs. Arthur Sherman, Mr. Henry Reed Bowen (advisory member), Dr. I. George Nace, Dr. Samuel McCrea Cavert, Dr. Gilbert Q. LeSourd; (third row) Dr. Ivan M. Gould, the late Dr. William E. Lampe, Miss Sue Weddell, Dr. Paul H. Conrad, Dr. Harry S. Myers, Dr. Stanley I. Stuber; (last row) Miss Mable Head, Dr. Luther Gotwald, Dr. Arlo Ayres Brown.

BIOGRAPHICAL DATA ON
Convention Speakers

Dr. Ralph W. Sockman, Minister of Christ Church, New York City

Dr. Nevin C. Harner, Professor of Christian Education of the Theological Seminary of the Evangelical and Reformed Church of Lancaster, Pa.

Dr. Howard F. Lowry, President of the College of Wooster

Dr. John Deschner, Executive Secretary of the United Student Christian Council

Dr. Edwin T. Dahlberg, Minister of the Delmar Baptist Church, St. Louis, Missouri

Dean Acheson, Secretary of State

Rear Admiral Stanton W. Salisbury, Chief of Chaplains of the U. S. Navy, Chairman of the Armed Services Chaplain Board

Dr. Hermann N. Morse, Vice-president of the National Council of the Churches of Christ in the United States and General Secretary of the Board of Home Missions of the Presbyterian Church, U. S. A.

Miss Sarah Chakko, President of Isabella Thoburn College in Lucknow, India, is now on a year's leave of absence to serve as first secretary of the Commission on the Life and Work of Women in the Church of the World Council of Churches in Geneva, Switzerland

Dr. A. D. Stauffacher, Executive Secretary of the Missions Council of the Congregational Christian Churches

Dr. Toyohiko Kagawa, Japanese Christian leader. He has toured extensively both in Europe and the United States to further the cause of Christ and His Church

Dr. O. Frederick Nolde, Director of the Commission of the Churches on International Affairs of the World Council of Churches and the International Missionary Council and Associate General Secretary of the World Council of Churches with portfolio on international affairs

Dr. W. A. Visser 't Hooft, General Secretary of the World Council of Churches

Dr. Harold E. Stassen, Vice-president of the National Council of the Churches of Christ in the United States and President of the University of Pennsylvania

Honorable Francis B. Sayre, Delegate of the U. S. to the Trusteeship Council of the United Nations

Mrs. Douglas Horton, Vice-president of National Council of the Churches of Christ in the United States of America. Former President of Wellesley College, she also served as Commander of the Waves in World War II.

The Reverend Eugene Carson Blake, Minister of the First Presbyterian Church, Pasadena, California

The Right Reverend Henry Knox Sherrill, President of the National Council of the Churches of Christ in the United States and Presiding Bishop of the Protestant Episcopal Church

DR. RALPH W. SOCKMAN · · · · · · · THE HONORABLE DEAN ACHESON

THE REVEREND
EUGENE CARSON BLAKE · · · · · · · DR. O. FREDERICK NOLDE

Dr. W. A. Visser 't Hooft · · · · · Miss Sarah Chakko

Dr. Toyohiko Kagawa

This Nation Under God

AN ADDRESS BY DR. RALPH W. SOCKMAN

Pastor, Christ Church—Methodist, New York

FOUR SCORE and seven years ago, a sad-faced but stout-hearted Lincoln stood on the battlefield of Gettysburg and said: "Four score and seven years ago our fathers brought forth on this continent a new nation conceived in liberty and dedicated to the proposition that all men are created equal." The same stretch of years which intervened between Lincoln and the Liberty Bell now separates us from the graves of Gettysburg. Never more than now was it so imperative that we, in the spirit of Lincoln, "highly resolve that this nation, under God, shall have a new birth of freedom and that government of the people, by the people, for the people shall not perish from the earth."

This National Council of Churches is the fruition of a spirit of unity which has long been growing, and the seed for a greater harvest which only God can forecast. These church agencies are not weak organizations pooling their resources to save them from bankruptcy. The Protestant church was never farther from bankruptcy, financially or institutionally, than it is today. The growth of the church is the very cause of this consolidation.

The Protestant church has far more unity than many of its critics recognize. The various denominations are united in common objectives for saving the souls of men and the social systems under which they live. The increasing awareness of these common aims has led to a progressive strengthening of the ties that unite and a weakening of the barriers which divide. More and more churchmen are coming to realize that unity within the church must lead the way if there is to be unity within the world.

Since this great act of unifying is the fruit of a long growth and the seed of a future harvest, let us look at its roots. We go back to the sixty-first chapter of Isaiah, which was the seed-plot from which our Lord took his text for his first sermon.

When Jesus returned from the wilderness of temptation to his home town of Nazareth, he went into the synagogue as his custom was. There was delivered to him the book of the prophet Isaiah. And he read the words beginning, "The Spirit of the Lord is upon me, because he hath anointed me to preach the gospel to the poor." This is the passage with which the prophet Isaiah opened the sixty-first chapter. As the chapter progresses, it pictures the redeemed as "trees of righteousness, the planting of the Lord." And then in the ninth verse, the prophet makes this sweeping prediction: "All that see them shall acknowledge them, that they are the seed which the Lord hath blessed."

Whether we interpret the word seed as a figure of speech in the agricultural or in the biological sense, the principle is the same. The prophet saw a spiritual seed remaining from the reverses and devastation of his nation. This seed was taken up by the Divine Sower of Nazareth, who went forth to sow. Although some of that seed fell on stony ground and some was trampled under feet of men, enough took root to raise a crop of convinced and converted Christians, whose passion to share the bread of life sent bands of sowers through the Mediterranean world, Gaul and Northern Europe.

That seed of the spirit was carried across the Atlantic by a band of Pilgrims who, in the cabin of their little ship, the Mayflower, drew up a compact, declaring that the voyage had been undertaken "for the glory of God, the advancement of the Christian faith and the honor of King and country."

To be sure, the religious motives of the American colonists were not unmixed with commercial interests. The settlers were not pure saints, even though some of them bore the name of Puritans. The treatment of the Indians had some dark chapters. But, by and large, the founders of American society were a God-fearing people, and they looked upon their new homes as veritably God-given. The Congregationalists in New England, the Anglicans and Dutch Reformed in New York, the Quakers in Pennsylvania, the Roman Catholics in Maryland, the Hugenots in the Carolinas, the Lutherans in the lands to the West—these and others were sufficiently religious to realize that back of the royal arms emblazoned on their charters, the real title of ownership rested in a higher, a Divine Power. In a very real sense, this land was to them, "God's Country."

Despite the waning of religious fervor which affected Europe and America in the 18th century, the colonists of this Western world did not lose vital contact with God. This fact is attested, for example, by the contrast between France and America. The revolt of liberty against tyranny caused a revolution on both sides of the Atlantic. But, whereas the French Revolution led to the enthronement of a Goddess of Reason, a resultant Reign of Terror, and eventually a dictator in the person of Napoleon, over here in America the Revolutionary War was followed by a Constitution, a Bill of Rights and a Washington.

Without attributing the difference wholly to religious influence, we can, nevertheless, say that the American spirit of independence never ignored dependence on God. We think of Franklin, one of the seemingly least religious, calling for prayer in the Constitutional Convention. We think of Jefferson, whose orthodoxy was cruelly questioned by his critics, struggling to keep breath in his aging body until the fiftieth anniversary of the Declaration of Independence, and then repeating the prayer of Simeon, "Now, Lord, lettest thou thy servant depart in peace." We think of John Marshall, often called the father of American Constitutional law, sitting in the room of his deceased wife and reading aloud from the Prayer Book of his church to his beloved Mary, absent in body but present in spirit.

The laws, the institutions, the ideals of America stem from the soil of belief in a sovereign God. From that conviction come the criteria for determining the ideas of right. From it came also the human dignities calling for recognition in constitutional rights. From the soil of our religious faith has grown an American way of life wherein the individual can live in a home free from unwarranted search, cast his secret ballot in free election, plead his case in court before a jury of his peers, receive instruction in a free public school, and worship his God in a free church. While this American way of life is still far from perfect and its promises have not been fulfilled for all, nevertheless, it is growing toward its ideals, and much of its social ferment is the yeasty germination of the principles put by Jesus in the faith of our fathers.

John Hersey in his novel, *The Wall*, pictures the fate which befell a community of Jews in a Warsaw ghetto during the war. Quentin Reynolds in a review said: "In that tragic hour, they drew strength from the only reservoir that remains—the past. They now realize that they had never, nor could they ever, divorce themselves from their spiritual and cultural heritage."

We of America are not walled in any ghetto. But we are in need of strength to endure these difficult days and to deliver these pregnant hours of promise. And we, too, can draw strength from the reservoir of our heritage. We do not think of our fathers as a "chosen people" in the sense that they were the special favorites of a divine champion. God is no respecter of persons. But he is a respecter of principles. And our fathers, though not "chosen favorites" were a choosing people, whose choice of principles enabled God to use them as chosen seed. And when we look back at those who, in "this nation under God," have given us our heritage, we humbly and gratefully acknowledge "that they are the seed which the Lord hath blessed."

And now it is our turn to sow. If we do not take our turn, we forfeit the name of Christian. Paul wrote to the Corinthians, that "as workers together with God, we beseech you that ye receive not the grace of God in vain." The person who receives the inheritance of his fathers and does nothing to pass it on to others is something less than a Christian, something less than a good citizen, something less than a decent man. We cannot be followers of Christ unless we are sowers with Christ.

I

We must go forth to sow with a missionary motive. How often it happens that when the words "missions" or "missionary" are mentioned, the temperature of a congregation falls, especially when that temperature is not too high anyway. So many conventional church members say, "I believe in the church, but I am not interested in missions." In the mind of the pew, the church and missions are held in separate compartments. The support of the local church is regarded as an obligation which rests on the member as a debt of honor. But many seem to feel that missions are just an extra interest for those who care for that sort of thing.

Maybe one reason that missions are not generally regarded by the pew as an integral part of the church support is that we have not clearly preached it as such from the pulpit. Perhaps it would help if we ceased using the word "missions" in the plural and started to use it in the singular, "mission." What we need is to talk about the church's mission rather than the church's missions.

What is the church's mission? Do you say, it is to save the souls of those who belong to it? But is a person saved until he becomes interested in saving others? Not if I read my New Testament aright. According to the teachings of Jesus, we are saved for service.

Of course, in our modern churches we do not talk so much as our fathers did about saving our members. We talk now about serving them. The up-to-date churchman seems to demand service rather than salvation. He wants the church to give him health for his body, peace for his mind, prosperity for his business. He wants to be relieved from his frustrations, his anxieties, his hardships and all the other "ills that flesh is heir to." The heritage of the soul doesn't bother him too much. But to pour pleasing services into the Dead Sea of self-centered listeners is not preaching the Gospel of Christ. If "the Son of Man came not to be ministered unto but to minister," certainly the sons of men cannot be his followers unless they too are ministers in his service.

To me, this fact is symbolized in the formation of this National Council of Churches. We are not merely co-ordinating the work of the Foreign Missions Conference, the Home Missions Council and the Missionary Education Movement. We are saying to the world that missions are integral to the church. To use a homely figure, we are bringing missions from the baggage car, where so many of our members think it is carried, into the passenger car. Nay, into the engine itself. For the church cannot run with-

70

out a mission. Its mission is to save the children of God, and the children of God are not saved until they are concerned to save other members of God's family, even to the ends of the earth.

If we would be followers, we ought to be his missionaries, sowing with him. Then we, too, become "the seed which the Lord hath blessed."

II

And along with the missionary motive must go an informed mind. We must have a reason for the hope that is in us, if it is to take root deeply enough to bring forth enduring results.

One significant aspect of our time is its spiritual emptiness. Back in the 1920's, T. S. Eliot wrote:

> *"We are the hollow men,*
> *We are the stuffed men*
> *Leaning together,*
> *Headpieces filled with straw."*

A national business depression with its panaceas and a second World War with its promises have not filled that emptiness. Many signs indicate that America is ready for a great religious revival. Certain popular evangelists are drawing large crowds. Religious and semi-religious books are widely read. More significant is the increased number of courses in the religious field now being offered at our colleges and universities. And we know how the preaching missions led by Dr. Bader have been stirring many of our cities.

Mere interest and inquiry, however, do not always lead to spiritual commitment. A major weakness of Protestantism has been that it has counted too much on popular preaching. Crowds drawn by spectacular or entertaining or eccentric preachers do not generate church strength.

We must advance from mass meetings of the curious to mass movements of the consecrated. A religious revival worthy of the name must lead to an informed, devoted and organized churchmanship.

In the Soviet section of Germany we are told by Dr. Paul Payne that the communists are focusing their heaviest propaganda on children from seven to twelve years of age. The Christian church must multiply its efforts to capture the imagination and inform the minds of the youth. It is becoming trite to say that American education must be redeemed from its present pagan tendencies if this is to remain "a nation under God."

It augurs well that religious education is to be so central in the program of this National Council. We surely have the genius to find a place for spiritual nurture in the schooling schedule of our children, if we give to religious education a prestige, efficiency and urgency comparable to that devoted to secular education.

71

But with all our talk about it, religious education, like the missionary movement, has not been really integrated into our churchmanship. How well we know the parent who sees that his children go to Sunday school but feels no personal need to attend a Bible Class or even to go to church. How well we know the layman, perhaps active, who regards religious education as something limited to little children. How well we know the businessman or professional man who through ability and application has risen toward the top, but who has left his study of religion back in the high school stage. He goes to a luncheon club, hears a speaker close a talk with a pious appeal that America must "get back to God" if it is to get ahead in business, and he joins in the applause, without giving any further serious thought about what "getting back to God" means.

Or perhaps at his luncheon club or Chamber of Commerce, he hears a speaker who finds it popular and profitable to attack the church as being socialistic or communistic. Having, however, no inside knowledge of what the church's general teaching and program are, this otherwise honest man can be easily terrified by some quotation torn from its context and twisted by clever speakers and writers.

To be sure, we preachers are not infallible in our pronouncements on politics and economics. We are not economic experts. The laymen see to it that we do not have very much experience in handling big money! But if we would be true to the prophetic tradition, we are called to cry out against evils when we are not competent to furnish the specific prescription for their cure.

The Christian church should expect criticism. The servant is not above his Master, and if our Lord had his critics so must his church. Oh, I am not saying it is always the church's Christ-likeness which brings its enemies. Let us, as Christians, humbly admit our lack of Christian perfection. Let us hear others who honestly differ with us as they view the "Road Ahead." But let us all remember that in this hurrying time when we try to read the signs on the road ahead we should ride forward and not backward.

I am not pleading a defense of the church tonight. I am pleading with the host of well-meaning but ill-informed people now critical of the church to come in and learn what it is teaching, see what it is seeking, share in what it is doing. I am pleading for a churchmanship intelligent enough to know what the church is about, and devoted enough to do something about what the church knows.

We look to the laymen rather than to the ministers for the new force in this spiritual advance. The recent conventional church program has too much deteriorated into a professional propaganda financed by silent spectators. The Christian movement began as a company of Christ's followers each telling what he knew about his Lord. And the World Council of Churches makes one of its major objectives the recovery of the lay witness.

72

When laymen get to talking about religion in the same simple, matter-of-fact way they talk about their secular interests, when laymen think through and talk out what it means to be a Christian business man or a Christian doctor or a Christian trade-unionist, then we shall start a real revival of religion in "this nation under God."

The dangers and tensions of our time may prove to be godsends in driving Christians to a clearer understanding of their faith and a deeper devotion to it. In competing with communism for the minds of millions, Christians ought to be learning what Christ has that the Kremlin lacks. The compassion of the cross has more power and appeal than the compulsions of the crescent and the sickle. And we can demonstrate this to the people of China and Africa and our own America if we churchmen will match the zeal and speed of the Communists. Then all that see us shall acknowledge that we are "the seed which the Lord hath blessed."

III

Not only with a missionary motive and an informed mind, but also with a unifying spirit must our seed be sown.

This National Council parallels in American Protestantism the position of the United Nations in the international realm. But let us remember that the United Nations is not set up to create a spirit of unity, but rather to realize a unity which God created. The United Nations is not out to make one world; God made us one world.

Likewise this Council represents more than a spirit of unity which we are trying to create. We are here to keep "the unity of the spirit" which we have as an existing fact in the family of God. And the hopeful aspect is that more and more churchmen are coming to recognize this basic divine unity of the church. They are talking more of "the church" and less of "the churches."

With all our talk about unity, most of us do not realize its necessity or its essence. I think of two contrasted statements of our Lord. On one occasion, a disciple came saying, "We saw one casting out devils and we forbade him because he followed not with us." Jesus replied: "Forbid him not. He that is not against us is for us." Jesus was not greatly concerned about labels, but about direction. The other healer was working in the right direction. He was, therefore, for Christ, regardless of his label.

On another occasion, when Jesus was being heckled by spectators, he said: "He that is not with me is against me; he that gathereth not with me scattereth." Jesus was condemning those who were headed in the wrong direction. And he was saying that the spirit has but two directions to choose—the gathering or the scattering. We cannot be neutral. Christian unity is found in direction not in definition. The important matter is not

73

where the headquarters of this Council are located, but in what direction are its headquarters headed.

And when our direction is that of gathering rather than scattering, we find our fulfillment. Antoine de Saint-Exupery, the French aviator whose mystical insights matched physical bravery, wrote in *Flight to Arras:* "But this is veritable love, a web woven of strands in which we are fulfilled. Through my comrades I was woven into the whole of my country."

Man is not made to be a unit. He is made for unity. He finds his freedom and fulfillment in togetherness. The child finds his freedom and fulfillment in the family, not in individual isolation. The citizen finds his freedom and fulfillment in a nation, not as a man without a country. The Christian finds his freedom and fulfillment in the church, the family of God, the body of Christ.

This is a principle we Protestants have hitherto not been appreciating. We have sought freedom by separation. If we felt ourselves limited in any group, we went off and started another. But now we are rediscovering the Christian principle that the freedom of the Christian man is in the unity of the spirit and the service of the Lord. This is the "new birth of freedom" which I have in mind when I repeat Lincoln's resolution that "this nation under God shall have a new birth of freedom."

May this be the new birth of freedom signalized by this National Council. The religious world has been waiting and calling for some great act of faith to arouse and inspire the churches. This is the greatest forward step toward church unity which America has yet seen, and it may well prove epochal.

Never since the first century have conditions been so ripe for a new Apostolic Age. The dangers which threaten the world, the longing for peace and brotherhood in the hearts of common men, the vision of unity caught by Christian leaders—all furnish a striking parallel to the conditions facing Christ's first disciples. If one million of the thirty-four million represented in this National Council became fired with the passion of the apostle, a new Book of Acts would be written.

And think what it would mean to the world if word went out that America was experiencing a vast deep religious revival. The Kremlin propagandists might sneer at it, but the hungry hearts of the Orient, of Africa, and of Europe would take new hope.

A few weeks ago, at a great Reformation service in this auditorium, an open Bible was carried on the shoulders of marchers in the procession. It symbolized the truth which John Robinson told the Pilgrims when he said that "the Lord hath more light to break forth from his Holy Word." The Bible is still open. The light is still breaking. And if we follow as faithful pilgrims, we shall be "the seed which the Lord hath blessed."

74

Religious Education—
Foundation of the National Life

FROM AN ADDRESS BY PROFESSOR NEVIN C. HARNER

Theological Seminary of the Evangelical and Reformed Church
Lancaster, Pennsylvania

IN THIS HOUR of crisis for the world and our own country, it seems clear that our national life cannot hope to maintain itself without a widespread and vital religious faith.

Without such a faith, we cannot hope to keep our democracy. For democracy at root is respect for persons, and the only real guarantee that such a respect will persist is a continuing belief in God who creates each person and endows him with immeasurable worth.

Without such a faith, we cannot hope to achieve the basic morality essential to our national life. Fundamental honesty and integrity are greatly needed in every walk of life—the family, the professions, industry, and politics. But there is no assurance that we can get or keep such morality apart from a continuing firm belief that God wills it to be so.

Without such a faith, we cannot hope to develop the spiritual stamina necessary to see us through the years ahead. The worst we can anticipate is the sudden eruption of a third world war; the best is a long hard pull. In either case we shall need inner resources of stability and comfort. Where shall they be found except in reliance upon a God who holds nations as well as individuals in the hollow of his hand?

When we turn to the actual scene about us, what do we find?

I

We find widespread religious illiteracy. In a survey made among more than eighteen thousand high school students a few years ago, sixteen thousand could not name so many as three of the Old Testament prophets, and twelve thousand could not cite the titles of the four Gospels. We have largely divorced religion from general education; in church and synagogue we have reached only half of the children and youth of the nation; and this half we have taught only indifferently.

75

II

We find also widespread confusion on moral issues. The great absolute commands have evaporated for many people, and they have given themselves over to self-indulgence and the easiest way out. The net outcome is a good deal of crime and delinquency, a considerable amount of immorality in the broadest sense of the term, and a sizable quantity of undisciplined living.

III

Most serious of all, we find a widespread denial of the basic convictions of the Christian faith. We who are adults grew up in an era when virtually everybody rendered lip-service at least to the cardinal Christian doctrines. But now the situation has changed. From communism without and secularism within a challenge is hurled at things long taken for granted. Many persons do not really believe any longer even the opening verse of the Bible, "In the beginning God created the heavens and the earth."

These two lines of thought—what we need for the maintenance of our national life, and what we find as we look about us—converge on a single inescapable conclusion: the desperate necessity to take seriously our task of Christian nurture.

The Christian College and the National Life

AN ADDRESS BY HOWARD F. LOWRY

MANY OF YOU probably recall Carl Sandburg's poem in which he finds himself on a crack train headed West. The thought strikes him that inevitably, as time passes, the shining cars will have rusted away, and the passengers also. Deep in these thoughts of transition, he asks of a man in the smoking room, "Where are you bound?" and the man answers, "Omaha." The title of the poem, which is the main part of it, reads simply "Limited."

If your minds have gone beyond Omaha at the thought of this convention, if you are moved by the very implication of these days here, then let me make my speech in the first minute following Dr. Harner's statement. It is this: The commitment that brings this convention together is the commitment at the heart of every church college worth the name. If you believed that coming here was valid, then you are automatically concerned with the church college. Because the only kind of higher education in America that cares an iota in any central way—notice that distinction: in any central way—about what you are doing here this week is the church college. It is the only kind of higher education that puts Christ first and at the center of the whole educational process. If you are struck, as I am, by what Dr. Harner has said—if we have, percentage-wise, twice the number of Christians in America that we had in 1895, if we have poured our money and energy into so many forms of religious education within the church proper, and yet have produced a pagan mind in the country as a whole, you may seek the reason. Part of the reason could well be that higher learning, which does somehow deeply affect all the rest of learning in a commonwealth, has largely a pagan heart and soul.

I assume you do not share Mr. Dooley's thesis that all which unites America is a common impulse for the same money. Something better than that surely forms our community here today. And the community of this gathering in Cleveland is identically the community of a church college. Without any elaboration, think of what the elements of that community really are. What unites the minds of all Christian believers in this room

77

right now? A few plain concepts: (1) the world itself is not an accident, but has a mind behind it; (2) the deepest nature of that mind is love; (3) God is in partnership with free creatures—magnificently, dangerously free for sin or for righteousness, for misery or glory, abject waste or creative achievement; and (4) there was a great Event in history that means more than anything else has ever meant. There was One born, as someone has so strikingly put it, in Asia, but on "the very edge of Asia, in Palestine, whose face is towards Europe." The great highways linking Europe with Asia and Africa ran through this little country, and thus, quite literally it was "at the center of the known world that Jesus Christ was born." We meet here this week in the faith that this is so, that it can still be so. The church colleges have, as their main business, the faith that this is so. They are the only place in high learning where you will find this magnificent assumption at the center of things.

One of the most thoughtful men you and I know once said to me, "Why don't some of you put it as bluntly as this: secular education believes life is secular; Christian education believes life is sacred. Why blur the distinction?" In passing, I must say that Dr. George Buttrick, whom I have just quoted, perhaps has been made to feel the need for making things clear. He recently reported that one of his parishioners once stopped him after church to tell him she could not refrain from expressing her gratitude, "to tell you how much your sermons have meant to my husband ever since he lost his mind." Even so, let's follow his lead and the sharp truth he has suggested on the issue at hand.

In the community of the church college we need your clearer understanding. And we do not always have it. We wish you could see, for one thing, that a church college is not just a set of rules, eight hours of religion, or even just chapel and church services. If it were no more than these, it would be as Dr. Frank Caldwell has said, "just white icing on a black cake to make it look white." Or as another educator has put it, "A church college does not have a religious program; it is a religious program." It is a laboratory, a laboratory of study and living, operating in the belief that he who tries doing the will of the Father shall know of the doctrine. It will not always be a place where, as some wish and others fear, there is unalloyed sweetness and light. Not all who come to a church college fully share its purpose; and many of those who do share it are still human. Some of the best lads we have are still, at times, distinctly inclined to their own line. In view of one or two recent events on our own campus I am practically an authority on this subject. But whatever its shortcomings or its interruptions, the church college does try to point to the kind of life Dr. Harner has suggested real education ought to produce.

In so doing, it contributes immensely to the democratic society and to that decent, orderly world men dream of. The most searching remark

I ever heard on the subject of democracy—save perhaps one of Abraham Lincoln's—was made by Dr. William Ernest Hocking. It was made in conversation and has remained ever since in my mind. The essence of democracy, and the difficulty of securing it lies in this: it is an effort to obtain in human society "a maximum of self-realization with a minimum of self-interest." You and I know, as plainly as we know anything, that the only philosophy of life that has ever fully and richly attempted to make this almost paradoxical balance real in the lives of great numbers of men is the ideal of the Christian faith.

I wonder also, if another plain truth is not becoming clearer. If some of you go to as many meetings of educators as I do, you may be getting a little weary of hearing it said that the end of all education is the discovery of values. To be sure, this is so, in one sense. But it is not the whole sense. Indeed, one suspects sometimes that we already have the knowledge of more values than we know what to do with. What we do not have so often is the eternal sanction that makes these values real in human living— that makes them more than philosophical concepts professors can agree on, that makes them vital realities along the nerves and the bloodstream as well as in the mind. And, personally, I know of no other education that can give sanction to values as Christian education can.

Our church colleges have contributed something else to our national life, to higher learning itself. They have helped keep alive an adequate conception of what liberal education itself is: the twofold task of seeking new truth and of keeping alive old truths that have value for mankind. By the very nature of their Christian commitment, which is both revolutionary and conservative at once, both pioneering and yet proud of its human and divine inheritance, church colleges have an incentive for this double work. An education really liberal must be concerned about both sides of the task.

Yet many people—some of them my own best friends—believe what I have just said is nonsense. You cannot persuade them that a church college can be the home of liberal education. Its very Christian commitment prevents its being so, they say; and anybody who would retain his own faith in Christian, liberal learning should pay careful attention to their charge.

The charge rests upon a curious failure to understand the nature of Christian commitment. If a person becomes a Christian, his action is restricted. In all conscience there are things he can no longer do. But he is not cut off from freedom of thought and research. If he believes the world is God's, then there are no dark alleys of the mind down which he dare no longer to look. He carries a lantern in his hand and a passport in the search for truth, the free search that always is implicit in a reasonable faith. No microscope or test tube, no phenomenon of life, no ugly social fact is for-

79

bidden ground. If any group of men and women ought to be willing to look fearlessly and unafraid, it is Christians; and any church college that conspires against the free movement of intelligence and observation is conducting some kind of pious intellectual fraud. Any effort to put blinders on the human spirit is a plot against both God and man. No church college can engage in it with impunity.

On the other hand, a university—if it be a "university"—can hardly be called one if it asks the human spirit to stop short of its own deepest search for religious faith. Indeed, a university that will not admit the study of religion as a part of liberal education is simply not giving a liberal education. Nor can it take refuge in some cult of "objectivity." In the name of "objectivity" many educators leave religion out of their account on the ground, to use plain speech, that it is too hot to handle, too full of dynamite and human emotion. It is not bloodless enough to be made a part of liberal learning. But what kind of "objectivity" does one get from many of these men? I am not speaking here, of course, of many honest minds that have sought religious faith and not been able to accept it. I am speaking, rather, of men who pronounce on Christianity out of childish memories of what they thought it was, out of ideas they have never taken the trouble to ventilate; of men who make second, third, or fourth-hand judgments on Christian learning out of a free-wheeling ignorance and an innocence of first-hand documents that they would despise in their own field of study. Many a concealed "religion" of another sort often lurks beneath this "objectivity." I have heard men suggest, with perfect freedom, some nihilistic view of life in an academic lecture or recommend a philosophy that was little more than the philosophy of animals—and do all this without restraint in university halls where an open, forthright account of Christianity and its teachings would have been held to be impropriety and violation of good sense.

My thesis today is this: Our nation needs education that rules out no great area of human inquiry, that does not cut short the questionings of men. Simply because it entertains a complete investigation of man's mind and spirit, because it does not abandon our great inheritance, because it gives lively heed to the deep roots on which our highest culture has drawn, because it has concern for the possibility of man's immortal soul and the reality of a God behind intelligent life, Christian education may well turn out to be the only really liberal education we have left. It has its own obligations to verify its references as it can, to hear opposite sides of all questions, and not to close its own eyes. But the Socrates within its breast will insist on some examination of the spirit and life of Jesus Christ. This will be its ultimate inquiry and laboratory exercise.

The church college needs to be independent. This means to be free of government aid. I hasten to say this is a private judgment of my own; I do not presume to speak for anyone else. But I have a conviction that we should have some colleges which are not taking federal money, even should it require real sacrifice on their part to resist alluring temptation. On a principle of diversity which is important in our national life, if for no other reason, some colleges must keep their independence. And some of them will do well to be church colleges. One understanding, however, will be necessary. If the churches are to maintain private colleges and to take any significant part in the higher learning in America, they are going to have to pay for these colleges in a way they have hardly dreamed of. And I hope I speak not merely as a college president on a kind of busman's holiday. Our churches have treated the colleges as if they were little business instead of the big business they are, measured by their contribution to our nation's life. The churches must now stand up and pay for their colleges if they do not want to hand them over to the state or bury them altogether.

They can do this in two ways. They can do it as only a few denominations have done—you can count on one hand the denominations that have done it—actually look the bill in the face and pay it. I am not sure the churches of all denominations can or will ever do this. But, failing to do this out of the church treasuries, they can at least do the other thing: they can turn towards our church colleges the interest and concern of men and women who are capable of giving practical help, men and women who give money to every other kind of educational effort and to all kinds of gadget-hunting enterprises and let this cause go begging in vain.

As I was coming to this meeting I thought again of what has always seemed one of the best remarks ever made on education—Professor Whitehead's suggestion that true learning, after all, has the ultimate task of giving men an "habitual vision of greatness." The highest vision you and I know is, by our common consent here today, the One in whose name we are met. Years ago in Greece it was suggested that a democracy was a society existing within the sound of a man's voice. Perhaps we have not fully realized how difficult it is to extend throughout the world a kind of society thought of originally as something within the confines of a city. If this world is to be the city of our highest humanity, the City of God, only One Voice can make it so. If that Voice is lost it will be a city without light, whose doom is already written on its gates. Surely, we now know and feel this desperation. Surely, we realize that you cannot have Christian values in a society that has persistently been stripping its education of the religion that produces these values and makes them live among men. This would seem elementary logic, especially in this coming December season, when the symbols that illuminate Christ's name are moving forward into our consciousness in all their beauty and terrible virility. Out of the early century that gave them birth there went a passion, a force that has changed the world and remade man's very mind. It has given him high moments in his culture, in art, in sculpture, in painting and music. It has healed the rough places and made them plain. It has transformed men's lives and altered the face of nations. It has resisted evil and conquered hate with love. It has created martyrs and disciples. And every day it stands ready to renew its bet on the individual lives of all of us. This afternoon, as war and desolation seem not so far off as we might wish, it still says with its old quietude, without a touch of unrest at its heart, "Thy kingdom come, on earth as it is in heaven." It points to a mind and a faith. They are the mind and faith by which you and I have our chance of enduring in any important way.

Personally, at least, I shall never say again what I found myself saying this past summer. It seemed that, if every man must carry his own Geiger counter, if every house must have its bomb shelter, every block its warden (that, indeed, might be the worst of all), if we have to live in that kind of world for the next twenty years, perhaps we were little better than the cave man. That thought shall not tempt me again. For it is a wrong thought, a treasonous one. We are better than the cave man, no matter what happens to us now. We have a wonderful human heritage on which all good men can draw; and we have the knowledge of Jesus Christ. And what surprise could now come to us, even if the worst happened? The worst in human evil we saw long ago, two thousand years almost ago—when the creature hanged the highest image of his Creator on a cross. What happens now, by way of a bomb, is a small thing compared with that. Nor does modern man have, as we so often hear, some awful adjustment to make. What adjustment? That adjustment was made then, long ago. What we have is a memory. And the work of the churches meeting here this week, along with the colleges of the church, is to make that memory a living reality in the lives and minds of men. Through this memory we can, perhaps, still save ourselves from ignoble death as a civilization. And with it, we can surely save our souls and the immortal meaning that lies beyond all forms of death and resurrection. And my thesis this afternoon is this: the education which in 1950 ignores the chance of making Christianity a live consideration among men is not adequate to our nation or to that world of which we do not yet despair.

Christian Youth and the Nation

FROM AN ADDRESS BY JOHN DESCHNER

Executive Secretary, United Student Christian Council, New York

THE YOUNG PEOPLE of this nation are hungry for integrity, for hope, for certainty, for a costly faith. We cannot look only at the Christian youth when we think of the nation, for the hard fact is that most of this nation's young people are not in our churches. Jesus Christ loves both Christian and non-Christian young people. That is why we cannot be concerned only about the Christians.

The gospel is the same for every generation. But every generation is asked to obey God in a different way. Young people are not more prophetic, more enthusiastic, more creative than older people. What is true is that they have a new chance at the problems that have baffled their elders.

For example—young people are very critical of institutions. They are impatient with the disunity of the churches, not interested in denominational organizations. The ecumenical movement needs to capture their restlessness. Our young people are needed when the ecumenical movement becomes too sure of itself, too secure in its present solutions, too slow to change, too serious about its own achievements.

Let me give a second example. Young people are already re-thinking the basis of the ecumenical movement. They are sensing that the question of Christian unity is a missionary question. So long as we are unwilling to speak the gospel to every man and woman in every race, every class, every condition, we will not really find ways to manifest our unity as a church. The church must cross new boundaries—the ideas of freedom of faith in one Lord, one faith, one baptism is a gift not only to the church but to every man.

If ecumenical means missionary, it implies a mission of youth in each locality. That means that the task of evangelism is a task for the membership, not for professional ministers. The members are the ministers, the real field is the nation.

These young people realize that ecumenical work is missionary work. And that missionary work is local work. And that local work is the task of the membership. If we call the ecumenical movement a "top level movement" we simply fail to understand its real character.

We began by thinking of the youth of this nation—a silent generation, waiting for an authentic voice. Christian young people are beginning to speak to the young people of our nation under the slogan "youth going to youth." This is the best way to explain the unique character of the church's youth and student movements. They are the non-professional effort of youth to go to youth in their own idiom.

Do not expect great numbers and enthusiastic movements from these young people in the future. Hard work, small results, a purified movement, a tested membership—these are some of the things God has in the future for these young people.

We have about 2,500,000 students in the U.S.A. About 1,300,000 are willing to say that they are members of the largest Protestant churches. These churches maintain a professional ministry of more than 1,100 full and part-time ministers to minister to that constituency. Yet it is still true that when you ask for the striking force of the Protestant student movements—meaning by that the serious, inter-group, responsibility-bearing students—you find a movement of about 200,000 students. This is something like 15 per cent of our Protestant constituency.

Jesus Christ asks for a costly service; he asks for greatness. We must pray that the youth of today may be willing to accept the cross. We must show them a Christ worth following and worth serving.

The Nation's Dependence
on the Local Church

FROM AN ADDRESS BY THE REVEREND EDWIN T. DAHLBERG

Pastor, Delmar Baptist Church, St. Louis, Missouri

IT IS WELL to remember that what we are organizing here in Cleveland is a National Council of Churches and not a National Church. A national church would be fatal to religious freedom. Even if it were separated from the state it would tend to reflect the philosophy of the state and become a ready tool of a coercive totalitarianism.

The best guarantee of a free faith in a free society is a strong local church, completely sovereign, and close to the mind and heart of the people, a grass roots fellowship of the spirit. National religious and educational agencies may prepare the study curriculum for the churches. But it is in the local congregation and in the local Sunday school that pastors and teachers introduce young people to Christ and secure a warmhearted commitment to the Christian way of life. That is where character is formed and faith in God is nurtured.

America is suffering today from a lack of local initiative. Everything from department stores and newspapers to baseball chains and television is owned and operated by absentee interests that have very little personal association with the people back home. In fact, as soon as a store manager becomes acquainted with the community which he serves, he is transferred. The policies of capital and labor, too, are determined from far away. The consequence is a de-personalization of all life, with resulting cold wars in human relations on every hand.

This must never happen to the churches. At all costs, they must be vitally interested in the lives of people, one by one, and in the small business of living as well as the large.

The ecumenical movement, therefore, will be effective only in so far as it functions on the village and small town level and gives a high place to the pastors and laymen of the local churches.

This does not mean that the churches should be isolationist and unrelated to each other. For a minister to pray, as one pastor in the national capital actually did pray, for the churches as the "brides" of Christ is to be guilty of a kind of ecclesiastical polygamy. The church is basically one in spirit, in spite of its diverse local manifestations. Hence, the necessity for councils of churches, on the county, state and national levels, that shall correlate the message and ministry of the local congregations in an effective, co-operative witness of nation-wide character.

Let no one be frightened away from the ecumenical movement by unfounded rumors concerning what some call a super-church, or a Protestant Vatican. There is nothing whatsoever to that charge. The National Council of Churches, like the World Council of Churches, represents a free, voluntary family of churches, grouped together as trusting brethren in Christ, yet completely safeguarded in their liberties and sovereignty.

The National Council of Churches is something like the Colorado River, which begins in tiny rills and streams among the pine needles up on the Continental Divide. Before it reaches the sea it has carved out the tremendous formations of the Grand Canyon, watered the deserts, and become the subject of treaties governing the water and irrigation rights of seven western states. In the National Council of Churches, likewise, the local churches, schools and congregations are the fountains of our faith, far up among the watersheds of the Eternal. The ecumenical movement simply represents the efforts of Christian shepherds to get away from a scandalous competition around the water courses, and to enter into inter-denominational treaties that shall guarantee the right of all the flocks to the living water.

The Strategy of Freedom

FROM AN ADDRESS BY SECRETARY OF STATE DEAN ACHESON

I REGRET that I have not been able to come out to Cleveland to meet with the National Council of Churches, as I had hoped to do, and that it has been necessary for me to talk to you instead from my office at the State Department in Washington. The events of the past few days, as I know you well understand, raise innumerable questions which require almost hourly study, consultation, and decision.

This coming-together of many great sources of spiritual strength in our American community is an event of historic importance. The great increase in the power and the effectiveness of the Christian communions which are now uniting to form the National Council of Churches will encourage millions of people throughout the world.

The remarks that I had planned to make this evening were prepared several days ago. I had not planned to discuss current day-to-day developments on this occasion.

But now a serious situation has arisen, one which holds grave danger for the peace of the world.

I would like to talk to you about the meaning of this situation which has been created in Korea, before going on to discuss some of the broader questions I had in mind to raise with you this evening.

An act of brazen aggression has taken place in Korea, the second such act in five months.

After many discouraging weeks, the United Nations forces, under the command of General MacArthur, were approaching the successful conclusion of their mission, which was to enable the United Nations to help the people of Korea establish their own free and independent government. Plans were moving forward in the General Assembly for the reconstruction of the country, and the nations which had contributed forces to this heroic effort were looking forward to the return of their troops to their home countries upon completion of their mission.

Then came this second shocking act of aggression. This is a fresh and unprovoked aggressive act, even more immoral than the first.

In behalf of the United States, President Truman declared that it is the

87

intention of this country to localize the conflict and to withdraw its forces from Korea as soon as possible. In the Security Council, this Government was one of the sponsors of a proposed resolution which affirmed that the policy of the United Nations was to hold the Chinese frontier with Korea inviolate, and that legitimate Chinese and Korean interests in the frontier zone would be fully protected.

The peaceful nations of the world made it unmistakably clear that if the Chinese Communist intervention had a limited motivation, if it sprang from an uncertainty regarding the intentions of the United Nations forces, the matter could be settled without enlarging the conflict.

But, at the very moment when representatives of these Chinese Communist authorities appeared at the headquarters of the United Nations, claiming the right to speak before this world organization in the name of the Chinese people, the cloak of pretense had been thrown off and the armies of the Chinese Communists have streamed across the Manchurian border, engaging the forces of the United Nations in a new encounter.

We have had dark days before in Korea, and I am confident, too, that the United Nations will not be found lacking in firmness of spirit or determination in responding to this new aggression. Now this new act of aggression has created a new crisis, a situation of unparalleled danger. For if the Chinese Communist authorities continue to impose upon their people this warring against the United Nations, they will vastly increase the danger to the whole fabric of world peace. This is their hour of decision. The authorities of Communist China stand before the bar of the judgment of mankind. If they defy the United Nations and mock the Charter then no lies, no bluster, and no veto will conceal from the people of the world the evil of their action.

These are questions that affect all the members of the United Nations. The United States has no special interests or interests different from those of the majority. From the very beginning of the Korean crisis, the United States has sought complete solidarity with the majority of members.

World Endangered by Communist Design

The questions raised by these acts of aggression in Korea go far beyond the contours of this small and remote peninsula. They have to be viewed as part of a world picture. To be fully understood, they must be seen as part of the worldwide operations of the international Communist movement. According to the Bolshevist interpretation, history points to the collapse of non-Soviet states and their replacement by Soviet-style and Soviet-controlled states. The combination of these intentions and Soviet military power creates very grave danger to the survival of free nations and free institutions, a danger which must not be underestimated.

Our essential purpose is to preserve our free institutions, so that freedom and justice may survive and continue to flourish. We wish to do this peacefully, but if we must, we will fight. The course of action we have chosen is to join with our allies in building the strength of the free world as a bulwark against Soviet aggression. The purpose of this strength is to deter such aggression. This involves building military strength, but it requires no less the buttressing of all the other forms of power—economic, political, social, and moral—and the utmost resolution and unity among the free nations of the world.

Over the period of time the rulers of the Soviet Union, confronted by a strong and confident free world, may be obliged to abandon their expansionist aims. To build the strength of the free world is a hard course. It involves great effort and much sacrifice both by our own people and by all the people of the free world. It offers no promise of relief from these burdens in the near future. It makes no guaranty of peace. But it is rooted in the principles by which we live, and it offers us the best realistic approach to the problem of peace, and the preservation of our freedom.

Elements in Strategy of Freedom

There are six main elements of the strategy by which we are seeking to carry out this course of action—the Strategy of Freedom.

First is the development of an international order for the preservation of peace and freedom under the United Nations. Our action in Korea is intended to support the authority of the United Nations against aggression. In the current session of the General Assembly, we have initiated a number of measures designed to increase the effectiveness of the United Nations action against aggression. We intend to do our full part in helping the United Nations to grow in strength.

The second element in the Strategy of Freedom is the development of regional groupings, within the framework of the United Nations. To insure their collective security, free nations are engaged in cooperative defense measures, not possible on a universal basis at the present time. The keystone of the defense system of the free world is being built in the North Atlantic community, and among the states of the Western Hemisphere.

The development of further regional organizations depends in the first instance upon the existence of this community sense among the people of other areas.

The third element in our Strategy of Freedom is the rapid building up of military strength at home and among our allies.

So measured, the defense efforts of the United States and other free nations are inadequate. A greatly increased scale and tempo of effort is required on the part of all free nations to enable them to overcome this inadequacy at the earliest possible moment.

The fourth element is economic cooperation. This has a dual character. It contributes powerfully to the building of our defenses against external attack. It also is an instrument for helping to build healthy societies in which the vitality and the promise of freedom find practical expression— in comparison with which the decadence and despair of Communist tyranny is starkly exposed.

So far as possible, economic cooperation, like defense cooperation and collective security programs, is being carried on through the United Nations and regional organizations in order to strengthen international institutions devoted to peace and security.

The fifth element in the Strategy of Freedom is a readiness at all times to negotiate just settlements of international disputes and to find just accommodations of conflicting interests. With the confidence that comes of strength and the humility that comes from our devotion to Christian principles, we shall be endlessly patient in working for peace. And we shall at the same time be endlessly alert to defend the bases of our national life.

The sixth element in the Strategy of Freedom is a firm adherence in all our actions, at home and abroad, to the moral values which give meaning to our lives.

The principles to which our common life is dedicated are powerful forces for good in the world, but we do not always present our best side to the world. In our enthusiasm and drive we often do not take care to make ourselves understood, and expect others to recognize us for what we are. We have launched a greatly expanded information program to bring knowledge of ourselves to other peoples, a program which the President has called "The Campaign of Truth." What is even more important than what we say to the world is how we conduct ourselves at home and abroad. The force of example and action is the factor which finally determines what our influence is to be. If we are to be worthy of the leadership that derives from our power, we must be sure that we are true to the values and principles upon which our society is founded.

Without this, which depends on every one of us, on the everyday conduct of each citizen, the Strategy of Freedom would "become as sounding brass or a tinkling cymbal."

These are the elements of our national foreign policy of the Strategy of Freedom. This is the course by which we seek to avoid war and to secure peace. We must hope and strive for the best while we prepare for the worst.

This is a responsibility, not just of a few public officials, not just of the Congress, but of the whole American people. The qualities we must demonstrate—steadiness, moderation, restraint, constancy of purpose, and flexibility in action, imagination, wisdom, maturity—these qualities are possible for us as a nation only if the American people participate as individuals in striving to make our society worthy of the hopes that free men everywhere have placed in it.

A deep understanding of the forces we are dealing with, and the role we must play, must be acquired by each of us. Every single individual has a share of this responsibility.

The six elements of the Strategy of Freedom—support of the United Nations, development of regional organizations, the rapid building up of our strength in partnership with our allies, economic cooperation, readiness to negotiate, and a firm adherence to the fundamental purposes and principles of our society—constitute a national policy, not a party policy. They are rooted in our traditions. They find general support in both parties.

It is right and proper that there should be differences of opinion among us about the execution of this policy, and about questions of emphasis, priorities, application and administration. No one has a monopoly of wisdom and the vigor and vitality of a democratic society derived from free discussion and debate and the consent which flows from understanding. However vigorous our debates may be, it should be made clear to all that our country is united in its determination to hew to the Strategy of Freedom which is our national policy.

The nation's peril is our challenge. The united will of the people must be our answer.

The Ministry of the Christian Church in the Armed Forces

FROM AN ADDRESS BY REAR ADMIRAL STANTON W. SALISBURY, U.S.N.

Chief of Chaplains of the U. S. Navy, and chairman of the Armed Services Chaplain Board

THE CHAPLAINS who served in World War I and II added much luster to the record of the various corps, by their bravery, courage, effectiveness, spiritual consecration, and religious convictions. Their service to the religious welfare of the men in uniform was made at great cost to themselves, and some real sacrifice on the part of their churches. This same outstanding ministry must be provided and amplified in the dread days to come.

Since last June, when a new war came on the horizon, many of the former chaplains have returned to active service, because they could not be elsewhere in a time of emergency, when the Christian ministry is so greatly needed by our young people standing in our stead in places of danger and death.

In times such as this soldiers and sailors come from all types of families, they are a cross-section of America. That means a mingling of all races, for we have real integration in the Armed Forces. It means a melting pot where local prejudices are lost sooner or later. It means a confusion of standards and ideals. It means the association of persons holding various creeds and theological beliefs. It may mean a challenge to one's moral concepts. Religious convictions cannot be taken for granted, for there is always someone to defend other such convictions. These young people are at the age of doubt; they argue long and loud; they doubt the word of everyone—father, mother, preacher, teacher—and even presume to do so when they meet their first military instructor—but this happens only once!

The recruit attends a series of lectures given by the chaplains on the virtues of a religious man serving in the armed forces. These character guidance lectures stress a man's responsibility to his country, to his comrads and shipmates, to his family, and to himself as a child of God. . . .

The young service people find the chaplain to be one of them. They discover that he is friendly, understanding, and sympathetic. He listens to their troubles and takes the place of parents in time of trial. He wears a uniform to mark him as one of the same force. Some day they will meet him out in the military establishment. They know that he will suffer the same hardships, undergo the same trials, be present in time of battle; the man of God going everywhere, even though danger is nigh and Death stalks close at hand. It may be his portion to be wounded, and it may be that he will be killed. Here is Christianity in action; the church following and serving its sons and daughters through its representatives, the clergymen in uniform loaned to the military establishment to make real and effective the words of our Master: "I came not to be ministered unto, but to minister."

In the military establishment there are the same proportion of church members as in the civilian community, but there is a better opportunity to reach the unchurched. The latter meet the impact of religion and are faced with the necessity of considering its value when they have their interview with the chaplain at the recruit training station. But the ministry is continued wherever the service man or woman goes. They meet the chaplain again and again. He is at hand when they become ill; he will be at the scene of any accident almost as soon as the doctor and the crash crews; he will give lectures on the true way of life; he will provide means of securing knowledge of culture, education, and advancement; and by personal example the chaplain will be the living representative of him whom we call Master. In fact, the chaplain is in truth a missionary to the largest and most responsive mission field in the world today. By deed and word, by precept and example, the chaplain will endeavor to bring light to those in darkness, knowledge to the ignorant, and salvation to the lost.

The Church in the Nation

FROM AN ADDRESS BY HERMANN N. MORSE

THIS PROGRAM is devoted to the place of the mission enterprise of the church in the concern of the National Council, of which the Home Missions Council and the Foreign Missions Conference are two of the component elements. Since the National Council is designed to serve the whole range of the vital interests of the Christian churches of America, our question is as to the significance of missions in the life and work of the church and as to the contribution of the missionary program to such an organization as this.

Our greatest hope for the National Council is not in the field of organizational mechanics. Our great purpose is to create an organization which will stimulate and lead in a great forward movement of the church to win America and the world for Christ. What we do here must finally be judged on its contribution to the spiritual life of our time. In that effort the missionary enterprise must have a central place.

This is a National Council of Churches. That is, its field of operation is the United States of America. But in saying that, we see America both as a field and a force. It is a field in that here, as much as in any country, we need a revitalization of religious faith and a renewed effort to win our people to a convinced and courageous discipleship. It is a force in that, with our newly won place of world leadership and influence, the spiritual character of America may well have a decisive effect upon the future of the whole world. We dare to believe that a Christian and a Protestant America can be the strongest force in the world against the new and the old paganisms that are contending for the mastery of the world.

My particular function is to speak for the home mission enterprise. One might describe the essential contribution of that enterprise to the church which it serves as three basic concerns: first, for its foundations, second, for its outlook on contemporary life, and, third, for its ultimate boundaries. These are the three oldest concerns of Home Missions, and the three newest and most urgent: to establish and maintain the church as an intimate part of the life of every community; to make its mission and its service relevant to the needs of the people in every time and place; and to keep it always pressing forward, always pushing its boundaries out to the far side of every frontier of life.

Of necessity, these basic concerns have made Home Missions continent-minded. It has had to think of the entire nation. It has refused to accept any lesser objective than to win the whole nation for Christ, to make this a Christian nation. While this objective has not been achieved, there is no reason to believe that it is impossible of achievement.

I

The Home Mission enterprise grew up with the nation. Throughout its history its basic objectives have been to extend the preaching of the gospel, to establish and maintain the church, and to perform a ministry of Christian service to provide for the fundamental needs of Christian living. In the beginning its efforts were directed toward the American Indians and the frontier settlements. As the nation expanded, it pressed forward with the job of churching the continent, the tempo of which steadily increased as the population flowed westward. With this went a concern for education, health and community life.

The passing years brought a great variety of problems: the changing character of immigration from abroad, the constant movement of people within the United States, the freeing of the Negro slaves, the development of industry and the great growth of cities, the changing status of rural areas, the rapid development now of this section and now of that, the blight of isolation or retardation that afflicted particular areas or groups, the acquisition of Alaska and the opening of the West Indies, the effects of wars and depressions. Obviously, the missionary task was one that could never be finished. As we move into the era just before us, we realize that we are in a period of more profound and far-reaching change than in any earlier period in our history.

II

There are new elements in our problem today, but this does not mean that we have those missionary needs in increased measure and urgency. Actually, there are more people outside the churches and, because of the tremendous movement of population, more people living in unchurched communities than ever before. Every other characteristic problem—ministry to special groups, pioneer evangelization, service in every field of human need— is more difficult to cope with and has increased urgency.

The new factor today is in the circumstances which condition our performance of the missionary task. That is, the new factor is in the nature of social development, the unprecedented mobility both of people and of ideas, the prevailing secularism, and the undermining of traditional standards and loyalties in many fields. Of course, it is not religion alone that is confronted with this sort of a dilemma.

95

1. New Patterns of Population Distribution

Nothing is of more primary concern to the church than the question of where and how people live. Broadly speaking, the strength of the Protestant church is in its ministry to people in the setting of their home communities. That is what gives such high importance to the tremendous reshuffling of population that has been going on in this country. Striking instances are the great growth of Negro population in Northern and Western cities and the increase of Puerto Ricans in New York.

Four things of great practical importance to the mission of the church stand out in this situation: (1) The very great number of people who have settled in new residential communities where new churches must be established and equipped for their ministry. (2) The many millions of others who have moved out of contact with the churches of which they have been members constitutes a great problem both for the churches they have left and for those in the communities to which they have gone. (3) The thousands of instances in which churches have been surrounded by an entirely different type of population than they had known or in a steadily declining population. (4) The great numbers of people who cannot be adequately reached by existing churches but require special types of pioneer evangelization.

2. The New Form and Significance of Inter-group Relations

We often speak very glibly and condescendingly of what we call "minority groups." Some of the most thrilling chapters of home missionary history deal with the ministry of the church to such groups—Indians, Negroes, Orientals, Spanish-Americans; various groups of European immigrants; disadvantaged elements of our native white population, as Southern mountaineers, migrant workers, lumberjacks.

This whole matter of inter-group relations is become one of the critical social issues of our day which compels a fundamental re-examination of our position and policy in the work of the church. Here the National Council can render a very great service.

3. The Changing Intellectual and Spiritual Climate

This is too familiar a theme to require elaboration here. That secular society often shows high regard for basic human values proves no more than that society is still living on its inherited spiritual capital. When concern for human welfare is torn from its natural rootage in the love of God, it becomes little more than a political or, at best, an ethical generalization.

Another oft told tale concerns the lag in spiritual and ethical insight compared with our marvellous achievements in the scientific realm. Still another familiar aspect is concerned with the vast increase in educational

96

General Secretary Cavert and President Sherrill

Entering the hall for the Constituting Service

A summer view of the Public Auditorium

Snow did not daunt the delegates

and cultural opportunity for the mass of our people coupled with a high-powered type of mental conditioning through various communications media the net result of which is of doubtful moral and spiritual value.

In larger communities there is an anonymous character to life that makes it easy to insulate oneself from spiritual influences. At the same time men, increasingly immersed in the flood of mass society, find it more and more difficult to assert themselves as individuals.

Once we could assume the secure anchorage of the Christian church in the main stream of American life; could assume the general acceptance of the centrality of spiritual values. Today we have to be concerned about the ability of the church, not so much to maintain itself as an institution, which it can very well do, but to be a vital, controlling force in our total life.

4. New Concepts of Social Responsibility and Collective Action

Everyone is familiar with the extent to which we have gone in asserting the responsibility of the state for fundamental social welfare. The social gains at many points have been impressively great. At the same time, there is a serious threat to individual initiative and self-reliance. Important questions are raised as to the future place of voluntary organizations and private initiative within the broad area of social welfare.

III

It is against such a background that we can most clearly see the need and place of such an organization as the National Council of Churches. The insight of the founding fathers of the nation that liberty and union are one and inseparable has deep meaning for the church today. Liberty is a precious heritage of the Protestant churches but will have its fullest expression in the unity of the spirit.

Our social conscience has been sufficiently alerted to make us acutely embarrassed by inconsistent practices which we are organizationally not able to control. Because in theory we make worship and fellowship interdependent, we cannot easily adapt ourselves to a stratified society of sharply distinguished groups.

Formerly we were apt to think of most forms of Home Mission service as something that the privileged made possible for the underprivileged. Today the distinction between the privileged and the underprivileged is not so clear and, in any event, they are mingled in most communities, so that we have to think of Home Missions as something we all do, all the time, everywhere. We have to try to make worship and fellowship, evangelism and fellowship, service and fellowship inter-dependent. Without fellowship, much of the significance of worship, evangelism and service, as parts of a missionary program, is lost. This is essentially a Protestant concept which becomes increasingly important as the lines of social demarcation are sharpened.

When we put our Home Mission enterprise over against this whole modern, changing situation, the problems of greatest long-range significance emerge:

1. The first is our oldest problem—the problem of sheer extension. We confront this problem on a vaster scale than ever before in three characteristic forms:

The problem of new church development.
The problem of evangelistic extension into the secularized community.
The problem of pioneer evangelization.

2. The second is the problem of stabilizing and undergirding the churches in rapidly changing or undeveloped situations.

3. The third we may simply describe as the problem of bridging the gulfs between races and classes that cut across American life.

4. The fourth and last that we will mention is the problem of our missionary outposts. International developments as well as internal factors have given to Alaska, Hawaii, and the West Indies a new and greatly increased significance.

It is in relation to such problems as these that we have already made our greatest advances in the development of co-operative programs and procedures, and it is here that interdenominational co-operation can make its most direct and practical contribution. Because these are all problems that concern the total interests of the church, this more comprehensive organization in the National Council points the way to greater effectiveness. In the greater interest of our total Christian mission we must now find the means of making our growing sense of unity in faith and effort really come alive in the everyday life and work of the church at the grass roots as well as in the strategy and plans of our general agencies. Thus we may hope that we are here launching a great forward movement for the extension of the gospel into all the life of the world in our time.

The Church in the World

FROM AN ADDRESS BY MISS SARAH CHAKKO

*President of Isabella Thoburn College, India; Secretary of the
World Council's Commission on the Life and Work of Women in the Church*

Is this civilization worth saving?

Frankly, many of us do not act as if Christian groups can do much to save our civilization. We put our faith elsewhere. We depend upon human wisdom, upon diplomatic negotiations, collective security, large armies. We are not far removed from the Jews of Jesus' day who counted on the might of armies for the realization of Jewish safety and security. Looked at from the worldly point of view this may be justified.

The little group of Christians who resisted the Nazi oppression and paganism certainly did not stop World War II. The same may be said of the Japanese Christians before the last war. Looked at soberly, one has no earthly reason to believe that the Christians in China or Russia can avert World War III.

But the still more basic question is if this civilization as we know it is worth saving. Does it fulfill in its essence the purposes of God? With the several centuries of opportunity, what have we done with the life-giving word of God? The small minority who have cared have worked toward a world-wide church. But have enough of us cared about the hungry peoples of the world? Have we given them a chance at a decent living? Have we not taken possession of good land and driven the weaker peoples out? Have we not grabbed the persons of human beings and used them for our profit, and turned against them the moment we find them getting self-conscious enough to assert their rights? Do we not justify this very iniquity by quoting the Holy Word of God? Have not saints and martyrs cried out against such iniquities and gone to their deaths? If we wish to preserve such a civilization, why should we expect the God of justice to befriend us at this hour? Let us ask ourselves what it is that we wish to save in our civilization and for whom are we saving these values?

The Christian church is a minority movement.

The Christian church has always been a minority movement. There have been periods in the history of Europe and America when people

99

thought it was not so and that they were secure in their numbers. But I believe that in all of history the real believers have always been a minority. To the Christian from the areas of the younger churches where he knows he is in a minority, it comes as a shock that it is so in America. The neo-paganism which has come into existence has come because the church has lost the purity of her faith and because we have let ourselves be captured by the all-powerful state, or by money, or by social status and respectability. The fact of the minority church all over the world gives a new meaning to that term that came alive at Whitby a few years ago—"partnership in obedience"—a new relation between the older and the younger churches, between what used to be thought of as sending and receiving missions. The missionary work of our day thus finds a new relationship of giving and receiving for the mutual strengthening that comes out of the pooling of resources in men, money, experience, ideas. Thus no Christian groups remain as purely giving or receiving groups.

What is the function of the church in the world today?

1. What it always has been: to call people once again to the love of God, to an appreciation of the right sense of values in life and to commitment of themselves once again to God.

2. In these days of tension, to listen attentively to those who criticize the church, criticize our nation, to understand if they have the truth on their side and to use them as a corrective agency in our church, national and personal lives.

3. To maintain spiritual lines of communication between people who are behind the various kinds of curtains, not to let national policies interfere with Christian fellowship. This is not an easy thing in times of tension, as we in India have learned to understand.

4. To influence our nations in right public policies and yet not be captured by the national interests, thus letting the church be captured.

With all this we may be too late to save this civilization. If so, the function of the Christian is to stand firm in his faith and see the emergence of a new one which has shed the shackles of the corruption of the old. The future that God has for redemption may perhaps not be through this civilization which has not risen to its responsibilities. The important thing is not for a civilization to be saved, but for God's scheme of redemption to be worked —through us, if we can fulfill our obligations, but in spite of us, if that is necessary. Whatever the case, the Christian's hope is always there; it is in the ultimate purposes of God, not in saving his skin. Therefore the Christian has no panic. He follows the path blazed by his Lord.

CHRISTIAN FAITH IN ACTION

Our Missionary Responsibility to the Nation and the World

FROM AN ADDRESS BY DR. ALBERT D. STAUFFACHER

*Minister and Executive Secretary of the Missions Council
of the Congregational Christian Churches*

THE CHURCHES that have constituted this National Council of the Churches of Christ in the United States of America are in the nation and in the world but not of the nation and of the world. They are of God. The Christian religion is a missionary religion, a religion with a mission. The mission is from God to men and to nations on the earth. God is the Initiator of the mission which brought the world, the prophets and the Church into being. There followed the Book, the organization, the strategy and the program, all created to serve and expedite the mission. "Mission is to the Church what flame is to fire."

Thirty-one million, nine hundred and ninety-seven thousand members of the churches of this National Council are not here. There are some ten thousand people back home for each one of us here. They constitute the home base of this Council, the "Church's Second Foundation." They too belong to the mission of God and they too are called to the missionary responsibility. We shall succeed only as we are successful in bringing them, along with us, to fulfill the mission and the missionary obligation of this Council. They, with us, must see clearly the urgency and relevancy of this responsibility and be motivated to respond to it. For "mission" is the very essence of their lives in the fellowship of the church.

The task of the missionary enterprise has been set before us as "the bold intention of Christianizing the life of our nation" on the one hand and "One World in Christ" on the other. . . . At least one-half the people in the nation are in no vital touch with the church; three-fifths of the world's population live in the lands of the Younger Churches, and 97 per cent of these are unreached by the church, Catholic and Protestant. To proclaim the Gospel and extend the benefits of the church to all these people, to call forth and train leadership, and to apply the Gospel to all the involved institutions and relationships adds up to a stupendous responsibility. Yet

101

these are the tasks to which we have set our hands in the nation and in the world.

To bring the whole church with us, all the 32,000,000, so that the whole church may be activated to receive, embody and transmit the mission of God is our missionary responsibility. We need "Christian communities" sharing their life with others.

This missionary responsibility breaks down into five areas of concern.

I

The churches of this National Council are established of God to proclaim the good news of reconciliation, unity and peace, available for men and nations through Jesus Christ and his gospel. This is a mission of incomparable relevancy and urgency to the condition of man and the world today.

To make known and observed this Gospel of God is the missionary responsibility to which our churches are "sent" of God.

II

The churches of this National Council are commissioned of God to demonstrate to the nation and the world the effectiveness of the Gospel to provide the things essential to the good life. The good life calls for more than security, plenty, and political freedom, or liberation from enthralling fetters and entanglements; it calls for a world order wherein justice can function and peace can live; for a vital faith, a meaningful purpose and a program for effective and creative living. Jesus staked his divine credentials upon the power of his gospel to achieve these things for all men. In the world conditions under which we live, this commission to demonstrate the power of the religion of Jesus to produce the good life calls for the full strength of the whole church.

III

The churches of this National Council are called, by the fact of their missionary responsibility, to exalt God above all other priorities in the nation and the world. The history of nations affirms that primary reverence for God with obedience to his will is the key to enduring life; neglect thereof is the forerunner of bankruptcy, decay and defeat. Breach of the covenant with God leads to division, captivity and ruin.

The worship of gods of man's creation rather than the living God who created man is the major threat of today. Historians centuries hence may say that the central question before our generation was, "Will man worship God or collective man?"

In a world where a religion of godlessness is rampant and where the honor, dignity and freedom of man are violated, the church must confront

102

the nation and the world with the living God, the sovereign Lord of the affairs of men.

IV

The churches of this National Council are charged by the gravity of their missionary responsibility to discipline their life to the operation of the Holy Spirit. "When the Gospel makes no advance in our days we must not seek for excuses in the pagan world around us, but try to find the real obstacles inside the church. We have neglected the Holy Spirit."

There is a growing concern in missionary circles today, in some cases amounting to a conviction of sin, lest, in our eagerness to get on with the job, we rely too much on our own wisdom, education and know-how and trust too little to the Holy Spirit. We do too much for people and too little with them. We speak too much for God and do not permit him to speak through us. As a result there is a severance of the branch from the vine, and the Spirit cannot get through. It is our missionary responsibility to the Holy Spirit of the Living God to maintain the inner quality and to keep the channel open.

V

The churches of this National Council are summoned by their Lord, the Head of the church, and through the achievements, the open doors, and the resources God has given, to bring an offering, continuous and dependable, sufficiently worthy and costly to match his sacrifices and promises in the gospel.

This is a time for great giving. God has done so much with the little we have given, what would he not do with the sacrificial dedication of our total lives and resources? Assuming that our church members are average citizens, the annual income of the church members co-operating in this Council is at least $32,000,000,000. Everything needed to fulfill our missionary responsibility is ours save the dedication of life and resources, in true Christian stewardship, to the discipline of God's Holy Spirit.

In this National Council, "missions" occupy their rightful place in the body of the church. It is a great asset to the Divisions of Home and Foreign Missions that the missionary enterprise is no longer an elective to the members of this Council. Henceforth it is evident that missionary responsibility inheres in membership in the church. Moreover, this Council, not an end in itself, is now a mission of God to the nation and the world.

103

God and the Nations

FROM A REPORT OF THE ADDRESS BY DR. TOYOHIKO KAGAWA OF JAPAN

"HOLY FATHER, keep through thine own name those whom thou hast given me, that they may be one, as we are." I bring thanks to the churches of the U. S. for all you have done for us; since the war you have in the name of Christ helped us. You have proved to us that we are workers together with Christ.

There have been four occasions in history when the Church has proved stronger than the armies: (1) When the Roman Empire was conquered in 410 (Augustine's *City of God*); (2) When the hordes of Mohammedans attacked Constantinople. The Crusades failed adequately to meet the emergency, but St. Francis did not; (3) When The Thirty Years' War between the Catholics and the Protestants devastated Europe, the final answer was given by new religious movements, as the one led by John Wesley; (4) When the Industrial Revolution has led to the rise of Communism, the whole world is again in danger. The answer will again be given in a religious movement matching the need of the time.

We forget that God is amongst us. The destiny of Jesus is to unite God and man. Properly speaking, we should all be punished to cleanse and heal all that is wrong. God is at the disposal of all the universe. Our world is in a terrible fever, whose remedy—the Cross of Christ—is hidden in the body of the Church. When the body is wounded or infected, the blood goes to the diseased spot and dies that the body may live. This is God's plan for the salvation of the world; Jesus Christ came to die for the world, that the world might be reunited with God. The whole Gospel of John most effectively illustrates this fact.

Born in the country of Buddhism, Confucianism and Shintoism, I am a product of Christian missions. I found that the Christian religion was the only one which could free mankind and cure him of his sins. . . .

In trying to destroy China, Japan is going to be destroyed. This was my burden when, in the spirit of Christ, I went to Shanghai to ask forgiveness for the sins of my country. Upon my return to Japan, I was arrested, jailed for 18 days; for two days I could not lie down; "Lie down," the guards said, "you will be socked!" But I could not lie down because Japan's destiny was so heavy on my mind. I put my head between my knees, I was so weighed down with sorrow and shame for my country. Then came the words to me, "That he would grant you, according to the riches of his glory, to be strengthened with might by his Spirit in the inner man; That Christ may dwell in your hearts by faith. . . . " Eph. 4:16, 17. Then Christ came with inexpressible joy. If I had been assassinated then, still I would have been overjoyed; for I then realized that Christ was in my heart—that he lived within me, and hope came again to me for my country.

Communism is based on class consciousness, which never makes for a happy society. Communism's destiny is clear: class consciousness becomes suicide—only a universal consciousness can survive, which is the reason the Gospel is so pertinent, for it brings the sinner and God together and all the classes in between.

Universal consciousness of Christ—the redemptive love of Christ—is the only way to redeem and save the world. Are you Americans willing to bear the cross of Jesus in order to unite all nations into one?

Prayer: Unite us again with God; unite us with the churches in Hungary, Czechoslovakia, Poland—with all European countries; with China, Japan and Korea; and bless us all that we may go back to our churches with the fire of the Gospel."

A Christian View on the International Crisis

AN ADDRESS BY DR. O. FREDERICK NOLDE

Director of the Commission of the Churches on International Affairs of the World Council of Churches and the International Missionary Council

You WILL NOT misunderstand me when I say at the outset that I approach my task tonight with fear and trembling. My disturbance does not arise from the limited time available for preparation but rather from the subject which I have agreed to propose for your consideration. I would be at measurable ease in describing for you the program of the Churches' Commission on International Affairs, a joint agency of the World Council of Churches and the International Missionary Council—the manner in which the Commission is developing a structure for continuing Christian testimony to the world of nations and the representation it is making on world problems currently before the United Nations and related bodies. That easy course is not open to me tonight. In face of tangled evidence and obvious ignorance of details, I am forced by request and circumstances to attempt an appraisal of the present critical situation, and to suggest lines of procedure which will reflect Christian conviction. In this effort, I do not speak officially as Director of the C.C.I.A. I approach my task as an individual Christian and a citizen of the United States, remembering that my recent activities have permitted exposure to points of view held by Christian leaders in many parts of the world.

My approach to the present situation is on the background of two presuppositions. The first is my conviction that God in his goodness makes available strength in proportion to the needs of the hour. Christianity was born and bred in adversity, and Christians have risen to greatest heights when confronted by the most critical tests. God will provide strength at this moment of history if we will only use what he places at our disposal. In the second place, I hold to the belief that even in this trying hour a third world war is not inevitable. In accepting that view, we must not delude ourselves. Events of the last few days have considerably diminished the margin of possibility. We are on the brink of a precipice. To avoid being plunged into the abyss, we must exploit to the full every possibility which that thin margin affords us.

THE SITUATION

The broad outlines of the world's dilemma are generally known. With full recognition that we are not without guilt with regard to the total situation that has arisen, we are convinced that an act of aggression has been committed. The United Nations authorized an international police action which has, on varying grounds and in various ways, been opposed and resisted by North Korea, by the Peoples' Government of China, and by the U.S.S.R. In the United States as well as in other countries, a far-flung program of military preparation is under way. While there are some who believe that force should never be used, the preponderant majority reluctantly accepts the necessity of military strength to serve as a deterrent to aggression and, wherever aggression occurs, as a means of opposing it. The reality of the situation is that the world is divided into two armed camps and that the United States and other governments are making every effort to have a military power sufficient for any emergency. In face of these circumstances, the definition of our problem is not too difficult. We must find those affirmative steps which will decrease the need for using military measures now under way and, if further need does arise, to keep such military measures at every point to the absolute minimum which circumstances will allow.

In seeking to determine these affirmative steps, we must ask ourselves what can be done by the people to whom we can speak and who will listen to us. We cannot at this time hope to get sympathetic audience from Soviet controlled areas. What we can do is so to govern our own immediate actions by justice and goodwill as progressively to extend the area of our influence and ultimately win a hearing from those who now oppose us.

Before proposing concrete steps, let me stress the importance of building into the fabric of our individual and community life the two presuppositions which I previously mentioned. Our people need the comfort and inspiration which come from the conviction that God does make available the strength which the emergency requires. The knowledge that there still remains a marginal possibility of averting a global war should intensify their efforts in this critical time.

In suggesting eight possible lines of procedure, I shall first of all indicate the danger against which we should guard and then explain or illustrate the positive means by which this may be done. Needless to say, isolation of any one proposal from the others may lead to a faulty conception of what is intended.

107

I

Guard against hysteria which robs action of moral perspective and political wisdom. Confronted by imminent danger, people are disposed to cast reason and judgment to the wind. In alarming proportions, there is for example the demand that we should now drop atomic bombs on Communist China and promptly invade Manchuria. I unhesitatingly express my personal opinion that these are the very things which we should not at this moment do. In the first place, until all other means have been explored and found impossible, the dropping of atomic bombs would not be morally justifiable. In the second place, we would be veritably playing into the hands of those who want to pin upon us the tangible responsibility for starting a world war. Be it noted that, in saying this, I speak in the light of conditions as they exist today and allow that the conditions of tomorrow may be different. I would not give to those who are resisting the decisions of the United Nations the comfort and assurance of a pledge not to resort to drastic measures if their actions leave us no reasonable alternative. By calmness and confidence, born of the conviction that God will ultimately prevail, we must meet our responsibility in a way that reflects moral principles to the fullest possible extent permitted by a tragically evil situation.

II

Guard against self-righteousness and hatred which give impulse to the monstrosity of a holy war or a preventive war. We cannot overlook evils in others; in fact, we must condemn them. But the conviction of our implication in world guilt and the knowledge of what total global war means rule out any possibility of war ever being holy or of a preventive war ever being justified. If war should come, and God forbid that it may, it must be irrevocably thrust upon us by others than ourselves and every alternative recourse which our interpretation of God's will for man can entertain must first have been honestly explored.

III

Guard against unilateral action which rejects a moral judgment as reflected by majority opinion in the United Nations. One hopeful factor in the United Nations decision to recommend military measures against aggression by North Korea was the emergence for the first time in history of international police action, imperfect though that recognizedly was. That new factor must be retained and improved. The General Assembly, by action on November 3, has invited each member of the United Nations to maintain in its national armed forces elements for service as a United Nations unit or units. If military forces stronger than those now operating in Korea are needed, they should be provided in accordance with this action of the

United Nations. If when all such designated forces have been made available, even more are needed, additional forces should be provided within that same framework. The United States, as a government of preponderant power, must submit its actions to international consideration and decision. The day when any one country has the right by itself to declare war on another is past.

IV

Guard against false pride and face-saving tendencies which close the door to open-minded and effective negotiation. We must be constantly willing to review our policies, especially as they apply to particular situations. For example, an original commitment may have called for military action embracing all Korea. Alternate possibilities should not be arbitrarily discarded, such as the creation of a buffer strip to be controlled by the United Nations for a cooling-off period. Great importance must in this connection be attached to the offers by intermediate or small governments to negotiate differences between the major powers. Moreover, other nations respect us when we respond to such proposals by the U.S.S.R. as hold promise of offering effective solutions. The mood of the United States Congress will be a crucial factor in determining what our foreign policy can be, and public opinion should make unmistakably clear that critical international issues must be settled on merit and not become the football of party politics.

V

Guard against complacency which comes with increasing military strength and which may bring a disposition to risk an incident or even to create an incident for inciting conflict on a world scale. The United States must indicate readiness to expose its action to impartial scrutiny. The United Nations has provided a medium for this by setting up a Peace Observation Commission to be located at every potential danger spot throughout the world, a plan which was originally proposed by the Churches' Commission on International Affairs. With the accusations and counter-accusations on rearmament by occupying powers in the Eastern and Western zones, Germany is in a critical position so long as the tensions between the Soviet Government and the Western Powers continue. It offers a logical point at which to inaugurate the Peace Observation Commission's operations. Informal conversations with church and political leaders in Western Germany reveal that such a Commission would be welcome. It should be located in both the Eastern and Western zones but could serve a useful purpose even if its establishment were limited to the Western zone. The United States can demonstrate readiness to expose its actions in Germany to international scrutiny by taking the initiative in calling for a Peace Observation Commission in both the Eastern and Western zones and by

109

agreeing to the operation of such a Commission in the Western zone, no matter what the decision by the U.S.S.R. may be. Once the start has been made, similar commissions can be located in other areas.

VI

Guard against making our economy so dependent upon military production as to give the impression that we are unprepared to recognize the importance of economic health throughout the world. The President of the United States has expressed before the United Nations our desire to achieve a real disarmament which will include *all kinds* of weapons; be based on *unanimous* agreement, and be *foolproof*. He has further held out the hope that our armaments would be transferred into food, medicine, tools for use in under-developed areas, and into other aids for human advancement. Numerous leaders in the United States have publicly professed that our war preparations are designed in the interest of peace.

So long as the marginal possibility of averting war remains, these commitments must be kept prominently before the world. We must let it be known that we have not forgotten our promises and that we continue to study ways whereby the goal of diverting our resources to constructive enterprises may be achieved. In so doing we would provide much needed assurance to our own people and to the people and governments of every country throughout the world. At all times we must indicate our willingness to beat swords into plowshares at any moment when reconciliation has reached the point of providing convincing evidences that aggression need no longer be feared.

VII

Guard against the prejudice which refuses to see the evils in a situation which is predominantly good and thus deserving of support. Rarely if ever is one party to a dispute entirely right and the other party entirely wrong. Few situations may be described as completely "black and white." The mixture of the good and the evil which characterized virtually every international issue is a substantial obstacle to effective solutions. Christians must be particularly vigilant in making sharp distinctions so that, in supporting a predominantly just cause, they will not condone the injustices which are inherent or which emerge in the situation.

Many illustrations could be cited. I mention only one. When the churches commended the United Nations' action in Korea they felt justified because two new factors had appeared—the presence on the scene of a neutral international commission and the effort to take action by international police measures. This commendation may in no sense be taken as a cloak to cover subsequent mistakes or injustices. Christians must now insist that (1) the benefits of the land reforms which were effected in North

Korea must be conserved, allowing that injustices worked while instituting those reforms cannot go unheeded; (2) the principles of justice and law as relating to reported atrocities must be equally applied in North and in South Korea; and (3) provisions must be made for North Koreans freely to exercise their electoral right in determining the government of a free and unified Korea. Such impartiality is incumbent upon Christians if they seek a just settlement of world issues. Clear cut political planning along these lines would tend to ease many fears.

VIII

Guard against impatience in seeking a sound conclusion of the world's present plight. Americans by tradition want to get a job done quickly and to have it out of the way. If we are bent upon creating a world atmosphere in which conflicting ideologies can compete peacefully, we cannot expect a speedy conclusion. It is in large part this lack of patience that makes some people contend that communism can be successfully combatted by military action. The result of a global war, even though we were victorious, would probably be to spread communism far more quickly and widely than has been possible through Soviet tactics of coercion, infiltration, revolution and deceit.

We must be prepared in patience to persevere in what may continue to be a long drawn-out struggle. In this connection, two lines of activity are imperative. Because of their intrinsic merit they would be imperative even if there were no need to oppose communism. The program of economic assistance to under-developed areas of Africa, Asia and the Far East is the only just and e fective answer to the upsurging demand for independence and for an acceptable standard of living. Equally important is the universal observance of human rights and fundamental freedoms. We must guard against the totalitarian methods which we condemn in others, set an example of true democracy in our domestic practice, and speed the completion of an adequate International Covenant on Human Rights.

Measures such as these require patience, and their fruits are not always readily apparent. Nevertheless their inherent rightness calls for patient continuance in well-doing.

CONCLUSION

I have sought to outline for you certain measures which it is within our power to undertake. If time permitted, the illustrations I have cited could be further developed and other measures added. I do not presume to say that these steps will prove effective. I recognize that full catastrophe may break upon the world at any time. Nevertheless I make bold to contend for my fundamental thesis. So long as there remains even a marginal possibility of averting total global war, we must utilize every means which will not betray conviction or offend conscience. In this process and even if war should come—we must penetrate the artificial curtains by which we are momentarily separated and experience the bonds of humanity and faith which unite men of different nations and races.

The struggle for peace must go forward unremittingly, and men must be driven by the conviction that the peace can yet be won. In these trying days and always, we pray God, through Jesus Christ our Lord, for the faith which will enable us to stand in face of principalities and powers of darkness. From Him alone can come strength to make the expression of our faith adequate for the needs of our day.

The Church in the World of Nations

AN ADDRESS BY DR. W. A. VISSER 'T HOOFT

General Secretary, World Council of Churches

As WE CONSIDER the present situation of the Church in the world of nations our temptation is to concentrate our attention on the dramatic and perhaps catastrophic developments in the political realm rather than on the less sensational events in the life of the church. But we must resist that temptation. Now, if ever, we must keep our sense of Christian perspective. And that means that we remain sensitive to that specific history within and behind general history, which is the history of God's dealings with his people. In fact, we will never understand the deeper meaning of this historical hour nor grasp the significance of the signs of the times—unless we seek to hear what the spirit is saying to the churches in and through the convulsions of our time.

We ask therefore: What are the decisive events and developments in the life of the Church in our day? What are the greatest things which God does in and for His church in our time?

THE CHURCH LEARNS AGAIN TO FIGHT

The first of these crucial facts is, surely, that the church learns again to fight.

From the days of Constantine the Great until our own days the normal situation of the church has been that it lived in relatively peaceful relations with the world. Sometimes the church and the world embraced each other as in the Middle Ages; sometimes the world ignored the church as in modern secularism, but there are few examples on record in that whole long period of a systematic attempt to destroy the Christian church. Thus, during that period, the church has had a relatively tranquil and protected life. And the biblical view of a church which must expect open hostility or even persecution from the *kosmos* surrounding it seemed often distant and unreal.

But in our day and generation this situation has changed radically. The rise of totalitarianisms that demand complete and exclusive loyalty of whole nations brings the church once again in open conflict with the world. From the zonal demarcation lines in Germany to the Pacific Ocean, the church confronts a powerful ideology which considers that religion is an obstacle on the road to happiness and that the struggle against religion is an imperative duty for those who would liberate man. At the same time, in large areas where the Christian church was indirectly protected by the existence of at least nominally Christian colonial governments, it is now up against majority-religions with a strong and new self-consciousness which considers Christianity as a foreign and dangerous intruder in their national cultures.

This puts the church in a new situation which is at the same time a very old situation. The church must learn to fight again. It must remember its origins. It must learn to live wholly and exclusively upon its own inner strength. It must again meet the great test and demonstrate that its Lord has once for all overcome the world.

Pascal said: "Wonderful situation, when the Church depends upon God alone." The fighting church discovers that God's word is really not bound. At first sight it seems ludicrous to speak of the freedom of the fighting churches. Are they not surrounded by obtsacles and held by insuperable chains? Still, it is a fact that these churches discover a deeper freedom, a freedom which no one can take away from them. Let me quote the words of one of their leaders. He says: "It is precisely when we enter in conflict with powerful enemies that we discover whether we live in the liberty which is in Christ. We are liberated from cowardice, for we are being held. We are liberated from fear; for we become ready to suffer; we are liberated from the spirit of revenge, for we pray for our enemies whom Christ would save."

It is a paradoxical fact that it is in these fighting churches where so much suffering takes place that we find a Christian joy and a Christian hope such as we meet too rarely in other churches. But for those who know their Bible that paradox is familiar. It is the joy of those who find God faithful in the hour of need. It is the hope of those who see God's history going on in spite of all "the raging of the heathen." In one of the last persecutions in the early Christian era, Cyprian, who died later as a martyr, wrote: "Let us stand upright amidst the ruins of men's world and not lie down with those who have no hope left." That experience is once again made in the Church of Christ today.

The whole Church of Christ should share in that joyful knowledge. We should not get obsessed with all that we hear about political compromises made by church leaders. These are indeed serious matters, but they do not reflect the true and deep life of the church. The real story of the churches under pressure is the story of new life, of true revival, yes, and of evangelism and growth in spite of the totalitarian attempt to eradicate Christianity. The real story is that, instead of slowly dying out, the church demonstrates once again that (in the words of Calvin) its history is a history of resurrections. For this is the unanimous judgment of friend and foe; this is what fills Christians with joy and Marxists with indignant surprise: where the church accepts to fight the great spiritual battle, its strength is renewed. This is a great fact in our time which should bring us deep and powerful encouragement.

THE CHURCH AS THE GUARDIAN OF THE HUMAN VALUES

The second important fact about the church in our time is that it becomes increasingly the chief guardian of the human values. Let me explain. Until quite recently, it was the general assumption monotonously expressed in thousands of books, plays and poems that the church was the enemy of the typically human values. The abundant life—as they repeated in unison —could only be lived outside the church. For the church did not allow that uncontrolled and unrestrained self-expression which seemed the greatest good of human existence.

Why is it that we find, in so many places and among the very best of our modern spokesmen, a new awareness that self-expression may not lead to true abundance of life and that after all the church may be right in its claim that only those who lose their life for the sake of God will find it? The answer is given in that moving book made up of pieces of paper which Dietrich Bonhoeffer scribbled during the years of war when he was sought by the Gestapo. Bonhoeffer, who paid for his convictions by his death, wrote in those dark days: "It is not that the Church looks for the production of and the alliance with those (human) values. It is those values which *having become homeless* seek refuge within the Christian realm and in the shadow of the Christian Church."

Yes, the great human values—truth, freedom, justice, the dignity of man—these values which so many humanists and secularists sought to defend apart from the church, have suddenly proved to be homeless and rootless. They cannot live by themselves. They are swept away when the storm comes—unless they are strongly anchored in a faith which can stand any storm, a faith which knows of eternal divine and therefore unshakable standards and commandments.

It is a remarkable phenomenon of our time, that the most far-sighted and profound interpreters of our predicament have nearly all come to the conclusion that only a new rooting of the most precious human elements of our heritage in the Christian soil in which they grew originally can save our civilization. Is it not significant that it is the Orthodox priest in Giorgiu's *Twenty-Fifth Hour*, the Roman Priest in Graham Greene's *The Power and the Glory*, and the Protestant pastor in Paton's *Cry the Beloved Country* who are the advocates of man against the inhuman and anti-human powers of our times?

Similarly, in Asia where our Western democracy is tried out without acceptance of the faith out of which the basic democratic convictions have grown, there is an increasing questioning whether Hinduism, Buddhism or Mohammedanism can really provide the framework for a society of free and responsible persons, and the Christian church has in that situation an unparalleled opportunity for a relevant Christian witness.

But it is especially in the totalitarian situation that the church's role as guardian of the human values stands in clear outline. Where man is seen "merely as a member of a collectivist society," there the church comes in the unique position of being the one and only advocate and defender of man as a person. When I asked leaders of Christian youth movements in Eastern Germany how they explained the fact that in spite of all the ideological pressure they reached as many young people as ever before—their answer was: "The boys and girls say that it is only in the Church that they are treated as human beings." In other words, even if the field of action of the church is narrowed down by all sorts of obstacles, its basic witness remains, and that witness cannot fail to have its long-range repercussions.

When the Roman empire fell, it was the church that built the bridge between the old civilization and the new. May it not be that once again the church is called to carry that great responsibility?

The Church Rediscovers its Essential Unity

The third great fact about the church in our time is that it rediscovers its essential unity. Let us not think that the ecumenical movement is merely a religious replica of the political movements toward unity which have grown up in the last decades. If it were, it would have collapsed during the last World War and it would not be able to maintain its cohesion in the present deeply divided state of the world. No, the deepest motive of the ecumenical movement is that fundamentally biblical motive that there is only one body of Christ and that those who call themselves by his name dare not rest until they have demonstrated that oneness. Nothing less is at stake than the Glory of God. Our Lord says that he has given the glory which the Father gave him to his disciples so that they may be one. And the purpose of this oneness is no less than that the world may believe.

What does this ecumenical movement mean for the churches? It means that they learn again to share the human gifts which they have received from God, not for themselves alone, but for the whole body.

St. Paul tells us that each receives his spiritual gifts for the common good. But we have imprisoned our gifts within our denominational or national frontiers.

When Archbishop Soderblom presented for the first time the plan to create a World Council which he wanted to call, The Ecumenical Council," a German printer made the excusable mistake to print, *"Okonomischer*

Rat" (economic council). That was really a prophetic error. For the ecumenical movement is the attempt to restore the true economy of God's plan. The function is to tear down the tariff walls which keep the riches of each church from enriching the other churches. The purpose is to build up the Body in which all serve each other and in which no member can ever say to other members: "I have no need of thee."

We are only beginning to recapture that essential truth about the Church of Christ. We are still far too proud and too preoccupied with our ecclesiastical institution to avail ourselves fully of the great gift which God offers to us through his wonderful and sacred mystery: The Church Universal and the communion of saints. But we begin to see what it might mean if all our denominations, all our parishes would accept joyfully to live as conscious and grateful members of the world-wide body. We begin to realize what would happen if the churches, which still live in outward freedom, would learn the secret of the deeper freedom from the churches under great pressure. We become aware of the gifts which the youngest churches have to give—that truly apostolic sense that the church exists to evangelize, that a church which is not a missionary church is no church at all. And we begin to see that the oldest churches help us to understand better that ours is a historical religion based on the great facts and events of the divine revelation. We know already how much the poorer and the richer churches need each other, how both have to give and to receive in the process of interchurch aid. And so this new ecumenical fact slowly but surely penetrates the life of our churches.

Dare we believe that these facts are really important enough to figure in the world's history alongside of the dramatic developments in the realm of politics? We must not only dare to believe that they are as important as the things we read about in the newspapers; we must believe that they represent the essential, the truly significant history of our time.

George Bernard Shaw, who did not pretend to be a Christian but who had extraordinary moments of deep insight, put these words in the mouth of a cowboy who had committed a crime:

"There are two games—the one we play—and the one which is played *upon* us." Let us turn our eyes to that second, that deeper history. As the shadows darken, it becomes easier to see the light of God's action in this world. Let us be grateful that we have received the faith which opens our eyes to that light.

117

CHRISTIAN FAITH IN ACTION

The Laity and the National Council

FROM AN ADDRESS BY HAROLD E. STASSEN

President of the University of Pennsylvania

THE NEWS from Cleveland this week has been very good news. The joining together of eight inter-church groups and twenty-nine denominations with thirty-two million members into one magnificent structure in this nation under God is the best news of the last half century to the laymen of America. But the news for the world this week has been very bad news. The sudden savage onslaught of large Communist Chinese armies in flagrant disregard of the decision of fifty-three United Nations is grave aggression. This is the worst news of the last half century. Future history may record this coincidence and report a significant relationship between this good news and this bad news.

Because America needs, in this hour, above all else, a clarification of its moral principles, a deepening of its fundamental faith and a reflection, in resourceful action and unshakeable determination, of its superb philosophy. No method could be found for a greater impact on the moral foundations, the faith and the philosophy of America than this superb structure of the National Council of Churches with its own focus and also with its potential of increased co-ordination, in these underlying questions, with our fellow citizens of the Catholic and Jewish and other religions.

It is not and it will not be easy to interpret the great moral concepts of our religion into action on the difficult national and world-wide questions of the day. It is not within the power of any mortal man to make such an authoritative interpretation, but if millions of men earnestly try, then I believe it will be made with reasonable success. It is to stimulate that process of moral interpretation that I give my own views in clear and forthright manner on the most grave and difficult of current questions.

It has been suggested that, in view of the attack of Chinese Communist forces upon our American soldiers in the United Nations forces in North Korea, we should now carry the war into China itself and include in that action the use of the atomic bomb in China.

I have carefully and prayerfully considered that course of action. I have conferred by telephone with others across the country in whose judg-

118

ment I have confidence. I have come to this conclusion. These Chinese Communist armies are clearly attacking under orders from the Russian Communist Politburo in the Kremlin. The Chinese people are under a dictatorship which, in turn, is subservient to that Russian Communist Politburo. If America carries atomic war to China, millions of Chinese civilians will be killed who are themselves now the victims rather than the agents of communism. America would, for the first time, incur the enmity of the Chinese people and lose moral standing in the world, without any gain against the real source of the world danger. Thus it is my judgment, on moral grounds and on other grounds, that the United States should not carry atomic war to the people in China.

There are, in my humble view, just two circumstances in which the use of atomic weapons would be morally justified. If they can be used effectively to assist American soldiers to escape the trap in North Korea, then use for this purpose in North Korea is justified. And most important of all, if, at any future time, the United States and the United Nations conclude that the Russian Communist Politburo has directly or indirectly started World War III with world domination as their objective, then the use of atomic weapons to destroy the centers of communist atomic power, and the centers of communist war-making power, and the Kremlin itself, would be justified. I do not believe that point has arrived. But it may come.

I believe there is only one way to nurse the last tender hopes of world peace. The United Nations should promptly issue new directions to General MacArthur that he should draw his land forces back to a point where he believes he can stabilize a ground front with minimum casualties and continue to attack the opposing forces in North Korea by air and sea. All of the peace-desiring members of the United Nations should then promptly break off all diplomatic and trade relations with the Communist Chinese government. The Communist Chinese delegation should be promptly expelled from the United Nations sessions and deported from the United States. Ground reinforcements of the United Nations should be promptly sent to relieve the forces which have fought so hard for so long. And an extensive, resourceful program should be instituted to assist and encourage the millions of freedom-loving Chinese in their efforts by counter-revolution to throw off the oppressive communist dictatorship. This may take years to accomplish, but the tide of opposition to the communist dictators and to Russian imperialism is rising fast in China, and it will eventually sweep over them.

This slow process is the only way to cope with the Chinese situation. A war now with China is not the way. Above all, appeasement of the Chinese Communists is not the way. If the above course is followed, then whether or not a third world war started would depend upon whether or not the Russian Communist Politburo made another major move of aggression. This may come. We must arm rapidly to meet it. In so rearming we may also prevent it. Just as Munich led to World War II, appeasement now would pave the way for World War III. No settlement with them would be worth a thimble full.

There will undoubtedly be those who will scoff at the moral restraint which I have here urged as America's course of action, but I feel that those instances in recent history in which we departed farthest from our own moral standards led to the most tragic results: the doctrine of unconditional surrender; the agreements which consigned millions of the peoples of the Balkans to the loss of their liberties; the veto provision of the United Nations charter.

On the other hand, those instances in which America came the closest to interpreting the moral concepts of our religion in action have been the most successful: the mediation provisions of the Charter; the dependent peoples sections with their insistence that independence should be the goal and that all men are entitled to fundamental freedoms; the Marshall plan; the kindly occupation of Japan.

It is my view that the insistence of the founding fathers of our country upon translating the great concepts of our religion into a governmental, economic and social system was the key to the success of America. The key to success for our foreign policy in this crucial period will be found in sincere and ingenious efforts to translate the great moral concepts of our religion into specific courses of action in world affairs. If we do that, we may well win through without the tragedy of a third world war. But with or without war we will win. This I believe, because I have a deep and abiding faith that there is a God, and man was meant to be free!

There is a tremendous need and in inspiring challenge before the National Council of Churches. As a layman speaking for laymen, we pledge co-operation and we are humbly thankful it has come into being at this critical time.

The Christian Witness in the National Life

AN ADDRESS BY AMBASSADOR FRANCIS B. SAYRE

United States Representative in the United Nations Trusteeship Council

IT IS GOOD to be a part of this great Christian gathering. As the world storm gathers ominously around us, it is of utmost value to share our thinking in the light of our Christian convictions.

You have listened over the air to our Secretary of State who has brilliantly reviewed for us this nation's basic "strategy of freedom" and the ways in which our country is trying to uphold it under the Charter of the United Nations. You heard last night Dr. Nolde's able presentation of the Christian's reaction to this present crisis and what our practical course of action should be. You heard also from Dr. Visser 't Hooft of the valiant fight which the Christian church is making in those dark areas of the world where its witness is sorely needed. Our subject for this afternoon is "The Christian Witness in the National Life."

Today our nation stands before the world, as our President said yesterday, as "the keystone of the hopes of mankind for peace and justice." It is imperative that it stand as a Christian nation.

Indeed, it makes me very humble to be given the opportunity to speak to this great gathering of eminent men and women, drawn from many different walks of life by a common consecration to the cause of Christ. We are met to help unify and thus to strengthen the Christian forces of America. For we are conscious that human greed and selfishness and unconcern for God's moral law are on the way to wreck the civilization we know—unless men and women can somehow make the forces of Christianity more vital and more telling in their impact upon the life of America.

How can men and women like ourselves put Christianity more actively into play in America? That is the question, I take it, to which my title, "The Christian Witness in the National Life," refers.

I

The title poses a profound question. Has the Christian witness a real significance in our national life, and, if so, what? Is it a valid assumption

121

that we may look to Christianity for practical guidance in our national problems?

Is Christianity, when all is said and done, merely a form of idealistic escapism from the terrifying problems and suffering and hard realities of present existence? Or is it something more? Can it be a divine revelation of the only way of life in this work-a-day world which can ever satisfy the deep insistent longings of the human heart and upon which alone, consequently, an enduring human society can be built?

Certainly no true and sincere Christian can believe that Christ was an escapist. He faced life foursquare. He plunged into the very thick of its hard realities; he faced the evil of it with his eyes wide open. He did not seek, like some religious leaders, to withdraw from life's intensities and urge, as the divine solution, the overcoming of all desire. Instead, he taught Christians to heal the sick, to feed the hungry, to live more vividly. He taught that men and women should meet life realistically, seeing and fighting its evil without flinching. "I have come that they might have life and have it more abundantly."

Christ lost his life; but he measured values with such sure accuracy that the victory of the cross has built incomparable power—power that again and again has overthrown kingdoms and changed the course of empires, power that has proved unconquerable and undying through the centuries. It is the problem, as well as the responsibility, of every one of us Christians, to find practical ways and means of releasing and utilizing this incomparable power, not only in our individual contacts and relationships, but also in the policies and secular activities of our nation.

It will not do to hold the principles taught by Christ applicable to individual men and women and not to nations. Nations are men and women; and moral standards and basic principles of moral law, which in a world created by God are as immutable and eternal as the law of gravity, are just as applicable to collections and groups of individuals—to nations and peoples and races—as they are to single individuals.

Christ was profoundly conscious of the fact, inescapable and incontrovertible, that as long as human life endures, greed and the service of self repel men, whereas self-sacrifice and devotion to humanity win them. In consequence, evil and self-seeking are, and eternally will be, disruptive forces, whereas goodness will forever be a unifying and strengthening power. Since Christianity is the very essence of goodness, it follows that a world society to be enduring must be built upon the uniting and strengthening power of the basic principles which Christ summed up and embodied in his life—whether these be recognized and labelled as Christian, or whether they be tagged as Buddhist or Mohammedan or Hindu, or simply recognized without religious tags as fundamental and eternal reality. The supreme dominance of God in this world, the consequent brotherhood of all

122

men, the conquering power of goodness—these are principles of universal validity.

II

These basic Christian principles are unique in their power to solve and to heal. They are applicable to every field of human endeavor—to business, to industry, to government administration, to national and international issues. Therefore, in spite of the singularly baffling problem of translating them into concrete policies and deeds in given situations—the problem is no less than trying to find a finite application of an infinite principle—nevertheless, this must eternally be the task of each Christian man and woman, helping to build the Kingdom of God.

If what Christ taught is true, a tremendous and breath-taking conclusion follows. Upon these fundamental principles alone can an enduring society or enduring institutions be built, and such policies as depart from these principles lead in the end to sure failure or disaster.

Is this really true?

In the international field for over twenty years I have studied intensively in many lands the effects and repercussions of international movements and policies. From this long first-hand experience I am utterly convinced that the only policies upon which a lasting world peace can possibly be maintained are those based upon Christian fundamentals as I have just stated them.

Let me be concrete.

There was a time when the absolute nature of the sovereignty of independent states was conceived to be the very cornerstone of a sound structure for world peace. In the Nineteenth Century it was a point of honor for every sovereign state to brook no derogation or infringement of its sovereignty. Every nation asserted a divine right to act in complete disregard of the interests of other states or of other peoples. Yet such a conception strikes at the very heart of brotherhood. In our Twentieth Century we are fast learning that moral obligations may be actually of more compelling force than legal ones—that only those nations can grow great which are highly sensitive to the obligations of humanity, since these states alone will attract and win an ever-increasing host of other peoples to their side.

Today we have come to realize that international collaboration—recognition of the viewpoints and needs of others—offers the only practical hope for the survival of our civilization. The United Nations is built upon that thesis. The Charter of the United Nations is a veritable catalog of the over-ruling obligations owed to society by sovereign states. Listen to the Charter: "All Members (States) shall settle their international disputes by peaceful means in such a manner that international peace and security, and justice, are not endangered.

"All Members shall refrain in their international relations from the threat or use of force. . . .

"All Members . . . shall refrain from giving assistance to any state against which the United Nations is taking preventive or enforcement action." And so forth and so on. And these telling words have again and again been translated into very concrete action.

The Nuremberg trials are another Twentieth Century manifestation that the sovereign powers of an independent state are not in fact absolute. So is the International Trusteeship System, under which colonial states administering non-self-governing peoples are held to international accountability. The Declaration of Human Rights looks in the same direction. The Genocide draft convention is still another example. The outdated imperialism, based upon this non-Christian conception of the absolute and untrammeled right of sovereign nations to be guided by self-interest alone, irrespective of moral principle, is every day becoming more and more thoroughly discredited.

Another conception, unquestioned among the hard-headed realists of an earlier day, was that peace must rest upon a delicately adjusted "Balance of Power" between separate sovereign states or military alliances of states. Nineteenth Century peace hung upon the balance between the Triple Alliance and the Triple Entente. That conception bore its deadly fruit in the First World War. It led to disaster. Tragic experience proved it utterly impractical as a means for the keeping of the peace.

Today we are coming to realize with ever-growing clarity that peace cannot be achieved by one part of the world becoming ranged against another. World stability can come only as nations work shoulder to shoulder together for common ends. One thinks at once of the United Nations. The crucial world problems of our day, such as Korea, China, Germany or Japan, can never be solved on the basis of national self-interest. Lasting peace can be built only when nations shift their supreme objectives from the satisfaction of their own selfish interests to promoting the welfare and meeting the genuine needs of all mankind, without regard to race or color or creed. No other approach—and least of all military alliances for purely selfish power—will ever bring to us stable world peace.

A third outlived conception was that of so-called Nineteenth Century "colonialism." A hundred years ago there lurked in many minds the idea that Europe possessed a divine right to exploit Asia and Africa for her own profit. To the "realists" of that day the exploitation of alien races for the building of an empire seemed the road to unbreakable power. It led to deep and lasting racial bitterness. It led to the rankling poison of racial inferiority complexes. We are paying the price today in Asia with blood. Happily the so-called Nineteenth Century "colonialism" is dead or dying fast everywhere today, except behind the Iron Curtain. It has been sup-

124

planted by an altogether different conception, based upon the assumption that the interests of non-self-governing peoples constitute a "sacred trust" which must be observed by all administering powers. The United Nations Trusteeship Council is bringing new hope to the peoples of the trust territories. In constant touch with them through visits, petitions and reports, it keeps a friendly and watchful eye on their progress and advancing welfare. The Charter provides as one of the basic objectives of the Trusteeship system the promotion of "the political, economic, social and educational advancement of the inhabitants" and the encouragement of "respect for human rights and for fundamental freedoms for all without distinction as to race, sex, language or religion." That comes close to Christian principle.

Every one of these outworn conceptions, upon which Great Powers once built basic international policies, has, under Twentieth Century strains and pressures, proved either disastrous or unworkable, and today among free peoples is thoroughly discredited.

The meaning of fundamental Christian principles in terms of broad international policies is becoming ever clearer. A stable world society cannot be established except as sovereign states turn from the pursuit of purely selfish national ends to serving the needs of humanity—to promoting human welfare and human progress. In Korea, for instance, as President Truman recently declared, "We have absolutely no interest in obtaining any special position for the United States . . . nor do we wish to retain bases or other military installations in that country." America poured into Korea her manpower and her resources under the United Nations for no purpose other than to build common security for all free peoples. Again, lasting peace cannot be built upon carefully balanced military alliances but only upon genuine brotherhood. The Marshall Plan, the Point Four program, the International Refugee program, the World Health Organization, the International Labor Organization, the International Children's Emergency program, all look in that direction. Also, we have come to realize that the exploitation of other peoples or of other nations for selfish interest or profit can yield only racial bitterness, international unrest and often fighting. Among free peoples, international trusteeship opens up new vistas.

III

It is when we turn to concrete problems in specific countries and try to work out black-and-white solutions that we are beset with difficulty. The international problems of today are so amazingly complex, so tremendous in their scope, that one cannot expect Christianity overnight to yield a simple or rule-of-thumb answer in each case. Turning one's other cheek, for instance, is manifestly not the sound solution for the problem of Korea. Christ did not turn his other cheek to the money-changers in the Temple. He never surrendered to evil.

How should a Christian nation or how should the United Nations deal with an anti-Christian nation, bent upon world mastery involving the destruction everywhere of moral standards and of human freedom? Clearly we must maintain, unyielding, our Christian ideals and objectives. But that is not enough. We must use our wits and our brains in working out practicable ways and means for achieving these objectives. And this may require considerable time.

Each case is a problem *sui generis;* and on its best concrete solution Christians may well differ. But on the over-all objectives to be reached there can be no difference of opinion.

In the time which remains, may I clarify this thought by touching very briefly upon one or two urgent problems now pressing upon us.

Here, for instance, is the problem of Japan. In Japan some 80,000,000 human beings, who have passed through the valley of humiliation and disaster, are ready to begin a new life. They ask for the right to determine what this new life shall be—to decide their own future destiny. Five years have passed since their defeat, and they are still held under military occupation as enemies. Can anyone question what a Christian policy toward these defeated people would be?

Surely it is high time to conclude a peace treaty with Japan. And, if we would build firm foundations for the future, has the time not come when we should welcome Japan back as a full-fleged member into the Family of Nations, with full sovereignty? In the peace treaty the Japanese people must be treated on the basis not of master and inferior but of full equality. The Japanese people, under post-war arrangements, clearly must be given the right to live; and since the Japanese people cannot subsist upon their very limited agricultural resources, Japan must be helped to a position where she can support herself by trade abroad. If we would follow the Christian pathway, she must not be barred from foreign markets by tariff discriminations or excessive trade barriers.

The problem of Germany is still more complex and challenging. From the Christian viewpoint, the German people have a fundamental right to unite into a single nation. Doubtless some day they will. But at present the East Germans are forbidden to do so by their Soviet slavemasters. As soon as a free and democratic method can be found, the German people should be united. In the meantime, distinctions between British, French and American zones in Germany are being eliminated in so far as possible, and a united Western Germany is being encouraged to go forward in building up a political, economic and social life of her own. The solution of the German problem is the key to the solution of the problem of Europe. It is only along the line of Christian principle that we shall ever attain solutions that will prove lasting.

The present world crisis, brought on by the utterly unprovoked attack

126

by organized Chinese troops against the forces of the United Nations, valiantly fighting for human freedom in Korea, tests to the utmost the nature and the reality of our Christian convictions. In the present crisis we are confronted with as grave and as tragic a problem as any America has ever faced. If Christian principles have validity in international issues such as we face today, in what direction shall we now turn?

The problem is too complex, too far-reaching in its countless issues, to expect a simple or a quick solution. The ultimate solution, depending upon gradually unfolding developments, no one can yet see. But Christians can take their stand upon certain fundamental principles.

At the outset, we must keep our minds clear as to our relationships with the Russian people. No major difference—no unbridgeable chasm—exists between the Russian people, as distinct from the Soviet Government, and the American people. The masses of Russian people have probably no comprehension of the Soviet Union's aim to gain world mastery by conquest through the use of unbridled force—no share in the Government's irreligious designs. The Russian people are fundamentally mystical and religious. I remember standing, one day before the Second World War, in the Anti-Religious Museum in Moscow, where were displayed various sticks and bones, emptied from relic boxes taken from the churches, to prove the falsity of religion. As I stood there, in the center of the Anti-Religious Museum, a Russian peasant woman, evidently fresh from the fields, went down on her knees to pour out her heart in prayer before them.

The world is torn in two today not by a struggle of people against people, but by a profound contest of ideology against ideology.

It is only the ideology of the Soviet Union and the perverted effort to enslave the world on the basis of that ideology that America must fight—and fight to the death. For international communism is first of all atheism, a profound and rationalized disbelief in God. It teaches that the fundamental realities of the world rest on man-created force and not on God—on material power and not on the things of the spirit.

When man rejects God, moral standards disappear. Might replaces right. Absolute dictatorship becomes the only alternative to hopeless confusion and inaction. Purges and liquidations necessarily become part of the program.

In spite of its false and glittering promises to the contrary, international communism is essentially an attack against the very objectives for which Asians, peoples of the West, and free men everywhere, must struggle —improved living standards, security against aggression, freedom for every people to develop their own cultures. The victory of communism in its Moscow form would mean the end of human freedom everywhere.

A Christian program of national action will be based upon certain inescapable principles. In the first place, our course of action, as Secretary

127

Acheson put in on Wednesday evening, must be determined by "a firm adherence in all our actions, at home and abroad, to the moral values which give meaning to all our lives."

Christians will not capitulate to evil. They will not surrender to those who would enslave the human spirit. They will not fear those whose only power is the doing of bodily harm. Their faith is in God; and those who really live with God have no room in their lives for fear or despair.

In the second place, we recognize, as one of the basic principles of Christianity, freedom of the human spirit—the sanctity of each individual personality. America was born of this concept of human freedom. Americans have laid down their lives before in defense of human freedom. If it should become necessary, we shall not shrink from doing so again.

But, in the third place, although fighting to prevent unprovoked aggression is sometimes necessary, as it is in Korea today, although against the Soviet attempt to destroy human freedom, a Christian America must stand firm, Christians nevertheless now recognize that war does not solve problems.

The future still lies dark. But in spite of the gravity of present issues, war between the United States and either Russia or China is still, we believe not inevitable. War would not stop the spread of communism. Military force to prevent aggression is necessary now and again; but only a force as tremendous as the power of ideas can prevent the spread of communism.

In the face of a world crisis such as now confronts us, the task of Christians must be tirelessly to apply their brains and their ingenuity to the finding of practical ways and means other than war to prevent the wrecking of our world by Soviet Russia.

America has faced grave crises before. We remember Valley Forge, Gettysburg, Verdun, Pearl Harbor. Whatever may come, there is nothing to fear, if only we have a stalwart faith in God, and the courage to uphold Christian principles, even if necessary at the cost of life.

"Be strong in the Lord, and in the strength of his might."

IV

In conclusion, may I come back to the thought with which I began. We are met here in Cleveland at a critical time to unify and to strengthen the forces of Christianity in America. We shall be learning to understand each other's viewpoints, to combine our efforts and to forget smaller sectarian differences in the larger vision. That, in the political field, is precisely what we are at, day by day, in the United Nations. But here at Cleveland we have the inestimable advantage of a common religious faith. Christianity, if we have the faith to see it, lights the way forward.

Yet there is danger. Often in this hard-driving mechanical age we

Americans get the idea that we can generate spiritual forces by organization and outward form. We cannot.

I keep thinking of Christ and wondering which way he would lead were he physically present today. I feel confident that problems of organization would play the least part in his thinking.

What he would be tremendously concerned about would be individual lives. He would be turning to this man and to that woman and bidding each to follow him, to live more gallantly in his companionship, to help weave him into the pattern of the life of each community.

The saving of Western civilization can come only through the powerful strengthening of spiritual forces. And this can come, as we know full well, only through the utter consecration to God of individual men and women, fighting the good fight in every walk of life—whether in business or law or diplomacy or engineering or homemaking or the bringing up of children. On a thousand fronts, each of us must be more terribly concerned with the building of God's Kingdom.

God waits upon us for the doing of his work. Are we in dead earnest? Are we prepared to take the hand of Christ and go forward?

The Witness of the Church in Public Affairs

FROM AN ADDRESS BY MRS. MILDRED MCAFEE HORTON

President of Wellesley College and Former War-Time Commander of the Waves

THE CHURCH makes a witness in public affairs because it is, itself, a public institution. No one institution functions independently of all the rest. What we do as business men and women affects our lives as parents. What we do as parents affects the life of our schools. What our church does, affects in some measure at least, the kind of society in which the home, the state, the economic order functions.

Churchmen in America recently re-activated a plan for a great Christian University in Japan. Churchmen sponsored the dream and were quick to respond to the appeal to help build a better Japan than our bombs destroyed. We were quick to respond but slow to give our money to be sent to Japan, saying, "This is a great idea, but this is a bad time to raise money. This is something which must be done, but how about next year?"

Communists, smarting under the charge of being untrustworthy, have been asking in Japan, "Why do you charge us with deception? Did Christians not say they would give money for a Christian University? Where is that money?" Our church venture in goodwill has become a matter of truly grave public concern. The gifts of our churches are involved with the prestige of our nation in that land of magnificent and fearful responsibility for America.

Challenging messages come from our Christian Colleges behind Communist lines in China. These colleges are one of the few remaining links of disinterested friendliness between peoples of East and West. Listen to excerpts from an indoctrination course under the auspices of the People's Government.

Question: Does science support the idea of God?

Communist Answer: No. . . . If God is an objective reality . . . why are there so many denominations? These prove that Christians cannot agree among themselves about God. Therefore God cannot exist objectively.

130

Question: Christians talk about love. Is that not good?

Communist Answer: Christians talk about love, but do not act on it. Christians talk about service, but in fact they only serve the upper classes.

The answers are not sound, but they offer evidence that the role of the church and of church members is not ignored in public affairs. The church is inextricably involved in the social order. I say this with full awareness of and adherence to the doctrine of the separation of church and state which is, I suppose, as widely supported as any of our American doctrines.

There is an interpretation of the doctrine to which I do not subscribe —that religion functions in a tight little compartment of one's life, relating man to an other-worldly existence, and identified with a church which is cut off from contact with a state. This interpretation of separation keeps church and state separate by making one or the other irrelevant to life as men choose to live it. Separation through this kind of isolation comes oddly close to the notion of separation through domination. It makes one institution important to life—the other separated from it by irrelevance!

The Minister of Education in the Central Peoples' Government of China has said: "Religion and school education are two things which must be clearly separated," and yet it seems quite clear from reports from our Protestant colleges that freedom of religion is still tolerated in China.

Our concern for the future arises from the difference between what communists and Christians mean by "religious freedom." Their assumption seems to be that religion is a purely private, personal, individual affair which may do something satisfying for the worshipper but must not be allowed to affect his public behavior. Our interpretation of the separation of church and state presumes constant contact between them as institutions serving the same people but performing separate functions for and by them without domination of either one by the other. Each recognizes a standard of justice and authority higher than itself since our historic tradition includes the recognition of the existence of God.

We assume that we live as a nation, as a world, within the framework of God's universe—the kind of God revealed by Jesus Christ. Our standards, therefore, derive from a source beyond and above our own judgment, from God. Someone has defined an atheist as a "man with no invisible means of support," but there lies deep within our national tradition the conviction that we do have an invisible means of support, that we operate under the judgment of God.

The citizens who object to the appointment of an official governmental ambassador to the Vatican do so on the grounds that it is not good policy to mix ecclesiastical and political government. The use of diplomatic channels to transmit ecclesiastical convictions puts church and state in the relation of institutions which, in a bargaining position, are negotiating in the area of political activity. What seems to many people the more distinctive American position is that the church is not in politics versus the state but is in society together with the state. The church cannot function adequately unless it is free to proclaim the sovereign will of God as judgment on the state.

How Can the Church Proclaim that Will?

At a Detroit conference on The Church and Economic Life there was drafted a statement about the role of the church which seems to apply as well to other aspects of public affairs:

"The Church . . . is charged with a fourfold duty, . . . to be the teacher of the principles of conduct; a voice of judgment; a guardian of moral and spiritual values already won; and the herald of a better day."

Who would challenge that statement? But how can the church exert positive, intentional influence on the whole of society without violating individual rights of people who differ from the judgment of the church spokesmen? The fact is that no group of representatives—in or out of the church—can be held responsible for expressing the mind of everybody they represent. It is high time that in intelligent America people should learn to differentiate between spokesmen and reporters. If we don't agree with what the commissions of this National Council say on behalf of church people of America I suggest that

(1) we make sure they said it;

(2) if they really said what we don't like, let's tell the responsible officers and give them a chance to explain or to answer our objections;

(3) elect another set of representatives if we are in sufficient strength to do so or, if we are not numerically strong enough, present our minority report as freely as we like, but without impugning the motives of the people who disagree with us.

We need to bring to bear on controversial issues all the discriminating judgment of which we are capable. Churchmen and women ought to be among those who always believe the best until they know the worst and then forgive the wrong-doer while they strive valiantly to prevent the wrongs which the wrong-doer does!

The give and take between institutions is one of the ways in which people get perspective on the job in hand. The church which will challenge government representatives, college presidents, school teachers, lawyers, doctors, business men, laborers to take their religion seriously and consider God's will in their daily occupation—that church will perform a more con-

132

structively effective function than the church which undertakes to tell each of these groups what it ought to do.

Some churchmen will see ills others will not see. None can see them from God's total point of view. Let the church speak, therefore, whenever its responsible, thoughtful spokesmen feel a concern for expressing God's will as they see it. The Protestant church claims no infallibility, and there will surely be contradictory insights among free men seeking God's will for men. But Christians, secure in their faith in God's ultimate control of His universe, will not fear the power of mistaken interpretations of God's will. We know that the God of love will prevail and we can therefore, at our best, refuse the way of hate and cruelty toward those with whom we disagree.

In crisis days like these we know God's will will seem to some to point toward military service. Some servants of the same God will refuse to fight. May the church keep all of us in fellowship as seekers for God's will, critics of each other's judgments frequently, but ever respectful of each other as objects of the same Father's love. How he can love some of us is hard to understand! That he does so gives us hints of values in the worst of us which all of us do well to recognize.

The Cost of Discipleship

AN ADDRESS BY DR. EUGENE CARSON BLAKE

Pastor, Pasadena Presbyterian Church, Pasadena, California

THIS WEEK has derived not a little of its inspiration from the numbers of those gathered here in the name of Jesus Christ. It has been heartening to sense the potential power of the Christian faith here represented when that power shall have been brought to bear upon our nation in this new unity of spirit and organization which here in Cleveland has been achieved.

It is altogether proper that much of the program of this week has been in the nature of a celebration of a great achievement. Congratulations have been in order to all those whose efforts in negotiations through many years have now borne fruit. Mutual congratulations have been in order for us all in that now, at last, a very large part of the ecumenical and inter-denominational interests of non-Roman Christianity in the nation has been merged into the National Council of the Churches of Christ in the U. S. A. It has been indeed an historic occasion, and the last thing I would want to do would be in any way to belittle it or, in this final sermon, to sound an unharmonious note.

And yet a cursory examination of the Gospel indicates that Jesus himself was never overly impressed with numbers. At the very height of his popularity in Galilee he turned away from the enthusiasms of the crowd and concentrated his attention upon twelve men only in whom he detected a potential quality of faith and loyalty which he did not find in the multitude. It is peculiarly important that we Americans, who are noted by critics in other lands as being a people dazzled by size and organization, should pause now to consider the "Cost of Discipleship," not taking it for granted that the magnitude or complexity of our achievement guarantees any signal advance in the Lordship of Jesus either over us as individuals or over our churches or nation. For there is an individual price to be paid by every man who would follow him, and the long range significance of this new council of churches will be measured by the quality and persistence of the individual Christian discipleship of us who are leaders in our churches and in this Council, and by that same quality of faith and loyalty in many men and women throughout all our churches whose eyes are upon us and whose prayers have sustained our endeavors here.

I

In the 14th Chapter of St. Luke's Gospel at the 25th verse, we find these words: "And there went great multitudes with him." This sounds as if it might be the introduction to a hopeful passage dwelling upon the attractiveness of Jesus and his personal power and influence over the hearts of men. But you know, as you listened to me read just now, that that verse is the immediate introduction to one of the most embarrassing passages in the Gospels. "And there went great multitudes with him; and he turned, and said unto them, If any man come to me, and hate not his father, and mother, and wife, and children, and brethren, and sisters, yea, and his own life also, he cannot be my disciple. And whosoever doth not bear his cross, and come after me, cannot be my disciple."

It is not surprising, after that, that the great crowd soon melted away and Jesus was left with a very few willing to pay the price demanded. To hate my own family, the father who begot me, the mother from whom I first heard the very name of Jesus! To turn my back upon the responsibilities of parenthood, to forsake the companionships of those bound to me by the ties of blood and by the stronger ties of love made binding upon me in my earliest associations? "This is too much," said the crowds in Galilee, and they went their several ways apart from him.

Even if you and I reduce the impact of these words of Jesus by agreeing that they are hyperbole—an exaggeration designed to shock us into a realization of the high cost of Christian discipleship—even when we agree that Jesus could not have meant literal hatred of those closest to us, still we must ask ourselves why Jesus felt it necessary so to shock men with such an extreme expression of his demand for single-hearted loyalty.

And when we ask ourselves this question we can come quickly to an answer. Of all the sins to which mankind is subject, none is more subtle and more entangling than the sin of misplaced loyalty. It was not too hard for Jesus to win a number of men away from their natural greed for material things. In his company gold always is revealed for the tinsel that it is, and with him near, food and clothes cannot be valued more than the life of which they are but the necessary support. It is not too hard for Jesus to change in a man the natural hatred of an enemy (I mention the hardest of the accepted and agreed upon Christian attitudes), to transform that natural attitude of antipathy into forgiveness and concern and generosity. Again and again we have seen it done.

But even to get us to consider whether our loyalties may be sinful, this required the strongest words even Jesus could muster. And yet we all know, as we judge others, that many a man's Christianity is hindered or distorted by his family loyalty. Nor does it seem out of place or overdone to find in the very beginning of *Pilgrim's Progress* that Christian's family was almost his first obstacle. "So I saw in my dream that the man began to run," wrote Bunyan. "Now he had not run far from his own door, but his wife and children, perceiving it, began to cry after him to return; but the man put his fingers in his ears, and ran on, crying, *Life! Life! Eternal Life!* So he looked not behind him. . . . "

The suggestion here is not the common one that family love may be distorted, as the father's was in "Edward, My Son," or the mother's in "The Silver Cord," or the son's in "Oedipus." It is, rather, that the very virtue of family love and devotion can stand in the way of God. It is the attitude so common that I knew not what to say nor how to say it to an officer of my church who accompanied his refusal of a task with, "But my family comes first."

It is the attitude so generally accepted as virtuous that anyone who does transcend it soon earns the name of saint. One such among us here wrote out of his own renunciation:

> *Love, linger not to whisper your temptation*
> *Seek not to bind me with your heavy chain*
> *I would be free to seek the world's salvation*
> *I would be free to rescue men from pain!*[1]

In contrast to that quality of discipleship, again and again the long-range victory of the whole family of God is prevented by our narrower family loyalty. The brotherhood of all mankind is blocked by nationalism and provincialism, and by that over-concern for intimates which reads out of consideration those who happen to be beyond that too restricted pale.

Certainly it is not stretching the meaning of this passage to extend its application by reminding ourselves now of the fact that denominational loyalty can stand in the way of true discipleship to Christ. By this I do not imply that every co-operative effort is always more Christian than every denominational program. I do not mean to suggest that always the denominational interest should be sacrificed to the interest of the National Council of Churches. Nor do I believe that every union of two churches is necessarily the immediate will of God. But you and I know that the cause of Christ is hindered again and again by the too narrow loyalty of us all. Even within my own church, which I believe is no worse in this than yours, good men, sometimes, on behalf of the Educational program, or the Foreign Missions program, or the National Missions program block the larger cause of our whole church. How much more often do good men fail to follow Christ because they refuse to give sufficient loyalty beyond their own denomination to him, the Lord of all our churches. Must we not, therefore, in honesty say that a part of the cost of Christian discipleship must be our willingness to hate our intimates in our own church family whenever loyalty to them stands in the way of the cause of Jesus Christ?

[1] Kagawa

II

In this same passage Jesus uses two brief illustrations which suggest further costs of discipleship—costs which the crowd would not pay—costs which we must reckon if we would be his disciples. "For which of you, intending to build a tower, sitteth not down first, and counteth the cost, whether he have sufficient to finish it? Lest haply, after he hath laid the foundation, and is not able to finish it, all that behold it begin to mock him, saying, This man began to build, and was not able to finish."

Our endeavor here begun at Cleveland runs this second danger, too. Unless our discipleship to Jesus is willing to pay the material costs of an effective program in this Council, it would have been better that we had not, with all this fanfare and publicity, begun to erect this ecumenical tower. Not only have too many of us been faithless to Christ because of too narrow loyalties but also because of an unwillingness to pay the cost.

It is not that we do not have the resources to make this Council a most effective instrument. We represent twenty-nine denominations totaling a membership that runs to thirty-one million. The income of our combined membership must be reckoned in the billions of dollars. Our problem is not whether we have sufficient resources to build our tower but whether we intend to make them available. If we have been sincere in what we have been saying here all this week, it means that no longer are we going to continue on the old paths of denominational rivalries where as separate churches any one of the larger of us has much more of resources than our interdenominational agency. Let me remind you of the disgraceful way we have but recently allowed Church World Service to be starved to ineffectiveness in a time of national and denominational prosperity. And this is not merely an administrative mistake; this has been a sin against Jesus Christ.

In his name then, tonight, as you dedicate yourselves anew to him in this Council, I call upon you to count the cost of this that we have begun to build. Do you intend to pay for it in dollars appropriated from our churches, or do you intend to let the nation later mock us, when having failed to meet our united opportunities and obligations, they say of us, "They began to build and were not able to finish." This, my friends, is not merely a matter of strategy and judgment and administration, it is one of discipleship to Jesus Christ, and loyalty.

III

Once more Jesus continued, as he spoke to the crowd who had too lightly begun to follow him without reckoning the cost, "Or what king, going to make war against another king, sitteth not down first, and consulteth whether he be able with ten thousand to meet him that cometh against him with twenty thousand?" This is a third consideration that we need to take to mind when we would add up the whole cost of our discipleship. Dare we with our ten thousand march to meet the forces ranged in battle against us?

At first estimate, I confess that the forces of evil and opposition seem entirely too great. Despair so easily seems but realistic wisdom. Perhaps we had best capitulate and send an embassage to the Prince of Darkness, asking his conditions of peace. I do not refer here to the political enemies of our nation represented by Russia and world wide communism. I remain, even this week, quite optimistic about the long-range defeat of Communism on the military and even on the diplomatic front. We should not be so much affected as we have been by hysterical exaggeration of Russian power and Communist cleverness. I expect to see the collapse of the Russian empire and her satellites while the Western democracies (if they are true to their Christian heritage) grow in strength.

Nor do I refer here to any competing ecclesiastical groups, either Protestant or Catholic, whom some would list as our enemies and as evil forces. The free churches we represent are stronger and will remain stronger than any religious rivals in America not by attacking others but by increased devotion to our own tasks and to him who leads us in them. No, I refer to those forces of evil both at home and abroad, both within and without our own churches when I say that at first estimate the enemy appears to be too strong for us, the power of the secular society which, without regard to God or duty, supports criminal racketeering and open gambling, and a liquor traffic that makes money by debauching character. I mean those forces of evil represented by the corruption in all our cities where, in police departments, councils, legislatures, the festering sores from time to time break out into public notice.

Against these forces of materialism, where is the sufficient resource in all our churches? The lethargy of Christian people and our materialistic preoccupations do not finally add up to enough in most of our communities to do very much to win the battle for right and decency in which we should be engaged. In the face of the power of evil, the strength of the Christian church seems pitifully inadequate.

But this despair is not well-founded. We believe in a sovereign God and in Jesus Christ, his Son, our Lord. If we are willing to follow Jesus Christ, we will find ourselves always, in the long run at least, with the preponderance of strength. This is our faith. God rules, not Satan. God and one man dedicated to him—even that is enough. The victory belongs to those who at last find themselves ranged on the side of God.

If we are willing to pay the price of discipleship, willing to dedicate ourselves once more to learn of him, to make loyalty to him transcend all our lesser loyalties, to devote ourselves and our possessions to the building

of his Kingdom, to wage all the battles which we fight under his cross as
our standard, then and only then have we the right to hope that this meeting has been an historic meeting and that this task accomplished has been
significant.

> To whom shall the world henceforth belong
> And who shall go up to possess it?

So asked John Oxenham and replied in his truly Christian verse:

> To the men of Good Fame
> Who everything claim—
> This world and the next—in their Master's great name—
> To these shall the world henceforth belong,
> And they shall go up and possess it;
> Over much, o'erlong, has the world suffered wrong,
> We are here by God's help to redress it.

But must we not speak one final word to be quite true to the Gospel
as we try to assess the full cost of discipleship? In the passage we have been
examining, so far I have rather slurred over two verses: "Whosoever doth
not bear his cross, and come after me, cannot be my disciple"; and later
this: "Whosoever he be of you that forsaketh not all that he hath, he cannot
be my disciple."

If, in our enthusiasm or faith, we, like Peter, protest our Lord's
cross, saying, "Be it far from thee, Lord," looking for our successes and
satisfactions and victories, like Peter, too, we must expect to hear him
say to us, "Get thee behind me, Satan, for thou savourest not the things
that be of god. . . . " Above all, we need to remember that God's way to
victory often looks to men like a road to ruin; that the indestructible city,
though visible to Pilgrim from the delectable mountains, is reached by
climbing lucre's hill, over hard ways, not stopping there; and that always
in this world, for Christ and for his disciples, there falls the shadow of a
cross. Yes, and for this victory, Jesus had to follow steadfastly in that shadow to where its substance stood unyielding, planted in the soil of Golgotha.
His cross was part of the cost of our Lord's own triumph and "the servant
is not greater than his master."

Let us therefore remember as we now renew our pledges of loyalty
to Jesus Christ, that a cross is part of the cost of discipleship to him and
that Christian triumph is ever through the cross and beyond it.

O God, Whose love has drawn us to Thyself and Whose power alone
can sustain us on the Christian way, by Thy grace enable us to follow
Jesus in all our ecclesiastical efforts that our churches and this Council
may be true instruments of Thine. Through that same Jesus Christ our
Lord. AMEN.

The Presidential Message

BY THE RIGHT REVEREND HENRY KNOX SHERRILL

First President of the National Council of the Churches of Christ in the U. S. A.

THIS WEEK an historic event in the life of the Church has taken place. The formation of this National Council of Churches in a time of universal confusion and discord is a promise of high hope for the future. The churches here represented are determined, without compromise in those areas in which differences are to be found, to cooperate wholeheartedly in those great fields of practical endeavor in which we are essentially as one. For this spirit of understanding and of mutual trust on the part of the churches and of well and long established organizations we can thank God.

For these days we have met. Old friendships have been renewed, new ones made. We have adopted a constitution and by-laws; officers have been elected. Inspiring addresses have been made. Such is the universal and necessary pattern of all conventions of every kind and in every field of endeavor. But on this occasion a further question must be asked. Is there a deeper meaning and purpose in a gathering of the representatives of the Christian churches? Can we penetrate beneath the matters of procedure and of organization and find the inner life of the Spirit?

We are all of us necessarily children of our own age. The attitudes, the methods of the day profoundly affect the experience and the program of the churches. Much of this is helpful if kept in proportion and balance. But we must constantly beware lest the Church lose sight of her primary function and purpose. As a student of the first centuries of the history of the Church has written of the recognition of the Church by the Roman Empire, the effect "was not so much to Christianize civilization as to civilize Christianity, it was not to consecrate human institutions to the service of God but rather to identify God with the maintenance of human institutions." We talk justifiably of the many millions of church people associated in this council. We rightly speak of more efficient organization, we wisely use modern methods of publicity and of promotion. But we must be very certain that there is more than organization, promotion and activity to the National Council of Churches. For without a deeper reality of the

Spirit, all our plans and methods are but sounding brass and tinkling cymbals.

The Christian religion is of great depth and complexity. But there is also a central simplicity which so often escapes the wise and prudent. Christianity proclaims God, Creator of heaven and of earth, an eternal and everlasting God, yet our Father, who so loved the world that He gave. We would do well at this hour to meditate beside the manger of Bethlehem, to hear the young Master in the synagogue of Nazareth read words which might well be guiding principles of this council: "The Spirit of the Lord is upon me . . . to preach good tidings to the poor, to proclaim release to the captives and recovery of sight to the blind, to set at liberty them that are bruised, to proclaim the acceptable year of the Lord." We must with repentant hearts stand in the shadow of the Cross and then with joy announce the great act of God: "He is risen. The Lord is risen indeed." We are of the company of those who received the promise, "Lo, I am with you alway to the end of the world." We are the spiritual successors of that group who were all filled with the Holy Ghost. These are very familiar, perhaps too easily familiar, truths. But in these realities of the Spirit are to be found our power and purpose. In them is the only abiding source of our fellowship.

The greatest tragedy of our world is that God is forgotten. We have had pride in our human power, knowledge and strength. While Christianity has been recognized in a conventional sense, in reality in many cases it has had no more influence upon men, nations and institutions than did the Pantheon of Gods upon the conduct of the Roman Empire or the every day life of the Roman citizen of the second or third century. This is a hard fact but must be faced incisively if we are to know where we stand. Even now with the terrible experience of the past three decades, when we should have learned the actual truth, still we fail, even in despair and fear, to heed the supreme warning and lesson of our times, that all our striving, our planning and labor are in vain without God. We struggle in the international field for a reign of law and order, through countless negotiations and conferences. But as yet the great majority of men do not seem to realize practically that there can be no law without a Law Giver in whose sight even the nations are a very little thing. We speak constantly of democracy and of human rights but there can be no dignity to man as merely a child of nature. His worth comes as a child of God. What is needed supremely is the northwest wind of the cleansing grace and power of God. The churches themselves must constantly be reminded of this fact within their own confines. This National Council of Churches in the years to come will have pronouncements to make upon many matters of grave importance. We must never forget that the authority for these will not rest simply in the Constitution of this assembly but far more in how sincerely and humbly

141

testimony can be given out of the vital spiritual experience of the churches. "Thus saith the Lord." A church historian recently said to me, "The greatest thing about the Apostolic Church was the realization of its own insufficiency." Some one has said that "God is often present when human success is less evident." So it will be with us in our day! By ourselves we can do little or nothing. Our strength cometh from the Lord.

The truth of the matter is that we need constantly the rebirth of conviction. In our day due to many causes religion has become with a great many people a kind of vague and general goodwill—a somewhat shallow humanitarianism, mixed with democratic idealism and national pride. "My religion is in doing good," is an oft-repeated phrase without any understanding of how difficult it is to do good, not to say be good. We are familiar with the statement of a committee seeking a pastor: "We want a good preacher but one who does not preach theology." The church becomes a respectable and secondary institution in society, a friendly meeting place but certainly not an heroic company nor a dynamic force. That kind of pleasant self-satisfied laissez faire Christianity is far removed from those Christians of another century who were said to have turned the world upside down.

The era in which we live is stern. The forces of evil are powerful and relentless. Only a church of deep conviction and spiritual experience can meet the necessities of our time. The age-long questions of the nature of God and man, the Person of Christ, of good and evil, of sacrifice and of redeeming love must be faced with new intensity and poignancy. These imperatives of God must be answered and the issue at least primarily and partially concluded in the secret recesses of the heart and mind of each individual. Large generalities are not enough, for the relationship to God in Christ cannot be second-hand but must be living and personal. I realize that I am speaking to clergy, laymen and women who are leaders of the churches. But all the more as a result we must be on our guard against large professional generalities. We have an accepted and accustomed role to play. But we must not become so conventionalized that we eliminate the deep personal wellsprings of the spirit—communion with God, companionship with the living Christ—which will cause men to take knowledge of us that we have been with Jesus.

If we have met here and have been only concerned with the necessary machinery of ecclesiastical cooperation, having gone merely through the forms of religious observance so characteristic of many invocations on secular occasions, then we shall have missed a great opportunity. Here we should be conscious of the overshadowing and indwelling presence of God, here in the fellowship of the churches, we should experience the gift of power. The real problem which confronts the churches is not the strength of the enemy without but the quality of the spiritual life within. This council can only be strong as the churches are strong for water cannot rise above its level. Nothing added to nothing still remains nothing. The churches can only be strong as there is strength and intensity of conviction and experience.

Before the Gospel can be extended or applied there must be the realization that there is a transforming Gospel. There cannot be a nation under God without there being first churches under God with all that implies in intellectual and spiritual strength and discipline. There can be no artificial division between the sacred and the secular. The churches if they are expressions of the purpose and the will of God cannot be limited as some would declare to special fields of worship. For if worship is real, then action must follow—for all of life belongs to God. Once we have the conviction that there is a saving Gospel then that Gospel must be extended and applied to every aspect of life. The task is horizontal for we may say with John Wesley, "The world is the field," but it is also vertical, touching all strata of society. The Gospel has to do with international relations, with peace or war, with the atom bomb, with economic conditions, with family life, for nothing human can be alien to the love of God in Christ. The churches cannot be simply a reflection of the prejudices, opinions and standards of contemporary society. For the church has the task of being the light of the world, and must view life in so far as this is possible within the limits of humanity from the point of view of the eternal.

With lives dedicated to God we can face even our disordered society with courage, even with joy. We shall face cruelty, selfishness, pride of power, exploitation in ourselves and in others in the consciousness of the judgment of God. We shall be touched by His compassion and forgiveness, never forgetting that God so loved the world. Together we shall strive sincerely to build here the city of God for, with all our differences which should not be minimized or exaggerated, we share these ideals and aspirations as the Spirit of God moves and unites us in a common purpose. Because we do not rely upon our own strength, we meet manifold difficulties of today with more than the resignation of the stoic but with the conviction that the unseen forces of the Spirit are more than those that be against us.

My friends, a nation or a world, or a church under God rests upon dedicated men and women. If we here and our brethren in the churches we represent can at this time experience the gift of God's grace, then we can make the words of another our own, "We shall this day light a candle by God's grace that I trust shall never be put out." Together we shall move forward with renewed resolve and great hope in the building of a Christian America in a Christian world.

SECTION IV

The Outreach

November 18, 1950

Dear Dr. Morse:

I extend heartiest congratulations to the National Council of the Churches of Christ in the U.S.A. as it begins its task of drawing twenty-nine great communions into united action on on a still greater scale than in the past. I have followed with warm appreciation the work which has been done in recent years by the interdenominational agencies which now combine their forces in a new Council. I hope and believe that this step will enable the American churches to exert a greater influence in the strengthening of the spiritual foundation of our national life at a time when a materialistic philosophy is rampant.

I am grateful for the contributions which the churches of the National Council are making to the faith of our people, to the maintenance of freedom throughout the world, to social welfare and to interracial and international good will. I hope the coming years will bring still greater unity of purpose and effort among the religious forces of America.

Very sincerely yours,

HARRY TRUMAN

Rev. Dr. Hermann N. Morse,
Secretary,
Planning Committee for the National Council
of the Churches of Christ in the U.S.A.
156 Fifth Avenue
New York 10, N. Y.

PLANNING COMMITTEE
NATIONAL COUNCIL OF THE CHURCHES OF CHRIST
IN THE UNITED STATES OF AMERICA

November 30, 1950

Dear Mr. President:

In this hour of crisis for the peace of the world, the National Council of the Churches of Christ in the United States of America, in session in Cleveland, is keeping you in its prayerful remembrance. May the God who holds the nations in the palm of His hand and from whom, in times past, our fathers sought wisdom and understanding, guide you and your advisers to the end that peace may be vouchsafed to the people of the earth.

The delegates here assembled, representing twenty-nine communions whose combined membership exceeds thirty-one millions, express the fervent hope that the United Nations, assured of the full participation of our country, may act under God, to secure with justice, the enduring welfare of mankind. The responsibilities which are yours can be borne only with the aid that comes from God and to Him we commend you in our prayers.

Sincerely yours,

Earl F. Adams
Executive Secretary

Mr. Harry S. Truman,
President of the United States
The White House
Washington, D. C.

December 5, 1950

Dear Dr. Adams:

The earnestness and spiritual power of your message
sent in behalf of the National Council of the Churches of Christ
in the United States of America in this hour of crisis for the
peace of the world has brought me strength and given me new
courage in these difficult days. I am indeed grateful -- more
grateful than I can say -- for the advice that I was kept in
prayerful remembrance during the assembly in Cleveland. With
true insight your thoughtful body perceives that the United
Nations, under God, is the world's last, best hope for peace
and for the welfare of the human race.

I can in these grave days when upon me devolves the
responsibility of office but reiterate the prayer which I uttered
before the Congress when I was called so unexpectedly to assume
the duties of the Presidency: "Give therefore thy servant an
understanding heart."

I trust that this latest union representing twenty-
nine communions and a combined membership exceeding thirty-one
millions, will make the National Council of Churches a powerful
agency for peace. Only through an honorable and enduring world
peace can we hope to hasten the day when the kingdoms of this
world shall become the Kingdom of God and His Law the law of
nations.

Very sincerely yours,

Harry Truman

Reverend E. F. Adams, D.D.,
Secretary, Planning Committee,
National Council of the Churches of Christ
   in the United States of America,
156 5th Avenue,
New York 10, N. Y.

To the People of the Nation

The NATIONAL COUNCIL OF THE CHURCHES OF CHRIST
IN THE UNITED STATES OF AMERICA

Sends Greetings:

This Council has been constituted by twenty-nine Churches for the glory of God and the well-being of humanity. It manifests our oneness in Jesus Christ as divine Lord and Saviour; his is the mandate we obey and his the power upon which we rely. It is designed to be an instrument of the Holy Spirit for such ministries of evangelism, education, and relief as are better achieved through Christian cooperation than by the labors of separated groups. It coordinates and continues the work of eight interdenominational agencies ministering in as many fields of Christian usefulness.

The Council is linked in spirit with the world-wide ecumenical organizations which provide for interdenominational cooperation at the international level. It is likewise similar in purpose to the federations of churches in state, county and city through which the several communions do their common work in our land. So it becomes the national unit of a system of unified Christian enterprise which circles the inhabited earth.

For the denominations which compose it the Council opens an avenue for mutual confidence, a widening way along which potential controversy among them may be wrought into concord, and unhappy competition into emulation in pursuit of whatsoever things are true, honest, just, pure, lovely, and of good report.

The Council itself, however, is not a denomination, not a Church above the Churches. The autonomy of each communion is assured by constitutional provision. The Council is an agency of cooperation—not more but magnificently not less.

THE FUNCTIONS OF THE COUNCIL

In behalf of the denominations the Council continues and develops many services. It assists in the preparation of materials for the Church School, and through its scholars it is making ready for the world the Revised Standard Version of the Bible; it serves as a clearing house for full reports and statistics bearing upon church membership, denominational

150

organizations and programs, and social trends of interest to Christians; it seeks to aid the Churches in undergirding and coordinating their home and foreign missions; it searches out and trains leadership for Christian undertakings; it lifts up its voice in behalf of the Christian way of life in messages to the people of the country; it provides a single inclusive agency through which, if they wish, the denominations may nominate and support chaplains and minister to the men and women of the armed forces of the United States; it offers a means of approach to agencies governmental and civil in matters of justice and goodwill; it devotes itself to the presentation of Christian ideals through radio, television and motion pictures; it is an organ of evangelism both specifically and broadly conceived, standing ready to serve the cause of Christ in every area as need arises, to the end that the entire country may be permeated by the blessings of His Gospel. Through these and other means it gives help to the churches, bringing the experience of all to the service of each.

THE SPIRIT OF THE COUNCIL

The Council has nothing to fear from the times, though it has much to desire of them. Being the servant of One who holds in His hand all the nations, and the isles, as a very little thing, it is free from the apprehensions of those who, taking counsel of men alone forget that no age is isolated from God's ageless purpose. We call our fellow citizens to Christian faith: this will defend them from groundless social dreads and lift them to concerns worthy and productive.

The Council stands as a guardian of democratic freedom. The revolutionary truth that men are created free follows from the revelation of God in Jesus Christ, and no person who knows that God as Father has given him all the rights of sonship is likely to remain content under a government which deprives him of basic human rights and fundamental freedoms. The nation may expect in the National Council a sturdy ally of the forces of liberty.

The Council stands for liberty with the richest content. It stands for the freedom of men to be as the Lord God meant them to be. It stands for Christian freedom—including the freedom to pursue happiness and with justice and sympathy to create conditions of happiness for others. It therefore stands against the misuse of freedom. The nation may expect from the National Council, in the name of One who suffered death upon a cross, an unrelenting, open-eyed hostility, as studious as it is deeply passionate, to all of man's inhumanity to man.

The Council opposes materialism as an end in itself. It is the foe of every political system that is nourished on materialism, and of every way of living that follows from it. From that smug idealism which is a form of selfishness, the Council prays to be protected; but danger on this hand does not lessen the necessity it feels to fight a constant fight against all kinds of secular materialism which demolish the slowly built edifice of Christian morality and fair dealing.

Through the Council the churches, as they are dedicated to the doing

151

of God's will, must increasingly become a source of spiritual power to the nation. The American Churches, of which the Council is one of the visible symbols, are in their true estate the soul of the nation. When those Churches take their true course, they draw their standards not from the world around but from the guiding mind of Christ. The Church is not the religious phase of the civilization in which it finds itself; it is the living center out of which lasting civilizations take life and form. In this sense the Council will be an organ through which the will of God may become effective as an animating, creative and unifying force within our national society.

The Council gives thanks to God for all those forces which make for harmony in our society. When, for example, science employs its ingenuity to knit the world together in bonds of communication, when business and industry make a like contribution through the life-bringing mutuality of commerce, when the arts depict the beauty and the tragedy of our existence which draw us into unity with one another, when the many professions and occupations recognize themselves as callings to human usefulness, then the Council salutes and supports them. By word and deed and in the name of Christ who gave his life for all mankind it affirms the brotherhood of men and seeks by every rightful means to arrest those forces of division which rend the nation along racial lines and stay its growth toward unity.

THE PRESENT CRISIS

Because this message is sent at a moment when clouds arising from the war in Korea threaten to darken the entire sky, the time is big with peril and with opportunity.

To the leaders we have set in authority in our government is committed the solemn and momentous task of making necessary choices in the political and military spheres.

We who are the people of the country, however, have a part to play as well. The call of Christ to us all seems clear, that we play it with calmness, self-control, courage, and high purpose, as becomes those whose lives are in the hands of God. Without hysteria, without hatred, without pride, without undue impatience, without making national interest our chief end but shaping our own policies in the light of the aims of the United Nations, without relaxing our positive services to the other peoples of the world, and in complete repudiation of the lying dogma that war is inevitable, let us live and, if need be, die as loyal members of the world community to which Christ summons us and to which we of the Council are dedicated.

THE LARGER SIGNIFICANCE OF THE COUNCIL

We of the National Council of the Churches of Christ in the U.S.A. begin our work in humility as we see the magnitude of the task ahead. We are not unconscious of our own short-comings. Knowing that men too often dream in marble and then build with straw, we whose very human lives are not separate from sin and ignorance can make no boast of past or future excellence.

But this we have done: by God's grace we have forged an implement

152

for cooperation such as America has never seen before. Into it have been poured the thoughts of wise and noble men and women, the prayers and consecration of the faithful, and the longing of all the participating Churches to serve the spiritual needs of all the people. The Council is our Churches in their highest common effort for mankind.

Our hope is in Jesus Christ. In Him we see the solution of the world's ills, for as human hearts are drawn near to him, they are drawn near in sympathy and understanding to each other. The Council itself is a demonstration of his power to unite his followers in joyous cooperation. Let nation and nation, race and race, class and class unite their aims in his broad purposes for man, and out of that unitedness there will arise new strength like that of which we ourselves already feel the first sure intimations.

In this hope we commend you, our fellow citizens, to God's mercy, grace and peace.

SECTION V

The Personnel of the Constituting Convention

The Personnel

OF THE CONSTITUTING CONVENTION

The National Council of the Churches of Christ in the U.S.A. was constituted by 29 communions to carry on and extend the work of many interdenominational agencies. The Council has no authority or administrative control over the constituent churches; no authority to prescribe a common creed, form of church government or worship or to limit the autonomy of the cooperating churches.

The Council's governing body is the General Assembly which meets biennially. In the interim, the General Board is the policy-making body. Official representatives, on the basis of proportional representation, are named to both the General Assembly and the General Board by the constituent communions. Other members are the Council's officers, three representatives each from the four divisions; the chairmen of certain departments and commissions, and representatives of the cooperative work of the churches in states, cities and counties.

The General Board meets bi-monthly.

157

Constituting Convention of the

NATIONAL COUNCIL OF THE CHURCHES OF CHRIST
IN THE UNITED STATES OF AMERICA

GENERAL ASSEMBLY

* Indicates persons who were unable to be present.
† Indicates persons appointed by State and Local Councils of Churches as approved by denominational bodies in the respective areas.

Denominational Appointments

AFRICAN METHODIST EPISCOPAL CHURCH
Representatives

Sadie T. M. Alexander, Philadelphia, Pa.
A. J. Allen, Cleveland, Ohio
G. W. Baber, Detroit, Mich.
L. L. Berry, New York, N. Y.
Russell S. Brown, St. Louis, Mo.
W. A. Fountain, Atlanta, Ga.
Joseph Gomez, Waco, Texas
S. L. Greene, Birmingham, Ala.
J. A. Gregg, Jacksonville, Fla.
Annie E. Heath, Philadelphia, Pa.

Nora Link, Philadelphia, Pa.
D. Ward Nichols, New York, N. Y.
Kay B. Nichols, New York, N. Y.
Alma Polk, Pittsburgh, Pa.
F. M. Reid, Columbia, S. C.
C. E. Stewart, Buffalo, N. Y.
D. Ormond Walker, Wilberforce, Ohio
A. Wayman Ward, Chicago, Ill.
W. R. Wilkes, Atlanta, Ga.
R. R. Wright, Atlanta, Ga.

Alternate Representatives

John D. Bright, Philadelphia, Pa.
Mrs. S. L. Greene, Birmingham, Ala.
E. L. Hickman, Louisville, Ky.

S. R. Higgins, Columbia, S. C.
J. L. Roberts, Chicago, Ill.
A. C. Sumpter, Toledo, Ohio

AFRICAN METHODIST EPISCOPAL ZION CHURCH
Representatives

Cameron C. Alleyne, Philadelphia, Pa.
H. J. Callis, Washington, D. C.
Rufus E. Clement, Atlanta, Ga.
A. L. Cromwell, Winston-Salem, N. C.
S. E. Duncan, Reedsville, N. C.
J. W. Eichelberger, Chicago, Ill.
Robert Fisher, Washington, D. C.
*B. F. Gordon, Charlotte, N. C.
G. F. Hall, Charlotte, N. C.

M. Anna Hauser, Winston-Salem, N. C.
J. Clinton Hoggard, Yonkers, N. Y.
J. W. Martin, Chicago, Ill.
A. A. Perry, Rozbury, Mass.
J. H. Satterwhite, Salisbury, N. C.
S. G. Spottswood, Washington, D. C.
James Clair Taylor, Memphis, Tenn.
W. J. Walls, Chicago, Ill.
E. B. Watson, Greensboro, N. C.

Alternate Representatives

C. C. Coleman, Mobile, Ala.
*E. J. Hayes, Williamston, N. C.
Abbie Clement Jackson, Louisville, Ky.

B. M. Montgomery, Charlotte, N. C.
Victor J. Tulane, Washington, D. C.

AMERICAN BAPTIST CONVENTION

Representatives

Dana M. Albaugh, New York, N.Y.
B. C. Barrett, Bakersfield, Calif.
G. P. Beers, New York, N.Y.
Mrs. Howard G. Colwell, Loveland, Col.
Paul H. Conrad, New York, N.Y.
Edwin T. Dahlberg, Syracuse, N.Y.
R. N. Dutton, Topeka, Kansas
Sanford Fleming, Berkeley, Calif.
*Joseph C. Hazen, Summit, N.J.
Marguerite Hazzard, Pelham, N.Y.
Cay Hermann, Philadelphia, Pa.
Richard Hoiland, Philadelphia, Pa.
James L. Kraft, Wilmette, Ill.
William B. Lipphard, New York, N.Y.
A. H. Lofgren, Troy, N.Y.
R. R. Mixon, Newton, Kansas
Reuben E. Nelson, New York, N.Y.
Edwin W. Parsons, New York, N.Y.
E. H. Pruden, Washington, D.C.

Mrs. C. H. Sears, New York, N.Y.
C. L. Seasholes, Dayton, Ohio
Hazel Shank, New York, N.Y.
Luther Wesley Smith, Philadelphia, Pa.
Harold E. Stassen, Philadelphia, Pa.
Dorothy A. Stevens, New York, N.Y.
Mrs. L. E. Swain, Craigville, Mass.
Mrs. Milo E. Wenger, New York, N.Y.
Jesse R. Wilson, New York, N.Y.
†J. Burt Bouwman, Lansing, Mich.
†Hugh Chamberlin Burr, Rochester, N.Y.
†Gilbert B. Christian, Portland, Ore.
†Frank Jennings, Boston, Mass.
†J. O. Nelson, Des Moines, Iowa
†Russell Orr, Springfield, Ill.
†Arthur A. Schade, Huron, S.D.
*†Mrs. William Sale Terrell,
West Hartford, Conn.

Alternate Representatives

Benjamin P. Browne, Philadelphia, Pa.
Dorothy O. Bucklin, New York, N.Y.
H. R. Bowler, New York, N.Y.
D. B. Cloward, New York, N.Y.
M. D. Farnum, New York, N.Y.
Wallace Forgey, Melrose, Mass.
R. D. Goodwin, New York, N.Y.
V. C. Hargroves, Philadelphia, Pa.
Isaac Higginbotham, Boston, Mass.
Irene A. Jones, New York, N.Y.
*Mrs. John Killian, New York, N.Y.
Mrs. E. R. McCarthy, St. Louis, Mo.
George B. Martin, Summit, N.J.
George Moll, Philadelphia, Pa.

H. F. Osteyee, Philadelphia, Pa.
Annie E. Root, New York, N.Y.
Ivan Murray Rose, Philadelphia, Pa.
*W. E. Saunders, Rochester, N.Y.
Frank Sharp, New York, N.Y.
J. E. Skoglund, New York, N.Y.
W. E. Smith, San Francisco, Calif.
Stanley I. Stuber, New York, N.Y.
*†Harvey W. Hollis, Albany, N.Y.
†Robert L. Kincheloe, South Bend, Ind.
†Mrs. A. B. Stenger, Wheeling, West Va.
†Earl Hollier Tomlin, Providence, R.I.
†Edwin H. Tuller, Hartford, Conn.

AUGUSTANA EVANGELICAL LUTHERAN CHURCH

Representatives

Mrs. John S. Benson, LeSueur, Minn.
Conrad Bergendoff, Rock Island, Ill.
P. O. Bersell, Minneapolis, Minn.
Rudolph Burke, Minneapolis, Minn.
S. E. Engstrom, Minneapolis, Minn.

Emory Lindquist, Lindsberg, Kansas
Richard B. Pearson, Forestville, Conn.
S. H. Swanson, Minneapolis, Minn.
Emil Swenson, Minneapolis, Minn.
Lael H. Westberg, Minneapolis, Minn.

Mrs. MacLeod and Dr. Ross lead the staff for the induction ceremony

Seated: Miss Edith E. Lowry, Dr. Roy G. Ross, Dr. Samuel McCrea Cavert, Dr. Earl F. Adams, Mrs. W. Murdoch MacLeod. Standing: Dr. George Nace, Dr. J. Quinter Miller, Dr. Roswell P. Barnes, Dr. Philip C. Landers.

A busy spot in the Exhibition Hall

Part of the Exhibition Hall

A group of Choristers at the Altar

Alternate Representatives

Victor E. Beck, New York, N.Y.
C. O. Bengtson, Chicago, Ill.
Oscar A. Benson, Worcester, Mass.
Mrs. Leslie A. Carlson, Kansas City, Mo.
Martin E. Carlson, Minneapolis, Minn.

Mrs. Walter Ekelund, Minneapolis, Minn.
Eskil G. Englund, Worcester, Mass.
R. L. Fredstrom, Lincoln, Neb.
T. A. Gustafson, East Orange, N.J.
*George Hall, St. Peter, Minn.

CHURCH OF THE BRETHREN

Representatives

Rufus D. Bowman, Chicago, Ill.
C. Ernest Davis, Elgin, Ill.
*C. N. Ellis, Huntingdon, Pa.
Mrs. Everett Fisher, Huntington, Ind.

R. E. Mohler, McPherson, Kansas
Raymond R. Peters, Elgin, Ill.
Paul M. Robinson, Hagerstown, Md.
†Jesse D. Reber, Harrisburg, Pa.

Alternate Representatives

D. W. Bittinger, McPherson, Kansas
†Frank B. Durand, Phoenix, Ariz.

†Minor C. Miller, Richmond, Va.

COLORED METHODIST EPISCOPAL CHURCH

Representatives

Curtiss Battle, Jersey City, N.J.
M. L. Breeding, Cleveland, Ohio
Henry C. Bunton, Denver, Col.
Bertram W. Doyle, Nashville, Tenn.
June Dwellingham, Little Rock, Ark.
W. M. Frazier, Holly Springs, Miss.
J. Arthur Hamlett, Kansas City, Kansas
Mrs. R. Thompson Hollis, Oklahoma City, Okla.

C. A. Kirkendoll, Jackson, Tenn.
Mrs. Benjamin Mays, Atlanta, Ga.
E. P. Murchinson, Jackson, Tenn.
L. H. Pitts, Cordele, Ga.
B. Julian Smith, Chicago, Ill.
Wheatley C. Stewart, Odessa, Texas
J. L. Tolbert, New Albany, Miss.

Alternate Representatives

*W. H. Amos, Detroit, Mich.
Sadie Gray Mays, Atlanta, Ga.
*Amos Ryce, 2nd, Gary, Ind.

*Thelma N. Watson, Memphis, Tenn.
*Mrs. A. A. Womack, Little Rock, Ark.

CONGREGATIONAL CHRISTIAN CHURCHES

Representatives

Ronald Bridges, Sanford, Maine
Alfred E. Buck, Brooklyn, N.Y.
Fred S. Buschmeyer, New York, N.Y.
Athern P. Daggett, Brunswick, Maine
Truman B. Douglass, New York, N.Y.
Mrs. James F. English, Hartford, Conn.
George E. Forbes, Lakewood, Ohio
Walter A. Graham, Pembroke, Ky.
Henry David Gray, Pasadena, Calif.
Mrs. Walter Judd, Washington, D.C.
Helen Kenyon, New York, N.Y.
Samuel C. Kincheloe, Chicago, Ill.
Mrs. E. E. McClintock, New York, N.Y.

David McKeith, Jr., Boston, Mass.
Mrs. William H. Medlicott, Boston, Mass.
Liston Pope, New Haven, Conn.
Henry Rust, Boston, Mass.
Mrs. Henry W. Schneider, Grand Rapids, Mich.
Charles H. Seaver, Scarsdale, N.Y.
Kenneth Stokes, Philadelphia, Pa.
*Luther A. Weigle, New Haven, Conn.
†Ellis H. Dana, Madison, Wis.
†John Montgomery, Des Moines, Iowa
†Arthur Seebart, Livingston, Mont.
†Harold R. Semple, Providence, R.I.

161

Alternate Representatives

Harold B. Belcher, Boston, Mass.
Mrs. E. E. Briggs, Sioux City, Iowa
Hilda Camp, Waterbury, Conn.
Mrs. Thomas L. Crosby, La Grange, Ill.
Arthur E. Elmes, Washington, D.C.
Joseph H. Evans, Cleveland, Ohio
Ray Gibbons, New York, N.Y.
George B. Hastings, Grant, Neb.
Mrs. N. W. McBeath, Des Moines, Iowa
Stanley U. North, New York, N.Y.
Albert D. Stauffacher, New York, N.Y.

Frederick H. Thompson, Portland, Maine
Albert B. Tucker, Wilmette, Ill.
Arthur E. Wilson, Providence, R.I.
†Henry Reed Bowen, Newark, N.J.
†S. W. Keck, Huron, S.D.
†Mrs. Ralph B. Lunt, South Portland, Maine
†Claton S. Rice, Seattle, Wash.
†Mrs. R. S. Scott, Spokane, Wash.
†Arthur W. Taylor, Lincoln, Neb.

CZECH-MORAVIAN BRETHREN

Representatives

Josef A. Barton, Belleville, Texas

DANISH EVANGELICAL LUTHERAN CHURCH OF AMERICA

Representatives

A. E. Farstrup, Des Moines, Iowa
Agnes Holst, Cedar Falls, Iowa
Alfred Jensen, Des Moines, Iowa

Johannes Knudsen, Des Moines, Iowa
Clayton Nielson, Withee, Wis.
H. O. Nielsen, Cedar Falls, Iowa

INTERNATIONAL CONVENTION OF DISCIPLES OF CHRIST

Representatives

Hampton Adams, St. Louis, Mo.
Genevieve Brown, Indianapolis, Ind.
Alice Gadd Buckner, Indianapolis, Ind.
George Walker Buckner, Jr., Indianapolis, Ind.
Mrs. Harry E. Burch, Winterset, Iowa
Lin D. Cartwright, St. Louis, Mo.
Gaines M. Cook, Indianapolis, Ind.
James A. Crain, Indianapolis, Ind.
Hugh D. Darsie, Brooklyn, N.Y.
Hayes Farish, Lexington, Ky.
Mrs. James T. Ferguson, Kansas City, Mo.
A. Dale Fiers, Cleveland, Ohio
Robert A. Fudge, Indianapolis, Ind.
C. O. Hawley, Indianapolis, Ind.
E. K. Higdon, Indianapolis, Ind.
Laurence V. Kirkpatrick, Enid, Okla.
H. B. McCormick, Indianapolis, Ind.
Glenn McRae, St. Louis, Mo.
Riley B. Montgomery, Lexington, Ky.

William T. Pearcy, Indianapolis, Ind.
Parker Rossman, Indianapolis, Ind.
Marvin O. Sansbury, Des Moines, Iowa
Virgil A. Sly, Indianapolis, Ind.
Harlie L. Smith, Indianapolis, Ind.
Julian E. Stuart, Indianapolis, Ind.
T. T. Swearingen, Kansas City, Mo.
George Oliver Taylor, Indianapolis, Ind.
Mrs. Gerard Taylor, Enid, Okla.
Jessie M. Trout, Indianapolis, Ind.
Hollis L. Turley, Indianapolis, Ind.
Willard W. Wickizer, Indianapolis, Ind.
Mrs. James D. Wyker, Mount Vernon, Ohio
†Raymond Baldwin, Topeka, Kansas
†Abbott Book, San Francisco, Calif.
†John Harms, Chicago, Ill.
†Carroll H. Lemon, Lincoln, Neb.
†Forrest L. Richeson, Minneapolis, Minn.

Alternate Representatives

John Francis Bellville, Elmira, N.Y.
W. B. Blakemore, Chicago, Ill.
Robert W. Burns, Atlanta, Ga.
Merrill L. Cadwell, Warren, Ohio

J. Eric Carlson, St. Louis, Mo.
Myron C. Cole, Portland, Ore.
F. E. Davidson, South Bend, Ind.
*Stephen J. England, Enid, Okla.

162

Warren Grafton, Kansas City, Mo.
Perry Epler Gresham, Detroit, Mich.
Mrs. J. Warren Hastings, Washington, D.C.
D. Ray Lindley, Wilson, N.C.
John E. McCaw, Des Moines, Iowa
Irwin Miller, Columbus, Ind.
Franklin H. Minck, Akron, Ohio
Edward S. Moreland, Cincinnati, Ohio
Charles Clayton Morrison, Chicago, Ill.
*Warner Muir, Los Angeles, Calif.
Lee C. Pierce, Jackson, Miss.

M. E. Sadler, Fort Worth, Texas
*O. L. Shelton, Indianapolis, Ind.
Roy Snodgrass, Fort Worth, Texas
*John A. Tate, Richmond, Va.
William R. Vivrett, Jr., Pittsburgh, Pa.
Mae Yoho Ward, Indianapolis, Ind.
H. T. Wood, Memphis, Tenn.
*C. M. Yocum, Indianapolis, Ind.
†Reuben W. Coleman, Dayton, Ohio
†Dale Dargitz, Denver, Col.
†Harry H. Rogers, San Antonio, Texas
†George H. Wilson, St. Joseph, Mo.

EVANGELICAL AND REFORMED CHURCH

Representatives

Mrs. E. Roy Corman, Pittsburgh, Pa.
Barbara Deitz, Bowling Green, Ohio
Purd E. Deitz, St. Louis, Mo.
Dobbs F. Ehlman, Philadelphia, Pa.
L. W. Goebel, Chicago, Ill.
Mrs. F. A. Goetsch, St. Louis, Mo.
Gerhard W. Grauer, Chicago, Ill.
Nevin C. Harner, Lancaster, Pa.
Willard A. Kratz, Catasauqua, Pa.

J. N. LeVan, Philadelphia, Pa.
John W. Mueller, St. Louis, Mo.
Florence Partridge, Cleveland, Ohio
Henry J. Schlundt, Evansville, Ind.
F. W. Schroeder, Webster Groves, Mo.
Paul M. Schroeder, Rochester, N.Y.
Fred C. Schweinfurth, Cleveland, Ohio
Franklin I. Sheeder, Philadelphia, Pa.
James E. Wagner, Lancaster, Pa.

Alternate Representatives

Reginald H. Helfferich, Bath, Pa.
*T. W. Hoernemann, New Philadelphia, Ohio
Huber F. Klemme, Cleveland, Ohio
Mrs. Milton C. Lang, Baltimore, Md.
Roy W. Limbert, Dover, Pa.
William Nelson, Akron, Ohio

Paul H. Schulz, Detroit, Mich.
*H. L. V. Shinn, Toledo, Ohio
G. Siegenthaler, Baltimore, Md.
Stephen Szabo, Cleveland, Ohio
Richard Van Voorhis, Tiffin, Ohio
Calvin H. Wingert, Canton, Ohio

EVANGELICAL UNITED BRETHREN CHURCH

Representatives

Harold E. Davidson, Columbus, Ohio
O. T. Deever, Dayton, Ohio
Fred L. Dennis, Dayton, Ohio
G. E. Epp, Naperville, Ill.
Janet Gilbert, Dayton, Ohio
D. T. Gregory, Dayton, Ohio
Carl Heinmiller, Dayton, Ohio
U. P. Hovermale, Dayton, Ohio
L. L. Huffman, Dayton, Ohio

Torrey A. Kaatz, Toledo, Ohio
R. H. Mueller, Dayton, Ohio
Walter Muller, Peoria, Ill.
E. W. Praetorius, St. Paul, Minn.
J. B. Showers, Harrisburg, Pa.
C. H. Stauffacher, Kansas City, Mo.
Roy D. Stetler, Harrisburg, Pa.
Ira D. Warner, Puente, Calif.

Alternate Representatives

M. N. Berger, Dayton, Ohio
B. H. Cain, Dayton, Ohio
Mrs. H. S. Frank, Farmington, Minn.
Ralph M. Holdeman, Dayton, Ohio
J. Gordon Howard, Westerville, Ohio
W. R. Montgomery, Dayton, Ohio
Paul Price, Reading, Pa.

J. Allan Ranck, Dayton, Ohio
*Paul E. V. Shannon, York, Pa.
Mrs. J. B. Showers, Harrisburg, Pa.
*Richard Tholin, Chicago, Ill.
*J. Britain Winter, Baltimore, Md.
S. G. Ziegler, Dayton, Ohio
†Alvin S. Haag, Redlands, Calif.

163

RELIGIOUS SOCIETY OF FRIENDS (FIVE YEARS MEETING)

Representatives

*A. Ward Applegate, Wilmington, Ohio
*Merle L. Davis, Richmond, Ind.
Errol T. Elliott, Richmond, Ind.
*Samuel Levering, Ararat, Va.

Russell E. Rees, Chicago, Ill.
Helen E. Walker, Whittier, Calif.
†John J. Haramy, Indianapolis, Ind.
†Clyde A. Milner, Guilford College, N.C.

RELIGIOUS SOCIETY OF FRIENDS OF PHILADELPHIA AND VICINITY

Representatives

Anna C. Brinton, Wallingford, Pa.
Dorothy A. James, Wallingford, Pa.
*Grace E. Rhoads, Jr., Moorestown, N.J.

Lydia B. Stokes, Moorestown, N. J.
*Richard R. Wood, Moorestown, N.J.
*Gertrude M. Woodruff, Philadelphia, Pa.

Alternate Representative

Howard G. Taylor, Jr., Philadelphia, Pa.

THE METHODIST CHURCH

Representatives

Merrill R. Abbey, Madison, Wis.
Charles V. Adams, Montoursville, Pa.
Leon M. Adkins, Syracuse, N.Y.
L. Scott Allen, Atlanta, Ga.
Benjamin F. Allgood, Haddon Heights, N.J.
Mrs. Benjamin F. Allgood, Haddon Heights, N.J.
Mrs. Paul Arrington, Jackson, Miss.
James C. Baker, Los Angeles, Calif.
Mrs. M. H. Baxley, Columbia, S.C.
Chilton G. Bennett, Chicago, Ill.
Harold A. Bosley, Evanston, Ill.
Charles F. Boss, Jr., Chicago, Ill.
C. A. Bowen, Nashville, Tenn.
J. W. E. Bowen, Atlanta, Ga.
M. W. Boyd, Morristown, Tenn.
Charles W. Brashares, Des Moines, Iowa
Walter M. Briggs, Colorado Springs, Col.
Mrs. Frank G. Brooks, Mount Vernon, Iowa
Arlo Ayres Brown, Chestertown, Md.
Earl R. Brown, New York, N.Y.
Harvey C. Brown, Nashville, Tenn.
Ira A. Brumley, Conway, Ark.
Frank T. Cartwright, New York N.Y.
Harold D. Case, Pasadena, Calif.
Charles A. Chappell, Syracuse, N.Y.
*Fred P. Corson, Philadelphia, Pa.
Weldon Crossland, Rochester, N.Y.
*M. S. Davage, Nashville, Tenn.
Dana Dawson, Topeka, Kansas

Matt L. Ellis, Conway, Ark.
Arthur S. Flemming, Delaware, Ohio
Charles Wesley Flint, Washington, D.C.
Mrs. Earl Foster, Oklahoma City, Okla.
Denson N. Franklin, Gadsden, Ala.
Henrietta Gibson, New York, N.Y.
W. K. Greene, Spartanburg, S.C.
Wilbur D. Grose, St. Paul, Minn.
John O. Gross, Nashville, Tenn.
J. C. Haley, Tacoma, Wash.
Laura B. Hazley, Edna, Texas
Amos L. Heer, Kent, Ohio
Mrs. E. L. Hillman, Durham, N. C.
Mrs. Frank I. Hollingsworth, Denver, Col.
Fred G. Holloway, Madison, N.J.
Ivan Lee Holt, St. Louis, Mo.
*Gurney P. Hood, Raleigh, N.C.
Mrs. H. A. Hudspeth, Dallas, Texas
Walter L. Hunt, Unadilla, N.Y.
H. L. Johns, New Orleans, La.
Mrs. A. C. Johnson, Bowling Green, Ky.
E. Shurley Johnson, Detroit, Mich.
David D. Jones, Greensboro, N.C.
*Jameson Jones, Nashville, Tenn.
*E. W. Kelly, St. Louis, Mo.
Leon V. Kofod, New York, N.Y.
James Lawson, Berea, Ohio
W. Earl Ledden, Syracuse, N.Y.
Elizabeth Lee, New York, N.Y.
*Umphrey Lee, Dallas, Texas
Mrs. Howard M. LeSourd, Newton, Mass.
Henry V. Loeppert, Chicago, Ill.

164

*John Wesley Lord, Boston, Mass.
Thomas B. Lugg, Chicago, Ill.
J. Ralph Magee, Chicago, Ill.
A. W. Martin, Dallas, Texas
*William C. Martin, Dallas, Texas
Paul E. Martin, Little Rock, Ark.
James K. Mathews, New York, N.Y.
Dorothy McConnell, New York, N.Y.
Sallie Lou McKinnon, New York, N.Y.
Mrs. Charles W. Mead, Omaha, Neb.
Joseph J. Mickle, Shreveport, La.
Arthur J. Moore, Atlanta, Ga.
Aubrey S. Moore, Chicago, Ill.
J. Earl Moreland, Ashland, Va.
*John R. Mott, New York, N.Y.
*Julia Parr Naftzger, Kokomo, Ind.
Fred D. Newell, New York, N.Y.
Ray H. Nichols, Vernon, Texas
G. Bromley Oxnam, New York, N.Y.
Theodore H. Palmquist, Los Angeles, Calif.
Charles C. Parlin, New York, N.Y.
S. Stewart Patterson, Washington, D.C.
Lovick Pierce, Nashville, Tenn.
*Ira S. Pimm, Trenton, N.J.
Samuel Pinkerton, St. Paul, Minn.
*A. E. Pruner, Carpinteria, Calif.
William F. Quillian, Atlanta, Ga.
Karl Quimby, New York, N.Y.
Marshall R. Reed, Detroit, Mich.
Mrs. Fred C. Reynolds, Washington, D.C.
Mrs. C. N. Richmond, Chicago, Ill.
Sumpter M. Riley, Jr., Chicago, Ill.
Cecil F. Ristow, Seattle, Wash.
J. Callaway Robertson, Alexandria, Va.
Mrs. E. U. Robinson, Cookeville, Tenn.
Mildred Rydmark, Flint, Mich.

John Q. Schisler, Nashville, Tenn.
W. Taylor Seals, Lexington, Ky.
*Alexander P. Shaw, Baltimore, Md.
*Hammell P. Shipps, Delanco, N.J.
A. Frank Smith, Houston, Texas
*Alexander K. Smith, Ardmore, Pa.
Eugene L. Smith, New York, N.Y.
W. Angie Smith, Oklahoma City, Okla.
W. T. Smith, Peoria, Ill.
J. Richard Spann, Nashville, Tenn.
Norman Spellman, Kerrville, Texas
R. B. Spencer, Fort Morgan, Col.
Marshall T. Steel, Dallas, Texas
Thelma Stevens, New York, N.Y.
Ralph Stoody, New York, N.Y.
Mrs. Ellsworth M. Tilton, Springfield, Ore.
Earl V. Tolley, Binghamton, N.Y.
*Irwin Trotter, New Haven, Conn.
*R. Carter Tucker, Kansas City, Mo.
King Vivion, Nashville, Tenn.
Mrs. Edwin Voight, Indianola, Iowa
Hazen G. Werner, Columbus, Ohio
Lloyd C. Wicke, Pittsburgh, Pa.
Robert M. Williams, Washington, D.C.
Paul D. Womeldorf, Oklahoma City, Okla.
Robert Woods, Toledo, Ohio
†Gertrude L. Apel, Seattle, Wash.
*†Wilbur T. Clemens, Albany, N.Y.
†Jennie M. Doidge, Bridgeport, Conn.
†B. F. Lamb, Columbus, Ohio
†Grove Patterson, Toledo, Ohio
†William J. Scarborough, Buckhannon, W. Va.
†O. M. Walton, Pittsburgh, Pa.
†Chauncey D. Wentworth, Augusta, Maine

Alternate Representatives

W. S. Boyd, Pittsburgh, Pa.
G. Alfred Brown, Fort Worth, Texas
T. T. Brumbaugh, New York, N.Y.
Dawson C. Bryan, Nashville, Tenn.
R. C. Calkins, Des Moines, Iowa
Allen Claxton, New York, N.Y.
*Russell D. Cole, Mt. Vernon, Iowa
M. Earl Cunningham, Nashville, Tenn.
*Ralph S. Cushman, St. Paul, Minn.
Harry Denman, Nashville, Tenn.
*Wilbert H. Dougherty, Freeport, Pa.
George A. Fallon, Worcester, Mass.
*Mrs. Lacy W. Goostree, Fort Worth, Texas
W. Emory Hartman, Columbus, Ohio
Mrs. J. Theron Illick, Syracuse, N.Y.
George H. Jones, Nashville, Tenn.
Elmer D. Landreth, Abilene, Texas
*Leo H. McKay, Sharon, Pa.

*Mrs. C. A. Meeker, New York, N.Y.
Marjorie Minkler, New York, N.Y.
Mrs. James Oldshue, Chicago, Ill.
J. Manning Potts, Nashville, Tenn.
Ralph H. Richardson, Burlingame, Calif.
H. Conwell Snoke, Philadelphia, Pa.
Howard E. Tower, Nashville, Tenn.
Walter Towner, Nashville, Tenn.
*Harry L. Williams, Nashville, Tenn.
Horace Williams, Nashville, Tenn.
†C. A. Armstrong, Fargo, N.D.
*†John Keith Benton, Nashville, Tenn.
†Gay H. Brown, Troy, N.Y.
†Alice M. Chappell, Portland, Ore.
†Adlai C. Holler, Myrtle Beach, S.C.
*†Ralph B. Huston, Jacksonville, Fla.
†Mrs. Lowell Johnson, Butte, Mont.
†Arlie H. Krussell, Beloit, Wis.

165

†Harry J. Lord, Lansing, Mich.
†Chester McPheeters, Detroit, Mich.
†Harry W. McPherson, Springfield, Ill.

†Henry Shillington, Columbus, Ohio
†Dillon W. Throckmorton, Sacramento, Calif.

MORAVIAN CHURCH IN AMERICA

Representatives

John S. Groenfeldt, Bethlehem, Pa.
Kenneth G. Hamilton, Bethlehem, Pa.
George G. Higgins, Winston-Salem, N.C.

Edwin W. Kortz, Bethlehem, Pa.
R. Gordon Spaugh, Winston-Salem, N.C.
F. P. Stocker, Bethlehem, Pa.

Alternate Representatives

W. H. Allen, Bethlehem, Pa.
I. Richard Mewaldt, Madison, Wis.

*J. Kenneth Pfohl, Winston-Salem, N.C.
*Edwin A. Sawyer, Winston-Salem, N.C.

NATIONAL BAPTIST CONVENTION OF AMERICA

Representatives

Henry A. Boyd, Nashville, Tenn.
J. N. Byrd, San Antonio, Texas
C. D. Pettiway, Little Rock, Ark.

G. L. Prince, Crockett, Texas
P. S. Wilkinson, San Antonio, Texas

NATIONAL BAPTIST CONVENTION, U.S.A., INC.

Representatives

C. C. Adams, Philadelphia, Pa.
J. Timothy Boddie, Baltimore, Md.
W. H. Borders, Atlanta, Ga.
Nannie H. Burroughs, Washington, D.C.
B. W. Coates, Meridian, Miss.
E. C. Estell, Dallas, Texas
J. W. Gayden, Greenwood, Miss.
*E. L. Harrison, Washington, D.C.
William J. Harvey, III, Oklahoma City, Okla.
J. L. Horace, Chicago, Ill.
W. H. Jernagin, Washington, D.C.
Mrs. C. J. Jernagin, Washington, D.C.
D. E. King, Louisville, Ky.

O. C. Maxwell, New York, N.Y.
Benjamin E. Mays, Atlanta, Ga.
M. M. Morris, Greenville, Miss.
C. T. Murray, Washington, D. C.
Homer E. Nutter, Lexington, Ky.
*J. W. Parrish, Columbus, Ohio
B. J. Perkins, Cleveland, Ohio
*U. J. Robinson, Mobile, Ala.
E. C. Smith, Washington, D.C.
Roland Smith, Atlanta, Ga.
I. A. Thomas, Evanston, Ill.
William Prince Vaughn, Birmingham, Ala.
J. F. Walker, Cincinnati, Ohio
W. L. Wilson, Spartanburg, S.C.

Alternate Representatives

L. G. Carr, Philadelphia, Pa.
J. F. Clark, Pine Bluff, Ark.
J. F. Green, Detroit, Mich.
T. E. Huntley, St. Louis, Mo.
J. V. McIver, Orange, N.J.

Annette H. Officer, East St. Louis, Mo.
A. J. Payne, Baltimore, Md.
C. H. Pearson, Washington, D.C.
G. Taylor, Brooklyn, N.Y.
*C. R. Williams, Memphis, Tenn.

THE PRESBYTERIAN CHURCH IN THE UNITED STATES

Representatives

John M. Alexander, Atlanta, Ga.
S. Hugh Bradley, Decatur, Ga.
Jas. R. Bullock, Houston, Texas
C. Darby Fulton, Nashville, Tenn.
Edward D. Grant, Richmond, Va.

Clarence S. Johnson, Kirkwood, Mo.
Ben R. Lacy, Jr., Richmond, Va.
Mrs. A. Walton Litz, Little Rock, Ark.
J. P. McCallie, Chattanooga, Tenn.
Janie W. McGaughey, Atlanta, Ga.

Bernard A. McIlhany, Louisville, Ky.
M. A. MacDonald, Clinton, S.C.
J. G. Patton, Jr., Decatur, Ga.
Claude H. Pritchard, Atlanta, Ga.
J. McDowell Richards, Decatur, Ga.

Ferguson Wood, Johnson City, Tenn.
†Dorothy Blount, Mobile, Ala.
*†James W. Jackson, Columbia, S.C.
†Albert J. Kissling, Jacksonville, Fla.

Alternate Representatives

Mrs. F. R. Crawford, Farmville, Va.
Mrs. John L. Parkes, Atlanta, Ga.

†Frances C. Query, Durham, N.C.
†J. W. Witherspoon, Beckley, W. Va.

THE PRESBYTERIAN CHURCH IN THE U.S.A.

Representatives

Charles H. Albers, Chicago, Ill.
Edward J. Ardis, Mechanicsburg, Pa.
Jesse H. Baird, San Anselmo, Calif.
Clifford E. Barbour, Knoxville, Tenn.
Eugene C. Blake, Pasadena, Calif.
*Gale B. Braithwaite, Sioux Falls, S.D.
Mrs. J. Hastie Brown, Syracuse, N.Y.
Mrs. W. Verne Buchanan, New
Philadelphia, Ohio
E. Fay Campbell, Philadelphia, Pa.
Mrs. J. M. Douglas, Weirsdale, Fla.
Mrs. Walter B. Driscoll, St. Paul, Minn.
E. L. R. Elson, Washington, D.C.
Hugh Ivan Evans, Dayton, Ohio
Clayton T. Griswold, New York, N.Y.
Jack Hart, Chicago, Ill.
Mrs. John M. Irvine, Wexford, Pa.
Lem T. Jones, Kansas City, Mo.
Mrs. Paul K. Justus, St. Louis, Mo.
*Patricia Kimble, St. Paul, Minn.
Charles T. Leber, New York, N.Y.
*Ganse Little, Columbus, Ohio
Ralph Waldo Lloyd, Maryville, Tenn.
Allan D. Locke, New York, N.Y.
John A. Mackay, Princeton, N.J.
Jean S. Milner, Indianapolis, Ind.

Hermann N. Morse, New York, N.Y.
Mrs. Paul Moser, New York, N.Y.
Paul Calvin Payne, Philadelphia, Pa.
*John T. Peters, New York, N.Y.
Elinor K. Purves, Princeton, N.J.
Mrs. J. T. Robison, Texarkana, Texas
Mildred Roe, Philadelphia, Pa.
Lloyd S. Ruland, New York, N.Y.
*Harrison M. Sayre, Columbus, Ohio
Margaret Shannon, New York, N.Y.
Alexander E. Sharp, New York, N.Y.
C. Ralston Smith, Oklahoma City, Okla.
James W. Smith, Sr., Charlotte, S.C.
Henry P. Van Dusen, New York, N.Y.
Robert B. Whyte, Cleveland, Ohio
Paul A. Wolfe, New York, N.Y.
†Joseph Bachman, Bismarck, N.D.
†E. C. Farnham, San Francisco, Calif.
*†George Hunter Hall, Phoenix, Ariz.
†Marion E. Mansell, Rockwood, Tenn.
†T. H. McDowell, Oklahoma City, Okla.
†Glenn W. Moore, Los Angeles, Calif.
†Edward Allen Morris, Trenton, N.J.
†Dan M. Potter, Attleboro, Mass.
†Mrs. R. V. Rorabaugh, Tulsa, Okla.

Alternate Representatives

Robert G. Andrus, Lake Forest, Ill.
*John O. Bigelow, Newark, N.J.
Donald F. Campbell, Stamford, Conn.
Merlyn A. Chappel, New York, N.Y.
Henry Sloane Coffin, Lakeville, Conn.
*Peter K. Emmons, Scranton, Pa.
Mrs. Frederick W. Evans, Springfield, Pa.
Margaret Flory, New York, N.Y.
Ray J. Harmelink, Philadelphia, Pa.

Walter L. Jenkins, Philadelphia, Pa.
Daniel M. Pattison, New York, N.Y.
Paul N. Poling, Philadelphia, Pa.
Harold B. Walker, Evanston, Ill.
Mrs. Ralph E. Weber, Summit, N.J.
*William G. Werner, Cincinnati, Ohio
William N. Wysham, New York, N.Y.
*†Raymon M. Kistler, Jenkintown, Pa.
†J. T. Morrow, Tulsa, Okla.

THE PROTESTANT EPISCOPAL CHURCH

Representatives

Karl M. Block, San Francisco, Calif.
John M. Burgess, Washington, D.C.

Charles C. J. Carpenter, Birmingham, Ala.
*Mrs. Francis O. Clarkson, Charlotte, N.C.

167

*W. A. Cochel, Parkville, Mo.
Mrs. Clifford C. Cowin, Lakewood, Ohio
Gardiner M. Day, Cambridge, Mass.
Peter Day, Milwaukee, Wis.
*Hubert T. Delaney, New York, N.Y.
Clarence Wallace Hayes, Berkeley, Calif.
John S. Higgins, Providence, R.I.
Henry W. Hobson, Cincinnati, Ohio
Scott N. Jones, Ripon, Wis.
*Clark G. Kuebler, Ripon, Wis.
Mrs. Edward G. Lasar, St. Louis, Mo.
*Nancy Miller, Durham, N.H.
Spencer Miller, Jr., South Orange, N.J.
R. Bland Mitchell, Little Rock, Ark.

G. Gardner Monks, Washington, D.C.
*Thomas B. K. Ringe, Philadelphia, Pa.
Noel Sargent, New York, N.Y.
William Scarlett, St. Louis, Mo.
Henry K. Sherrill, New York, N.Y.
Mrs. Harper Sibley, Rochester, N.Y.
Claude W. Sprouse, Kansas City, Mo.
Frank W. Sterrett, Bethlehem, Pa.
Harwood Sturtevant, Fond du Lac, Wis.
Charles P. Taft, Cincinnati, Ohio
Beverley D. Tucker, Cleveland, Ohio
Frederick J. Warnecke, Newark, N.J.
†Frederick D. Goodwin, Richmond, Va.

Alternate Representatives

Stephen F. Bayne, Seattle, Wash.
*Paul F. Good, Omaha, Neb.
R. O'Hara Lanier, Houston, Texas
*John E. Large, New York, N.Y.
*C. Avery Mason, Dallas, Texas
Bernard C. Newman, New York, N.Y.
G. Ashton Oldham, Norfolk, Conn.

*Anthony R. Parshley, Providence, R.I.
*Thorne Sparkman, Bryn Mawr, Pa.
*Donald H. Wattley, New Orleans, La.
*†R. A. Kirchhoffer, Indianapolis, Ind.
†Ruth Custis Kitchen, Philadelphia, Pa.
†Glenn F. Lewis, St. Paul, Minn.

REFORMED CHURCH IN AMERICA

Representatives

Helen Brickman, New York, N.Y.
Mrs. John A. Dykstra, Grand Rapids, Mich.
James Gray, Schenectady, N.Y.
James E. Hoffman, New York, N.Y.
Bastian Kruithof, Holland, Mich.

Bernard J. Mulder, New York, N.Y.
Mrs. Norman V. Peale, New York, N.Y.
Francis M. Potter, New York, N.Y.
R. J. Vandenberg, Forest Hills, N.Y.
Gerrit Vander Lugt, Pella, Iowa

Alternate Representative

Henry A. Vruwink, Brooklyn, N.Y.

ROMANIAN ORTHODOX EPISCOPATE OF AMERICA

Representatives

*Nicholas Moldovan, Farrell, Pa.
*John Stanila, Youngstown, Ohio

Viorel Trifa, Cleveland, Ohio
John Trutza, Cleveland, Ohio

RUSSIAN ORTHODOX CHURCH OF NORTH AMERICA

Representatives

Ralph Montgomery Arkush, New York, N.Y.
Ivan Michaelson Czap, Philadelphia, Pa.

Georges Florovsky, New York, N.Y.
Stephen Rusiniak, Lakewood, Ohio
Nicholas Vansuch, New York, N.Y.

Alternate Representatives

Lewis Nescott, McKeesport, Pa.

SEVENTH DAY BAPTIST GENERAL CONFERENCE

Representatives

Elmo F. Randolph, Milton, Wis.
*Mrs. James L. Skaggs, Salem, W. Va.

George B. Utter, Westerly, R.I.

SYRIAN ANTIOCHIAN ORTHODOX CHURCH

Representative

James C. Meena, Cleveland, Ohio

UKRAINIAN ORTHODOX CHURCH

Representative

Peter Kieluch, New York, N.Y.

UNITED LUTHERAN CHURCH IN AMERICA

Representatives

Mrs. C. W. Baker, Jr., Duquesne, Pa.
Nona M. Diehl, Philadelphia, Pa.
Paul C. Empie, New York, N.Y.
Henry Endress, New York, N.Y.
Wallace E. Fisher, Gettysburg, Pa.
Franklin Clark Fry, New York, N.Y.
R. H. Gerberding, New York, N.Y.
Luther A. Gotwald, New York, N.Y.
James F. Henninger, Allentown, Pa.
James C. Kinard, Newberry, S.C.
C. Franklin Koch, New York, N.Y.
M. P. Moller, Jr., Hagerstown, Md.
O. Frederick Nolde, Wyndmoor, Pa.

F. Eppling Reinartz, New York, N.Y.
S. White Rhyne, Philadelphia, Pa.
Mrs. O. A. Sardeson, New York, N.Y.
G. Morris Smith, Selinsgrove, Pa.
Mary Helen Smith, Philadelphia, Pa.
Robert W. Stackel, Pittsburgh, Pa.
Clarence C. Stoughton, Springfield, Ohio
L. Ralph Tabor, Washington, D.C.
S. Frederick Telleen, New York, N.Y.
H. Torrey Walker, Philadelphia, Pa.
Gould Wickey, Washington, D.C.
†Alvin D. Havekost, Denver, Col.

Alternate Representatives

Mary E. Anstadt, Philadelphia, Pa.
Mrs. Howard S. Bechtoldt, Chicago, Ill.
David H. Bremer, Washington, D.C.
Hugo L. Dressler, Hickory, N.C.
Frances Dysinger, Philadelphia, Pa.
Charles H. Esser, Kutztown, Pa.
Fred F. Fielder, New York, N.Y.
Mrs. Howard R. Gold, Williamsport, Pa.
Ernst P. Hoeppner, Philadelphia, Pa.
E. E. Keister, Strasburg, Va.
Paul Andrew Kirsch, New York, N.Y.
Clarence E. Krumbholz, New York, N.Y.
Harold U. Landis, Lebanon, Pa.

Harold C. Letts, New York, N.Y.
John M. Mangum, Philadelphia, Pa.
Lawrence W. Reese, Philadelphia, Pa.
G. Elson Ruff, Philadelphia, Pa.
W. Carl Satre, Toledo, Ohio
Francis A. Shearer, New York, N.Y.
Lawrence F. Speckman, Louisville, Ky.
William H. Stackel, Rochester, N.Y.
Zeb. B. Trexler, Concord, N.C.
Paul C. White, New York, N.Y.
*William F. Zimmerman, Greenville, Pa.
†Frederick E. Reissig, Washington, D.C.

UNITED PRESBYTERIAN CHURCH OF NORTH AMERICA

Representatives

T. Donald Black, Philadelphia, Pa.
James M. Guthrie, Long Island, N.Y.

William M. Hendricks, Brooklyn, N.Y.
Mrs. Gordon Jackson, Pittsburgh, Pa.

169

James R. Lee, Bellerose, N.Y.
John L. McCreight, Clifton Heights, Pa.
*William F. Rotzler, Pittsburgh, Pa.

Ernest Tilford, Industry, N.Y.
†M. Earl Collins, Kirkwood, Mo.

Alternate Representatives

Mrs. H. H. McConnell, Sr., New York, N.Y.
George D. Munro, Drexel Hill, Pa.

William H. Neebe, Bloomfield, N.J.
*Charles D. Skuce, Youngstown, Ohio
†John Meloy, Louisville, Ky.

MERGING AGENCIES
Consultants

CHURCH WORLD SERVICE, INC.

Robbins W. Barstow, New York, N.Y.   *W. Harold Row, Elgin, Ill.

FEDERAL COUNCIL OF THE CHURCHES OF CHRIST IN AMERICA

*T. C. Allen, New York, N.Y.
Margaret T. Applegarth, New York, N.Y.
J. C. Austin, Chicago, Ill.
Jesse M. Bader, New York, N.Y.
Roswell P. Barnes, New York, N.Y.
Nadine Blair, Washington, D.C.
Donald C. Bolles, New York, N.Y.
Beverley M. Boyd, New York, N.Y.
Samuel McCrea Cavert, New York, N.Y.
Theresa Capell, New York, N.Y.
G. A. Crawley, Baltimore, Md.
Ralph E. Diffendorfer, New York, N.Y.
H. Paul Douglass, New York, N.Y.
*John E. Easter, Roanoke, Va.
Deane Edwards, New York, N.Y.
Richard M. Fagley, New York, N.Y.
Hamilton P. Fox, Wilmington, Del.
Edward W. Gebhard, Chicago, Ill.
Albea Godbold, St. Louis, Mo.
Elma L. Greenwood, New York, N.Y.
Cameron P. Hall, New York, N.Y.
Mrs. William C. Hanson, Kansas City, Kan.
Nolan B. Harmon, New York, N.Y.
Thomas S. Harten, Brooklyn, N.Y.
Mary Elizabeth Hillman, New York, N.Y.
Howard W. Hopkirk, New Rochelle, N.Y.
Laurence T. Hosie, Syracuse, N.Y.
John M. Johansen, New York, N.Y.
F. Ernest Johnson, New York, N.Y.
H. H. Kalas, Chicago, Ill.

George D. Kelsey, New York, N.Y.
*Clarence W. Kemper, Boulder, Col.
George F. Ketcham, New York, N.Y.
J. Oscar Lee, New York, N.Y.
Nellie Lind, New York, N.Y.
E. Burns Martin, Hammond, Va.
Thomas B. Mather, Kansas City, Mo.
H. H. McConnell, New York, N.Y.
J. Quinter Miller, New York, N.Y.
Paul Moser, New York, N.Y.
John Oliver Nelson, New Haven, Conn.
Marion Nelson, New York, N.Y.
*Justin Wroe Nixon, Rochester, N.Y.
Laurence E. Nye, Portland, Ore.
Emelie F. Paky, New York, N.Y.
*Mrs. Ellis L. Phillips, New York, N.Y.
*Harold Quigley, New York, N.Y.
Otis R. Rice, New York, N.Y.
Mrs. William W. Rockwell, New York, N.Y.
Aenid A. Sanborn, New York, N.Y.
C. Clark Shedd, Toledo, Ohio
John S. Stamm, Harrisburg, Pa.
James L. Stoner, New York, N.Y.
Paul L. Tilden, Brooklyn, N.Y.
Walter W. Van Kirk, New York, N.Y.
A. Dudley Ward, New York, N.Y.
Forrest C. Weir, Atlanta, Ga.
Armond D. Willis, New York, N.Y.
L. Foster Wood, New York, N.Y.

FOREIGN MISSIONS CONFERENCE OF NORTH AMERICA

E. M. Aitken, Ontario, Canada
Roger Altman, Washington, D.C.
Harry B. Ansted, Chicago, Ill.

Mrs. L. B. Arey, Chicago, Ill.
Jesse H. Arnup, Ontario, Canada
*James E. Bear, Richmond, Va.

Edna Beardsley, New York, N.Y.
R. Pierce Beaver, New York, N.Y.
*Albert E. Beebe, New York, N.Y.
*E. C. Bender, Martinsburg, Pa.
Clara L. Bentley, New York, N.Y.
John B. Bentley, New York, N.Y.
Kathryne Bieri, New York, N.Y.
Margaret Billingsley, New York, N.Y.
*Mrs. H. C. Bleckschmidt, St. Louis, Mo.
*Marion A. Boggs, Little Rock, Ark.
W. P. Bradley, Washington, D.C.
Mrs. Art Brandon, Ann Arbor, Mich.
*Leland S. Brubaker, Elgin, Ill.
William W. Cadbury, Moorestown, N.J.
Helen B. Calder, Auburndale, Mass.
Alice E. Cary, Boston, Mass.
A. V. Casselman, Philadelphia, Pa.
Nelson Chappel, New York, N.Y.
*J. Calvitt Clarke, Richmond, Va.
George E. Coleman, Memphis, Tenn.
Lucile Colony, New York, N.Y.
Elizabeth Congdon, Oak Lawn, R.I.
*Mrs. John T. Connell, Butler, Pa.
Charles H. Corbett, New York, N.Y.
E. H. Cressy, Hartford, Conn.
Rowland M. Cross, New York, N.Y.
L. A. Dixon, Ontario, Canada
M. C. Dixon, Minneapolis, Minn.
Ralph E. Dodge, New York, N.Y.
Agnes C. L. Donohugh, New York, N.Y.
Mildred G. Drescher, New York, N.Y.
Raymond A. Dudley, Boston, Mass.
Rhoda Edmeston, Nashville, Tenn.
*Helen Eklund, New York, N.Y.
Ruth Elliott, New York, N.Y.
James E. Ellis, New York, N.Y.
Mabel E. Emerson, Cambridge, Mass.
*Henry S. Evans, New Concord, Ohio
Charles J. Ewald, Cleveland, Ohio
Wynn C. Fairfield, New York, N.Y.
*D. J. Fleming, New York, N.Y.
*Mrs. D. J. Fleming, New York, N.Y.
Arva C. Floyd, Emory University, Ga.
Elmer W. Fondell, Chicago, Ill.
J. Earl Fowler, New York, N.Y.
Helen M. Franck, New York, N.Y.
*T. P. Fricke, Columbus, Ohio
D. H. Gallagher, Ontario, Canada
Henry F. Garber, Mt. Joy, Pa.
F. F. Goodsell, New York, N.Y.
Florence Gordon, New York, N.Y.
Frances Gray, New York, N.Y.
Ralph P. Hanson, Chicago, Ill.
Richard E. Hanson, New York, N.Y.
R. A. Harrisville, Minneapolis, Minn.
*Mrs. H. E. Harwood, Columbus, Ohio
H. K. Heebner, Philadelphia, Pa.

*E. M. Hodgeboom, Huntington, Ind.
Conrad Hoffman, Jr., New York, N.Y.
Garland E. Hopkins, Chicago, Ill.
Henry N. Hostetter, Washington Boro, Pa.
H. R. Howden, Ontario, Canada
*Walter M. Howlett, New York, N.Y.
Edward H. Hume, New York, N.Y.
Mrs. Leslie P. Hunt, Ontario, Canada
M. T. Jenson, Alexandria, Minn.
Mrs. Jacob Juist, Detroit, Mich.
Thomas B. Keehn, New York, N.Y.
E. R. Kellersburg, New York, N.Y.
Peter Konsterlie, Minneapolis, Minn.
*Lewis H. Lancaster, Nashville, Tenn.
*Frank C. Laubach, New York, N.Y.
Charles H. Long, Jr., New York, N.Y.
Ward N. Madison, Philadelphia, Pa.
O. R. Magill, New York, N.Y.
Alfred Mathes, Birmingham, Ala.
Arleigh G. Matlock, Memphis, Tenn.
*Mrs. Arthur B. McBride, Sewickley, Pa.
James O. McDonald, Wilmington, Del.
Mrs. John McKillop, Ontario, Canada
R. G. McMillan, Ontario, Canada
Robert J. McMullen, New York, N.Y.
Mrs. Robert J. McMullen, New York, N.Y.
*Jean McVeety, Minneapolis, Minn.
F. J. Michel, Chicago, Ill.
Orie O. Miller, Akron, Pa.
Ira W. Moomaw, New York, N.Y.
Alfred Moore, New York, N.Y.
Mrs. John B. Moore, Columbia, S.C.
*John H. Mosemann, Goshen, Ind.
Mrs. Robert Muller, Bayside, N.Y.
*Mrs. Thomas Nicholson, St. Paul, Minn.
Joel Nystrom, New York, N.Y.
Mrs. Arthur W. Pae, Ontario, Canada
R. M. Paty, New York, N.Y.
Laura K. Pelton, Ontario, Canada
D. C. Pope, Washington, D.C.
*C. Lowrey Quinn, Anderson, Ind.
Glenn P. Reed, Philadelphia, Pa.
John H. Reisner, New York, N.Y.
C. H. Rice, Wooster, Ohio
Mrs. C. H. Rice, New York, N.Y.
Louise Robinson, New York, N.Y.
E. E. Roenfelt, Washington, D.C.
Emory Ross, New York, N.Y.
Mrs. L. R. Rounds, New York, N.Y.
W. Stanley Rycroft, New York, N.Y.
Harry W. Seamans, Washington, D.C.
*Mrs. Howard W. Selby, West Newton, Mass.
*Mrs. H. Ray Shear, Pittsburgh, Pa.
Helen M. Shirk, New York, N.Y.

171

*J. Edgar Smith, Anderson, Ind.
John C. Smith, New York, N.Y.
Wendell C. Somerville, Washington, D.C.
Mrs. Lloyd Sprague, Corning, N.Y.
John H. Stanton, Johnstown, Pa.
*L. M. Stavig, Sioux Falls, S.D.
Hugh C. Stuntz, Nashville, Tenn.
R. A. Syrdal, Minneapolis, Minn.
Mrs. Hugh D. Taylor, Ontario, Canada
*Robert Taylor, New York, N.Y.
C. J. Ulery, Springfield, Ohio
John C. Van Wyk, Oskaloosa, Iowa

Arnold B. Vaught, New York, N.Y.
A. L. Warnshuis, Bronxville, N.Y.
Mrs. A. L. Warnshuis, Bronxville, N.Y.
Sue Weddell, New York, N.Y.
Mrs. Charles E. Wegner, St. Paul, Minn.
John B. Weir, New York, N.Y.
*Charles A. Weishaupt, Columbus, Ohio
Mrs. Roscoe M. White, Richmond, Va.
M. O. Williams, New York, N.Y.
*Edmund S. Wolfe, Bridgeport, Conn.
Wayland Zwayer, New York, N.Y.

HOME MISSIONS COUNCIL OF NORTH AMERICA

E. F. Adcock, Anderson, Indiana
Mrs. A. J. Allen, Cleveland, Ohio
C. Harry Atkinson, New York, N.Y.
Mrs. L. M. Awtrey, Acworth, Ga.
Everett A. Babcock, Cleveland, Ohio
Marion Baker, Dayton, Ohio
Harold H. Baldwin, New York, N.Y.
Mrs. A. A. Banks, Jr., Detroit, Mich.
Mrs. M. J. Battle, Milwaukee, Wis.
Elsie C. Beckett, Washington, D.C.
Adam D. Beittel, Talladega, Ala.
Mrs. Fred Berry, Woodriver, Ill.
Mrs. L. L. Berry, New York, N.Y.
J. L. Black, Cleveland, Ohio
Mrs. S. T. Boone, Detroit, Mich.
John T. Broek, Plainfield, N.J.
Charles L. Brooks, Indianapolis, Ind.
Mrs. Harry Buis, Brooklyn Village, Ohio
Emma Burris, New York, N.Y.
G. Bruce Cameron, Cincinnati, Ohio
*Henrietta Carey, Brooklyn, New York
E. Russell Carter, Lawrence, Kan.
Ione Caton, New York, N.Y.
Tollie L. Caution, New York, N.Y.
Mrs. Matthew C. Cavell, Evansville, Ind.
Mrs. Rollin T. Chamberlin, Chicago, Ill.
Mrs. F. A. Chappelle, Brooklyn, N.Y.
James V. Claypool, Chicago, Ill.
William W. Clemes, New York, N.Y.
*Mrs. C. C. Coleman, Tupelo, Miss.
Ralph Collins, Cleveland, Ohio
Elbert M. Conover, New York, N.Y.
*S. B. Copeland, Pittsburgh, Pa.
*Mrs. J. Crewse, Cleveland, Ohio
Frederick W. Cropp, New York, N.Y.
Muriel Day, New York, N.Y.
George Dorey, Ontario, Canada
J. F. Dunn, Akron, Ohio
J. M. Ellson, Richmond, Va.
*Charles Enders, Washington, D.C.
E. L. Fisher, New York, N.Y.
Mrs. W. A. Fountain, Atlanta, Ga.

*Isabelle M. Gates, New York, N.Y.
H. R. Gebhardt, St. Louis, Mo.
Hazel Gomez, Waco, Texas
Merle Gripman, New York, N.Y.
*Mrs. J. Gros, Lakewood, Ohio
*Oscar C. Grueninger, St. Louis, Mo.
Clifford G. Hansen, New York, N.Y.
Joseph H. Heartberg, New York, N.Y.
Mrs. L. H. Hemingway, Washington, D.C.
Mrs. G. Henry, Brooklyn Village, Ohio
W. A. Hilliard, Detroit, Mich.
V. C. Hodges, Cleveland, Ohio
Elizabeth Howell, New York, N.Y.
Wesley Hotchkiss, New York, N.Y.
*Mrs. G. Virgil Hutchison, Imperial, Pa.
Hal Hyde, Atlanta, Ga.
J. Earl Jackman, New York, N.Y.
Mrs. E. M. Kaigler, Detroit, Mich.
*Paul S. Kershner, Akron, Ohio
Benson Y. Landis, New York, N.Y.
Ruth Landis, Cleveland, Ohio
Laurence W. Lange, New York, N.Y.
*Wilbur Larson, New York, N.Y.
Theodore R. Leon, Indianapolis, Ind.
James K. Leitch, Pittsburgh, Pa.
G. E. E. Lindquist, Lawrence, Kan.
Anna D. Locker, Cincinnati, Ohio
Edith E. Lowry, New York, N.Y.
Mrs. C. Maxwell Loveys, Ontario, Can.
Alice Maloney, New York, N.Y.
*Ellis Marshburn, Chicago, Ill.
Mrs. Daniel T. Martin, Minneapolis, Minn.
*George U. Martin, Steubenville, Ohio
Mrs. A. M. F. Mason, Cleveland, Ohio
Mary McLanachon, Dayton, Ohio
Dale W. Medearis, Indianapolis, Ind.
Fred W. Michel, Indianapolis, Ind.
*W. Vernon Middleton, Philadelphia, Pa.
Beulah Miller, Columbus, Ohio
Ruth E. Milner, Indianapolis, Ind.
Barney N. Morgan, New York, N.Y.

172

Edna Morris, Philadelphia, Pa.
Beata Mueller, New York, N.Y.
*Alice Murdock, New York, N.Y.
*Mrs. Edgar B. Murdoch, Washington, Pa.
I. George Nace, New York, N.Y.
*Mrs. Alvin J. Neevel, Tarrytown, N.Y.
James Z. Nettinga, Pasadena, Calif.
Lyle V. Newman, Indianapolis, Ind.
Mrs. C. S. Patterson, Ontario, Canada
Elsie R. Penfield, New York, N.Y.
Don F. Pielstick, New York, N.Y.
*Glen E. Pierson, Elmhurst, N.Y.
*Paul Reid Pontius, Greensburg, Pa.
Henry S. Randolph, New York, N.Y.
Beatrice Reid, Columbia, S.C.
William H. Rhoades, New York, N.Y.
Mark Rich, New York, N.Y.
Mary O. Ross, Detroit, Mich.
Harry V. Richardson, Atlanta, Ga.
*Clifford L. Samuelson, New York, N.Y.
Ross W. Sanderson, New York, N.Y.
Harold Schultz, St. Louis, Mo.
Julia Baum Shaw, Columbia, S.C.
Rolland H. Sheafer, Indianapolis, Ind.
Mrs. F. E. Shotwell, Los Angeles, Calif.
Louisa R. Shotwell, New York, N.Y.

Claude J. Snyder, St. Louis, Mo.
*Loretta Spencer, Frankfort, Ky.
Dorothy Stabler, New York, N.Y.
Archibald K. Stewart, Pittsburgh, Pa.
Mrs. Robert Stewart, New York, N.Y.
Mrs. George Terbeek, Cleveland, Ohio
Ross Thornton, Cleveland, Ohio
W. C. Timmons, New York, N.Y.
Alex Toth, Lancaster, Pa.
*Thomas Alfred Tripp, New York, N.Y.
R. J. Vanden Berg, New York, N.Y.
Mrs. Bert E. Van Soest, Cleveland, Ohio
Lincoln B. Wadsworth, New York, N.Y.
Mabel Wagner, New York, N.Y.
Paul L. Warnshuis, Los Angeles, Calif.
Corenne Watts, Birmingham, Ala.
F. C. Weigman, Akron, Ohio
Ralph S. Weiler, Philadelphia, Pa.
George A. Wieland, New York, N.Y.
S. B. Williams, Kansas City, Mo.
Lillian A. Windham, New York, N.Y.
Ernest C. Witham, New York, N.Y.
W. E. Woodbury, New York, N.Y.
Annie Wortham, Detroit, Mich.
Charles E. Zunkel, Elgin, Ill.

INTERNATIONAL COUNCIL OF RELIGIOUS EDUCATION

*Joe Allen, New Haven, Conn.
Benjamin V. Andrews, Indianapolis, Ind.
*O. O. Arnold, Dayton, Ohio
Joe R. Babb, Indianapolis, Ind.
William E. Barrick, Evanston, Ill.
*A. C. Baugher, Elizabethtown, Pa.
*David H. Bradley, Bedford, Pa.
H. C. Bradshaw, Topeka, Kan.
Mary Margaret Brace, New York, N.Y.
Rachel M. Brant, Dayton, Ohio
Ralph P. Bridgman, Toledo, Ohio
W. H. Buckner, Franklin, La.
Elizabeth Bulkeley, Detroit, Mich.
Roy A. Burkhart, Columbus, Ohio
Charles A. Butts, Boston, Mass.
Robert J. Campbell, Chicago, Ill.
J. Henry Carpenter, Brooklyn, N.Y.
*Dora P. Chaplin, Greenwich, Conn.
A. Wilson Cheek, Chicago, Ill.
Cautious A. Choate, Wichita, Kan.
*Homer N. Clark, Pittsburgh, Pa.
J. S. Clarke, Ontario, Canada
*Henry E. Cole, Pittsburgh, Pa.
Jonathan A. Dames, Indianapolis, Ind.
Floyd Q. Davidson, Wichita, Kan.
Claud King Davis, Sisterville, W. Va.
Roy E. Dickerson, Cincinnati, Ohio
Emmett S. Dickson, Indianapolis, Ind.

Ralph E. Dodge, New York, N.Y.
Bryant Drake, Chicago, Ill.
*Francis A. Drake, Lake Geneva, Wis.
Franklin Duncombe, Bala-Cynwyd, Pa.
Frances W. Eastman, Boston, Mass.
Merle L. Easton, Boston, Mass.
*Mrs. L. D. Edwards, Nashville, Tenn.
Elmer O. Ellefson, Minneapolis, Minn.
*J. M. Ellison, Richmond, Va.
Herbert F. Evans, Whittier, Calif.
Harold W. Ewing, Nashville, Tenn.
Newton C. Fetter, New York, N.Y.
Ernest H. Fledderjohn, Plymouth, Wis.
*J. Emerson Ford, Nashville, Tenn.
David Forsyth, Ontario, Canada
Virgil Foster, Chicago, Ill.
*H. Clifford Fox, Findlay, Ohio
Mrs. Wallace Frasher, Los Angeles, Calif.
Harlan M. Frost, Buffalo, N.Y.
Lee J. Gable, Chicago, Ill.
F. L. Gibbs, Pittsburgh, Pa.
Robert W. Gibson, Pittsburgh, Pa.
Alice L. Goddard, Chicago, Ill.
*Oliver B. Gordon, Philadelphia, Pa.
Evelyn Green, Atlanta, Ga.
Leonard R. Hall, Richmond, Ind.
Carl A. Hansen, Hartford, Conn.
Joseph John Hanson, Philadelphia, Pa.

Ronald I. Hargis, Alfred, N.Y.
Frank E. Harris, Lebanon, Illinois
Russell F. Harrison, Indianapolis, Ind.
J. A. Heck, Reading, Pa.
Donald F. Heldt, Chicago, Ill.
*A. W. Henshaw, Schenectady, N.Y.
Ray Henthorne, St. Louis, Mo.
*Harry Hines, Dallas, Texas
*Mell W. Hobart, Minneapolis, Minn.
Ralph L. Holland, Indianapolis, Ind.
Robert M. Hopkins, New York, N.Y.
Walter M. Howlett, New York, N.Y.
Mrs. C. L. Johnson, Marion, Ind.
Frank E. Johnston, Philadelphia, Pa.
Mary Harker Jones, Sharon, Pa.
Raymond B. Kearns, Jr., Philadelphia, Pa.
*Russell M. Kerr, Winnsboro, S.C.
John B. Ketcham, Chicago, Ill.
Mrs. Joseph H. Kindle, Wooster, Ohio
Helen F. Kindt, Chicago, Ill.
Paul Ring, Lakewood, Ohio
*Herman A. Klahr, Columbus, Ohio
Forrest L. Knapp, New York, N.Y.
Gerald E. Knoff, Chicago, Ill.
Josephine A. Kyles, Washington, D.C.
Philip C. Landers, Chicago, Ill.
Mary Edna Lloyd, Nashville, Tenn.
Addison Leitch, Pittsburgh, Pa.
Richard E. Lentz, Chicago, Ill.
Hazel A. Lewis, St. Louis, Mo.
Edwin B. Lindsay, Davenport, La.
John Leslie Lobingier, Boston, Mass.
B. G. Locher, Glasgow, Va.
C. W. Longman, Cleveland, Ohio
Mildred A. Magnuson, Chicago, Ill.
*J. Norman Martin, Newark, N.J.
Ralph N. McEntire, Topeka, Kan.
Robert McFadden, North Manchester, Ind.
F. B. McIntosh, Ada, Ohio
*Mrs. Morris McKean, Grand Rapids, Mich.
Frank M. McKibben, Evanston, Ill.
*Vernon C. McMaster, Montgomery, Ala.
*Jesse Jai McNeil, Detroit, Mich.
Fred E. McQueen, St. Louis, Mo.
Francis Pickens Miller, Charlottesville, Va.
*T. Franklin Miller, Anderson, Ind.
J. Dexter Montgomery, Indianapolis, Ind.
Samuel S. Morris, Sr., Nashville, Tenn.
J. T. Morrow, Tulsa, Okla.
Anna B. Mow, Chicago, Ill.
Ruth Elizabeth Murphy, Chicago, Ill.
J. J. Murray, Lexington, Va.
*Malcolm V. Mussina, Williamsport, Pa.
E. Lee Neal, St. Louis, Mo.

*E. E. Nietz, Columbus, Ohio
Estel I. Odle, West Lafayette, Ind.
*Walter Overstreet, Buchhannon, W. Va.
W. T. Packer, Granville, Ohio
*E. B. Paisley, Philadelphia, Pa.
C. D. Pantle, St. Louis, Mo.
Wilbur C. Parry, Chicago, Ill.
Mrs. Leon Roy Peel, Minneapolis, Minn.
*Morris Pepper, McKenzie, Tenn.
Lemuel Petersen, Chicago, Ill.
Ray Petersime, Gettysburg, Ohio
Hugh D. Pickett, Parkersburg, W. Va.
*Paul Popenoe, Altadena, Calif.
*Merrill Powers, Chicago, Ill.
Hollis F. Price, Memphis, Tenn.
*H. L. Pritchett, Dallas, Texas
Mrs. Henry Radloff, Eitzen, Minn.
Mrs. E. R. Reno, Oklahoma City, Okla.
Paul R. Reynolds, Chicago, Ill.
*R. W. Riley, Nashville, Tenn.
*M. Leo Rippy, Nashville, Tenn.
Charles Marion Ross, Indianapolis, Ind.
Roy G. Ross, Chicago, Ill.
Pearl Rosser, Chicago, Ill.
D. P. Rudisill, Hickory, N.C.
*Oscar J. Rumpf, Philadelphia, Pa.
Dennis Savage, Chicago, Ill.
Charles E. Schofield, Nashville, Tenn.
*Roy Schreiner, Harrisburg, Pa.
Irene Scudds, Cincinnati, Ohio
Mrs. H. C. Shaffmaster, Detroit, Mich.
Erwin L. Shaver, Chicago, Ill.
F. B. Shelton, Sweetwater, Tenn.
*H. Shelton Smith, Durham, N.C.
Mrs. Orville Smith, Chicago, Ill.
Richard B. Smith, Chicago, Ill.
*Roy L. Smith, Chicago, Ill.
Guy E. Snavely, Washington, D.C.
Clark L. Snyder, Chicago, Ill.
Helen F. Spaulding, Chicago, Ill.
Edward D. Staples, Nashville, Tenn.
*A. O. Steele, Charlotte, N.C.
Carlyle Stewart, Detroit, Mich.
Murray C. Stewart, Homer City, Pa.
Harry Thomas Stock, Boston, Mass.
Fred D. Stone, Chicago, Ill.
Gene Stone, Columbus, Ohio
H. L. Stright, Minneapolis, Minn.
C. O. Strohl, Des Moines, Iowa
Erlo E. Sutton, Boulder, Col.
John Edward Thomas, Boston, Mass.
James V. Thompson, New York, N.Y.
W. Taliaferro Thompson, Richmond, Va.
John L. Tilley, Baltimore, Md.
Charlotte C. Tompkins, New York, N.Y.
Norman E. Tompkins, Chicago, Ill.
John C. Trever, Chicago, Ill.

174

Frank C. Tucker, St. Louis, Mo.
Maynard P. Turner, Kansas City, Mo.
Esther W. Tyree, Columbus, Ohio
*Milton R. Vogel, Topeka, Kan.
*Raymond A. Vogeley, Columbus, Ohio
*Ralph N. Voorhis, Hackensack, N.J.
George W. Wade, Oklahoma City, Okla.
Lee Edwin Walker, Pittsburgh, Pa.
V. O. Ward, Greenwich, Conn.
Edith F. Welker, Hartford, Conn.
*James F. Wertz, Charlotte, N.C.
Thomas H. West, Chicago, Ill.
E. L. Whittemore, Berkeley, Calif.

Mildred C. Widber, Boston, Mass.
*Henry Lee Willett, Philadelphia, Pa.
A. M. Williams, Memphis, Tenn.
E. B. Williams, Philadelphia, Pa.
Lillian Williams, Chicago, Ill.
*Frank T. Wilson, Washington, D.C.
U. G. Wilson, Portsmouth, Va.
Mildred E. Winston, Washington, D.C.
Dorothea K. Wolcott, Findlay, Ohio
Herman E. Wornom, New York, N.Y.
J. C. Wynn, Philadelphia, Pa.
Mrs. Dempster Yinger, Dubuque, Iowa

INTERSEMINARY MOVEMENT

R. H. Edwin Espy, New York, N.Y.
Ellen B. Gammack, New York, N.Y.
Douglas Horton, New York, N.Y.

*Wilbert B. Smith, Wilmington, Del.
Arch McD. Tolbert, New York, N.Y.

MISSIONARY EDUCATION MOVEMENT

Hazel Anderson, Pittsburgh, Pa.
Pat Beaird, Nashville, Tenn.
Kenneth J. Beaton, Ontario, Canada
Juanita Brown, New York, N.Y.
Priscilla Chase, New York, N.Y.
Franklin D. Cogswell, New York, N.Y.
D. J. Cumming, Nashville, Tenn.
Lucy Eldredge, New York, N.Y.
J. A. Engle, New York, N.Y.
Burnice Fjellman, Chicago, Ill.
Mary E. Frizzell, Philadelphia, Pa.
*Charles H. Gibboney, Atlanta, Ga.
Leona Hansen, Dayton, Ohio
C. P. Hargraves, Nashville, Tenn.
Avis Harvey, New York, N.Y.
Frances M. Hill, Indianapolis, Ind.
*H. S. Hillyer, Ontario, Canada
Armstrong Hunter, Boston, Mass.
*Helen L. Johnson, New York, N.Y.
William J. Keech, New York, N.Y.
Gilbert Q. LeSourd, New York, N.Y.
S. Franklin Mack, New York, N.Y.
*Mae McAlpine, Dayton, Ohio
Mrs. Leighton McCutchen, Nashville, Tenn.
Nina Millen, New York, N.Y.
Hubert Morrow, Memphis, Tenn.

*Anetta C. Mow, Elgin, Ill.
Hazel V. Orton, New York, N.Y.
Neva Palmeter, Philadelphia, Pa.
Mrs. Kenneth Rystron, East Orange, N.J.
Leslie C. Sayre, New York, N.Y.
Helen C. Schmitz, New York, N.Y.
Gilbert Schroer, St. Louis, Mo.
Ruth Isabel Seabury, Boston, Mass.
Mrs. Arthur M. Sherman, New York, N.Y.
Ralph R. Shrader, Boston, Mass.
Harry C. Spencer, New York, N.Y.
Ada P. Stearns, New York, N.Y.
Mrs. E. LeRoy Stiffler, Cincinnati, Ohio
William H. Stimming, Newark Valley, N.Y.
Elizabeth Stinson, New York, N.Y.
Grace Storms, Boston, Mass.
Edwin F. Tewksbury, Nashville, Tenn.
*Frederick R. Thorne, New York, N.Y.
Samuel Thorne, New York, N.Y.
May R. Titus, Nashville, Tenn.
*Ruby Van Hooser, New York, N.Y.
Walter N. Vernon, Jr., Nashville, Tenn.
*Helen L. Woodward, Georgetown, Ill.
Eloise A. Woolever, New York, N.Y.
E. Mae Young, Nashville, Tenn.

NATIONAL PROTESTANT COUNCIL ON HIGHER EDUCATION

Heil D. Bollinger, Nashville, Tenn.
Herbert J. Burgstahler, Delaware, Ohio
Donald Herges, Chicago, Ill.
Weimer K. Hicks, Beaver Dam, Wis.
*H. D. Hopkins, Defiance, Ohio

*W. Bay Irvine, Marietta, Ohio
S. T. Ludwig, Kansas City, Mo.
George Michaelides, Cleveland, Ohio
J. C. K. Preus, Minneapolis, Minn.
Kenneth Reeves, Philadelphia, Pa.

Paul R. Shelly, Bluffton, Ohio
Ronald von Riesen, Newton, Kansas
David Andrew Weaver, Alton, Ill.

Mrs. Gould Wickey, Washington, D.C.
E. W. Willcox, Kent, Ohio

STUDENT VOLUNTEER MOVEMENT FOR CHRISTIAN MISSIONS, INC.

Paul E. Converse, New York, N.Y.

E. H. Johnson, New York, N.Y.

UNITED COUNCIL OF CHURCH WOMEN

Mrs. R. O. Anthony, Miami, Ariz.
Mrs. Jesse M. Bader, New York, N.Y.
*J. Marion Bailey, So. Charleston, W. Va.
Mrs. George Barbour, Cincinnati, Ohio
*Mary McLeod Bethune, Washington, D.C.
Mrs. Roy C. Bishop, St. Petersburg, Fla.
Mrs. A. L. Blackstone, Waukesha, Wis.
Mrs. J. I. Blount, Birmingham, Ala.
Mrs. Earl Breeding, New York, N.Y.
Mrs. T. Smith Brewer, Huntington, W. Va.
*Mrs. Allan Knight Chalmers, Newton-ville, Mass.
Loran Cockrell, Madison, Wis.
Mrs. F. R. Crawford, Farmville, Va.
Mrs. W. L. Crowding, Sunbury, Pa.
Mrs. C. B. Currence, Phillipsburg, Kansas
Mrs. Charles Dengler, Jackson, Mich.
Mrs. Roy A. Dillon, Oklahoma City, Okla.
Mrs. James M. Dolbey, Cincinnati, Ohio
Mrs. W. W. Draper, Forrest City, Ark.
*Mrs. John Dunn, New York, N.Y.
Mrs. W. E. DuRant, Elliott, S.C.
Mrs. J. M. Edenfield, Jacksonville, Fla.
Mrs. Charles G. Eidson, Waco, Texas
Mrs. James M. Evans, New York, N.Y.
Mrs. H. G. Fisher, Grand Rapids, Mich.
Louise M. Gridley, Rutland, Vermont
Edith L. Groner, New York, N.Y.
Mrs. Henry D. Haberyan, Shreveport, La.
Mrs. Allan S. Hackett, New Orleans, La.
Mrs. Otto Hackman, Lincoln, Neb.
Mrs. B. W. Hamilton, New York, N.Y.
Mrs. G. A. Hample, Bismarck, N.D.
Mrs. John M. Hanna, Dallas, Texas
Ruth M. Harvey, Minneapolis, Minn.
Mable Head, New York, N.Y.
Mrs. Charles M. Henderson, Memphis, Tenn.
*Mrs. Charles S. Johnson, Nashville, Tenn.
Mrs. David D. Jones, Greensboro, N.C.
Mrs. Ralph W. Jordan, Columbus, Ohio

Mrs. David F. Jorgensen, Altadena, Calif.
Mrs. E. Lester Keyser, Baltimore, Md.
Sylvia H. Knowles, New Bedford, Mass.
Mrs. W. R. Lee, Denver, Col.
Mrs. Abram LeGrand, New York, N.Y.
*Mrs. Floyd E. Logee, Orrville, Ohio
Mrs. John O. Mabuce, Buffalo, N.Y.
Mrs. Chester E. Martin, Atlanta, Ga.
Mrs. George B. Martin, Summit, N.J.
Mrs. John E. Martin, Royal Oak, Mich
Mrs. C. A. McKinlay, Minneapolis, Minn.
Mrs. W. Murdoch McLeod, New York, N.Y.
Mrs. Earle L. Menker, Oakland, Calif.
Mrs. John Merrick, Seattle, Wash.
Mrs. J. Quinter Miller, Tuckahoe, N.Y.
*Mrs. Robert L. Moore, Los Angeles, Calif
Mrs. Ralph H. Mort, Portland, Ore.
Mrs. Ocie G. Perry, Washington, D.C.
Mrs. Vernon Phillips, Francestown, N.H.
Mrs. S. M. Pronko, Brentwood, Mo.
Miss Luella Reckmeyer, New York, N.Y
Mrs. Harry Rosengrant, Verona, N.J.
Mrs. Emory Ross, New York, N.Y.
Mrs. H. I. Rudduck, Mishawaka, Ind.
Mrs. Galen Russell, Southport, Conn.
Mrs. Gilbert W. Schroer, Webster Groves Mo.
Mrs. Cyrus F. Springall, Malden, Mass
Esther C. Stamats, New York, N.Y.
Mrs. A. H. Sterne, Atlanta, Ga.
Mrs. Wallace H. Streeter, Washington D.C.
Mrs. Charles P. Taft, Cincinnati, Ohio
Mrs. M. Edwin Thomas, St. Petersburg Fla.
Mrs. Irving L. Walker, Rochester, N.Y
Nina T. Wensley, Cleveland, Ohio
Mrs. Fred H. White, Buffalo, N.Y.
Mrs. E. E. Whiteside, Claremont, S.D.
Mrs. F. M. Wilson, Albuquerque, N.M
Mrs. John C. Young, Royal Oak, Mich
Mrs. Edwin B. Zeller, Cedar Rapids, Iowa

UNITED STEWARDSHIP COUNCIL

*James W. Bright, Norristown, Pa.
W. Rolfe Brown, Chicago, Ill.

Wesley O. Clark, Dayton, Ohio
*Archbishop Clement, New York, N.Y.

176

H. D. Davies, Chicago, Ill.
Velva Dreese, Indianapolis, Ind.
Frank L. Edwards, Chicago, Ill.
Mrs. John B. Frantz, Pottstown, Pa.
James E. Gayle, New Orleans, La.
E. Lamont Geissinger, Chicago, Ill.
C. W. Hatch, Anderson, Ind.
Bob S. Hodges, Jr., Decatur, Ga.
Vernon Kenneth Hoover, New York, N.Y.
*D. V. Jemison, Selma, Ala.
Arthur E. Kewley, Ontario, Canada
G. P. Krebs, Omaha, Neb.
T. A. Krueger, Columbus, Ohio
*Loren E. Lair, Des Moines, Iowa
Arthur H. Limouze, East Marion, N.Y.
Carolyn Mathews, New York, N.Y.
*Thomas B. Mc Dormand, Ontario, Canada
W. J. H. McKnight, Pittsburgh, Pa.
Mrs. W. J. H. McKnight, Pittsburgh, Pa.

*H. Spencer Minnich, Elgin, Ill.
Harry S. Myers, Hillsdale, Mich.
Mae Steele Myers, Hillsdale, Mich.
Stan Nichols, Medina, Ohio
James F. Riggs, New York, N.Y.
Wallace Robertson, Ridgewood, N.J.
*Henry F. Schuh, Columbus, Ohio
G. S. Schultz, Columbus, Ohio
*Curtis R. Schumacher, Bayside, N.Y.
Mrs. H. L. V. Shinn, Toledo, Ohio
*Marie Sievert, Columbus, Ohio
John E. Simpson, Oak Park, Ill.
*Tom A. Smith, Anderson, Ind.
Shelby E. Southard, Chicago, Ill.
John Stockton, Kansas City, Mo.
Paul Strauch, Buffalo, N.Y.
James H. Touchstone, Chicago, Ill.
John R. Weaver, New York, N.Y.
Mrs. Edwin B. White, Jacksonville, Fla.

STATE AND LOCAL COUNCIL OF CHURCHES

Lawrance S. Ashley, Ocala, Fla.
Bedros Baharian, Quincy, Wis.
Howard J. Baumgartel, Indianapolis, Ind.
*H. W. Becker, Kirkwood, Mo.
George Boardman, Brooklyn, N.Y.
Theodore W. Boltz, New Brunswick, N.J.
Fred L. Broad, Jr., Lansing, Mich.
Robert Byerly, Kokomo, Ind.
J. Albert Clark, Columbus, Ohio
*Clarence W. Crawford, Washington, D.C.
*Roy C. Crouch, Los Angeles, Calif.
Mrs. Elmer Davis, Harrisburg, Ill.
Marjorie Dickinson, Springfield, Ill.
D. Allen Easter, Honolulu, T.H.
Frank J. Fell, Jr., Philadelphia, Pa.
Mrs. Fenton Fish, Columbus, Ohio
Howard R. Gold, Williamsport, Pa.
*Erastus H. Green, Scranton, Pa.
*Arthur M. Guttery, Pittsburgh, Pa.
W. Bruce Hadley, Omaha, Neb.
Clement F. Hahn, Worcester, Mass.
*Lincoln B. Hale, Evansville, Ind.
G. Weir Hartman, Erie, Pa.
*Mrs. William J. Heydrick, Philadelphia, Pa.
Harvey E. Holt, Youngstown, Ohio
Mrs. Carl H. Hoy, Chicago, Ill.
*George T. Hubbard, Nashville, Tenn.
E. J. Johnson, Bakersfield, Calif.
Irene E. Johnson, Staten Island, N.Y.
*Ralph M. Johnson, Sacramento, Calif.
*Herbert W. Kendall, Kearney, Neb.
Hughbert H. Landram, Chicago, Ill.
G. Merrill Lenox, Detroit, Mich.
Julian Linkous, New Castle, Ind.

Lelia Lytle, Decatur, Ill.
Jessie G. Martin, Walton, Ind.
Mrs. Clyde Matheny, Columbus, Ohio
Douglas McCreight, Wooster, Ohio
Joseph Warren Merchant, New Bedford, Mass.
*Martha M. Miller, Mexico, Mo.
M. H. Morrison, Cedar Rapids, Iowa
Wayne A. Neal, San Diego, Calif.
T. Ross Paden, Wilkes Barre, Pa.
*D. S. Peterson, Odessa, N.Y.
Eleanor Peterson, Piqua, Ohio
William D. Powell, Lansdowne, Pa.
Daniel R. Price, Birmingham, Ala.
William W. Richardson, West Barrington, R.I.
Kenneth A. Roadarmel, Albany, N.Y.
Clyde N. Rogers, Columbus, Ohio
*A. S. Ross, Joplin, Mo.
Frank B. Ruf, Fort Wayne, Ind.
Donald M. Salmon, Seattle, Wash.
L. G. Shannon, Williamsport, Pa.
Lillian White Shephard, Columbus, Ohio
Ivey J. Shuff, Harrisburg, Pa.
John C. Smith, Hartford, Conn.
Mrs. James Speer, Pasadena, Calif.
Mark A. Talney, Portland, Ore.
*Norma H. Thompson, New York, N.Y.
Donald Timerman, Columbus, Ohio
Mrs. E. M. Van Scoyk, Cleveland, Ohio
Clarence I. Vessey, Colorado Springs, Col.
Loyal H. Vickers, Tacoma, Wash.
Catherine Lee Wahlstrom, Los Angeles, Calif.
S. Allan Watson, Elgin, Ill.

177

Harold P. Williams, Cleveland, Ohio
Goodridge A. Wilson, Nashville, Tenn.
Mrs. S. R. Wilson, Newton, N.J.

David W. Witte, Peoria, Ill.
Joseph M. Woods, Jr., Harrisburg, Pa.
Whitney S. K. Yeaple, Concord, N.H.

PLANNING COMMITTEE STAFF

Earl F. Adams

B. Margaret Rieber

Fraternal Delegates

William Barclay, Toronto, Canada — *Canadian Council of Churches*
*Eugene E. Barnett, New York, N.Y. — *Nat'l Council of Y.M.C.A.*
*Robert S. Bilheimer, New York, N.Y. — *World Council of Churches*
Eleanor Kent Browne, New York, N.Y. — *World Council of Churches*
Daniel Burke, New York, N.Y. — *American Bible Society*
Edward Cary, Cleveland, Ohio — *Salvation Army*
Gilbert Darlington, New York, N.Y. — *American Bible Society*
*Mark A. Dawber, Long Island, N.Y. — *Internat'l Council of Community Churches*
John W. Decker, New York, N.Y. — *Internat'l Missionary Council*
Mrs. Harrison Elliott, New York, N.Y. — *National Board of Y.W.C.A.*
W. J. Gallagher, Toronto, Canada — *Canadian Council of Churches*
*Norman Goodall, New York, N.Y. — *Internat'l Missionary Council*
*Marie Jeanne de Haller, Dallas, Texas — *World's Student Christian Federation*
J. Ruskin Howe, Joplin, Mo. — *Internat'l Council of Community Churches*
William Keys, New York, N.Y. — *World Council of Churches*
Henry Smith Leiper, New York, N.Y. — *World Council of Churches*
Fred Poulton, Toronto, Ont., Canada — *Canadian Council of Churches*
Fred W. Ramsey, New York, N.Y. — *Nat'l Council of Y.M.C.A.*
*Oscar L. Rand, Washington, D.C. — *Internat'l Council of Community Churches*
Charles W. Ranson, New York, N.Y. — *International Missionary Council*
E. V. Rasmussen, Cleveland, Ohio — *National Council of Y.M.C.A.*
J. Edward Sproul, New York, N.Y. — *National Council of Y.M.C.A.*
Tracy Strong, Geneva, Switzerland — *World's Alliance of Y.M.C.A.*
Miss Glora M. Wysner, New York, N.Y. — *International Missionary Council*

Invited Guests

Sarah Chakko, New York, N.Y.
John Deschner, New York, N.Y.
Hans von Hase, Marburg, Germany
Mrs. Clifford Heinz, Pittsburgh, Pa.
Toyohiko Kagawa, New York, N.Y.
Morris N. Kertzer, New York, N.Y.
J. K. Lilly, Indianapolis, Ind.

Mrs. J. K. Lilly, Indianapolis, Ind.
J. Howard Pew, Philadelphia, Pa.
Stanton W. Salisbury, Washington, D.C.
Francis B. Sayre, Washington, D.C.
Mrs. Francis B. Sayre, Washington, D.C.
W. A. Visser 't Hooft, Geneva, Switzerland

Visiting Delegates

Shiro Abe, New York, N.Y.
C. W. Abington, Nashville, Tenn.
*A. E. Acey, Portsmouth, Va.
Clarence Achberger, Cleveland, Ohio
Paul J. Acker, Cuyahoga Falls, Ohio
*C. Kenneth Ackerman, Tarrytown, N.Y.

Paul H. Ackert, Pittsburgh, Pa.
James A. Ackroyd, Needham, Mass.
Mrs. Charles V. Adams, Montoursville,
    Pa.
Charles H. Addleman, Portland, Ore.
*A. Carl Adkins, Mobile, Ala.

Mrs. Leon M. Adkins, Syracuse, N.Y.
Dora Ahrens, Cleveland Heights, Ohio
*Donald F. Alber, Canfield, Ohio
Andrew Albrechet, Evansville, Ind.
*Mrs. Charles G. Albury, Cranford, N.J.
Daniel B. Aldrich, Jr., Riverside, Calif.
Raymond L. Alexander, Peoria, Ill.
*Theophilus D. Alexander, North Little
Rock, Ark.
Thurman Alexander, Willoughby, Ohio
*Mills B. Alldredge, Des Moines, Iowa
*C. L. Allen, Akron, Ohio
*Mrs. C. L. Allen, Akron, Ohio
*Bettye Lee Alleyne, Philadelphia, Pa.
Fred C. Allrich, Highland, Ill.
*Ellen S. Alston, Raleigh, N.C.
Roger Altman, Washington, D.C.
*Mrs. John Amen, New York, N.Y.
Charles C. Amendt, Brecksville, Ohio
*S. A. Amos, Scranton, Pa.
A. Robert Anderson, Niles, Ohio
H. L. Anderson, Oak Hill, Ohio
Howard Anderson, Bloomington, Ind.
J. Lowrie Anderson, New Wilmington, Pa.
James Anderson, Wooster, Ohio
Lavern C. Anderson, Wilmette, Ill.
O. V. Anderson, La Grange, Ill.
William B. Anderson, Beaver, Pa.
*Edward F. Andree, Van Wert, Ohio
*Mrs. Edward F. Andree, Van Wert, Ohio
*R. M. Andrews, Cleveland, Ohio
*Richard Parker Andrews, Beaver Falls, Pa.
R. T. Andrews, Sr., Indianapolis, Ind.
B. Kenneth Anthony, Waterbury, Conn.
*Lois R. Anthony, Latrobe, Pa.
*Robert W. Anthony, Sr., New York, N.Y.
Henry D. Appenzeller, New York, N.Y.
*Fred L. Applegate, Trenton, N.J.
A. C. Archibald, Cleveland, Ohio
Bryan F. Archibald, Springfield, Ill.
*A. Burd Arganbright, Springfield, Ill.
*Mrs. A. Burd Arganbright, Springfield, Ill.
*L. M. Arksey, Greenville, Ill.
*Mrs. E. F. Armington, Euclid, Ohio
Homer J. Armstrong, Minneapolis, Minn.
M. F. Ashbrook, New York, N.Y.
*Mrs. M. F. Ashbrook, Cleveland, Ohio
John N. Ashley, Compton, Calif.
William A. Askew, Lawrenceville, Ill.
*Carl Asmus, East Palenstine, Ohio
Glenn H. Asquith, Syracuse, N.Y.
*Anna Astroth, St. Louis, Mo.
*Helen Atkinson, Sharpsville, Pa.
Spencer P. Austin, Indianapolis, Ind.
Clifford Ayers, Independence, Ohio
Mrs. I. J. Ayers, El Paso, Texas
Frederick W. Backemeyer, Gary, Ind.

Mrs. Wayne Badolett, South Bend, Ind.
S. H. Baer, St. Louis, Mo.
George T. Baggs, Cleveland, Ohio
Robert E. Baggs, Lynn, Mass.
*Joyce J. Bailey, Crown Point, Ind.
Keith Bailey, Jamestown, N.Y.
Mrs. Keith W. Bailey, Jamestown, N.Y.
Mart Bailey, Iowa City, Iowa
Mrs. Moses Bailey, West Hartford, Conn.
Oren Bailey, Bay City, Mich.
*R. L. Bailey, Columbus, Ohio
John Baiz, Warren, Ohio
*Gaynell L. Baker, Oxford, Ohio
Mrs. Herbert C. Baker, Cleveland, Ohio
Myrtle I. Baker, South Whitley, Ind.
Roberta E. Baker, Tiffin, Ohio
Miloslav Baloun, New York, N.Y.
Jacob F. Balzer, Crete, Neb.
*E. Dow Bancroft, Urbana, Ohio
A. A. Banks, Detroit, Mich.
*A. A. Banks, Jr., Detroit, Mich.
Charles Banning, Norwich, Conn.
*Wilbur M. Bantz, Decatur, Ill.
Franklin Barber, Battle Creek, Mich.
*Earle Barclay, Benton, Ill.
Harold Barger, Independence, Ohio
Mrs. Roswell P. Barnes, New York, N.Y.
E. S. Barnett, Reno, Nev.
Herbert L. Barnett, Wheeling, W. Va.
Wilbur Barnhart, Indianapolis, Ind.
Mrs. W. S. Barnhart, Indianapolis, Ind.
Mary L. Barnwell, New York, N.Y.
Charles B. Barr, Palestine, Ill.
William R. Barr, Bluffton, Ind.
Mrs. Donald J. Barrett, Cleveland, Ohio
*Everett R. Barrows, Concord, N.H.
*Mrs. Herman Bartels, Cleveland, Ohio
Mrs. Henry S. Barth, Wheeling, W. Va.
F. S. Bartlett, Jr., Hamilton, Ohio
Gene E. Bartlett, Evanston, Ill.
John L. Barton, Sioux Falls, S.D.
Marian C. Bascom, Baltimore, Md.
*Edward E. Bassett, North Royalton, Ohio
*T. V. Bastel, Cleveland, Ohio
Alex R. Batchelor, Atlanta, Ga.
*Terry M. Batts, Mobile, Ala.
L. W. Bauerle, Wichita, Kansas
Mrs. L. W. Bauerle, Wichita, Kansas
*Harry W. Baumer, West Bend, Wis.
Mrs. Howard J. Baumgartel, Indianapolis,
Ind.
Mrs. W. M. Baumheckel, Indianapolis,
Ind.
Samuel M. Baxter, Buffalo, N.Y.
Mrs. James Beach, Savannah, Ga.
Mrs. O. W. Beach, New York, N.Y.
Raymond K. Beals, Findlay, Ohio

*Arthur E. Bean, Greenville, Pa.
*Mrs. Arthur E. Bean, Greenville, Pa.
*Harry Charles Beard, Medina, Ohio
Clarence Beasley, Brookline, Mass.
Mrs. Shubael T. Beasley, Memphis, Tenn.
Mrs. Clarence Beaumont, Euclid, Ohio
*Mrs. Carl S. Bechberger, Shaker Heights, Ohio
James G. Beck, Knoxville, Tenn.
Robert T. Beck, Fort Wayne, Ind.
Mrs. Robert T. Beck, Fort Wayne, Ind.
Axel Beckman, Cleveland, Ohio
Alva E. Beers, Cleveland, Ohio
*Paul C. Bekeschus, Pittsburgh, Pa.
John Bell, New York, N.Y.
C. F. Bellows, Cleveland, Ohio
Richard C. Belsan, Cleveland, Ohio
Eugene W. Beltz, Cleveland Heights, Ohio
Mrs. Earl Benjamin, Cleveland, Ohio
J. S. Benn, Jr., Philadelphia, Pa.
Mrs. M. O. Bennett, Memphis, Tenn.
Wilson Bennett, Binghamton, N.Y.
Howard Benson, Evanston, Ill.
William E. Berg, Rock Island, Ill.
Ewald G. Berger, Toledo, Ohio
*Wilton Bergstrand, Minneapolis, Minn.
Gail Bergstresser, Cleveland, Ohio
Margaret Bergstresser, Cleveland, Ohio
William G. Berndt, Newton Lower Falls, Mass.
Gerald Berneking, Colorado Springs, Col.
Fred F. Berry, Wood River, Ill.
*Ralph M. Besse, Shaker Heights, Ohio
Albert D. Betts, Travelers Rest, S.C.
Vanna L. Bewell, Madison, Wis.
F. H. Biederstedt, Syracuse, N.Y.
August E. Binder, Mt. Vernon, Ind.
*R. F. Binder, Oak Park, Ill.
*Mrs. R. F. Binder, Oak Park, Ill.
David Paul Birch, Pittsburgh, Pa.
Mrs. Philip Smead Bird, Cleveland, Ohio
Kenneth Birnbaum, Cleveland, Ohio
*Vivian Birnbaum, Richmond, Va.
*Paul E. Bishop, Minneapolis, Minn.
Roy C. Bishop, St. Petersburg, Fla.
*Walter Bishop, Las Vegas, Nev.
*Mrs. Charles L. Bitzer, Harrisburg, Pa.
Mrs. M. F. Bixler, Cleveland, Ohio
C. G. Blackman, Berea, Ohio
Corliss G. Blackman, Berea, Ohio
R. Richmond Blake, Plymouth, Ind.
G. Wayman Blakely, Little Rock, Ark.
Robert I. Blakesley, Wellesley Hills, Mass.
Mrs. Robert I. Blakesley, Wellesley Hills, Mass.
Ferdinand Q. Blanchard, Cleveland, Ohio

Roger W. Blanchard, New York, N.Y.
*Herbert W. Bletson, St. Joseph, Mo.
John F. Blewitt, Fairview, Pa.
R. Banks Blocher, Neillsville, Wis.
*M. E. Blocker, Miami, Fla.
Herbert Bloesch, Chicago, Ill.
Wilbur W. Bloom, Detroit, Mich.
R. B. Blyth, St. Louis, Mo.
*Roy D. Boaz, Cloverdale, Va.
*Mrs. Roy D. Boaz, Cloverdale, Va.
Walter Boeckh, Chicago, Ill.
Mrs. Heil D. Bollinger, Nashville, Tenn.
Paul M. Bolman, Oak Park, Ill.
Albert A. Bolton, New York, N.Y.
Harold Z. Bomberger, Westminster, Md.
*Ruth E. Bond, Lewistown, Pa.
William Bonnema, Oak Park, Ill.
Edward H. Bonsall, Jr., Greenbelt, Md.
*Mrs. P. W. Book, Grove City, Pa.
Emmer Henri Booker, Brooklyn, N.Y.
*T. S. Boone, Detroit, Mich.
*Mrs. A. R. Booth, Springfield, Ill.
*A. R. Booth, Springfield, Ill.
Jay N. Booth, Ashland, Ohio
John W. Borders, Kokomo, Ind.
A. G. Bossenbrock, Hastings-On-Hudson, N.Y.
Kenneth B. Bowen, Chicago, Ill.
Clarence R. Bowman, Johnstown, Pa.
Elwood L. Bowman, New York, N.Y.
*Mrs. E. M. Bowman, Chicago, Ill.
Ernest E. Bowman, Virden, Ill.
Frederick W. Bowman, New York, N.Y.
Paul H. Bowman, Timberville, Va.
Sara A. Bowman, Cleveland, Ohio
J. H. M. Boyce, Houston, Texas
Charles A. Boyd, Elgin, Ill.
James M. Bracey, St. Louis, Mo.
*John W. Bradbury, New York, N.Y.
*Mary E. Bradfield, Cleveland, Ohio
James C. Bradshaw, Fort Worth, Texas
Mrs. Earle W. Brailey, Cleveland, Ohio
Earle W. Brailey, Shaker Heights, Ohio
*Hayes M. Braker, Pittsburgh, Pa.
I. J. Brams, Nampa, Idaho
Earl W. Brandenburg, New York, N.Y.
Mrs. H. F. Brandt, Cleveland, Ohio
*Wesley H. Bransford, Anderson, Ind.
Mrs. E. P. Brasseur, Lakewood, Ohio
M. E. Bratcher, New York, N.Y.
Theo. F. Braun, Cleveland, Ohio
Richard Bredenberg, S. Amherst, Ohio
M. L. Breeding, Cleveland, Ohio
V. E. Breidenbaugh, Terre Haute, Ind.
*Earl H. Brendall, Salisbury, N.C.
W. Earl Breon, Pomona, Calif.
Mrs. Emil Bretz, Cleveland, Ohio

Emil Bretz, Cleveland, Ohio
Mrs. Clair H. Brewer, Lakewood, Ohio
Eugene S. Briggs, Enid, Okla.
Mrs. Raymond S. Briggs, Lewiston Heights, N.Y.
Charles Bright, Maple Heights, Ohio
*Alice W. S. Brimson, Chicago, Ill.
*C. E. Brockway, Sharon, Pa.
*R. E. Brogdon, Charleston, S.C.
*A. C. Brooks, Indianapolis, Ind.
Mrs. James A. Brooks, Endicott, N.Y.
Mrs. A. N. Brown, Bryan, Texas
Aubrey N. Brown, Richmond, Va.
Carl R. Brown, Lakewood, Ohio
*Edwin A. Brown, Berea, Ohio
Mrs. Harold L. Brown, Upper Nyack, N.Y.
Mrs. Harry B. Brown, Wichita, Kansas
Howard J. Brown, Cleveland Heights, Ohio
*Mrs. Lloyd Brown, Lakewood, Ohio
Raymond R. D. Brown, Cleveland, Ohio
*W. Don Brown, Los Angeles, Calif.
Mrs. William P. Brown, Cleveland Heights, Ohio
Dallas L. Browning, Indianapolis, Ind.
Mrs. Dallas L. Browning, Indianapolis, Ind.
Marie H. Brubaker, Elgin, Ill.
*John Bruere, Cleveland, Ohio
*Ernest R. Bryan, Columbus, Ohio
H. C. Bryant, Burlington, Vermont
Harrison J. Bryant, Baltimore, Md.
Jerrus M. Bryant, Indianapolis, Ind.
Marian F. Bryant, Indianapolis, Ind.
*Mrs. L. C. Bryenton, Lakewood, Ohio
Albert W. Buck, Chicago, Ill.
*Harold E. Buckey, Rocky River, Ohio
Mrs. Paul K. Buckles, Newport News, Va.
Anna J. Buckner, Franklin, La.
*Bernice A. Buehler, Philadelphia, Pa.
Mrs. Malcolm A. Buell, Milford, Conn.
L. W. Bumpus, Pittsburgh, Pa.
Mrs. Jesse W. Bunch, Forest Grove, Ore.
Lowell Densmore Burgeon, Wauseon, Ohio
Sadie B. Burgess, Cleveland, Ohio
Jesse R. Burke, Jr., Willoughby, Ohio
*Mrs. Sam F. Burnet, Webster Groves, Mo.
Mrs. Hugh C. Burr, Rochester, N.Y.
*C. A. Burrell, Pittsburgh, Pa.
*John H. Burt, Youngstown, Ohio
E. E. Burtner, Dayton, Ohio
T. J. Burwell, Wichita, Kansas
*Leonard V. Buschman, Summit, N.J.
V. E. Busler, Marion, Ohio
Mrs. V. E. Busler, Marion, Ohio
Don Buteyn, Holland, Mich.

*Mrs. Frances Butler, Dunkirk, Ind.
A. J. Buttrey, Montclair, N.J.
*Mrs. Robert L. Buxton, Columbus, Ga.
C. D. Cade, Pine Bluff, Ark.
Lyman V. Cady, Nashville, Tenn.
Elizabeth C. Cahoom, Racine, Wis.
*Mrs. C. R. Caldwell, Shreveport, La.
Herschel L. Caldwell, Seattle, Wash.
Oscar P. Campbell, St. Louis, Mo.
P. Cliffore Campbell, Tulsa, Okla.
Warren C. Campbell, Fall River, Mass.
Gene Canestrari, New Haven, Conn.
Mrs. L. E. Card, Urbana, Ill.
Mrs. Ernest Carey, Marion, Ind.
C. G. Carlfelt, Rock Island, Ill.
Thomas J. Carlisle, Watertown, N.Y.
Edgar M. Carlson, St. Peter, Minn.
C. Fridelf Carlson, Chicago, Ill.
John A. Carlstedt, Topeka, Kansas
Charles Carlton, Cleveland, Ohio
*Richard E. Carlyon, Hastings, Neb.
Mrs. Richard E. Carlyon, Hastings, Neb.
Paul C. Carpenter, Orlando, Fla.
Harold F. Carr, Lakewood, Ohio
*James M. Carr, Atlanta, Ga.
Mrs. Frank Carroll, Dayton, Ohio
Catherine Carter, Nashville, Tenn.
Dorethea Cary, Cleveland, Ohio
Mrs. Harold C. Case, Altadena, Calif.
Edward Catlos, New York, N.Y.
Twila Lytton Cavert, New York, N.Y.
*Clifford I. Cecel, Graeley, Col.
E. Robert Chable, Palmyra, N.Y.
*Charles G. Chakerian, Hartford, Conn.
Thomas C. Chamberlain, Bay Village, Ohio
D. C. Chandler, Cleveland, Ohio
Joseph I. Chapman, Minneapolis, Minn.
C. R. Chappell, Manchester, N.H.
Mrs. Merlyn Arms Chappel, New York, N.Y.
Frank D. Charlton, Brownsville, Texas
*W. Howard Chase, New York, N.Y.
Mary Ashby Cheek, Rockford, Ill.
John R. Cheney, Cleveland, Ohio
Maeanna Cheserton-Mangle, New York, N.Y.
*E. B. Childress, Kansas City, Kansas
*B. G. Childs, Durham, N.C.
Mrs. E. L. Chism, Los Angeles, Calif.
*Earl E. Chrisman, Painesville, Ohio
T. W. Chryer, Sandusky, Ohio
Sung C. Chun, Princeton, N.J.
Mrs. Fred J. Church, Kingston, Pa.
M. W. Clair, Jr., Chicago, Ill.
Charles W. Clark, Cleveland, Ohio
*Cornelius E. Clark, Portland, Maine

Elizabeth M. Clark, Mt. Vernon, N.Y.
*Elmer T. Clark, New York, N.Y.
Henry H. Clark, Holliston, Mass.
W. E. Clark, South Bend, Ind.
*W. C. Clark, Lakes Charles, La.
William H. Clark, Monroe, Conn.
Claude E. Clarke, Shaker Heights, Ohio
David S. Clarke, Westerly, R.I.
*G. E. Clary, Savannah, Ga.
*Otha R. Clary, Wilmington, Ohio
*Laura Clayton, Farnland, Ind.
Leroy G. Cleverdon, Savannah, Ga.
*Letta B. Clift, Greenfield, Ind.
*A. R. Clippinger, Dayton, Ohio
Mrs. Alvin T. Coate, Indianapolis, Ind.
Alvin T. Coate, Indianapolis, Ind.
*Kenneth L. Cober, Providence, R.I.
Mrs. Albert Buckner Coe, Boston, Mass.
Albert Buckner Coe, Boston, Mass.
Robert Wood Coe, Boston, Mass.
Mrs. Henry S. Coffin, Lakeville, Conn.
Mrs. Harry Coggins, Aurora, Neb.
Clifford A. Cole, Los Angeles, Calif.
Elbert C. Cole, Framington, Mo.
Howard W. Cole, Boston, Mass.
Horatius H. Coleman, Detroit, Mich.
R. W. Coleman, New Orleans, La.
W. C. Coleman, Wichita, Kansas
Frank P. Coleste, Cleveland, Ohio
*Thomas E. Colley, Erie, Pa.
Ralph Hall Collis, Chicago, Ill.
Paul A. Collyer, New York, N.Y.
W. E. Compere, Los Angeles, Calif.
James E. Compton, Cleveland, Ohio
Claude Congleton, Barberville, Ky.
*W. Ross Conner, Madison, Wis.
Donald Conrad, Rock Island, Ill.
Leslie Conrad, Jr., Philadelphia, Pa.
*Norman A. Constable, Oil City, Pa.
Allen R. Conway, Garrettsville, Ohio
*David C. Cook, Elgin, Ill.
Frederick B. Cook, Milroy, Pa.
Mrs. Gaines M. Cook, Indianapolis, Ind.
*James E. Cook, St. Louis, Mo.
Mrs. V. H. Cookson, Cleveland, Ohio
George Cooley, Chicago, Ill.
W. A. Cooper, St. Louis, Mo.
D. Stanley Coors, Lansing, Mich.
*Kenneth W. Copeland, San Antonio, Texas
J. P. Cordero, Bucyrus, Ohio
E. Roy Corman, Pittsburgh, Pa.
*James Cosbey, Jr., Cleveland, Ohio
*Harry Fulton Cost, Worthington, Pa.
J. D. Coston, Chicago, Ill.
*Clare Cotton, Tallahassee, Fla.
*Mrs. Clare Cotton, Tallahassee, Fla.

J. Paul Cotton, Cleveland, Ohio
John V. Cotton, Akron, Ohio
J. Horace Coulliette, Chattanooga, Tenn.
*Gilbert B. Courtney, Chauncey, Ohio
*Walter W. Cowen, Chicago, Ill.
Roysel J. Cowman, Cleveland, Ohio
Alva Cox, Akron, Ohio
Mrs. Dean H. Coy, Lakewood, Ohio
Mrs. J. B. Crabbs, Berea, Ohio
*W. H. Cramblet, Bethany, W. Va.
Gertrude Crandell, Wooster, Ohio
Harold R. Crandall, Rockville, R.I.
*Henry Hitt Crane, Detroit, Mich.
Jasper E. Crane, Wilmington, Del.
Benjamin F. Crawford, Harpster, Ohio
Mrs. R. S. Crawford, Lakewood, Ohio
R. S. Crawford, Lakewood, Ohio
Mrs. F. D. Crayton, Cleveland, Ohio
George H. Crayton, Philadelphia, Pa.
Ira D. Crewson, Little Rock, Ark.
William Crittenden, Cincinnati, Ohio
*Mrs. William Crittenden, Cincinnati, Ohio
Mrs. E. D. Cronon, Cleveland Heights, Ohio
Thomas Le Roy Crosby, La Grange, Ill.
Eason Cross, Boston, Mass.
Mrs. R. M. Cross, New York, N.Y.
George D. Crothers, New York, N.Y.
Dorr R. Crounse, Defiance, Ohio
*Chester L. Crow, Fort Worth, Texas
W. Lynn Crowding, Sanbury, Pa.
Mrs. Herbert W. Crowe, Peoria, Ill.
Mrs. A. J. Culler, Cleveland, Ohio
Kendig B. Cully, Haverhill, Mass.
Truman Cummings, Cleveland, Ohio
Wood B. Cundiff, Lorain, Ohio
D. S. Cunningham, St. Louis, Mo.
*J. R. Cunningham, Davidson, N.C.
Martha E. Cunningham, West Columbia, S.C.
W. J. Cunningham, Greenville, Miss.
Mrs. Wendell Cunningham, Olmsted Falls, Ohio
*R. F. Curl, San Antonio, Texas
A. Stauffer Curry, Washington, D.C.
Eleanor Neff Curry, New York, N.Y.
Mrs. S. T. Cushing, Upper Montclair, N.J.
Mrs. Austin Cutler, Laporte, Ind.
Francis G. Cutler, Boone, Iowa
*W. S. Dacons, Charlotte, N.C.
*Agnes Z. Daehn, Forest Park, Ill.
Fred Dahn, Cleveland, Ohio
Mrs. Andrew Dale, Columbia, Tenn.
*Lucille E. Dale, Washington, D.C.
Alfred S. Dalrymple, Patoka, Ill.

182

*Clarence B. Daniels, Pittsburgh, Pa.
*Kenneth Dannenhauer, Oak Lawn, R.I.
*Mrs. Kenneth Dannenhauer, Oak Lawn, R.I.
*Mrs. Lloyd Darling, Lansing, Mich.
Mrs. Hugh D. Darsie, Brooklyn, N.Y.
*W. E. Daugherty, R.M.S. Verona, Pa.
Mrs. Floyd Q. Davidson, Wichita, Kansas
*William F. Davidson, Newark, N.J.
A. Ralph Davis, Detroit, Mich.
Alan Davis, New Haven, Conn.
*Alvis J. Davis, Nashville, Tenn.
C. Clare Davis, Cleveland, Ohio
*D. W. Davis, Brownsville, Pa.
Gaar M. Davis, Cleveland, Ohio
*Gail Davis, New Haven, Ind.
*Hazel Davis, Arlington, Va.
J. C. Davis, Cleveland, Ohio
*Linda J. Davis, Brownsville, Pa.
*Olga Davis, Cleveland, Ohio
Orville L. Davis, Greencastle, Ind.
Richard H. Davis, Chicago, Ill.
*Thoburn Davis, Rocky River, Ohio
Mrs. Walter Aubrey Davis, Charleston, S.C.
Mrs. Ben Dawson, Ponca City, Okla.
C. Richard Dawson, Indianapolis, Ind.
*Joseph M. Dawson, Washington, D.C.
Mrs. O. G. Dawson, Pine Bluff, Ark.
Albert E. Day, Baltimore, Md.
T. Chipman Day, Boston, Mass.
*Mrs. Joseph Deal, London Bridge, Va.
*Milton DeAmand, Madison, N.J.
*E. M. Dean, Roanoke, Va.
Willis De Boer, Williamsville, N.Y.
Mrs. Willis De Boer, Williamsville, N.Y.
Donald S. Deer, Granville, Ohio
Roy B. Deer, New York, N.Y.
L. E. Deitzel, Cleveland Heights, Ohio
Ora Delauter, Bridgewater, Va.
H. P. Demand, Evanston, Ill.
A. R. DeMott, Rochester, N.Y.
*E. S. Dennis, Ardmore, Pa.
Henry P. Depree, Holland, Mich.
Arthur R. Detwiler, Lenoir, N.C.
*Freda Dexheimer, St. Louis, Mo.
Mrs. Orian I. Dhein, Madison, Wis.
Hoke S. Dickinson, Cleveland, Ohio
Frederick R. Diehm, Cleveland, Ohio
Henry W. Dieringer, Chicago, Ill.
E. W. Dillingham, Cleveland, Ohio
W. A. Diman, Chicago, Ill.
Gertrude Dimke, Indianapolis, Ind.
R. C. Ditter, Cleveland, Ohio
Witherspoon Dodge, New Haven, Conn.
Arthur S. Dodgson, Terre Haute, Ind.
Lee F. Doellman, Lakewood, Ohio

A. H. Doescher, Dayton, Ohio
Geo. Wallace Doherty, Troy, N.Y.
John E. Donovan, Wyoming, Pa.
Earl N. Dorff, Oklahoma City, Okla.
James Edward Doty, Salem, Mass.
*Virgil F. Dougherty, Oklahoma City, Okla.
*Ethel B. Douglas, Chicago, Ill.
*Maxwell Dowell, Shaker Heights, Ohio
*Mrs. Ward M. Downs, Fairmont, W.Va.
*E. M. Dozier, Detroit, Mich.
*Mrs. M. M. Dozier, Pasadena, Calif.
Alice M. Drake, Washington, Pa.
*E. P. Drake, Franklin, La.
*Mrs. E. P. Drake, Franklin, La.
*Mrs. Francis A. Drake, Lake Geneva, Wis.
Nelson C. Dreier, Los Angeles, Calif.
Bernard Drew, Hartford, Conn.
George E. Drew, Lakewood, Ohio
Oliver G. Droppers, Cleveland, Ohio
*Mrs. Maitland DuBois, Clearfield, Pa.
*Lauriston J. DuBois, Kansas City, Mo.
C. P. Dudley, Cleveland, Ohio
Tilford E. Dudley, Washington, D.C.
Robert Sheldon Duecker, Kokomo, Ind.
John F. Duffy, Jr., Granville, Ohio
George W. Dunn, Sioux City, Iowa
*W. F. Dunkle, Jr., Wilmington, Del.
Mrs. G. Eugene Durham, Evanston, Ill.
Lawrence L. Durgin, Norwich, N.Y.
*John Durno, Scranton, Pa.
*Ben J. DuVal, Springfield, Ohio
Mrs. John J. Eagan, Atlanta, Ga.
*Irving W. Eastman, Cleveland, Ohio
Mrs. W. Burnett Easton, Appleton, Wis.
H. Campbell Eatough, Cambridge, Mass.
Mrs. Oscar H. Eberhart, Evansville, Ind.
Mrs. Raymond L. Edie, Pittsburgh, Pa.
Mrs. Deane Edwards, Rye, N.Y.
V. A. Edwards, Nashville, Tenn.
Dan Ehalt, Oak Park, Ill.
Mrs. Adolph G. Ekdahl, Boston, Mass.
Alberta L. Elkins, Lexington, Ky.
Harrison S. Elliot, New York, N.Y.
*Mrs. Keith Elliott, Battle Creek, Mich.
Ezra Ellis, Minneapolis, Minn.
*Mrs. Francis D. Ellis, New Britain, Conn.
Mrs. Leon W. Ellis, Syracuse, N.Y.
*C. M. Ellisor, Montgomery, Ala.
Thomas V. Ellzey, Amarillo, Texas
Franklin D. Elmer, Flint, Mich.
Lois Anna Ely, Indianapolis, Ind.
Chester B. Emerson, Cleveland, Ohio
Richard Emery, Dubuque, Iowa
Ludwig C. Emigholz, Cleveland, Ohio
*Mrs. Leslie W. Emory, Lorain, Ohio

183

James F. English, Hartford, Conn.
Mayble M. Epp, Indianapolis, Ind.
Paul Erb, Scottdale, Pa.
Mrs. J. V. Ericsson, Chicago, Ill.
Bernhard Erling, Des Moines, Iowa
N. E. Escatt, Goshen, Ind.
*Mrs. Clayton D. Eulette, Chicago, Ill.
Arthur W. Evans, White Plains, N.Y.
Mrs. D. K. Evans, Akron, Ohio
Mrs. Hugh Evans, Dayton, Ohio
*Joseph M. Evans, Chicago, Ill.
Lorenzo Evans, Indianapolis, Ind.
G. B. Ewell, Rochester, N.Y.
Rolland G. Ewing, New Milford, Conn.
*Galen C. Fain, Rolla, Mo.
Mrs. Wynn Fairfield, Elmhurst, N.Y.
Mrs. Dan R. Fairfax, Cleveland, Ohio
*Paul H. Fall, Hiram, Ohio
Robert A. Fangmeier, Cleveland, Ohio
Mrs. Harry L. Farmer, Shaker Heights, Ohio.
*Mary Kelly Farquhar, Wilmington, Ohio
Mrs. Elizabeth Farran, Parsons, Kan.
*Mrs. Anna Farrell, East Cleveland, Ohio
*Edgar S. Faust, Kalamazoo, Mich.
*Mrs. Edgar S. Faust, Kalamazoo, Mich.
*Floyd Faust, Columbus, Ohio
*Don Wilson Fein, Decatur, Ill.
Ralph M. Felix, Plymouth, Ohio
Mrs. L. E. Fellows, Newton, Iowa
*George Fenstermacher, Upland, Ind.
*Alex Ferguson, New York, N.Y.
C. F. Ferguson, Sumter, S.C.
Rowena Ferguson, Nashville, Tenn.
W. Reid Ferguson, Denver, Colo.
Lexie Ferrell, New York, N.Y.
*Harold E. Fey, Chicago, Ill.
Mrs. Harold E. Fey, Chicago, Ill.
R. R. Fickling, Independence, Ohio
Judson E. Fiebiger, Grinnell, Iowa
Mrs. Judson E. Fiebiger, Grinnell, Iowa
H. Ellis Finger, Jr., Oxford, Miss.
Harold H. Fink, Hampton, Va.
Robert W. Fink, Gloversville, N.Y.
E. A. Finstrom, Minneapolis, Minn.
Mrs. T. G. Finzel, Westlake, Ohio
Julius Fischbach, Lansing, Mich.
E. R. Fisher, Huntington, Ind.
*Mrs. Fred B. Fisher, New York, N.Y.
J. Richard Fisher, Gettysburg, Pa.
Mrs. Frederick Flammer, Newark, N.J.
*Mary R. Fleming, St. Petersburg, Fla.
Paul O. Flemming, Cleveland, Ohio
L. J. Fletcher, Peoria, Ill.
*Mrs. N. J. Fletcher, Jr., Alliance, Neb.
Omar Fletcher, Lucerene, Ind.
*Carrel W. Flewelling, Decatur, Ill.

*Donald Flick, Grove City, Pa.
Mrs. Marjorie Flick, Lakewood, Ohio
George Y. Flint, Warren, Ohio
*Mrs. David S. Flinton, Charleston, S.C.
*George L. Florence, Seymour, Ind.
*Charles B. Foelsch, New York, N.Y.
Maurice W. Fogle, Dayton, Ohio
*Paul J. Folino, Avon Lake, Ohio
Gaston Foote, Dayton, Ohio
Willard Griffin Foote, De Kalb, Ill.
Alice P. Ford, Cleveland, Ohio
*David K. Ford, Cleveland, Ohio
Harry Ford, Columbus, Ohio
*Dennis W. Foreman, Canton, Ohio
Charles S. Forester, Montgomery, Ala.
Margaret E. Forsyth, New York, N.Y.
*Harold Forsythe, Evansville, Ind.
*Mrs. W. R. Forsythe, Bay Village, Ohio
George A. Foster, Ocala, Fla.
Robert Burch Foster, Dayton, Ohio
Laurence Foster, Lincoln University, Pa.
*David Fouts, Jr., Freeport, Ill.
Eleanor W. Foxworth, Richmond, Va.
Mrs. Burton L. Fralick, Detroit, Mich.
*Malissa Francis, Franklin, La.
*E. E. Franklin, Lafayette, Ind.
John B. Frantz, Pottstown, Pa.
Elmer S. Freeman, Chicago, Ill.
Gretna Freeman, Cleveland, Ohio
*Samuel F. Freeman, Jr., East Orange, N.J.
*Harold Wiley Freer, Westlake, Ohio
*Paul Frees, Ashland, Ohio
*Charles M. French, Cleveland, Ohio
Allan McLachlan Frew, Philadelphia, Pa.
Edward S. Frey, Lemoyne, Pa.
J. Thomas Frost, Warsaw, Ind.
Lucille D. Frost, Cleveland, Ohio
Clarence Fuller, Melrose, Mass.
Herbert H. Fuller, Independence, Ohio
R. L. Fuller, Cleveland, Ohio
*Weldon E. Fulmer, East Cleveland, Ohio
*Mrs. Fred C. Fulton, Cleveland, Ohio
Mary Beth Fulton, New York, N.Y.
A. R. Furnival, Jackson, Mich.
Mrs. A. R. Furnival, Jackson, Mich.
*Mrs. Maude M. Fyler, Berea, Ohio
G. A. Gabelman, Philadelphia, Pa.
Mrs. David P. Gaines, Gladwater, Texas
David P. Gaines, Waterbury, Conn.
Mrs. E. D. Galloway, Hope, Ark.
Eva Gamble, New York, N.Y.
J. Harold Gamble, Binghamton, N.Y.
*W. Ted Gannaway, New York, N.Y.
Mrs. William O. Gardiner, Stratford, Conn.
Frank W. Gardner, New York, N.Y.
John A. Gardner, Midland, Mich.

R. J. Gardner, Cleveland, Ohio
John G. Gaskill, Andover, Mass.
John Parmer Gates, Harrisburg, Pa.
*L. O. Gates, South Bend, Ind.
Mrs. Neil Gebhardt, Erie, Pa.
Mrs. Albert E. Gehrig, Millerburg, Ohio
W. Harold Geiser, Binghamton, N.Y.
Mrs. Robert Gemmer, Indianapolis, Ind.
Robert Gemmer, Indianapolis, Ind.
*W. Max Gentry, Gering, Neb.
*Mrs. W. Max Gentry, Gering, Neb.
Herta N. Genz, Jamaica, N.Y.
*Herman N. George, Youngstown, Ohio
Arnold Gerberding, Huron, S.D.
Mrs. Arnold Gerberding, Huron, S.D.
Mrs. Donald H. Gibbs, Rock Island, Ill.
J. M. Gibbs, Anniston, Ala.
Phyllis M. Gibbes, Spartanburg, S.C.
Edward C. Gibson, Waco, Texas
*George W. Gibson, Birmingham, Ala.
Martha Gibson, Jefferson City, Mo.
*G. W. Gideon, Atlanta, Ga.
*Raymond H. Giffin, Troy, Ohio
Robert B. Giffin, Atlanta, Ga.
Lewis L. Gilbert, Cleveland, Ohio
Andrew S. Gill, Cleveland, Ohio
Grace E. Gill, Kansas City, Kan.
Mrs. J. Lewis Gillies, Los Angeles, Calif.
*Paul McBride Gillis, Pittsburgh, Pa.
*J. E. Gillum, Farmington, Mo.
*Mrs. A. W. Gilmore, Bridgeport, Conn.
Mrs. M. D. Girardeau, Lakewood, Ohio
Lewis Gishler, Muncie, Ind.
Gerald Giving, Minneapolis, Minn.
G. Wayne Glick, Huntington, Pa.
Mrs. M. B. Glismann, Oklahoma City, Okla.
Cranston Earl Goddard, Ashtabula, Ohio
*Bob Godfrey, Beckley, W. Va.
Howard C. Goeringer, Reading, Pa.
H. C. Goerner, Louisville, Ky.
*Mary Goff, Cleveland, Ohio
Charles F. Golden, New York, N.Y.
J. W. Golden, Memphis, Tenn.
Gerould R. Goldner, Lakewood, Ohio
R. F. Goodnow, Lakewood, Ohio
Mrs. C. O. Goodwin, Los Angeles, Calif.
Paul V. Goodwin, Champaign, Ill.
Frank L. Gosnell, Carthage, N.Y.
Mrs. Frank L. Gosnell, Carthage, N.Y.
Mrs. Raymond Goss, Parma, Ohio
P. Gordon Gould, Philadelphia, Pa.
Philip L. Gould, Wadsworth, Ohio
Allena Grafton, Los Angeles, Calif.
H. Howard Graham, Cleveland, Ohio
*J. H. Graham, Amory, Miss.
*Kenneth L. Graham, Independence, Mo.

Olin M. Graham, Vancouver, Wash.
Thomas Graham, Wooster, Ohio
John Gratton, Pittsfield, Mass.
*Harry Wood Gray, Richmond, Va.
Joseph L. Gray, Lake City, Fla.
Mrs. Joseph L. Gray, Lake City, Fla.
Mrs. Walter Gray, Oklahoma City, Okla.
Marian Grayson, Cleveland, Ohio
James L. Grazier, Norristown, Pa.
John D. Green, Lorain, Ohio
*Sherman L. Greene, Wilmington, Del.
Theodore Ainsworth Greene, New Britain, Conn.
Mrs. Theodore A. Green, New Britain, Conn.
Theodore Greenhoe, Niles, Mich.
Horace C. Greensmith, Olmsted Falls, Ohio
George D. Greer, New Castle, Ind.
*B. S. Gregg, St. Louis, Mo.
Mason Gregg, Granite City, Ill.
John L. Gregory, Burlington, Vt.
Evylin R. Gribble, Indianapolis, Ind.
Robert Calvin Grier, Due West, S.C.
Mrs. Grievish, New Orleans, La.
James Smith Griffes, Greenville, Ohio
Ross J. Griffeth, Eugene, Ore.
Robert E. Grimm, Pickstown, S.D.
Jeannette Grimme, Findlay, Ohio
*James R. Grishman, Minter City, Miss.
Irwin Groetenstroh, Evansville, Ind.
John W. Grohne, Cleveland, Ohio
Ralph Gronseth, Madison, Wis.
William P. Gross, Willoughby, Ohio
*William E. Crote, Streator, Ill.
Barbara H. Groth, Oberlin, Ohio
*Herman Groth, Cleveland Heights, Ohio
Maurice Grove, Jackson, Miss.
Leon E. Grubaugh, Denver, Colo.
*Mrs. W. H. Grundmann, St. Louis, Mo.
Armand Guerrero, Chicago, Ill.
*Mrs. William Guier, Tulsa, Okla.
*H. Paul Guhse, St. Petersburg, Fla.
Edward Gunther, Bath, N.Y.
Lloyd A. Gustafson, Mason City, Iowa
Mrs. L. A. Gustafson, Mason City, Iowa
Nore G. Gustafson, Warren, Pa.
John R. C. Haas, Evansville, Ind.
John Hagans, Jackson, Mich.
Ben F. Hagelbarger, Mansfield, Ohio
Mrs. Roscoe Hagen, Hagerstown, Ind.
*Harvey Hahn, Dayton, Ohio
Barton Haigh, New York, N.Y.
A. T. B. Haines, Buffalo, N.Y.
*LeRoy Halbert, Sharon, Pa.
*Phale D. Hale, Columbus, Ohio
*C. W. Hall, Utica, N.Y.

185

Clarence E. Hall, Cleveland, Ohio
Herbert Hall, Saginaw, Mich.
John A. Hall, Indianapolis, Ind.
*Calvin F. Hamilton, Detroit, Mich.
*Stanley Hamilton, Richmond, Ind.
William J. Hamilton, Jr. West Roxbury, Mass.
*Mrs. J. A. Hamlet, Kansas City, Kan.
Melvin A. Hammarberg, St. Paul, Minn.
L. M. Hammerschmidt, South Bend, Ind.
E. H. Hammon, Dayton, Ohio
Kenneth W. Hamstra, Pittsburgh, Pa.
Carrie Dee Hancock, Indianapolis, Ind.
*Gordon B. Hancock, Richmond, Va.
Walter K. Handy, Arlington, Va.
Bertha A. Hanna, Lakewood, Ohio
*Othello E. Hannawalt, Kensington, Ohio
Harold S. Hannum, St. Johnsbury, Vt.
B. B. Hanscom, Chagrin Falls, Ohio
W. C. Hanson, Kansas City, Kan.
Mrs. John J. Haramy, Indianapolis, Ind.
Chan Harbour, Cleveland, Ohio
Elias S. Hardge, Philadelphia, Pa.
Mrs. Russel Hargate, Elyria, Ohio
George F. Harkins, New York, N.Y.
*Georgia Harkness, Evanston, Ill.
William O. Harless, Ames, Iowa
Ruth May Harner, Warren, Ohio
Janette T. Harrington, New York, N.Y.
*Mrs. W. W. Harrington, York, Neb.
Clara E. Harris, Baltimore, Md.
Marquis Lafayette Harris, Little Rock, Ark.
Neoma Harris, Cleveland, Ohio
*Thomas S. Harris, Troy, Ala.
Vi Mae Harris, Cleveland, Ohio
*William H. Harris, Jr., St. Louis, Mo.
Samuel J. Harrison, Adrian, Mich.
Mrs. Samuel J. Harrison, Adrian, Mich.
Shelby M. Harrison, New York, N.Y.
*W. E. Harrison, Detroit, Mich.
W. Oliver Harrison, Corpus Christi, Texas
Ernest L. Harrold, Dayton, Ohio
*Sidney Blair Harry, St. Louis, Mo.
Bessie Hart, Fort Worth, Texas
Mrs. Charles S. Hartman, Fort Wayne, Ind.
Charles S. Hartman, Fort Wayne, Ind.
*Vladimir Hartman, Columbia, Mo.
Stuart C. Haskins, Worcester, Mass.
Hugo B. Haterius, Avoca, Texas
*Orris W. Haulman, Akron, Ohio
*Mrs. M. E. Haulman, Akron, Ohio
Lawrence D. Hawkins, Cleveland, Ohio
Clarence Wallace Hayes, Berkeley, Calif.
Edward H. Hayes, Russell, Mass.
L. R. Hayes, St. Louis, Mo.

*Claud M. Haynes, Jacksonville, Fla.
*Darwin M. Haynes, Shelby, Ohio
L. L. Haynes, St. Louis, Mo.
Marjorie Haynes, East Cleveland, Ohio
Stanley B. Hazzard, New York, N.Y.
Mrs. Roy C. Heacock, Uniontown, Ala.
Paul F. Heard, New York, N.Y.
*William Thomas Heath, Buffalo, N.Y.
*George D. Heaton, Charlotte, N.C.
V. R. Hefner, Portsmouth, Ohio
*J. W. Heininger, Cleveland, Ohio
Frank H. Heinze, Pittsburgh, Pa.
*Mrs. C. A. Heirich, Muskogee, Okla.
Roy C. Helfenstein, Richmond, Va.
*Frederick W. Helfer, Baltimore, Md.
Walter E. Helfer, Chicago, Ill.
Mrs. Emil Helm, Cleveland, Ohio
Emil Helm, Cleveland, Ohio
Walter O. Helwig, Milwaukee, Wis.
Helen Hendershot, Alliance, Ohio
Eva Henderson, Medford, Mass.
Mrs. James Henderson, Chicago, Ill.
*Roy A. Hendrickson, Willmer, Minn.
Carl Henry, New York, N.Y.
Leland B. Henry, New York, N.Y.
*Lydia D. Henschen, Cleveland, Ohio
*C. C. Herbert, Salisbury, N.C.
*J. C. Herrin, Chapel Hill, N.C.
*Mrs. Allan Hersee, Pontiac, Mich.
Mrs. Robert D. Hershey, Lansing, Mich.
Paul M. Herrick, Dayton, Ohio
Russel Hetsler, Brazil, Ind.
*Rose L. Hettmansperger, Fort Wayne, Ind.
John Heuss, New York, N.Y.
*William J. Heydrick, Philadelphia, Pa.
Mrs. Edwin G. Hibbs, Wooster, Ohio
*H. Beecher Hicks, Columbus, Ohio
*Stanley High, New York, N.Y.
Hiro Higuchi, Oberlin, Ohio
C. D. W. Hildebrand, Greencastle, Ind.
Richard Allen Hildebrand, New York N.Y.
Ernest G. Hildner, Jacksonville, Ill.
Ben H. Hill, Tulsa, Okla.
E. H. Hill, Little Rock, Ark.
O. Blakely Hill, Wellsville, N.Y.
E. L. Hillman, Durham, N.C.
*Henry A. Hills, Jeanerette, La.
Van W. Hinckley, Muncie, Ind.
Mrs. Russell Hines, Cleveland Heights, Ohio
*Franklin J. Hinkamp, Poughkeepsie, N.Y.
Greta Hinkle, Philadelphia, Pa.
Mrs. Roy C. Hisel, Oklahoma City, Okla.
Alfred C. Hiser, Lakewood, Ohio
*Harold B. Hoag, Tampa, Fla.

186

*Mrs. Lowell F. Hobart, Jr., Cincinnati, Ohio
*Earle C. Hochwald, East Cleveland, Ohio
Richard J. Hoddinott, East Cleveland, Ohio
William Hodge, Cleveland, Ohio
*A. L. Hodges, St. Louis, Mo.
Chester E. Hodgson, Newark, N.J.
*Mrs. James E. Hoffman, Hasbrouck Heights, N.J.
Peter J. Hofman, Cleveland, Ohio
Mrs. Virgil Hogue, Rockwood, Tenn.
John S. Holcomb, Benton Harbor, Mich.
Thomas Holden, San Francisco, Calif.
Mrs. Thomas Holden, San Francisco, Calif.
*Gertrude I. Holland, Xenia, Ohio
Mrs. R. L. Holland, Indianapolis, Ind.
Mrs. O. J. Holliman, Savannah, Ga.
Mrs. F. G. Holloway, Madison, N.J.
Lloyd Holloway, Lewistown, Mont.
Bernice A. Holmes, Indianapolis, Ind.
Rexford C. S. Holmes, Saginaw, Mich.
*George H. Holwager, Rockwood, Tenn.
E. G. Homrighausen, Princeton, N.J.
*Kenneth M. Hooe, Rock Island, Ill.
*Archie H. Hook, Seattle, Wash.
*T. Leroy Hooper, Morgantown, W. Va.
*Donald D. Hoover, New York, N.Y.
*H. D. Hoover, Gettysburg, Pa.
Mrs. J. F. Hoover, Shaker Heights, Ohio
R. D. Hopkins, Detroit, Mich.
Myron Taggart Hopper, Lexington, Ky.
*Gerald K. Hornung, Oklahoma City, Okla.
Edwin A. Horst, Amherst, Mass.
Walter Marshall Horton, Oberlin, Ohio
Henry O. Hospers, Utica, N.Y.
Robert D. Hotelling, Midland, Mich.
Walter A. Hotz, Pana, Ill.
*W. E. Houston, Jr., New York, N.Y.
*Richard A. Howard, Westerville, Ohio
Charles E. F. Howe, Columbus, Ohio
*Edna R. Howe, New York, N.Y.
*Mrs. Edwin A. Howe, Cleveland, Ohio
Mrs. J. Ruskin Howe, Joplin, Mo.
J. D. Howell, Cleveland, Ohio
Wirth Howell, Lakewood, Ohio
D. Andrew Howey, Montpelier, Ohio
*Harriet M. Howey, Washington, D.C.
Mrs. H. R. Howland, Denver, Colo.
*Weyman C. Huckabee, New York, N.Y.
Herbert Beecher Hudnut, Detroit, Mich.
Paul E. Huffman, Indianapolis, Ind.
Harold H. Hughes, Roanoke, Va.
Henderson Hughes, New York, N.Y.
Norman Hughes, Bay City, Mich.
*Mrs. R. H. Hughes, Tulsa, Okla.

*A. A. Hughey, Pittsburgh, Pa.
Fred Hughey, Rankin, Pa.
Angus C. Hull, Jr., Peoria, Ill.
M. Dale Humbert, Niles, Ohio
Russell J. Humbert, Youngstown, Ohio
Myron K. Hume, East Cleveland, Ohio
Clark W. Hunt, Tuckahoe, N.Y.
Ernest Hunt, Holt, Mich.
Horace H. Hunt, New York, N.Y.
Melvin C. Hunt, Lakewood, Ohio
*J. Norman Hunter, Glenshaw, Pa.
Howard Huntington, Southport, Conn.
T. E. Huntley, St. Louis, Mo.
Daniel D. Hurst, Detroit, Mich.
Harold R. Husted, Plainfield, N.J.
John H. Huston, Cleveland, Ohio
Ezra Hutchens, Bedford, Ind.
Alva R. Hutchinson, New York, N.Y.
Carl R. Hutchinson, Columbus, Ohio
*Paul Hutchinson, Chicago, Ill.
*Mrs. Ralph Cooper Hutchison, Easton, Pa.
Roy E. Hutchonson, Cleveland, Ohio
Mrs. Dale D. Hutson, Lakewood, Ohio
Stanley B. Hyde, Maywood, Ill.
Thomas P. Inabinett, Wilson, N.C.
*Mrs. W. H. Ingham, Lakewood, Ohio
*S. M. Ingmire, Newark, Ohio
J. C. Inman, Ashland, Ohio
Samuel G. Inman, Bronxville, N.Y.
Kannel Ireland, Dayton, Ohio
*John W. Irwin, New York, N.Y.
John Iszler, Milbank, S.D.
Albert E. Iverson, New York, N.Y.
Hilda L. Ives, Portland, Maine
*Everett E. Jackman, Norfolk, Neb.
*Herbert Jackman, David City, Neb.
Gordon E. Jackson, Pittsburgh, Pa.
H. Ralph Jackson, Nashville, Tenn.
J. H. Jackson, Chicago, Ill.
L. K. Jackson, Gary, Ind.
Mabel Jackson, Cleveland, Ohio
Mansfield E. Jackson, Philadelphia, Pa.
*P. F. Jackson, Dallas, Texas
Bertha E. Jacobs, Columbus, Ohio
Carl H. Jacobson, Roselle, N.J.
Frank Jaggers, Cleveland, Ohio
*Mrs. Guy H. James, Oklahoma City, Okla.
A. Henson Jarmon, Cleveland, Ohio
Mildred Jarvis, Indianapolis, Ind.
Mrs. Mal Jefferson, Belleville, N.J.
Mrs. Frank Jennings, West Newton, Mass.
Louis P. Jensen, Los Angeles, Calif.
Herluf Jensen, St. Paul, Minn.
Melvin J. Joachim, Mt. Vernon, N.Y.
E. J. Johanson, Washington, D.C.

Mrs. H. L. Johns, New Orleans, La.
*Mrs. Ada Johnson, Columbus, Ohio
Alvin D. Johnson, Middletown, Conn.
*Emil Johnson, Bakersfield, Calif.
*J. Glover Johnson, Marietta, Ohio
Joseph A. Johnson, Jackson, Tenn.
Marcus W. Johnson, Indianapolis, Ind.
Philip A. Johnson, Rock Island, Ill.
Pierre Johnson, Pittsburgh, Pa.
R. C. Johnson, Rochester, N.Y.
*W. L. Johnson, Philadelphia, Pa.
*William A. Johnson, Chicago, Ill.
*Eldred Johnston, Dayton, Ohio
*Olav R. Jonasson, Chicago, Ill.
Alan T. Jones, Merom, Ind.
Mrs. C. I. Jones, New Orleans, La.
*Charles Frederick Jones, Coshocton, Ohio
Charles S. Jones, Burlington, Vt.
*Mrs. David E. Jones, Youngstown, Ohio
Edgar DeWitt Jones, Detroit, Mich.
Edward H. Jones, Grove City, Pa.
*Edward H. Jones, Bethel, Ohio
*Mrs. Esther B. Jones, Richmond, Ind.
Harold Jones, Claremont, Calif.
Ira Jones, Lima, Ohio
J. Glanville Jones, New York, N.Y.
Mrs. J. Lee Jones, Cleveland, Ohio
Mary Alice Jones, Chicago, Ill.
Ralph M. Jones, Indianapolis, Ind.
Rudolph Joop, Detroit, Mich.
*David F. Jorgensen, Altadena, Calif.
Dorothy Judd, Cleveland, Ohio
Fred M. Judson, Santa Monica, Calif.
Mrs. E. J. Kalal, Brecksville, Ohio
Elsie Kappen, New York, N.Y.
Verne P. Kaub, Madison, Wis.
A. W. Kauffman, Bancroft, Mich.
Harvey F. Kazmier, Brookline, Mass.
Finley Keech, Fall River, Mass.
Donald Keith, Williamson, N.Y.
Mrs. D. E. Keller, Hazleton, Pa.
*Eldon H. Keller, Cleveland, Ohio
Henry L. Kellogg, Chicago, Ill.
*Harold F. Kellogg, Athens, Ohio
Albert E. Kelly, Pittsburgh, Pa.
Clare M. Kelly, Lakewood, Ohio
Leonard Kendall, Minneapolis, Minn.
Richard V. Kendall, Oxnard, Calif.
Bentley Kennard, Cleveland, Ohio
James W. Kennedy, Lexington, Ky.
*Frank M. Kepner, Los Angeles, Calif.
Evelyn M. Kerr, Cleveland, Ohio
*George P. Kerr, Pittsburgh, Pa.
*J. Allen Kestle, Johnston, Pa.
*Charles B. Ketchum, Alliance, Ohio
*F. Del Kettening, Monmouth, Ill.
*Mrs. F. Del Kettening, Monmouth, Ill.

Hazel J. Key, Cleveland, Ohio
*William B. Key, Ironton, Ohio
George V. Kidder, Burlington, Vt.
Ray H. Kiely, Wausau, Wis.
*Andrew S. Kier, Tarentum, Pa.
H. F. Kilander, Arlington, Va.
*Robert Killam, Cleveland, Ohio
*Mrs. E. L. Killin, Cincinnati, Ohio
Harold C. Killpatrick, San Antonio, Texas
Mrs. Francis M. Kinch, Tacoma, Wash.
A. S. King, Columbus, Ohio
*Ben T. King, Kingsport, Tenn.
*Mrs. Ben T. King, Kingsport, Tenn.
*Bernard N. King, York, Pa.
*Carl H. King, Salisbury, N.C.
Mrs. Dorsey D. King, Indianapolis, Ind.
*Forrest L. King, Lexington, Ky.
Herbert King, New York, N.Y.
Lester F. King, Columbus, Ohio
Mrs. Lester F. King, Nashville, Tenn.
*Marion O. King, Elwood, Ind.
Mrs. Mary D. King, Memphis, Tenn.
*R. A. King, Jacksonville, Fla.
*William R. King, Church Hill, Tenn.
*Mrs. William R. King, Church Hill, Tenn.
Beryl S. Kinser, Youngstown, Ohio
*Mrs. Carl Kirby, Talulla, Ill.
*Kearney Kirkby, Lansing, Mich.
*Robert Kirkman, Indianapolis, Ind.
Dow Kirkpatrick, Young Harris, Ga.
*Edgar C. B. Kirsopp, Philadelphia, Pa.
Helen Kittredge, New York, N.Y.
*Mrs. Herman A. Klahr, Columbus, Ohio
Arnold H. Klaiber, Tiffin, Ohio
*Robert E. Kleesattel, Lexington, Ky.
Cleveland Kleihauer, Hollywood, Calif.
Carl W. Klein, St. Louis, Mo.
Ernest Klein, Webster Groves, Mo.
*Mrs. Robert G. Klein, Cleveland, Ohio
*Harry Byrd Kline, Dallas, Texas
Arthur J. Knape, Lakewood, Ohio
Charles G. Knapp, Lewisburg, Pa.
Mrs. Paul E. Knauss, Marion, Ohio
John L. Knight, Berea, Ohio
*Mrs. Gerald Knoff, Wilmette, Ill.
Alva W. Knoll, Tippecanoe, Ohio
*Louis R. Knowles, Cynthiana, Ky.
*J. Hugh Knox, Nashville, Tenn.
Arthur M. Knudsen, Oak Park, Ill.
Kent S. Knutson, St. Paul 8, Minn.
Marvin B. Kober, Cedar Rapids, Iowa
Henry C. Koch, St. Louis, Mo.
John G. Koehler, Edgewood, R.I.
Percy E. Kohl, Birmingham, Ala.
*Donald H. Koontz, LaGrange, Ind.
Stephen Koska, Cleveland, Ohio
Emil N. Krafft, Cleveland, Ohio

*Reinhard Krause, Dover, Ohio
Earl W. Krueger, Indianapolis, Ind.
Mrs. Elmer Krueger, Cleveland Heights, Ohio
Harry H. Kruener, Granville, Ohio
*Miles H. Krumbine, Cleveland, Ohio
Arlie H. Krussell, Beloit, Wis.
George Kuechle, Cleveland, Ohio
Herbert E. Kuhn, New Haven, Mo.
Edith Kuhns, Cleveland, Ohio
*S. H. Kuntz, El Paso, Ill.
*Andrew E. Kurth, Cedar Rapids, Iowa
George S. Lackland, Toledo, Ohio
*William I. Lacy, Detroit, Mich.
Rufus H. LaFevre, Tamaqua, Pa.
W. E. Laganke, Cleveland, Ohio
W. Franklin Lahr, Louisville, Ky.
*Mrs. E. C. R. Laidlow, Plainfield, N.J.
*Mrs. James Madison Laird, Charleston, W.Va.
Herbert J. Lambacher, Parma Heights, Ohio
M. Willard Lampe, Iowa City, Iowa
Mary Lampkins, Cleveland, Ohio
Ethna Landers, Oak Park, Ill.
Otis Landis, Cleveland Heights, Ohio
Mrs. Emory Lane, Denver, Colo.
*Mrs. J. F. Lane, Memphis, Tenn.
Herbert F. Langdon, Chicago, Ill.
*James W. Lantrip, Nashville, Tenn.
*Mrs. Fred Lanz, Rocky River, Ohio
Clarence H. LaRue, Cleveland, Ohio
Jacob M. Lashly, St. Louis, Mo.
Mrs. Jacob M. Lashly, St. Louis, Mo.
James W. Laurie, Buffalo, N.Y.
Ralph J. LaVallee, Washington, D.C.
Mrs. Ralph J. LaVallee, Washington, D.C.
T. Reid Lawrence, Detroit, Mich.
S. J. Laws, Chicago, Ill.
C. E. Lawson, Buffalo, N.Y.
*James Lawson, Frankfort, Ind.
LeRoy Lawther, Lakewood, Ohio
John H. Leamon, Cambridge, Mass.
Kenneth S. Learey, Middletown, Ohio
Keene R. Lebold, Webster Groves, Mo.
*R. D. Lechleitner, Columbus, Ohio
C. L. Lee, Cleveland, Ohio
*Mrs. Merrit R. Lee, Wichita, Kansas
*Cecil Leek, Hamersville, Ohio
Vernon F. Legg, Sioux Falls, S.D.
Galen T. Lehman, North Manchester, Ind.
Paul Lehmann, Princeton, N.J.
Murray H. Leiffer, Evanston, Ill.
*Hugo Leinberger, Park Forest, Ill.
C. E. Lemmon, Columbia, Mo.
*Harold H. Lentz, Ashland, Ohio
Mrs. Richard E. Lentz, Chicago, Ill.

C. Oscar Leonardson, Rock Island, Ill.
Otto Leonardson, Minneapolis, Minn.
Royal E. Lesher, New York, N.Y.
*John Less, Detroit, Mich.
Stiles Lessly, De Kalb, Ill.
Harold Levander, South St. Paul, Minn.
J. Lee Lewis, Alma, Mich.
John H. Lewis, Wilberforce, Ohio
*Mrs. McIlyar H. Lichliter, Brookline, Mass.
*John Clayton Lime, Canton, N.C.
Karen Lindberg, Holyoke, Mass.
Jonathan Lindell, Minneapolis, Ind.
Albert L. Linder, Youngstown, Ohio
Darrell Linder, Findlay, Ohio
Mrs. Edwin B. Lindsay, Davenport, Iowa
J. L. Link, Chester, Pa.
*B. H. Linville, Springfield, Ohio
*W. J. B. Linvingston, Logan, W.Va.
L. Austin Lippitt, Twinsburg, Ohio
Ruth Lister, Cleveland, Ohio
*Frank Little, Vincennes, Ind.
John F. Little, Braddock, Pa.
*Lawrence C. Little, Pittsburgh, Pa.
*Joseph H. Lloyd, Youngstown, Ohio
*Edward W. Lodwick, Freeport, Ohio
David Loegler, Shaker Heights, Ohio
*Ralph W. Loew, Buffalo, N.Y.
Rudolph Loidolt, Bloomington, Ill.
C. W. Lokey, San Antonio, Texas
Livingston H. Lomas, Lakewood, Ohio
Ruth A. Long, Cincinnati, Ohio
*S. Burman Long, South Weymouth, Mass.
John Longbon, Columbia Station, Ohio
Mrs. C. W. Longman, Cleveland, Ohio
*Anna H. Loofbourow, Richmond, Calif.
A. William Loos, New York, N.Y.
Vere V. Loper, Berkeley, Calif.
*R. G. Lord, Tupelo, Miss.
Edgar A. Love, New York, N.Y.
*John W. Love, Washington, Pa.
Otto R. Loverude, Lowell, Mass.
Virgil E. Lowder, Chicago, Ill.
*Ephraim D. Lowe, Indianapolis, Ind.
Mrs. F. C. Loweth, Cleveland Heights, Ohio
*Jack Lowry, Beaver Falls, Pa.
Mrs. Roswell Lowry, Cleveland, Ohio
*Irwin J. Lubbers, Holland, Mich.
*Mrs. Irwin J. Lubbers, Holland, Mich.
G. W. Lucas, Dayton, Ohio
*Mrs. Fred E. Luchs, Athens, Ohio
Mel Ludwig, Webster Groves, Mo.
Joseph R. Ludwigson, Shaker Heights, Ohio
*Roland A. Luhman, Youngstown, Ohio
W. W. Lumpkin, Pittsburgh, Pa.

G. Clarence Lund, Akron, Ohio
Ralph B. Lunt, South Portland, Maine
Mrs. O. Lutherer, Chagrin Falls, Ohio
S. Raymond Luthy, Newport, R.I.
Maurice F. Lyerla, Phoenix, Ariz.
*Mrs. Clarkson Lyons, Ashtabula, Ohio
H. M. McAdow, Columbus, Ohio
*C. O. McAfee, Macon, Ga.
Ralph C. McAfee, Erie, Pa.
Mrs. J. F. McAlear, Polson, Mont.
*F. B. McAllister, Cincinnati, Ohio
Cary S. McCall, Richmond, Va.
W. C. McCallum, Alliance, Ohio
*Robert J. McCandliss, Grand Rapids, Mich.
*Mrs. Robert J. McCandliss, Grand Rapids, Mich.
*John E. McCaw, Des Moines, Iowa
Mrs. S. W. McClary, Kent, Ohio
Lalah McClellan, Cleveland, Ohio
Dolton F. McClelland, New York, N.Y.
Mrs. Dolton F. McClelland, New York, N.Y.
*Mrs. Johnnie McClure, Russellville, Ark.
*D. K. McColl, Wichita, Kansas
Kemper G. McComb, Cincinnati, Ohio
*C. M. McConnell, Boston, Mass.
Charles McConnell, Dayton, Ohio
Mrs. J. V. McConnell, Shreveport, La.
Mrs. H. B. McCormick, Indianapolis, Ind.
John W. McCracken, Chicago, Ill.
Myrtle A. McDaniel, Bethlehem, Pa.
Bruce H. McDonald, Baltimore, Md.
T. H. McDowell, Oklahoma City, Okla.
*Minnie L. McEaddy, Washington, D.C.
Mrs. E. H. McFarland, Detroit, Mich.
Mrs. G. A. McGregor, Fargo, N.D.
*Elizabeth McGuffie, Chicago, Ill.
*Clive McGuire, Indianapolis, Ind.
J. Franklin McHendry, East Cleveland, Ohio
Jerry D. McInnis, Emory University, Ga.
*Alice D. McKee, Columbus, Ohio
E. Stanley McKee, Fort Wayne, Ind.
*Mary J. Todd McKenzie, Jacksonville, Fla.
Robert A. McKibben, Los Angeles, Calif.
Ruth B. McKinney, Cleveland, Ohio
W. H. McKinney, Cleveland, Ohio
William H. McKinney, Indianapolis, Ind.
*Frank S. McKnight, Brookville, Pa.
Wilford H. McLain, Norwood, Ohio
*Harold N. McLaughlin, Cleveland, Ohio
W. J. G. McLin, Milwaukee, Wis.
Mrs. A. McMillan, Cleveland, Ohio
Alan McMillan, Sewanee, Tenn.
Rosa McMillan, Thedford, Nebr.

*W. Scott McMunn, Butler, Pa.
Emmett A. McNabb, Atlanta, Ga.
P. M. McPheron, Plymouth, Mich.
M. Wayne McQueen, East Cleveland, Ohio
Eugene R. McVicker, Gettysburg, Pa.
George J. MacDonald, Chicago, Ill.
David S. MacInnes, Syracuse, N.Y.
Mrs. John MacKenzie, Cleveland, Ohio
Virginia L. MacLeod, New York, N.Y.
Grant A. MacMichael, Cleveland, Ohio
John W. MacNeil, Framingham, Mass.
Vernon H. MacNeill, Rock Island, Ill.
Walter O. Macoskey, Tacoma, Wash.
Paul G. Macy, Chicago, Ill.
Paul Madsen, Boulder, Colo.
Marlene Maertens, St. Louis, Mo.
*William Mager, Union City, N.J.
*Mrs. W. Mager, Union City, N.J.
Louis Magin, St. Louis, Mo.
Mrs. Thos. M. Magruder, Columbus, Ohio
Robert L. Main, Tahlequah, Okla.
Mrs. Robert L. Main, Tahlequah, Okla.
Lawrence H. Maines, Cleveland, Ohio
*Wilma Ruth Maledon, Little Rock, Ark.
*Van J. Malone, Memphis, Tenn.
Carl L. Manfred, Duluth, Minn.
Lillie Mae Mansell, Rockwood, Tenn.
*Effie Manuel, Cleveland, Ohio
E. W. Marcellus, Chicago, Ill.
*A. T. O. Marks, Philadelphia, Pa.
Louise Marks, Cleveland, Ohio
Roland C. Marriott, Philadelphia, Pa.
Owen Marsh, Springfield, Ill.
*Ross S. Marshall, Cleveland, Ohio
Mrs. Roy Marshall, Omaha, Nebr.
Frank Martick, South Bend, Ind.
Mrs. Frank C. Martick, South Bend, Ind.
Florence Martin, Dayton, Ohio
*George F. Martin, Kansas City, Mo.
J. Orville Martin, San Francisco, Calif.
Mrs. Miles J. Martin, Scotia, N.Y.
*Mrs. W. C. Martin, Jackson, Mich.
Mrs. Arthur L. Martsolf, Beaver Falls, Pa.
John E. Marvin, Adrian, Mich.
Mrs. H. B. Marx, Muncie, Ind.
*F. H. Mason, Columbus, Ohio
Lucy R. Mason, Atlanta, Ga.
Harry V. Masters, Reading, Pa.
*J. Stanley Mathews, Cincinnati, Ohio
Willis D. Mathias, Allentown, Pa.
J. H. Mathis, No. Manchester, Ind.
Mrs. J. H. Mathis, No. Manchester, Ind.
Sargis Matson, Torrington, Conn.
T. E. Matson, Chicago, Ill.

190

William H. Matthews, Jr., Spring Lake, N.J.
Karl E. Mattson, Rock Island, Ill.
Elwood Maunder, Columbus, Ohio
Kenneth L. Maxwell, Hartford, Conn.
Ralph L. Mayberry, Los Angeles, Calif.
Paul O. Mayer, Euclid, Ohio
*Theodore C. Mayer, Wooster, Ohio
John C. Mayne, Washington, D.C.
A. W. Meckstroth, Cleveland, Ohio
Frederick M. Meek, Boston, Mass.
Mrs. Robert L. Meeks, Lakewood, Ohio
Mrs. S. C. Meisburg, Jackson, Miss.
John W. Meister, Fort Wayne, Ind.
Karl P. Meister, Chicago, Ill.
John C. Melchert, Mansfield, Ohio
Mrs. T. G. Melkerson, E. Cleveland, Ohio
C. M. Meller, Cleveland, Ohio
Mrs. John W. Meloy, Louisville, Ky.
W. W. Mendenhall, Ithaca, N.Y.
Lewis Meskimen, Flint, Mich.
William K. Messer, Dayton, Ohio
*Mrs. Harold S. Metcalfe, Pittsburgh, Pa.
John D. Metzler, Chicago, Ill.
Calvin C. Meury, New York, N.Y.
Mrs. G. A. Meyer, Walsenburg, Colo.
Harry L. Meyer, Fall River, Mass.
Karl H. Meyer, Chicago, Ill.
Bruce L. Middaugh, Erie, Pa.
Mrs. H. C. Milam, San Diego, Calif.
J. Earl Milburn, Chattanooga, Tenn.
*Paul W. Milhouse, Decatur, Ill.
Alex Miller, Plymouth, Mich.
Alva B. Miller, Cleveland, Ohio
Benton B. Miller, Indianapolis, Ind.
Bernice Miller, New York, N.Y.
Clementine Miller, Columbus, Ind.
*DeWitt L. Miller, Washington, D.C.
*Mrs. DeWitt L. Miller, Washington, D.C.
Don Miller, Naperville, Ill.
Grace Miller, Independence, Ohio
Harold E. Miller, Jr., Princeton, N.J.
L. C. T. Miller, Philadelphia, Pa.
*Orville C. Miller, Shelbyville, Ill.
*Paul E. Miller, Sacramento, Calif.
Raymond W. Miller, Washington, D.C.
Ruth Miller, New York, N.Y.
*Ruth Miller, Hiram, Ohio
Thomas Miller, Schenectady, N.Y.
W. Frederic Miller, Youngstown, Ohio
*William George Miller, Shadyside, Ohio
*Frances Mills, Berea, Ohio
*Mrs. Spann W. Milner, Atlanta, Ga.
Louis O. Mink, Detroit, Mich.
Ohmer C. Minnich, Cleveland, Ohio
Wilson P. Minton, Milroy, Pa.
George Mitchell, Terre Haute, Ind.

H. B. Mitchell, Gary, Ind.
Roscoe M. Mitchell, Tarrytown, N.Y.
John L. Mixon, Chicago, Ill.
*Newton E. Moats, Des Moines, Iowa
*H. Eugene Modlin, Clarksburg, W.Va.
E. Harold Mohn, Chicago, Ill.
*Lloyd V. Mohnkern, Macon, Nebr.
W. Irving Monore, Jr., Bridgton, Maine
*Elizabeth Monroe, Albany, Mo.
*Herald B. Monroe, Cleveland, Ohio
*Mrs. Russell K. Montgomery, Pittsburgh, Pa.
Thelma Montgomery, Berea, Ohio
*J. G. Moody, Cleveland, Ohio
Melvin Moody, Beach City, Ohio
Mrs. Reed Moody, Nampa, Idaho
Otis V. Moon, Des Moines, Iowa
Ansley C. Moore, Pittsburgh, Pa.
Mrs. Ansley C. Moore, Pittsburgh, Pa.
Dale H. Moore, Allentown, Pa.
*Elsie Ellen Moore, High Point, N.C.
*George V. Moore, Lexington, Ky.
M. Irene Moore, Indianapolis, Ind.
Mrs. Merle Moore, Seattle, Wash.
Lee C. Moorehead, Ada, Ohio
*E. E. Morgan, Pittsburgh, Pa.
Mrs. Harry S. Morris, San Diego, Calif.
Paul J. Morris, Granville, Ohio
T. V. Morrison, Newport News, Va.
Glen E. Morrow, Rochester, N.Y.
Iva F. Morrow, Cleveland, Ohio
Franklin Morse, Fond du Lac, Wis.
*Ruth Morton, New York, N.Y.
*Mrs. J. Edward Moseley, Indianapolis, Ind.
*Mrs. Clyde Mosher, Cuba, Ill.
Gordon Motersbaugh, Olmsted Falls, Ohio
Mrs. I. S. Motz, Evanston, Ill.
A. L. Mould, Erie, Pa.
*Mrs. A. L. Mould, Erie, Pa.
*Mrs. Elmer W. K. Mould, Elmira, N.Y.
Mrs. Harold R. Moulton, Southbridge, Mass.
*Otto A. Muecke, Chicago, Ill.
Theodore Muehlhauser, Cleveland Heights, Ohio
*F. W. Mueller, Nashville, Tenn.
Fred Mueller, Springfield, Ohio
Mrs. John W. Mueller, St. Louis, Mo.
*Mrs. R. H. Mueller, Dayton, Ohio
Roy E. Mueller, Indianapolis, Ind.
James B. Mulder, Highland Park, N.J.
Louise E. Mulder, Metuchen, N.J.
Mrs. Holbrook Mulford, Oak Park, Ill.
Mrs. Frederick M. Mullino, Montezuma, Ga.

191

Herbert Munro, Granville, Ohio
Warren Vinton Murphy, Hamden, Conn.
*J. Victor Murtland, Pittsburgh, Pa.
A. J. Muste, New York, N.Y.
J. R. Mutchmor, Ontario, Canada
*H. T. Myers, Norfolk, Va.
Jay G. Myers, Akron, Ohio
*Minor M. Myers, Woodstock, Va.
*Charles Haddon Nabers, Greenville, S.C.
Mrs. I. George Nace, Mt. Vernon, N.Y.
*Leora Nagel, Dayton, Ohio
Mrs. Harold Naragon, Cleveland Heights, Ohio
Edith Nash, Cleveland, Ohio
Walter L. Nathan, Bradford, Mass.
Alford R. Naus, Merchantville, N.J.
Kurtis Frind Naylor, Denver, Col.
C. C. Neal, Pine Bluff, Ark.
Harold D. Neal, South Bend, Ind.
Arnold Nearn, Lancaster, Pa.
Harry M. Neely, Flint, Mich.
*Mrs. Ralph Neely, Sharon, Pa.
Clifford A. Nelson, St. Paul, Minn.
Frank A. Nelson, Racine, Wis.
*John F. Nelson, Clarksburg, W.Va.
Merrill E. Nelson, Cleveland, Ohio
*R. N. Nelson, Pittsburgh, Pa.
William W. Nelson, Ottawa, Kan.
E. M. Nesbitt, Beaver, Pa.
*J. H. Ness, Dayton, Ohio
*Glenn W. Nethercut, Chicago, Ill.
*Arthur W. Newell, Richmond, Va.
Mrs. Duncan H. Newell, Longmeadow, Mass.
*Robert C. Newell, Cleveland, Ohio
Wendell R. Newell, Bisbee, Ariz.
*J. Howard Nichols, Caney, Kansas
Harry Nicholson, Akron, Ohio
Mrs. Harry Nicholson, Akron, Ohio
Wesley G. Nicholson, Eugene, Ore.
James H. Nicol, Ithaca, N.Y.
*Bill Nighswonger, Oklahoma City, Okla.
*M. W. Nilson, Roswell, N.M.
*Fred B. Noble, Jacksonville, Fla.
Mrs. Max A. Noble, Wichita, Kan.
Roger T. Node, Nashville, Tenn.
Robert A. Nolte, Bloomington, Ill.
Mrs. J. E. Noran, Rocky River, Ohio
J. Vincent Nordgren, Annadale, Staten Island, N.Y.
J. A. Nordstrom, Casper, Wyo.
Jess H. Norenberg, Madison, Wis.
C. Gail Norris, Lock Haven, Clinton County Pa.
*Lester S. Norris, Delaware, Ohio
*Mrs. W. H. Norwood, New York, N.Y.
Dorothy Nyland, New York, N.Y.

Henry T. Nyland, Cleveland, Ohio
Arthur R. Oates, Marshfield, Wis.
A. Glen O'Dell, Indianapolis, Ind.
Carroll N. Odell, Warsaw, Ind.
*Harold L. Ogden, Salem, Ohio
*Tarrance F. Ogden, Schenectady, N.Y.
Emma Jessie Ogg, Brooklyn, N.Y.
Marguerite Ohm, Milwaukee, Wis.
Arnold T. Ohrn, Washington, D.C.
Annie J. Oldham, Euclid, Ohio
Karl J. Olson, East Orange, N.J.
Lloyd H. Olson, Toledo, Ohio
Oscar Thomas Olson, Cleveland, Ohio
Reuben Olson, Oakland, Calif.
Kelly O'Neall, Denver, Col.
G. Edwin Osborn, Enid, Okla.
Ronald E. Osborn, Indianapolis, Ind.
Russell G. Osgood, Saginaw, Mich.
Mrs. Russell G. Osgood, Saginaw, Mich.
Charles Osborn, Rochester, N.Y.
Mrs. Charles Osborn, Rochester, N.Y.
*Newell Yost Osborne, Alliance, Ohio
Mrs. Edwin G. Osness, Billings, Mont.
Edwin G. Osness, Billings, Mont.
R. C. Ostergren, Boston, Mass.
Angela C. Ostrander, Cleveland, Ohio
Laila M. Ostrom, Alliance, Ohio
Mrs. Verner Ott, Cleveland, Ohio
Paul N. Otto, New York, N.Y.
*Helen Oudeman, N. Royalton, Ohio
*J. B. Outlaw, Chattanooga, Tenn.
Mrs. Alan Owens, Cleveland, Ohio
John Paul Pack, Seattle, Wash.
J. A. Palmer, Thomasville, N.C.
Nellie M. Pardee, Cleveland, Ohio
*William Park, Omaha, Neb.
Joseph A. Parker, Pontiac, Mich.
W. John Parker, Pomona, Calif.
Mrs. William Parkhurst, Lansing, Mich.
*Raymond T. Parks, Louisville, Ky.
Mrs. C. C. Parlin, Englewood, N.J.
Sarah S. Parrott, New York, N.Y.
*Mark H. Parry, Ridgway, Pa.
Mrs. Wilber C. Parry, Palatine, Ill.
Mrs. Edwin Parsons, New York, N.Y.
Waymon Parsons, Shaker Heights, Ohio
Ira A. Paternoster, Dayton, Ohio
Mrs. W. C. Patre, Toledo, Ohio
Mrs. H. M. Patrick, Bernardsville, N.J.
Loyce Patrick, Nashville, Tenn.
Mrs. James Patterson, Olmsted Falls, Ohio
Merle C. Patterson, Columbia, Tenn.
Harry A. Pattison, Livingston, N.Y.
Herman Patton, Cleveland, Ohio
*Louise Patton, New York, N.Y.
Wayne Paulen, Huntington, Ind.

*Franklin R. Payne, Pittsburgh, Pa.
Mrs. J. W. Payne, Cherryville, N.C.
Mrs. Paul Calvin Payne, Philadelphia, Pa.
Malcolm E. Peabody, Syracuse, N.Y.
C. Baker Pearle, Chicago, Ill.
Felix B. Peck, Charlotte, N.C.
Mrs. Remington Peck, Rocky River, Ohio
Mrs. Kenneth L. Peek, Elgin, Ill.
Lee A. Peeler, Arlington, Va.
Jesse Pindell Peirce, Elgin, Ill.
O. A. Pendleton, Boston, Mass.
E. J. Penhorwood, Lima, Ohio
*Mrs. E. J. Penhorwood, Lima, Ohio
Almon R. Pepper, New York, N.Y.
Mrs. A. G. Perkey, South Bend, Ind.
*J. J. Perkins, Wichita Falls, Texas
Louis L. Perkins, Auburn, N.Y.
C. W. Perry, Marion, Ind.
Mrs. Raymond B. Perry, Brecksville, Ohio
S. P. Perry, Durham, N.C.
Peter Person, Chicago, Ill.
Edward E. Peters, Cleveland, Ohio
Mrs. Lemuel Petersen, Chicago, Ill.
*Ellwood Peterson, Rock Island, Ill.
*Howard Peterson, Cambridge, Ohio
*John B. Peterson, Trenton, N.J.
Victor Peterson, Cleveland, Ohio
Walter L. Peterson, Spokane, Wash.
Richard W. Pettit, Mentor, Ohio
Charles W. Phillips, Kingston, Pa.
Harold C. Phillips, Cleveland, Ohio
W. A. Phillips, Denver, Col.
W. H. Phillips, Berea, Ohio
Hulda M. Phipps, Cleveland, Ohio
Mrs. Don Pielstick, Madison, N.J.
*Arthur Carl Piepkorn, Carlisle Barracks, Pa.
*Mrs. A. E. Pierce, Tulsa, Okla.
I. Benjamin Pierce, Sewickley, Pa.
Robert B. Pierce, Indianapolis, Ind.
Carl T. Pierson, Rossford, Ohio
*Charles V. Pike, Cleveland, Ohio
I. S. Pinkett, Chicago Heights, Ill.
Louis W. Pitt, New York, N.Y.
Earle B. Pleasant, New York, N.Y.
Mrs. C. W. Plopper, Shreveport, La.
John R. Plummer, Cleveland, Ohio
Wynn Plummer, Orange, Calif.
Eugene Pocock, Cleveland Heights, Ohio
*Mrs. P. D. Pointer, South Bend, Ind.
*Daniel A. Poling, New York, N.Y.
*Mrs. Daniel Poling, New York, N.Y.
M. C. Pollock, Dayton, Ohio
John W. Pontius, Buffalo, N.Y.
*Mrs. Paul Reid Pontius, Greenburg, Pa.

Mrs. E. C. Pope, Shaker Heights, Ohio
Fred B. Porter, Fort Worth, Texas
*Fred D. Porter, Detroit, Mich.
W. H. Porter, Nashua, N.H.
C. F. Post, South Bend, Ind.
Mrs. Dan Potter, Attleboro, Mass.
*Rockwell Harmon Potter, Hartford, Conn.
P. L. Powell, Franklin, Ind.
Oliver W. Powers, Brooklyn, N.Y.
*Mrs. R. C. Powers, Wickcliffe, Ohio
Edwin E. Prange, Berea, Ohio
Ida Prather, Atlanta, Ga.
*J. Perry Prather, Waterloo, Iowa
*Mary E. Pratt, Minneapolis, Minn.
Ann Elizabeth Prescott, Cleveland, Ohio
William Ray Prescott, Grand Rapids, Mich.
Mrs. M. H. Preslan, Cleveland, Ohio
*Harry Allan Price, Pittsburgh, Pa.
John Price, Benton Harbor, Mich.
Walter B. Price, Coloma, Mich.
*Marion Prindell, Chicago, Ill.
*Jacob Prins, Grand Rapids, Mich.
Ralph Proud, Jr., Wickliffe, Ohio
Lillian I. Prowder, Chicago, Ill.
Cleon F. Prowell, Harrisburg, Pa.
Mrs. E. V. Pugh, Washington, D.C.
Martin A. Punt, Hasbrouck Heights, N.J.
*J. Arnold Purdie, New York, N.Y.
Mrs. George E. Purdy, Des Moines, Iowa
Mrs. Russell C. Putnam, Cleveland, Ohio
*C. Lynn Pyatt, Lexington, Ky.
*Edna Pyle, Tulsa, Okla.
*Anna M. Pyott, New York, N.Y.
George E. Quandt, Bridgeport, Conn.
*Oliver B. Quick, Cleveland, Ohio
*Mrs. Harold L. Quivers, Washington, D.C.
Lynn Radcliffe, Cincinnati, Ohio
*Raye Ragan, Springfield, Ill.
David Railsback, Corona, N.Y.
Oliver A. Rajala, Cleveland Heights, Ohio
J. R. Raker, Jr., Portland, Ore.
Philip Ramer, Cleveland, Ohio
*Donn Ramsdell, Lexington, Ky.
*John G. Ramsey, Atlanta, Ga.
Darrell D. Randall, Cleveland, Ohio
*Raymond C. Rankin, Memphis, Tenn.
*Walter W. Rankin, Philadelphia, Pa.
McCoy Ransom, Kansas City, Mo.
*A. H. Rapking, Madisonville, Tenn.
*Louis Rawls, Chicago, Ill.
*E. K. Reagin, Knoxville, Tenn.
Granville W. Reed, Los Angeles, Calif.
Ronald Reed, Kent, Ohio
George O. Reemsnyder, Cleveland, Ohio
Osa Rees, Cleveland, Ohio

193

Joseph W. Reeves, East Northfield, Mass.
*Mrs. W. A. Reeves, Columbus, Ohio
Arthur C. Rehme, Bath, N.Y.
S. Robert Reiber, Cleveland Heights, Ohio
Conrad R. Reisch, Bridgeport, Conn.
Mrs. F. E. Reissig, Washington, D.C.
Herman F. Reissig, New York, N.Y.
Mildred A. Renaud, Cleveland Heights, Ohio
Raymond C. Renaud, Cleveland Heights, Ohio
*Liola Repp, Lakewood, Ohio
Karl Rest, Port Huron, Mich.
O. G. Reuman, Ravenna, Ohio
Ruth Reynolds, Indianapolis, Ind.
*Francis A. Rhoades, LaPorte, Ind.
*H. Lawrence Rice, Pittsburgh, Pa.
*C. C. Rich, Garard's Fort, Pa.
*Cyril K. Richard, Chicago, Ill.
Frank G. Richard, Partridge, Kansas
Mrs. Fred S. Richards, Forest Grove, Ore.
H. F. Richards, North Manchester, Ind.
Lawrence H. Richards, Jersey City, N.J.
Mrs. Donald W. Richardson, Richmond, Va.
Laura Richardson, Mansfield, Ohio
Lester B. Rickman, Jefferson City, Mo.
*George F. Ricky, Washington, D.C.
James F. Riddle, Cleveland Heights, Ohio
*E. D. Riebel, Naperville, Ill.
Richard A. Risser, Jonesville, Mich.
Ethel Ristine, Nashville, Tenn.
A. Grieg Ritchie, St. Louis, Mo.
*Ruth V. Ritchie, Narengo, Ind.
A. L. Riter, Cleveland, Ohio
Irene Ritter, Cleveland, Ohio
*F. J. Roat, Cleveland, Ohio
A. L. Roberts, Lakeland, Fla.
*Carroll C. Roberts, Eugene, Ore.
*Fred R. Roberts, Kingston, Pa.
*James F. Roberts, Lynwood, Calif.
John C. Roberts, Muncie, Ind.
*Walter H. Roberts, Dayton, Ohio
*Mrs. Charles F. Robbins, West Orange, N.J.
George Robinson, Baltimore, Md.
H. N. Robinson, Cleveland, Ohio
S. W. Robinson, Vincennes, Ind.
U. S. Robinson, Evanston, Ill.
*W. L. Robinson, Corinth, Miss.
Mrs. W. W. Robinson, Vincennes, Ind.
*William B. Robinson, Steubenville, Ohio
William H. Robinson, Racine, Wis.
Henry Lee Robinson, Jr., Blacksburg, Va.
Mrs. Henry Lee Robinson, Jr., Blacksburg, Va.

Mrs. Kyle Adams Rodenbaeck, Claremont, Calif.
Richard R. Rodes, Cleveland, Ohio
Claude L. Roe, Cleveland, Ohio
Mrs. Charles F. Rogers, Cleveland, Ohio
Gladstone Rogers, Miami, Fla.
Jefferson P. Rogers, Cleveland, Ohio
*John Rogers, Tulsa, Okla.
Miriam E. Rogers, Cleveland, Ohio
William L. Rogers, New York, N.Y.
Gottfried Roller, Richmond, Va.
Mrs. Ralph A. Rood, Lakewood, Ohio
Galen Lee Rose, Cedar Rapids, Iowa
Kenneth Rose, Lewisburg, Pa.
George F. Roser, Rochester, N.Y.
Charles W. Ross, Macon, Ga.
Mrs. Roy G. Ross, Chicago, Ill.
Solomon D. Ross, Detroit, Mich.
Verla M. Ross, Washington, Pa.
Mrs. Philip M. Rossman, Rhinebeck, N.Y.
Vern Rossman, New Haven, Conn.
Rodney W. Roundy, Portland, Me.
Lester L. Roush, Columbus, Ohio
Porter Routh, Nashville, Tenn.
*E. C. Rowand, Jr., Sharon, Pa.
Mrs. Harold A. Royer, Bellevue, Ohio
L. C. Rudolph, Louisville, Ky.
John Rudyk, Cleveland, Ohio
*Mrs. Frank B. Ruf, Fort Wayne, Ind.
Raymond M. Ruhlman, Cleveland, Ohio
Paul N. Runk, Lima, Ohio
Mrs. H. S. Rusk, Pueblo, Col.
Arthur J. Russell, Cleveland, Ohio
Mark Rutherford, Indianapolis, Ind.
Mrs. Walter F. Rutter, Wakefield, Mass.
Mrs. Norman Ryan, Cleveland, Ohio
Mrs. Vernon Ryding, Chicago, Ill.
*Thomas A. Rymer, Washington, D.C.
Raleigh E. Sain, Independence, Ohio
Melba C. St. Clair, Verona, N.J.
Aileen May Sanborn, Detroit, Mich.
*Leon D. Sanborne, Berea, Ky.
William E. Sander, Seattle, Wash.
Carl H. Sandgren, St. Paul, Minn.
David H. Sandstrom, Massena, N.Y.
Glenn F. Sanford, New York, N.Y.
*Harry Sarles, Dallas, Texas
Mrs. W. C. Satre, Toledo, Ohio
Glenn M. Sauder, Muskegon, Mich.
Ivane T. Saulpaugh, New York, N.Y.
Theodore F. Savage, New York, N.Y.
*Thomas B. Sawyer, Durham, N.C.
Carlton W. Saywell, Phoenix, Ariz.
L. L. Scaife, Buffalo, N.Y.
*Mrs. William Scarlett, Webster Groves, Mo.

Howard C. Schade, Tarrytown, N.Y.
Paul G. Schade, South Norwalk, Conn.
*H. Brent Schaeffer, Jackson, Miss.
Harry G. Schairbaum, Alliance, Ohio
J. E. Schatz, Cleveland, Ohio
Gladys E. Scheer, Lexington, Ky.
Walter A. Scheer, St. Louis, Mo.
James Scherer, New York, N.Y.
Elwin H. Scheyer, Tacoma, Wash.
Mrs. S. Paul Schilling, Westminster, Md.
Walter Schlaretzki, Decatur, Ill.
Stanley W. Schmidt, Bangor, Maine
Francis J. Schnuck, Akron, Ohio
John Schott, Cleveland, Ohio
Mrs. Frederic P. Schrader, Los Angeles, Calif.
Mark Y. Schrock, Goshen, Ind.
Frank E. Schroeder, Hastings, Neb.
B. L. Schubel, St. Louis, Mo.
*Rudolph G. Schulz, Knoxville, Tenn.
Katherine Schutze, Indianapolis, Ind.
Helen C. Schwab, Topeka, Kan.
Charles Schwantas, Philadelphia, Pa.
Elizabeth Schwed, Warren, Ohio
*William G. Schwemmer, Kewaskum, Wis.
John R. Scotford, New York, N.Y.
*C. C. Scott, Richmond, Va.
Ernest P. Scott, Cleveland Heights, Ohio
George A. Scott, San Diego, Calif.
*John J. Scott, New Philadelphia, Ohio
*Mrs. John J. Scott, New Philadelphia, Ohio
William Merton Scott, Richmond, Ind.
*Robert W. Searle, New York, N.Y.
C. K. Searles, Toledo, Ohio
Charlotte S. Sears, Sidney, Ohio
Paul Secrest, Akron, Ohio
Mrs. Paul Secrest, Akron, Ohio
Kenneth B. Seeley, Kalamazoo, Mich.
Mrs. Kenneth B. Seeley, Kalamazoo, Mich.
Albert L. Seely, New Haven, Conn.
*Idelle Segar, Chicago, Ill.
W. C. Seitz, Gambier, Ohio
Nettie M. Senger, Fort Wayne, Ind.
Phoebe Settlage, Cleveland, Ohio
*Mrs. H. H. Settle, Greenville, N.C.
Charles Severns, San Diego, Calif.
*J. H. Seward, Memphis, Tenn.
*Mauddean T. Seward, Memphis, Tenn.
Leslie W. Seymour, Cisco, Texas
Mrs. Leslie W. Seymour, Cisco, Texas
*John Shaefer, Elgin, Ill.
Howard C. Shaffer, Jr., Bayside, N.Y.
Mrs. A. C. Shanks, Little Rock, Ark.
Mary E. Shannon, Topeka, Kan.
*Thompson L. Shannon, Dallas, Texas

Lawrie J. Sharp, Cleveland, Ohio
*D. R. Sharpe, Cleveland, Ohio
*Roger A. Sharpe, Erie, Pa.
*Henry K. Shaw, Elyria, Ohio
*William C. Shcram, N. Royalton, Ohio
M. Edith Shearer, Elmira, Ohio
*Mrs. Herman J. Sheedy, University Heights, Ohio
D. Ervin Sheets, Indianapolis, Ind.
Mabel M. Sheibley, New York, N.Y.
Mrs. Harold Sheldon, Olmsted Falls, Ohio
*Mrs. O. H. Sheldon, Tulsa, Okla.
Ethel A. Shellenberger, Philadelphia, Pa.
E. L. V. Shelley, East Lansing, Mich.
Gentry A. Shelton, Lexington, Ky.
*Arthur M. Shenefelt, London, Ohio
*H. Reed Shepfer, Erie, Pa.
*Wilbur Spencer Sheriff, Johnstown, Pa.
Arthur M. Sherman, New York, N.Y.
O. Sherman, N. Little Rock, Ark.
Henry Noble Sherwood, Louisville, Ky.
*Stanley L. Shippey, Stow, Ohio
*Herbert S. Shirley, Albany, Mo.
W. D. Shively, N. Royalton, Ohio
Robert C. Shoemaker, Worcester, Mass.
Mrs. Earl B. Shoesmith, Paso Robles, Calif.
John H. Shope, Chicago, Ill.
Mrs. John H. Shope, Chicago, Ill.
*Benjamin E. Shove, Camillus, N.Y.
*William Kyle Shown, Ava, Ill.
Mrs. I. J. Shumpert, North Little Rock, Ark.
P. Randolph Shy, Jackson, Tenn.
Earl H. Siebold, Fort Wayne, Ind.
Mrs. W. R. Sieplein, Lakewood, Ohio
Walter W. Sikes, Indianapolis, Ind.
Chester A. Sillars, Danbury, Conn.
A. J. Simmons, New York, N.Y.
*L. V. Simms, Dayton, Ohio
*Hans O. F. Simoleit, Rochester, Pa.
*A. E. Simon, New Castle, Pa.
*Audren Simpkins, Chauncey, Ohio
Abram L. Simpson, Washington, D.C.
W. F. Simpson, Monroe, Mich.
Jerry Singleton, Willoughby, Ohio
Gordon A. Sisco, Toronto, Canada
Mildred H. Sisson, Cuba, N.Y.
Clarence E. Sitler, Indianapolis, Ind.
John E. Sjauken, Syracuse, N.Y.
Mrs. Frank W. Skoog, Rumford, R.I.
*Frank J. Sladen, Grosse Pointe, Mich.
*Mrs. Frank J. Sladen, Grosse Pointe, Mich.
*Mrs. N. F. Slagel, Altoona, Pa.
*N. F. Slagel, Altoona, Pa.

195

Seth W. Slaughter, Columbia, Mo.
J. C. Slemp, Philadelphia, Pa.
Marie Smail, Mayfield Heights, Ohio
*C. Emerson Smith, Richmond, Va.
Carl R. Smith, Columbus, Ohio
*Mrs. D. Burt Smith, Mt. Airy, Philadelphia, Pa.
*Douglas C. Smith, Berea, Ohio
*Edgar B. Smith, Browning, Mont.
Edward C. Smith, Lakewood, Ohio
*Floyd F. Smith, Indianapolis, Ind.
*Mrs. Howard Wayne Smith, Ardmore, Pa.
Jackson E. Smith, Tulsa, Okla.
Jane Avery Smith, Columbus, Ohio
Mrs. John C. Smith, West Hartford, Conn.
John M. Smith, Cleveland, Ohio
Leslie R. Smith, Lexington, Ky.
Mariah O. Smith, Bloomington, Ind.
Martha C. Smith, Kansas City, Mo.
Robert W. Smith, Hannibal, Mo.
Rockwell C. Smith, Evanston, Ill.
Thomas H. Smith, Ypsilanti, Mich.
Mrs. Van S. Merle Smith, New York, N.Y.
Vernon T. Smith, Holt, Mich.
W. Stanley Smith, Columbus, Ohio
*William Martin Smith, Evansville, Ind.
Mareta Smoot, Indianapolis, Ind.
Mrs. Harry Smoyer, Cleveland Heights, Ohio
Thomas B. Smythe, Birdsboro, Pa.
*H. R. Snavely, Marshall, Ill.
*Glenn L. Sneed, Athens, La.
*Clair J. Snell, Jackson, Mich.
*John R. Snively, Rockford, Ill.
Ernest L. Snodgrass, Chicago, Ill.
E. J. Soell, Port Huron, Mich.
Mae Ida Solobillings, Chicago, Ill.
*Loren E. Souers, Canton, Ohio
Mrs. Walter C. Southwick, Cleveland-Rocky River, Ohio
*Mrs. Neal B. Spahr, Knoxville, Tenn.
William M. Spangler, Lexington, Ky.
Laren Spear, Decatur, Ill.
Mrs. Laren Spear, Decatur, Ill.
*Sholto M. Spears, Cleveland, Ohio
Mrs. Laurence F. Speckman, Louisville, Ky.
Mrs. Paul D. Spencer, Alliance, Ohio
Mrs. R. L. Spoerri, University Heights, Ohio
*George B. Spreng, Shaker Heights, Ohio
J. M. Springer, New York, N.Y.
*Henry C. Sprinkle, Jr., New York, N.Y.
*Walter P. Sprunt, Wilmington, N.C.
*Mrs. Walter P. Sprunt, Wilmington, N.C.
*Mrs. Alfred Srail, Sr., Cleveland, Ohio

*Mrs. Louis Staffel, Lakewood, Ohio
Russell H. Stafford, Hartford, Conn.
Calvin K. Stalnaker, Tulsa, Okla.
*Mrs. J. S. Stamm, Harrisburg, Pa.
*Forrest L. Standard, Webb City, Mo.
*J. T. Stanley, Greensboro, N.C.
Doris Stansbury, Granville, Ohio
Florence Stansbury, New York, N.Y.
*Mrs. Bayard Staplin, Buffalo, N.Y.
Evelyn Stark, Chicago, Ill.
Oscar G. Starrett, Schenectady, N.Y.
Mrs. Paul Statler, Cleveland, Ohio
Reuben A. Stauss, Versailles, Ohio
Elsie Stearns, Columbia Station, Ohio
Mrs. R. H. Stearns, Bronxville, N.Y.
Mrs. Edwin Allen Stebbins, Rochester, N.Y.
Joseph H. Stein, East Orange, N.J.
Luther E. Stein, Oak Park, Ill.
*Fred E. Stephens, St. Louis, Mo.
Mrs. Paul Stetler, Cleveland, Ohio
*Ruth Arnold Steva, St. Marys, Ohio
Edith M. Stevens, Worcester, Mass.
Mrs. Thomas Stevenson, Wooster, Ohio
*W. P. Stevenson, Philadelphia, Pa.
Donald H. Stewart, Houston, Texas
*F. G. Stewart, Brackenridge, Pa.
H. Walter Stewart, Cleveland Heights, Ohio
*John Stewart, St. Louis, Mo.
Henry A. Stick, Amherst, Ohio
*Leonard A. Stidley, Oberlin, Ohio
Lorin Stine, Dayton, Ohio
Jesse William Stitt, New York, N.Y.
*Paul R. Stock, St. Louis, Mo.
*Harold F. Stoddard, Newark, N.J.
Manfred Stoerker, Orrville, Ohio
R. R. Stokes, Philadelphia, Pa.
Mrs. John Paul Stone, San Diego, Calif.
Mrs. Howard E. Stowell, Niagara Falls, N.Y.
Helen Strasburg, Berea, Ohio
Hillyer H. Straton, Malden, Mass.
Rosa L. Strickland, Cleveland, Ohio
Donald W. Strickler, New York, N.Y.
Mrs. Tommie B. Stroud, Waco, Texas
Mrs. Paul Stuart, Birmingham, Ala.
Mrs. Hugh C. Stuntz, Nashville, Tenn.
*Roy Sturm, New York, N.Y.
*Mrs. W. B. Suddeth, Atlanta, Ga.
Mrs. Ed. Sunergren, Denver, Col.
*Trevah R. Sutton, Jackson Center, Ohio
Alfred W. Swan, Madison, Wis.
Walter W. Swank, Everett, Pa.
Carl B. Swanson, Peoria, Ill.
D. Verner Swanson, Geneva, Ill.
Cleon Swarts, Elkhart, Ind.

196

Romain A. Swedendure, Staten Island, N.Y.
Elsie Sweeney, Columbus, Ind.
H. Ray Sweetman, Briarcliff Manor, N.Y.
Birger Swenson, Rock Island, Ill.
Voggo Swenson, Harrisburg, Pa.
*Mrs. W. W. Swett, Takoma Park, Washington, D.C.
Okey R. Swisher, Cleveland, Ohio
*J. S. Sykes, Muskogee, Okla.
W. Clyde Sykes, Conifer, N.Y.
Kengo Tajima, Cleveland, Ohio
*Geza Takaro, New York, N.Y.
Norbert G. Talbott, Columbus, Ind.
Franklin C. Talmage, Decatur, Ga.
T. Markham Talmage, Hudson, N.Y.
George L. Tappan, Binghamton, N.Y.
*Mrs. John A. Tarvin, Cleveland, Ohio
Warren James Taussig, New York, N.Y.
*Ann Elizabeth Taylor, New York, N.Y.
Harry B. Taylor, Cleveland, Ohio
Mrs. Norman J. Taylor, Kenmore, N.Y.
Prince A. Taylor, Jr., New Orleans, La.
*Robert H. Taylor, Warren, Ohio
*Thomas H. Taylor, Cleveland Heights, Ohio
Thomas Hart Taylor, Paris, Ky.
Walter A. Taylor, Washington, D.C.
James W. Teener, Kansas City, Mo.
William H. Tempest, Buffalo, N.Y.
*Frank Templin, Jeffersonville, Ind.
Leslie G. Templin, Crossville, Tenn.
John S. Ter Louw, Brandon, Wis.
*Faith A. Terrell, New Vienna, Ohio
William Sale Terrell, Hartford, Conn.
Mrs. William Sale Terrell, West Hartford, Conn.
*F. Marion Tharp, Evansville, Ind.
Lucius E. Thayer, Boston, Mass.
Mrs. Raible C. Theurer, Lakewood, Ohio
Benjamin G. Thomas, South Bend, Ind.
*D. P. Thomas, Chicago, Ill.
David Thomas, Stillwater, Okla.
Grace Thomas, Erie, Pa.
Herman F. Thomas, Milwaukee, Wis.
J. W. Thomas, New York, N.Y.
*Mrs. W. W. Thomas, Oklahoma City, Okla.
*Calvin N. Thompson, Jr., Syracuse, N.Y.
E. Eugene Thompson, Greenville, Ohio
Frank Thompson, Muskogee, Okla.
*H. H. Thompson, Atlanta, Ga.
Herbert J. Thompson, Akron, Ohio
Mrs. Leland J. Thompson, Long Beach, Calif.
N. A. Thompson, Tulsa, Okla.
R. Melvyn Thompson, New Castle, Ind.

W. Paul Thompson, Reading, Pa.
Edgar T. Thornton, Lynchburg, Va.
*Cleveland T. Thrash, Birmingham, Ala.
Norris L. Tibbetts, New York, N.Y.
*Luther J. Tigner, Peoria, Ill.
Carl W. Tiller, Cheverly, Md.
Mrs. M. E. Tilly, Atlanta, Ga.
Ralph W. Tinsley, Dayton, Ohio
Paul A. Toaspern, New York, N.Y.
*Herrick L. Todd, Grove City, Ohio
Joseph C. Todd, Bloomington, Ind.
Mrs. Joseph C. Todd, Bloomington, Ind.
Mrs. J. B. Tomhave, Montevideo, Minn.
Mrs. James Town, Cleveland, Ohio
Edgar Towne, Pittsburgh, Pa.
Mrs. Walter Towner, Nashville, Tenn.
*John W. Townsend, Chagrin Falls, Ohio
William J. Townsend, Philadelphia, Pa.
Olin Tracy, Buffalo, N.Y.
*Roland M. Traver, Port Huron, Mich.
Mrs. Thomas Trayer, Kent, Ohio
Edward S. Treat, Burlington, Vt.
Percy J. Trevethan, Washington, D.C.
Francis W. Trimmer, Schenectady, N.Y.
J. H. L. Trout, Cleveland, Ohio
Ethel Troutman, Cleveland, Ohio
Lloyd B. Troutman, Ridgley, Mo.
*Thelma Tschabold, Akron, Ohio
Robert S. Tuck, Wooster, Ohio
Mrs. Henry H. Tucker, Little Rock, Ark.
Rex Tucker, Elyria, Ohio
D. W. Tull, Chester, Pa.
James E. Tull, Blacksburg, Va.
E. L. Tullis, Louisville, Ky.
Charles J. Turck, St. Paul, Minn.
*Herman L. Turner, Atlanta, Ga.
*J. J. Turner, Montgomery, W. Va.
*John C. Turner, Birmingham, Ala.
Harold W. Turpin, Hammond, Ind.
Morris Harrison Tynes, Staunton, Va.
George E. Ulp, Rochester, N.Y.
Mrs. Alvin Ulrich, Dearborn, Mich.
Thomas J. Updack, Fort Worth, Texas
*John C. Updegraff, Newark, Ohio
*William G. Upshaw, Davenport, Iowa
Ray S. Utterback, Painesville, Ohio
*Ralph E. Valantine, Huntington, W.Va.
J. J. Van Boskirk, Chicago, Ill.
Mrs. A. W. Van Dervort, Akron, Ohio
Reinhardt Van Dyke, Asbury Park, N.J.
*Marion Van Horne, New York, N.Y.
*Mrs. Roy Van Sant, Findlay, Ohio
*Mrs. P. J. Van Voorhis, Willoughby, Ohio
George Van Wingerden, Girard, Ohio
*Raymond M. Veh, Harrisburg, Pa.
*Mrs. Raymond M. Veh, Harrisburg, Pa.
S. C. Vernon, Cleveland, Ohio

197

Charles Vickrey, Scarsdale, N.Y.
Sidney R. Vincent, Columbia Station, Ohio
Mrs. J. Paul Visscher, Cleveland Heights, Ohio
Marideen Visscher, Kalamazoo, Mich.
John A. Visser, Detroit, Mich.
*Elmer Voelkel, Fort Wayne, Ind.
Guy H. Volpitto, Cleveland, Ohio
*Gertrude Von Riesen, London, Ohio
*Jerry Voorhis, Chicago, Ill.
*Mrs. Carl A. Voss, Pittsburgh, Pa.
Heber H. Votaw, Washington, D.C.
Mrs. George W. Wade, Oklahoma City, Okla.
Hazel Wade, Youngstown, Ohio
O. Walter Wagner, St. Louis, Mo.
Harvey E. Walden, Chicago, Ill.
Elsie K. Walenta, Cleveland, Ohio
Victor E. Walenta, Cleveland, Ohio
Mrs. Henry N. Walkden, Cleveland, Ohio
*Edgar A. Walker, Canton, Ohio
Gladys Walker, Cleveland, Ohio
J. C. Walker, Cleveland, Ohio
John C. Walker, Toledo, Ohio
Mrs. John C. Walker, Toledo, Ohio
*Charles B. Wall, Kenmore, N.Y.
Mrs. T. F. Wallace, Kansas City, Kansas
Judith Waller, Chicago, Ill.
Mrs. H. E. Walley, East Chicago, Ind.
*Karl F. Walter, Rocky River, Ohio
Bett V. Walton, Pittsburgh, Pa.
M. Louise Walworth, Newton Center, Mass.
*Mrs. W. J. Wanless, Glendale, Calif.
*Mrs. Charles C. Ward, South Bend, Ind.
Mrs. F. J. Warnecke, Newark, N.J.
*R. J. Warner, Xenia, Ohio
Hurley S. Warren, Plainfield, N.J.
Mrs. D. Washburn, Holyoke, Mass.
R. F. Washington, Detroit, Mich.
*Lovick P. Wasson, West Point, Miss.
*Mrs. John B. Waterman, Mobile, Ala.
Gerald Watkins, Rochester, N.Y.
*Sidney W. Watkins, Cleveland Heights, Ohio
*William H. Watson, Detroit, Mich.
A. C. Watters, Indianapolis, Ind.
*A. Alfred Watts, Chicago, Ill.
Mrs. Ernest W. Weaver, Toledo, Ohio
Galen R. Weaver, New York, N.Y.
Mrs. Galen R. Weaver, Scarsdale, N.Y.
Lance Webb, Dallas, Texas
Carlton N. Weber, Cleveland, Ohio
Mrs. Carlton N. Weber, Cleveland, Ohio
Clarissa E. Webster, Chicago, Ill.
Duane E. Webster, Worcester, Mass.

J. T. Weeden, Cleveland, Ohio
Russell M. Weer, Reading, Pa.
*C. A. Weesner, Indianapolis, Ind.
*A. H. Wegener, Edwardsport, Ind.
Mrs. Frank Weidman, Cleveland, Ohio
Mrs. Ralph S. Weiler, Lansdowne, Pa.
Mrs. R. T. Weills, Amarillo, Texas
Rosa Page Welch, Chicago, Ill.
Amy O. Welcher, Hartford, Conn.
Mrs. R. A. J. Wellington, Cleveland, Ohio
Mrs. H. J. Wells, Urbana, Ill.
Howard M. Wells, East Cleveland, Ohio
W. A. Welsh, Dallas, Texas
*L. E. Werner, Wilmington, Del.
*Mrs. David R. West, Minneapolis, Minn.
Donald F. West, Indianapolis, Ind.
Frank H. West, Evanston, Ill.
*George D. West, Nashville, Tenn.
Murray Guy West, Uniontown, Pa.
Samuel E. West, Wichita, Kansas
E. F. Westerberg, Bridgeport, Conn.
Mrs. Charles F. Weybright, Syracuse, Ind.
Francis C. Wheaton, Cleveland, Ohio
Chester A. Wheeler, Worcester, Mass.
*Guy R. Wheeler, Fairview Park, Ohio
Andrew White, Nashville, Tenn.
Robert J. White, Webster Groves, Mo.
Samuel White, Cleveland, Ohio
Mrs. Walter M. White, Nashville, Tenn.
Al Whitehouse, Cincinnati, Ohio
S. Lee Whiteman, Youngstown, Ohio
John S. Whiteneck, Bakersfield, Calif.
Mrs. H. R. Whiting, Cleveland, Ohio
B. Bruce Whittemore, Cincinnati, Ohio
*S. W. Wiant, Greenville, Ohio
*Mrs. S. W. Wiant, Greenville, Ohio
Norvell E. Wicker, Louisville, Ky.
Mrs. Norvell Wicker, Louisville, Ky.
Terry Wickham, Tiffin, Ohio
*Paul Wickman, Washington, D.C.
Raymond F. Wieder, Harrisburg, Pa.
E. G. Wiest, Cleveland, Ohio
Victor O. Wik, Des Moines, Iowa
*T. Winston Wilbanks, Denton, Texas
*Stewart L. Wile, Cleveland, Ohio
Carl H. Wilhelm, Chicago Heights, Ill.
William A. Wilkes, Cleveland, Ohio
Edith Wilkins, Cleveland, Ohio
*Harper S. Will, Chicago, Ill.
A. F. Williams, Cleveland Heights, Ohio
Benedict Williams, Sewickley, Pa.
C. Fred Williams, Arlington, Va.
E. C. Williams, Big Springs, Neb.
James F. Williams, Bay City, Mich.
*Mrs. John E. Williams, Western Springs, Ill.

198

John F. Williams, Newport News, Va.
*Morgan Williams, Kankakee, Ill.
*Ruth Williams, Cleveland, Ohio
Sudie H. Williams, Cleveland, Ohio
*Urban Williams, Pittsburgh, Pa.
W. B. Williams, Newport News, Va.
Mrs. W. B. Williams, Newport News, Va.
W. W. Williams, Roodhouse, Ill.
*Mrs. Zack A. Williamson, Beaumont, Texas
Edward B. Willingham, Washington, D.C.
Mrs. C. Leroy Wilson, Oakland, Calif.
Eugene T. Wilson, Atlanta, Ga.
*Mrs. Goodridge A. Wilson, Nashville, Tenn.
Janice M. Wilson, Cleveland, Ohio
*L. Elbert Wilson, Waynesboro, Pa.
*Moddie Wilson, Cleveland, Ohio
R. Norris Wilson, New York, N.Y.
*T. J. Wilson, Shadyside, Ohio
W. W. Wilson, North Royalton, Ohio
*J. Calvin Winder, Pittsburgh, Pa.
*Hayden B. Wingate, Flossmoor, Ill.
*Marshall Wingfield, Memphis, Tenn.
*Mrs. Harry Winsor, East Cleveland, Ohio
Mrs. F. J. Winter, San Antonio, Texas
*George W. Wise, Topeka, Kansas
*Howard B. Withers, Cleveland, Ohio
Frederic Witmer, Big Rapids, Mich.
Maurice E. Witmer, Portsmouth, N.H.
J. Louis Wolf, Lakewood, Ohio
*John D. Wolf, Martinsville, Ind.
Richard C. Wolf, New Haven, Conn.
*Charles Wolfe, Bay City, Mich.
Ray M. Wolford, Cleveland, Ohio
Mrs. Ray M. Wolford, Cleveland, Ohio
Louis R. Wolter, Toledo, Ohio

P. E. Womack, Austin, Texas
John A. Womeldorf, Princeton, W.Va.
*D. Finley Wood, Worthington, Ohio
W. D. Wood, Columbus, Ohio
*Mrs. R. F. Woodhull, Rockville Center, L.I., N.Y.
*Catherine T. Woods, Lewiston, Pa.
*Idalee Woodson, Peoria, Ill.
Groff L. Woodward, Cleveland, Ohio
*E. D. Worley, Morristown, Tenn.
William G. Worman, East Cleveland, Ohio
Ruth Mougey Worrell, Columbus, Ohio
Mrs. Paul Worthington, Englewood, Col.
*Matthew Worthman, Bluffton, Ind.
Donald G. Wright, Providence, R.I.
Helen Adeline Wright, Indianapolis, Ind.
Wallace M. Wright, Dayton, Ohio
Bige Wyatt, St. Louis, Mo.
Thomas Wylie, Kalamazoo, Mich.
*David J. Wynne, Pittsburgh, Pa.
*Allott W. Yadon, Arlington, Va.
Jobu Yasumura, New York, N.Y.
Mrs. W. S. K. Yeaple, Hillsboro, N.H.
Howard V. Yergin, New York, N.Y.
W. Ronald Yocom, Shillington, Pa.
Harvey O. Yoder, Lakewood, Ohio
Damon P. Young, Detroit, Mich.
J. Otis Young, Cincinnati, Ohio
Reuben Youngdahl, Minneapolis, Minn.
Robert N. Zearfoss, Buffalo, N.Y.
Albert A. Ziarko, Detroit, Mich.
Edward K. Ziegler, Bridgewater, Va.
William C. Zimmann, Dayton, Ohio
Donald E. Zimmerman, Dearborn, Mich.
Paul F. Zoschke, Cleveland, Ohio
*Howard C Zook, Wooster, Ohio
Charles R. Zweizig, Harrisburg, Pa.

SECTION VI

Executive Personnel of the National Council

THE RIGHT REVEREND HENRY KNOX SHERRILL
President, National Council of the Churches of Christ in the U.S.A.

MRS. DOUGLAS HORTON
Vice-President

MRS. ABBIE CLEMENT JACKSON
Vice-President

DR. M. E. SADLER
Vice-President

DR. HAROLD E. STASSEN
Vice-President

Biographical Data on Elected Officers

NATIONAL COUNCIL OF THE CHURCHES OF CHRIST IN THE UNITED STATES OF AMERICA

THE RIGHT REVEREND HENRY KNOX SHERRILL is the President of the National Council of the Churches of Christ in the United States of America. He is the Presiding Bishop of the Protestant Episcopal Church. Bishop Sherrill, who was consecrated Bishop in 1930, served as the ninth head of the diocese of Massachusetts until June 1947. He then became the twentieth presiding bishop of the Episcopal Church, one of the youngest men to hold that office. As Presiding Bishop, he is titular head of the Episcopal Church in the United States with its missionary work in many parts of the world. He serves as president of the church's National Council, the board of directors of the Domestic and Foreign Missionary Society. He served churches in Brookline and Boston, Mass., before becoming bishop. He was army chaplain during the First World War, and during the second World War, he was head of the Episcopal Church's Army and Navy Commission and later was chairman of the interdenominational General Commission on Army and Navy Chaplains. He has been a fellow of the corporation of Yale University since 1934 and is a trustee of Boston University, Masters School, General Theological Seminary, and the Groton School.

MRS. DOUGLAS HORTON is one of the Vice-Presidents of the National Council of the Churches of Christ in the United States of America. Mrs. Horton (then Mildred McAfee) was the first woman commissioned in the U. S. Navy and served as Commander of the Waves until 1946. During this time she was on leave of absence as President of Wellesley College, a position she held from 1936. She resigned in 1949 to join her husband, Dr. Douglas Horton, Minister and Secretary of the General Council of the Congregational Christian Churches. She is a member of the U. S. National Commission for UNESCO, a director of the New York Life Insurance Company, and a trustee of the New York Public Library. She was a vice-president of the Federal Council of the Churches of Christ in America (1948-1950), the first woman elected to office in the Federal Council.

MRS. ABBIE CLEMENT JACKSON is one of the Vice-Presidents of the National Council of the Churches of Christ in the United States of America. Mrs. Jackson is Executive Secretary of the Woman's Home and Foreign Missionary Society of the African Methodist Episcopal Zion Church since 1943. She has held this position since 1943. She was vice-president of the Home Missions Council in 1947-1948. She was recording secretary of the United Council of Church Women from 1948-1950, and a member of the national board for six years. She has been a member of the Board of Managers of the Missionary Education Movement of the United States and Canada and a member of the Committee on Reference and Counsel of the Foreign Missions Conference of North America. She is Vice-president of the Louisville Council of Churches.

DR. M. E. SADLER is one of the Vice-Presidents of the National Council of the Churches of Christ in the United States of America. Dr. Sadler is President of Texas Christian University and has held this position since 1941. He was formerly President of the International Convention of the Disciples of Christ. Previously he was also director of leadership training for the Disciples of Christ in Virginia and then for the nation. Successively he was Dean of Lynchburg College and minister of Central Christian Church, Austin, Texas. He has been active in the Y.M.C.A., American Red Cross, National Conference of Christians and Jews, and the Committee for Education on Alcoholism.

DR. HAROLD E. STASSEN is one of the Vice-Presidents of the National Council of the Churches of Christ in the United States of America. Dr. Stassen is President of the University of Pennsylvania. He has held this position since 1948. Previously he had been a candidate for the Republican nomination for the Presidency of the United States. He is former governor of Minnesota. During World War II, he was an officer in the United States Navy, serving on the staff of Admiral William Halsey in the Southwest Pacific. He has been an active Baptist layman and has been President of the International Council of Religious Education since 1942.

DR. ARTHUR S. FLEMMING is one of the Vice-Presidents of the National Council of the Churches of Christ in the United States of America. Dr. Flemming is President of Ohio Wesleyan University and has held his position since 1948. He is also Chairman of the Division of Christian Life and Work. Formerly he was a member of the U.S. Civil Service Commission, Director of the School of Public Affairs, a member of the editorial staff of the U.S. Daily (now U.S. News). During World War II, he held important posts in labor-management units of the Federal Government.

DR. CHARLES T. LEBER is one of the Vice-Presidents of the National Council of the Churches of Christ in the United States of America. Dr. Leber is General Secretary of the Board of Foreign Missions of the Presbyterian Church, U. S. A. He has been with the Board of Foreign Missions since 1936 serving in various administrative and promotional capacities. He has traveled extensively throughout Asia, the Near East, Africa, Latin America, and Europe. He has attended major world church and missionary meetings in recent years. Dr. Leber is a member of the General Council of the Presbyterian Church, U.S.A., and of the Department of International Justice and Goodwill of the Federal Council of Churches.

DR. HERMANN N. MORSE is one of the Vice-Presidents of the National Council of the Churches of Christ in the United States of America. He is also Chairman of the Division of Home Missions. Dr. Morse is General Secretary of the Board of Home Missions of the Presbyterian Church,

DR. ARTHUR S. FLEMMING
Vice-President

DR. CHARLES T. LEBER
Vice-President

DR. HERMANN N. MORSE
Vice-President

DR. PAUL CALVIN PAYNE
Vice-President

DR. REUBEN H. MUELLER
Recording Secretary

MR. CHARLES E. WILSON
Treasurer

MR. JAMES L. KRAFT
Associate Treasurer

Dr. Samuel McCrea Cavert
General Secretary

Dr. Roy G. Ross
Associate General Secretary

U.S.A. He has served as Secretary and Acting Chairman of the National Council's Planning Committee. He has been identified with the work of the Presbyterian national missions since 1912. In 1923 he became Secretary and Director of Budget and Research of the newly organized Board of National Missions. In 1930 he became Administrative Secretary and in 1949 General Secretary. He has been President of the Home Missions Council of North America and active on its committees.

Dr. Paul Calvin Payne is one of the Vice-Presidents of the National Council of the Churches of Christ in the United States of America. He is also Chairman of the division of Christian Education. Dr. Payne is General Secretary of the Board of Christian Education of the Presbyterian Church, U.S.A. He has held this position since 1939. He administers the nation-wide work in Christian Education among more than 2,500,000 persons affiliated with 8,600 Presbyterian churches and church schools. Previously he had been pastor of churches in New York, Oklahoma and Nebraska. He has been chairman of the International Council of Religious Education since 1948 and chairman of the Protestant Radio Commission.

Dr. Reuben H. Mueller is Recording Secretary of the National Council of the Churches of Christ in the United States of America. Dr. Mueller of Dayton, Ohio, is Executive Secretary of the Board of Christian Education of the Evangelical United Brethren Church. He served as General Secretary of Christian Education, Evangelical Church and also as General

Secretary of Evangelism, Evangelical Church from 1941-1946. Prior to this he was District Superintendent, Indiana Conference, Evangelical Church.

MR. CHARLES E. WILSON is Treasurer of the National Council of the Churches of Christ in the United States of America. Mr. Wilson is Chairman of the Defense Mobilization Board and former President of General Electric Company. He has been President of General Electric since 1940 and had served the company in other capacities for 40 years, having started with General Electric at 12 years of age. During World War II, he was chief of war production for the United States government. He then returned to General Electric as President. He has been active in many governmental and public organizations. He has been heading up the Religion in American Life campaign for the last two years.

MR. JAMES L. KRAFT is Associate Treasurer of the National Council of the Churches of Christ in the United States of America. Mr. Kraft is Chairman of the Board of Kraft-Phoenix Cheese Corp. Mr. Kraft has been in the cheese business since 1905, inventing the pasteurizing process as applied to the cheese industry. He organized a corporation in 1909, which is now the Kraft-Phoenix Cheese Corp. He was vice-president and for many years president. Mr. Kraft has been treasurer of the International Council of Religious Education since 1921. He was for many years a Sunday school superintendent in Chicago and active in the work of Baptist organizations.

DR. SAMUEL MCCREA CAVERT is the General Secretary of the National Council of the Churches of Christ in the United States of America. Dr. Cavert has been General Secretary of the Federal Council of the Churches of Christ in America since 1930. He joined the staff of the Federal Council in 1919 as Secretary of the Committee on the War and Religious Outlook. In 1921 he became one of two general secretaries, becoming the chief executive officer in 1930. He has been a delegate to many international church conferences and was active in setting up the World Council of Churches. He has served the U.S. Government as Protestant liaison officer in Germany, as a member of an Advisory Committee on Political Refugees, and on the U.S. Committee for the Care of European Children. He has been awarded honorary degrees by Lawrence College, Union College, Yale University, Ohio Wesleyan University and the University of Gottingen, in Germany.

DR. ROY G. ROSS is the Associate General Secretary of the National Council of the Churches of Christ in the United States of America. Dr. Ross has been General Secretary of the International Council of Religious Education since 1936. Prior to that, he was Executive Secretary for religious education of the Disciples of Christ and before that its director of youth work. He was pastor of churches in Illinois, Wisconsin, and Connecticut. His honorary doctor's degree was granted by Eureka (Ill.) College. He has built up the International Council from an organization of nine staff directors to 25, and a budget of $150,000 to more than $800,000.

MEMBERS OF THE GENERAL BOARD

By Denominational Appointments

AFRICAN METHODIST EPISCOPAL CHURCH

Rev. L. L. Berry, New York, N.Y.   Bishop D. Ward Nichols, New York, N.Y.
Bishop S. L. Greene, Atlanta, Georgia

AFRICAN METHODIST EPISCOPAL ZION CHURCH

Bishop Cameron C. Alleyne, Philadelphia, Bishop W. J. Walls, Chicago, Ill.
   Pa.

Alternates

Rev. James W. Eichelberger, Chicago, Ill. Rev. B. C. Robeson, New York, N.Y.

AMERICAN BAPTIST CONVENTION

Rev. George Pitt Beers, New York, N.Y.   Rev. Jesse R. Wilson, New York, N.Y.
Rev. Reuben E. Nelson, New York, N.Y.

Alternates

Rev. Joseph C. Hazen, Summit, N.J.   Rev. William B. Lipphard, New York,
                                              N.Y.

AUGUSTANA EVANGELICAL LUTHERAN CHURCH

Rev. P. O. Bersell, Minneapolis, Minn.

Alternate

Rev. Oscar A. Benson, Worcester, Mass.

CHURCH OF THE BRETHREN

Rev. Raymond R. Peters, Elgin, Ill.

COLORED METHODIST EPISCOPAL CHURCH

Bishop Bertram W. Doyle, Nashville, Tenn.   Rev. B. Julian Smith, Chicago, Ill.

CONGREGATIONAL CHRISTIAN CHURCHES

Mrs. William H. Medlicott, Boston, Mass.   Rev. Truman B. Douglass, New York,
Rev. Luther A. Weigle, New Haven, Conn.   N.Y.

EVANGELICAL UNITY OF THE CZECH-MORAVIAN BRETHREN CHURCH

Mr. Josef A. Barton, Bellville, Texas

DANISH EVANGELICAL LUTHERAN CHURCH OF AMERICA

Rev. Alfred Jensen, Des Moines, Iowa

INTERNATIONAL CONVENTION OF DISCIPLES OF CHRIST

Rev. Hampton Adams, St. Louis, Mo.
Rev. Gaines M. Cook, Indianapolis, Ind.
Rev. Hugh D. Darsie, Brooklyn, N.Y.

Pres. Riley B. Montgomery, Lexington, Ky.
Rev. Virgil A. Sly, Indianapolis, Ind.

EVANGELICAL AND REFORMED CHURCH

Rev. L. W. Goebel, Chicago 2, Ill.

Rev. James E. Wagner, Lancaster, Pa.

EVANGELICAL UNITED BRETHREN CHURCH

Bishop D. T. Gregory, Pittsburgh, Pa.

Bishop C. H. Stauffacher, Kansas City, Mo.

RELIGIOUS SOCIETY OF FRIENDS (FIVE YEARS MEETING)

Mr. Errol T. Elliott, Richmond, Ind.

RELIGIOUS SOCIETY OF FRIENDS OF PHILADELPHIA & VICINITY

Miss Anna C. Brinton, Pendle Hill, Wallingford, Pa.

THE METHODIST CHURCH

Rev. Leon M. Adkins, Syracuse, N.Y.
Bishop James C. Baker, Los Angeles, Calif.
Mrs. Frank G. Brooks, Mt. Vernon, Iowa
Rev. Earl R. Brown, New York, N.Y.
Dr. David D. Jones, Greensboro, N.C.
Bishop Arthur J. Moore, Atlanta, Ga.
Pres. J. Earl Moreland, Ashland, Va.
Mr. Ray H. Nichols, Vernon, Texas
Bishop G. Bromley Oxnam, New York, N.Y.

Rev. Theodore H. Palmquist, Los Angeles, Calif.
Mr. Charles C. Parlin, New York, N.Y.
Rev. William F. Quillian, Atlanta, Ga.
Bishop Marshall R. Reed, Detroit, Mich.
Rev. John Q. Schisler, Nashville, Tenn.
Bishop Alexander P. Shaw, Baltimore, Md.
Rev. Eugene L. Smith, New York, N.Y.
Bishop W. Angie Smith, Oklahoma City, Okla.
Rev. Paul D. Womeldorf, Oklahoma City, Okla.

MORAVIAN CHURCH IN AMERICA

Rev. F. P. Stocker, Bethlehem, Pa.

Alternate

Rev. R. Gordon Spaugh, Winston-Salem, N.C.

NATIONAL BAPTIST CONVENTION OF AMERICA

Rev. Henry A. Boyd, Nashville, Tenn.
Rev. J. N. Byrd, San Antonio, Texas
Rev. C. D. Pettiway, Little Rock, Ark.

Rev. G. L. Prince, Crocket, Texas
Rev. P. S. Wilkinson, San Antonio, Texas
Rev. John W. Williams, Kansas City, Mo.

NATIONAL BAPTIST CONVENTION, U.S.A., INC.

Miss Nannie H. Burroughs, Washington, D.C.
Mr. George A. Crawley, Sr., Baltimore, Md.
Mr. James E. Gale, New Orleans, La.
Rev. E. L. Harrison, Washington, D.C.

Rev. J. L. Horace, Chicago, Ill.
Rev. W. H. Jernagin, Washington, D.C.
Pres. Benjamin Mays, Atlanta, Ga.
Rev. U. J. Robinson, Mobile, Ala.
Rev. I. A. Thomas, Evanston, Ill.

PRESBYTERIAN CHURCH IN THE UNITED STATES

Rev. John M. Alexander, Atlanta, Ga.

Rev. J. McDowell Richards, Decatur, Ga.

PRESBYTERIAN CHURCH IN THE U.S.A.

Rev. Ganse Little, Columbus, Ohio
Mrs. Paul Moser, Jackson Heights, N.Y.

Rev. Harold E. Nicely, Rochester, N.Y.
Mr. J. Howard Pew, Philadelphia, Pa.

Alternates

Mr. Stewart Cort, Bethlehem, Pa.
Mrs. John M. Irvine, Wexford, Pa.
Pres. Ralph Waldo Lloyd, Maryville, Tenn.

Pres. John A. Mackay, Princeton, N.J.
Rev. Paul A. Wolfe, New York, N.Y.

PROTESTANT EPISCOPAL CHURCH

Rev. John S. Higgins, Providence, R.I.
Mr. Thomas B. K. Ringe, Philadelphia, Pa.

The Rt. Rev. Frank W. Sterrett, Bethlehem, Pa.
The Rt. Rev. Harwood Sturtevant, Fond du Lac, Wis.

REFORMED CHURCH IN AMERICA

Rev. Bernard J. Mulder, New York, N.Y

ROUMANIAN ORTHODOX CHURCH

Rev. John Trutza, Cleveland, Ohio

RUSSIAN ORTHODOX CHURCH

Mr. Ralph Montgomery Arkush, New York, N.Y.

SEVENTH DAY BAPTISTS

Rev. Elmo F. Randolph, Milton, Wis.

SYRIAN ANTIOCHIAN ORTHODOX CHURCH

Archbishop Antony Bashir, Brooklyn, N.Y.

UKRAINIAN ORTHODOX CHURCH OF AMERICA
Bishop Bohdan, New York, N.Y.

Alternate

Very Rev. Walter M. Propheta, South Plainfield, N.J.

UNITED LUTHERAN CHURCH IN AMERICA

Rev. Franklin Clark Fry, New York, N.Y.   Dr. H. Torrey Walker, Philadelphia, Pa.
Rev. E. Eppling Reinartz, New York, N.Y.

UNITED PRESBYTERIAN CHURCH OF NORTH AMERICA
Rev. James M. Guthrie, Floral Park, N.Y.

Alternate

Rev. James R. Lee, Bellerose, N.Y.

Representatives of the Cooperative Work of the Churches in States, Cities and Counties

Miss Gertrude Apel, METHODIST, Seattle, Wash.
Rev. J. B. Bouwman, AMERICAN BAPTIST, Lansing, Mich.
Rev. John W. Harms, DISCIPLES OF CHRIST, Chicago, Ill.
Rev. Frank Jennings, AMERICAN BAPTIST, Boston, Mass.
Mrs. William Sale Terrell, AMERICAN BAPTIST, West Hartford, Conn.
Rev. O. M. Walton, METHODIST, Pittsburgh, Pa.

Representatives of the Divisions

DIVISION OF FOREIGN MISSIONS

Mrs. Leslie E. Swain, AMERICAN BAPTIST, Craigville, Mass.
Mr. M. P. Moller, Jr., UNITED LUTHERAN CHURCH IN AMERICA, Hagerstown, Md.
Mr. James A. Gray, Schenectady, N.Y.

DIVISION OF HOME MISSIONS

Mr. A. H. Lofgren, AMERICAN BAPTIST, Troy, N. Y.
Mrs. Norman Vincent Peale, REFORMED IN AMERICA, New York, N. Y.

DIVISION OF CHRISTIAN LIFE AND WORK

Mrs. John M. Irvine, PRESBYTERIAN U.S.A., Wexford, Pa.
Mr. Charles P. Taft, PROTESTANT EPISCOPAL, Cincinnati, Ohio
Mr. Irwin Trotter, METHODIST, New Haven, Conn.

DIVISION OF CHRISTIAN EDUCATION

Mr. William Barrick, METHODIST, Evanston, Ill.
Dr. Edward D. Grant, PRESBYTERIAN U. S., Richmond, Va.
Mrs. Clifford Heinz, PRESBYTERIAN U.S.A., Pittsburgh, Pa.

Officers

President
Rt. Rev. Henry Knox Sherrill, PROTESTANT EPISCOPAL, New York, N. Y.

Vice-Presidents
Mrs. Douglas Horton, CONGREGATIONAL CHRISTIAN, New York, N.Y.
Mrs. Abbie Clement Jackson, A.M.E. ZION, Louisville, Ky.
Rev. Magruder E. Sadler, DISCIPLES OF CHRIST, Fort Worth, Texas
Pres. Harold E. Stassen, AMERICAN BAPTIST, Philadelphia, Pa.

Vice Presidents as Chairmen of Divisions
Pres. Arthur S. Flemming, METHODIST, Delaware, Ohio, *Division of Christian Life and Work*
Rev. Charles T. Leber, PRESBYTERIAN U.S.A., New York, N. Y., *Division of Foreign Missions*
Rev. Hermann N. Morse, PRESBYTERIAN U.S.A., New York, N. Y., *Division of Home Missions*
Rev. Paul C. Payne, PRESBYTERIAN U.S.A., Philadelphia, Pa., *Division of Christian Education*

Treasurer
Mr. Charles E. Wilson, AMERICAN BAPTIST, Washington, D. C.

Associate Treasurer
Mr. James L. Kraft, AMERICAN BAPTIST, Wilmette, Ill.

Recording Secretary
Rev. Reuben H. Mueller, EVANGELICAL UNITED BRETHREN, Dayton, Ohio

Chairmen of General Departments, Joint Departments, Central Departments and Commissions

General Department of United Church Women
Mrs. James D. Wyker, DISCIPLES OF CHRIST, Mt. Vernon, Ohio

General Department of United Church Men
Mr. Lem T. Jones, PRESBYTERIAN U.S.A., Kansas City, Mo.

Joint Department of American Overseas Communities
Bishop Ivan Lee Holt, METHODIST, St. Louis, Mo.

Joint Department of Evangelism
Prof. E. G. Homrighausen, PRESBYTERIAN U.S.A., Princeton, N. J.

Joint Department of Religious Liberty
Rt. Rev. Malcolm E. Peabody, PROTESTANT EPISCOPAL, Syracuse, N. Y.

Joint Department of Stewardship
Pres. Clarence C. Stoughton, UNITED LUTHERAN, Springfield, Ohio

Joint Department of Family Life
Rev. Joseph John Hanson, AMERICAN BAPTIST, Philadelphia, Pa.

Joint Department of Christian Vocation
Pres. Dale H. Moore, EVANGELICAL AND REFORMED, Allentown, Pa.

Commission on General Education
Rev. Harry T. Stock, CONGREGATIONAL CHRISTIAN, Boston, Mass.

Commission on Christian Higher Education
Rev. John O. Gross, METHODIST, Nashville, Tenn.

Joint Commission on Missionary Education
Dr. C. P. Hargraves, METHODIST, Nashville, Tenn.

Central Department of Field Administration
Rev. Hugh Chamberlin Burr, AMERICAN BAPTIST, Rochester, N. Y.

Central Department of Publication and Distribution
Mr. W. L. Jenkins, PRESBYTERIAN U.S.A., Philadelphia, Pa.

Central Department of Finance
Rev. Luther Wesley Smith, AMERICAN BAPTIST, Philadelphia, Pa.

NATIONAL COUNCIL OF THE CHURCHES OF CHRIST
IN THE UNITED STATES OF AMERICA

EXECUTIVE PERSONNEL

(Addresses given are for office headquarters. Where individual staff member is listed at Midwest office the address is 79 East Adams Street, Chicago 3, Ill. The list as given below includes all who were elected by the General Assembly and the General Board.)

GENERAL ADMINISTRATION

Samuel McCrea Cavert, *General Secretary*, 297 Fourth Ave., New York 10, N. Y.
Roy G. Ross, *Associate General Secretary*, 297 Fourth Ave., New York 10, N.Y.
Earl F. Adams, *Administrative Secretary*, 297 Fourth Ave., New York 10, N. Y.
Philip C. Landers, *Administrative Secretary*, 79 E. Adams St., Chicago 3, Ill.
J. Quinter Miller, *Administrative Secretary*, 297 Fourth Ave., New York 10, N. Y.
Wilbur C. Parry, (one-third time) *Associate Administrative Secretary*, 79 East Adams St., Chicago 3, Ill.
Mrs. B. Margaret Rieber, *Assistant to the General Secretary*, 297 Fourth Ave., New York 10, N.Y.

DIVISION OF FOREIGN MISSIONS,
156 Fifth Ave., New York 10, N. Y.

Sue Weddell, *Executive Secretary (for General Administration)*
Fred Field Goodsell, *Executive Secretary (for General Administration)*
Rowland M. Cross, *Executive Secretary of Far Eastern Joint Office*
Rev. Wallace C. Merwin, *Associate Secretary of Far Eastern Joint Office*
Emory Ross, *Executive Secretary of Africa Committee*
Clara L. Bentley, *Associate Secretary of Africa Committee*
A. Russell Stevenson, *Executive Secretary of Western Asia and Near East Joint Office*
Douglas H. Forman, *Executive Secretary of Christian Medical Council for Overseas Work*
J. Horton Daniels, *Director of Associated Missions Medical Office*
Frank S. Beck, *Staff Physician of Associated Missions Medical Office*
Josephine C. Lawney, *Staff Physician of Associated Missions Medical Office*
Eve J. Weddigen, *Staff Physician, Associated Missions Medical Office*
John H. Reisner, *Executive Secretary of Rural Missions Cooperating Committee*
Ira W. Moomaw, *Educational Secretary of Rural Missions Cooperating Committee*
Alfred D. Moore, *Executive Secretary of Committee on World Literacy and Christian Literature*
Arnold Vaught, *Executive Secretary of Committee on Relief and Reconstruction Services*
Helen M. Eklund, *Associate Secretary of Committee on Cooperation in Latin America*
Alberto Rembao, *Editor of* LA NUEVA DEMOCRACIA, *Committee on Cooperation in Latin America*

DIVISION OF HOME MISSIONS
297 Fourth Avenue, New York 10, N. Y.

Edith E. Lowry, *Executive Secretary*
I. George Nace, *Executive Secretary*

Louisa R. Shotwell, *Associate Secretary*
Benson Y. Landis, (half-time) *Secretary of Department of Town and Country*
Don F. Pielstick (half-time) *Secretary of Department of Town and Country*
Rev. William J. Villaume, *Secretary of Department of the Urban Church*
Mrs. F. E. Shotwell, *Western Supervisor for Migrant Work*
Ellis Marshburn, *Midwestern Supervisor for Migrant Work*
Merle Gripman, *Assistant Treasurer*
Rev. G. E. E. Lindquist, *Field Representative of Indian Work*
Rev. Harry V. Richardson (part-time) *Director of Sharecropper Committee*

DIVISION OF CHRISTIAN LIFE AND WORK
297 Fourth Avenue, New York 10, N. Y.

Roswell P. Barnes, *Executive Secretary*
C. Arild Olsen, *Associate Executive Secretary*
Walter W. Van Kirk, *Executive Director of Department of International Justice and Goodwill*
Cameron P. Hall, *Executive Director of Department of the Church and Economic Life*
A. Dudley Ward, *Director of Studies of Department of Church and Economic Life*
Elma Greenwood, *Assistant Executive Director of Department of the Church and Economic Life*
J. Oscar Lee, *Executive Director of Department of Racial and Cultural Relations*
Thomas C. Allen, *Director of Department of Racial and Cultural Relations*
Otis R. Rice (part-time) *Executive Director of Department of Pastoral Services*
Paul L. Tilden, *Associate Director of Department of Pastoral Services*
Beverley M. Boyd, *Executive Director of Department of Social Welfare*
Deane Edwards, *Executive Director of Commission on Worship*

JOINT DEPARTMENTS (*Administratively Related to Division of Christian Life and Work*)

Joint Department of Evangelism, 297 Fourth Ave., New York 10, N. Y.

Jesse M. Bader, *Executive Director*
H. H. McConnell, *Field Secretary*
Harry H. Kalas, *Director of Educational Evangelism* (Midwest office)
James L. Stoner, *Director of University Christian Missions*
Edward Gebhard, *Assistant Director of Educational Evangelism* (Midwest office)

Joint Department of Stewardship and Benevolence

Rev. Thomas K. Thompson, *Executive Director*

Joint Department of Religious Liberty, 297 Fourth Ave., New York 10, N. Y.

Armond D. Willis, *Executive Director*

DIVISION OF CHRISTIAN EDUCATION
79 East Adams Street, Chicago 3, Illinois

Central Administration and Operations

Roy G. Ross (half-time) *Executive Secretary*
Wilbur C. Parry (two-thirds time) *Associate Executive Secretary*
H. Leroy Brininger, *Director of Educational Promotion*
Mrs. Orville Smith, *Administrative Assistant*
Helen F. Kindt (one-third time) *Business Assistant*
Virgil Foster, *Editor of* INTERNATIONAL JOURNAL OF RELIGIOUS EDUCATION
Lillian Williams, *Managing Editor of* INTERNATIONAL JOURNAL OF RELIGIOUS EDUCATION

Commission on General Christian Education

Gerald E. Knoff, *General Director of Commission and Associate Executive Secretary of Division*

Alice L. Goddard, *Executive Director of Department of Children's Work and Vacation Religious Education*

Ruth Elizabeth Murphy, *Associate Executive Director of Department of Children's Work and Vacation Religious Education*

A. Wilson Cheek, *Executive Director of Department of Young People's Work*

Dennis Savage, *Associate Executive Director of Department of Young People's Work*

Richard E. Lentz (half-time), *Executive Director of Department of Adult Work*

Lee J. Gable, *Executive Director of Department of Leadership Education and Department of Church School Administration*

Paul King, *Associate Executive Director of Department of Leadership Education and Department of Church School Administration*

Mildred A. Magnuson, *Executive Director of Department of Curriculum Development*

Erwin L. Shaver, *Executive Director of Department of Weekday Religious Education*

John C. Trever, *Executive Director of Department of the English Bible*

Pearl Rosser, *Executive Director of Department of Audio-Visual and Radio Education*

Rev. Elmer Million, *Associate Executive Director of Department of Audio-Visual and Radio Education*

Rev. H. Leroy Brininger, *Director of Educational Promotion*

Helen F. Spaulding (one-third time), *Associate Executive Director of Department of Educational Program*

Luther A. Weigle, *Executive Chairman of Standard Bible Committee*

Fleming James, *Executive Secretary of Old Testament Section of Standard Bible Committee*

Commission on Christian Higher Education

Dr. E. Fay Campbell (part-time), *General Director of Commission and Associate Executive Secretary of Division*

Arch Tolbert, *Executive Director of Interseminary Committee*

JOINT COMMISSION AND JOINT DEPARTMENTS *(Administratively Related to Division of Christian Education)*

Joint Commission on Missionary Education, 156 Fifth Avenue, New York 10, N. Y.

Franklin D. Cogswell, *General Director of Joint Commission and Associate Executive Secretary of Division*

Gilbert Q. LeSourd, *Associate Director*

T. H. P. Sailer, *Honorary Secretary*

Nina Millen, *Director and Editor of Department of Children's Work*

Lucy M. Eldredge, *Director and Editor of Department of Youth Work*

Leslie C. Sayre, *Director and Editor of Department of Adult Work and Assistant Treasurer*

Hazel V. Orton, *Director of Production and Acting Director of Sales and Promotion*

Priscilla Chase, *Director of Order Department*

Joint Department of Family Life, 79 East Adams Street, Chicago 3, Illinois

Richard E. Lentz (half-time), *Executive Director*

GENERAL DEPARTMENT OF UNITED CHURCH WOMEN
156 Fifth Avenue, New York 10, N. Y.

Mrs. W. Murdoch MacLeod, *General Director*

Miss Edith L. Groner, *Associate General Director*

Miss Esther C. Stamats, *Director Christian Social Relations*

211

Miss Luella Reckmeyer, *Director of Christian World Relations*
Mrs. Emory Ross, *Director of Promotion and Education*
Mrs. James M. Evans, *Director of World Missions of the Church*
Mrs. Abram LeGrand (half-time), *Editor,* THE CHURCH WOMAN

CENTRAL DEPARTMENTS

Broadcasting and Films, 220 Fifth Ave., N. Y. 1, N. Y.

Ronald Bridges, *Executive Director*
Everett C. Parker, *Director of Program*
Albert Crews, *Director of Broadcasting and Television*
Arthur B. Rhinow, *Business Manager and Assistant Treasurer*
Wesley Goodman, *Director of Special Program*
Rev. Charles Schmitz, *Educational Director*
Mr. Arthur Austin, *Director of Special Events*

Field Administration, 297 Fourth Ave., New York 10, N. Y.

J. Quinter Miller, *Executive Director*
John B. Ketcham, *Associate Executive Director* (Midwest office)
George D. Kelsey, *Associate Executive Director*
Don F. Pielstick (half-time), *Director of Church Planning and Adjustment*
(to be filled), *Director of Field Program Coordination and Counseling*
Dr. Ernest J. Arnold, *Director of Southeastern Office*
Miss Theresa Capell, *Assistant to Executive Director*
Harry C. Munro (part-time), *Director of Southwestern Office*

Business and Treasury, 297 Fourth Ave., N. Y. 10, N. Y.

Earl F. Adams, *Acting Executive Director*
Mr. John K. Petersen, *Assistant Treasurer*
Helen F. Kindt (two-thirds time), *Associate Personnel and Office Manager* (Midwest
office)
Everett Crum (half-time), *Associate Director* (Midwest office)

Finance, 297 Fourth Ave., N. Y. 10, N. Y.

Richard B. Smith, *Executive Director*
Miss Josephine Little, *Associate Director*
Rev. Donald F. Landwer, *Director of Mid-west Office*
Clark L. Snyder, *Associate Director of Mid-west Office*
Mrs. Myra Amerman, *Assistant to the Executive Director*
Miss Edith Groner (one-quarter time), *Staff Member*

Research and Survey, 297 Fourth Ave., New York 10, N. Y.

F. Ernest Johnson, *Executive Director*
Benson Y. Landis (half-time), *Associate Executive Director*
David Barry, *Director of Field Research*
Helen F. Spaulding (two-thirds time), *Director of Research in Christian Education*
(Midwest office)
R. Pierce Beaver (half-time), *Director of Research in Foreign Missions*
Inez M. Cavert, *Research Associate*
Agnes Campbell, *Librarian*
Marion Nelson, *Assistant to the Executive Director*

Public Relations, 297 Fourth Avenue, New York 10, N. Y.

Donald C. Bolles, *Executive Director*
Lemuel Petersen, *Associate Director* (Midwest office)

212

William W. Clemes, *Associate Director*
Aenid A. Sanborn, *Associate Editor of* NATIONAL COUNCIL OUTLOOK
Beata Mueller, *Editorial Assistant*

Publication and Distribution, 297 Fourth Avenue, New York 10, N. Y.

Norman E. Tompkins, *Executive Director*
Donald F. Heldt, *Production Manager*
George Franklin Ketcham, *Assistant to the Executive Director*
Mrs. Elizabeth Dunn, *Administrative Assistant*
Everett Crum (half-time), *Director of Mid-west Office*

Ecumenical Relations, 297 Fourth Avenue, New York 10, N. Y.

Robbins W. Barstow, *Executive Director*

Church World Service, 350 Broadway, New York 13, N. Y.

Wynn C. Fairfield, *Executive Director*
Wayland Zwayer, *Assistant Executive Director*
Stanley I. Stuber, *Director of Information and Promotion*

Church Building and Architecture, 300 Fourth Avenue, New York 10, N. Y.

Elbert M. Conover, *Executive Director*

Washington Office, 122 Maryland Avenue, N.E., Washington, D. C.

Miss Nadine Blair, *Assistant Director*

SECTION VII

For the Record

The Official Minutes

NATIONAL COUNCIL OF THE CHURCHES OF CHRIST IN THE UNITED STATES OF AMERICA

in Convention assembled at Cleveland, Ohio

OPENING SESSION

Tuesday, November 28, 1950—8:00 p.m.

Cleveland Public Auditorium

THE OPENING SERVICE of worship and thanksgiving of the Constituting Convention of the National Council of the Churches of Christ in the United States of America was held in the Arena of the Cleveland Public Auditorium at 8:00 o'clock on the evening of November 28, 1950.

After the organ prelude, Dr. P. O. Bersell, President of the Augustana Lutheran Church, called the Convention to worship.

The congregation sang the hymn, "Praise to the Lord," led by Mrs. Rosa Page Welch, Convention song leader.

The responsive reading, "Act of Adoration" was led by Rt. Rev. Frank W. Sterrett, Bishop of the Protestant Episcopal Church.

Bishop John A. Gregg, Senior Bishop of the African Methodist Episcopal Church led the congregation in prayer. This was followed by the singing of the anthem "Praise We the Lord" by the Epworth-Euclid Methodist Church Choir under the direction of Mr. Elwin Haskin.

Dr. P. O. Bersell led the congregation in prayers of thanksgiving after which the choir sang the Doxology.

The scripture, Ephesians 4:1-7, 11-16, was read by President Benjamin R. Lacy, Jr., Moderator of the General Assembly of the Presbyterian Church in the United States.

The choir then sang the anthem, "God is a Spirit."

Reverend Ralph W. Sockman, minister of Christ Church (Methodist), New York, New York, preached the sermon.

The anthem, "Blessed be Thou, Lord God of Israel" was sung by the choir. Dr. Henry A. Vruwink, President of the General Synod of the Reformed Church in America then led the congregation in prayers of

217

intercession. The service closed with the singing of the hymn "All hail the power of Jesus' name!" and Dr. Ralph W. Sockman pronounced the benediction.

PLENARY BUSINESS SESSION OF THE GENERAL ASSEMBLY

Wednesday, November 29, 1950

Cleveland Public Auditorium

THE FIRST plenary business session of the General Assembly of the National Council of the Churches of Christ in the United States of America was called to order by Dr. Franklin Clark Fry, President of the United Lutheran Church in America who had been requested by the Planning Committee to preside at this session.

The Convention was led in a brief devotional service by Bishop John S. Stamm, of the Evangelical United Brethren Church.

Dr. Fry then introduced Dr. Hermann N. Morse as the Acting Chairman of the Planning Committee, who had been selected to serve in this capacity owing to the illness of Dr. Luther A. Weigle, the Chairman of the Committee.

CALL FOR THE CONVENTION Doc. Rec. A-101   Dr. Morse then read the Call for the holding of the Constituting Convention as prepared and sent out by the Planning Committee.

When the Planning Committee was constituted, it was authorized, among other things, "to arrange for and conduct a Constituting Convention." On the basis of this authorization, the Planning Committee has assumed responsibility for making arrangements in advance with regard to such matters as presiding officers, recording secretary, accreditation of voting representatives and other procedural matters. However, in order to regularize these advance arrangements, it is recommended that the General Assembly take the following actions:

1. To appoint those persons selected by the Program Committee as the presiding officers for the various sessions of the Constituting Convention;

2. To appoint Earl Frederick Adams, Executive Secretary of the Planning Committee, as Recording Secretary for the Constituting Convention and to authorize him to appoint such assistants as are necessary in order to keep an accurate record of business transactions and program items at the various sessions;

218

3. To approve as voting representatives for the Constituting Convention those accredited by the Committee on Registration and Credentials of the Planning Committee as having been duly appointed in accordance with the provisions of the proposed Constitution.

Following this statement, it was:

A-50-101   VOTED to approve the foregoing recommendations of the Planning Committee.

ACT OF   Dr. Fry, as the presiding officer, then led the
CONSTITUTING   Convention in a formal service wherein the National Council of the Churches of Christ in the United States of America was officially constituted and dedicated "to the glory of God and to the service of mankind."

Doc. Rec. 101A   The official text of this special service is made a Document of Record. The service included hymns, prayers, a roll call of the delegations, the signing of official documents by the representatives chosen by each communion, the presentation of documents by the representatives of the uniting agencies, a dedicatory prayer by a representative of state and city councils of churches and a benediction.

Those who signed the official book as representing the twenty-nine participating communions were as follows:

BISHOP S. L. GREENE—*African Methodist Episcopal*
BISHOP W. J. WALLS—*African Methodist Episcopal Zion*
DR. F. H. PRUDEN—*American Baptist Convention*
DR. P. O. BERSELL—*Augustana Evangelical Lutheran*
DR. DESMOND W. BITTINGER—*Church of the Brethren*
BISHOP BERTRUM W. DOYLE—*Colored Methodist Episcopal*
DR. VERE V. LOPER—*Congregational Christian*
REV. ALFRED JENSEN—*Danish Evangelical Lutheran Church of America*
DR. MARVIN O. SANSBURY—*Disciples of Christ*
DR. L. W. GOEBEL—*Evangelical and Reformed*
BISHOP IRA D. WARNER—*Evangelical United Brethren*
REV. JOSEF A. BARTON—*Czech Moravian*
ERROL T. ELLIOTT—*Five Years Meeting of Friends in America*
ANNA C. BRINTON—*Religious Society of Friends of Philadelphia and Vicinity*
BISHOP J. RALPH MAGEE—*Methodist*
DR. F. P. STOCKER—*Moravian Church in America—Northern Province*
DR. W. H. JERNAGIN—*National Baptist Convention USA, Inc.*
DR. HENRY A. BOYD—*National Baptist Convention of America*
DR. BEN R. LACY, JR.—*Presbyterian Church in the U.S.*
DR. HUGH IVAN EVANS—*Presbyterian Church in the USA*

219

RT. REV. HENRY KNOX SHERRILL—*Protestant Episcopal*
DR. HENRY A. VRUWINK—*Reformed Church in America*
REV. JOHN TRUTZA—*Roumanian Orthodox Church*
REV. NICHOLAS VANSUCH—*Russian Orthodox Church*
REV. ELMO F. RANDOLPH—*Seventh Day Baptists*
REV. JAMES C. MEENA—*Syrian Antiochian Orthodox Church*
REV. PETER KIELUCH—*Ukrainian Orthodox Church*
DR. F. EPPLING REINARTZ—*United Lutheran Church in America*
DR. J. LOWRIE ANDERSON—*United Presbyterian Church of N. A.*

Those who presented documents on behalf of the uniting agencies were as follows:

BISHOP JOHN S. STAMM—*The Federal Council of the Churches of Christ in America*
MRS. HUGH D. TAYLOR—*Foreign Missions Conference of North America*
DR. TRUMAN B. DOUGLASS—*Home Missions Council of North America, Inc.*
DR. PAUL C. PAYNE—*The International Council of Religious Education*
DR. KENNETH J. BEATON—*Missionary Education Movement of U.S. and Canada*
DR. BERNARD J. MULDER—*National Protestant Council on Higher Education*
MRS. HARPER SIBLEY—*United Council of Church Women*
DR. PAUL H. CONRAD—*United Stewardship Council of the Churches of Christ in the United States and Canada*

The prayer of dedication was led by Dr. Hugh C. Burr of the Rochester Federation of Churches. The Council was declared to be officially constituted by Dr. Fry as the Presiding Officer at this session.

On recommendation of Dr. Morse, it was

A-50-102   VOTED that Dr. Luther Weigle who has served for nine years as Chairman of the Planning Committee and its predecessor committees be elected as the Honorary Chairman for all sessions of the Constituting Convention and that the General Assembly record its deep appreciation for the far-reaching and significant service which he has rendered as Chairman of the Planning Committee and that the General Assembly also record its very sincere regret that, owing to illness, it was not possible for Dr. Weigle to be present at the Constituting Convention.

Dr. Morse then spoke of the splendid spirit of cooperation which has prevailed in all meetings of the Planning Committee and on his recommendation, it was also

A-50-103   VOTED that the General Assembly express and record its appreciation of and gratitude for the services rendered by the members of the Planning Committee in preparation for the Constituting Convention with special appreciation for the services rendered by the Executive staff of the Planning Committee and those staff executives of the uniting agencies who have carried special responsibilities in connection with the work of the Planning Committee.

On recommendation of the Planning Committee, it was

A-50-104   VOTED to adopt the program as recommended by the Committee on Program and Procedures subject to such changes as may be made on recommendation of the Committee itself or on recommendation of the Business Committee of the Convention.

On recommendation of the Planning Committee, it was

A-50-105   VOTED to appoint the following Committees to serve during the period of the Constituting Convention:

CONVENTION COMMITTEES

BUSINESS COMMITTEE

Dr. Hermann N. Morse, *Chairman*

Mr. Ralph Arkush	Dr. Glenn P. Reed
Dr. Arthur S. Flemming	Dr. Marvin O. Sansbury
Dr. Franklin Clark Fry	Dr. Luther Wesley Smith
Dr. Louis W. Goebel	Dr. Harold E. Stassen
Bishop G. Bromley Oxnam	Mr. Charles P. Taft
Mrs. Norman Vincent Peale	Bishop W. J. Walls

REGISTRATION AND CREDENTIALS

Dr. James E. Hoffman, *Chairman*

Dr. L. L. Huffman	Dr. Elmo F. Randolph
Dr. W. H. Jernagin	Mrs. Harper Sibley

RESOLUTIONS OF COURTESY

Dr. P. O. Bersell, *Chairman*

Mrs. Frank G. Brooks	Dr. Benjamin Lacy
Dr. Errol T. Elliott	Dr. Howard Taylor
Mr. Lem T. Jones	Mrs. William S. Terrell

COMMITTEE ON MESSAGE

(One member from each member-communion)

Dr. Douglas Horton, *Chairman*
(*Congregational Christian*)

Mrs. Sadie Alexander (*A. M. E. Church*)
A. Ward Applegate (*Friends—Five Years Meeting*)

221

Dr. Josef Barton (*Czech Moravian Brethren*)
President Conrad Bergendoff (*Augustana Lutheran*)
Dr. Henry A. Boyd (*National Baptist Convention of America*)
Miss Anna Brinton (*Friends—Philadelphia and Vicinity*)
Miss Nannie H. Burroughs (*National Baptist Convention USA*)
President Rufus E. Clement (*A.M.E. Zion*)
Bishop Fred P. Corson (*Methodist*)
Mrs. John A. Dykstra (*Reformed Church in America*)
President Calvert N. Ellis (*Church of the Brethren*)
Dr. Edward D. Grant (*Presbyterian U. S.*)
Rev. John S. Groenfeldt (*Moravian*)
Rev. Peter Kieluch (*Ukrainian Orthodox*)
Rev. Johannes Knudsen (*Danish Lutheran*)
Dr. Charles T. Leber (*Presbyterian U.S.A.*)
Very Rev. Elias Meena (*Syrian Antiochian Orthodox*)
Miss Florence Partridge (*Evangelical and Reformed Church*)
Rev. Elmo F. Randolph (*Seventh Day Baptist*)
Dr. F. Eppling Reinartz (*United Lutheran*)
Rev. William F. Rotzler (*United Presbyterian*)
Rev. B. Julian Smith (*Colored Methodist Episcopal*)
Rt. Rev. Harwood Sturtevant (*Protestant Episcopal*)
Mrs. Leslie E. Swain (*American Baptist*)
Very Rev. John Trutza (*Roumanian Orthodox*)
Rev. Nicholas Vansuch (*Russian Orthodox*)
Bishop Ira D. Warner (*Evangelical United Brethren*)
Mrs. James D. Wyker (*Disciples of Christ*)

NOMINATIONS COMMITTEE
Dr. Earl Moreland, *Chairman*

Dr. Gaines M. Cook   Dr. Raymond R. Peters
Bishop D. Ward Nichols   Dr. Dorothy A. Stevens

On recommendation of the Planning Committee, it was

A-50-106   VOTED to authorize the presiding officer at all
                    business sessions to rule that any matters presented
from the floor or other matters requiring extended debate shall be
referred to the Business Committee for study and recommendation,
with the understanding that the Business Committee may grant
hearings to those presenting such business items and to other persons
particularly concerned and with a further understanding that no new
business is to be presented from the floor after adjournment of the
Thursday morning session.

RESOLUTIONS   Dr. Morse then read the following statement prepared by the Planning Committee regarding reso-
lutions:

At future meetings of the General Assembly there will be opportunity
for reports from the various units of the Council and careful consideration
of possible resolutions dealing with various fields of interest or concern.

At this Constituting Convention, it will be necessary to devote a
major portion of time at plenary business sessions to organizational
matters. Furthermore, the various units will not have had adequate time
to give careful study to possible or proposed resolutions.

A special committee has been asked to prepare a message to the
churches. It is the opinion of the Planning Committee that for this Convention the message to the churches should receive the consideration of
the General Assembly rather than a long list of separate resolutions.
Therefore, the following recommendation is submitted by the Planning
Committee:

> *Recommended Action:* To refrain at this Convention from the adoption
> of resolutions on general matters, other than resolutions of cour-
> tesy, except as the Business Committee may for special reasons
> feel it wise to recommend action by the Assembly.

It was

A-50-107   VOTED to approve the foregoing recommendation
of the Planning Committee.

INCORPORATION   Dr. Morse then read the text of the proposed
Articles of Incorporation drafted by the Legal
Committee as a possible basis for incorporation in the State of New York.

Pursuant to this statement by Dr. Morse, it was

A-50-108   VOTED that, in accordance with recommendations
of the Planning Committee, an organization, which
shall be called NATIONAL COUNCIL OF THE CHURCHES OF
CHRIST IN THE UNITED STATES OF AMERICA, be forthwith incorporated under that name; and

that, to this end, the Planning Committee be authorized to proceed
forthwith with all the legal steps to create and bring into existence
such a corporation under the Membership Corporations Law of the
State of New York (or of such other state as the Planning Committee
may deem necessary); and

that John S. Stamm, Margaret M. Sherman, Truman B. Douglass,
Harold E. Stassen, Franklin D. Cogswell, Bernard J. Mulder, Georgi-
anna Sibley, Paul H. Conrad, Luther A. Weigle be and they hereby

are authorized and requested to act as incorporators of such corporation; and

that the certificate of incorporation be substantially in the form hereto annexed and made part of this resolution, it being understood that the Planning Committee and the aforesaid incorporators are authorized to make such textual changes therein as may be necessary to comply with legal requirements; and

that, as soon as the legal existence of such corporation is fully consummated, suitable announcement thereof be publicly made by the Chairman of the Planning Committee; and

that, pending consummation of the incorporation, the aforesaid incorporators shall, subject to formal ratification by them thereafter, have full power to proceed on behalf of this Constituting Convention with all the actions contemplated in paragraph 4 of the aforesaid certificate of incorporation, such actions to be given full and permanent legal status, after consummation of the incorporation, by prompt ratification by the incorporators and such representative persons as they may have associated with themselves as provided in such paragraph 4; and

that, upon such ratification, the actions thus provisionally taken be thereupon deemed consummated and deemed to be the actions of the corporation, National Council of the Churches of Christ in the United States of America.

RELATIONSHIPS WITH COOPERATING ORGANIZATIONS Regarding the relationships between the National Council of Churches and cooperating organizations, it was

A-50-109 VOTED that the relationship in fact and in law between the new National Council and each cooperating organization, and the work, assets and obligations thereof, shall be determined and formulated, and from time to time may be modified in whole or in part, by the General Board of the National Council in agreement with such cooperating organization; and

that, subject to like agreement, such cooperative organization may merge into the National Council as a corporation, and/or the National Council may assume from it all or specified assets and all or specified obligations; and

that, until the General Board has so acted in agreement with the cooperating organization, the National Council shall not be deemed to have assumed responsibility or obligation for the work, or to have assumed assets or commitments of such cooperating organization.

Dr. Morse then presented the following statement
prepared by the Planning Committee regarding
the election of representatives of the cooperative
work of the churches in cities and counties:

In Article IV, Section 2b, of the proposed Constitution there is provision for the election by the General Assembly of ten persons to represent the cooperative work of the churches in cities and counties.

There is further provision in Article IV, Section 2c, that each such representative shall be a member in good and regular standing of a communion included in membership of the Council and shall serve only when approved by action of his communion.

At the request of the Planning Committee, the Association of Council Secretaries nominated the ten persons who, in their judgment, might best be elected by the General Assembly to represent the cooperative work of the churches in cities and counties.

The Planning Committee has received official approval from the communions of which these respective nominees are members and, therefore, submits the following recommendation:

Recommended Action: To elect as members of the General Assembly the following persons as representatives and alternate representatives of the cooperative work of the churches in cities and counties as provided in Article IV, Sections 2b and 2c of the Constitution:

Hugh Chamberlin Burr, Chairman of Delegation, Rochester, N. Y.
E. C. Farnham................................San Francisco, California
John Harms.......................................Chicago, Illinois
John Montgomery.................................Des Moines, Iowa
Grove Patterson.....................................Toledo, Ohio
Dan M. Potter............................Attleboro, Massachusetts
O. M. Walton..............................Pittsburgh, Pennsylvania
Dorothy Blount......................................Mobile, Alabama
Jennie M. Doidge.........................Bridgeport, Connecticut
Mrs. R. V. Rorabaugh..............................Tulsa, Oklahoma

Alternates:

Reuben W. Coleman...................................Dayton, Ohio
Alvin S. Haag...................................Redlands, California
Harvey W. Hollis................................Albany, New York
Robert Kincheloe.............................South Bend, Indiana
Chester McPheeters.............................Detroit, Michigan
John Meloy.....................................Louisville, Kentucky
Frederick E. Reissig.............................Washington, D. C.

Harry H. Rogers.............................San Antonio, Texas
George H. Wilson..............................St. Joseph, Missouri
Ruth Custas Kitchen......................Philadelphia, Pennsylvania
Mrs. R. S. Scott..............................Spokane, Washington
Mrs. A. B. Stenger..........................Wheeling, West Virginia

It was explained that substitutions are to be made from the alternates if and when anyone nominated as a regular representative is nominated to the National Council under some other category or for any reason cannot continue to serve.

It was then

A-50-110   VOTED to adopt the recommendation of the Planning Committee concerning representatives and alternate representatives of the cooperative work of the churches in cities and counties as provided in Article IV, Sections 2b and 2c of the Constitution.

DIVISION MEMBERSHIP Dr. Morse then presented the following statement
ASSIGNMENTS   prepared by the Planning Committee regarding assignment of members of the General Assembly to membership in the four Divisions:

The Constitution provides in Article X, Section 4, for the assignment of each member of the General Assembly to membership in one of the four Divisions of the Council. The Planning Committee has sought to obtain from the member communions the suggestions of their officers regarding the allocation of voting representatives to membership in the four Divisions.

The task of allocating each person to the Division in which he or she might best serve involves in some cases rather difficult decisions, and it is quite probable that there will need to be a re-study of this matter subsequent to the Constituting Convention with possible change in assignments. Therefore, the Planning Committee makes the following recommendation:

> *Recommended Action:* To approve for purposes of divisional organization the assignment of members of the General Assembly to membership in the four Divisions as tentatively recommended by the Planning Committee and to authorize the General Board to change assignments as it may be deemed expedient or to make assignments in the case of those members not covered by the recommendations of the Planning Committee.

It was

A-50-111   VOTED to adopt the above recommendation.

PLANNING COMMITTEE On recommendation of the Planning Committee,
STATUS   it was

A-50-112   VOTED to grant the members of the Committee
the privileges of the floor at the Constituting Convention with the understanding that they will not have voting privileges except as they may have been chosen to serve as voting representatives of their respective communions.

RESOLUTION RE: Bishop G. Bromley Oxnam presented a resolution
INTERNATIONAL   for several members of the Convention as follows:
SITUATION

RESOLVED that messages be sent to the President of the United
States and his advisers and the Secretary General of the United
Nations assuring them of the prayers of this Convention in this
critical time and that the Chairman appoint a committee to
consider the advisability of drafting a statement on the present
international situation to the Convention.

It was

A-50-113   VOTED that the above resolution be referred to
the Business Committee.

CLEVELAND   Dr. Herbert J. Lambacher, President of the Cleve-
FEDERATION ADDRESS land Church Federation, welcomed the delegates
OF WELCOME   to Cleveland and brought greetings from the Cleveland Church Federation. Dr. Fry expressed the
appreciation of the Convention.

CONSTITUTION   Dr. Morse then read the following statement prepared by the Planning Committee regarding the
Constitution as amended:

The document published under date of April 25, 1944 and originally
submitted to the uniting agencies and to the various denominations included a draft of a proposed Constitution for the National Council of the
Churches of Christ in the United States of America. It was on the basis
of this proposed Constitution that actions were taken by the various
agencies and denominations. (See Convention Work Book for copy of the
Constitution as originally proposed.)

During the years since 1944 the Planning Committee has received
many suggestions for amendments to the Constitution. Those proposed
amendments which met with the unanimous approval of the Planning
Committee have been included in a tentative revision of the Constitution.
(See Convention Work Book for copy of the Constitution as revised to
include amendments unanimously approved by the Planning Committee.)
Copies of this revised Constitution were mailed to the offices of all de-

227

nominations anticipating membership in the National Council three months in advance of the Constituting Convention.

The Planning Committee recommends the adoption of all amendments included in the revised draft of the proposed Constitution.

It is recognized that the Planning Committee has had no right to amend the proposed Constitution which was submitted to the eight uniting agencies on April 25, 1944 and which was the basis of the actions taken by these agencies and their constituent bodies.

It is assumed that the Constituting Convention may receive the original Constitution, with amendments proposed by the Planning Committee of which due notice was given at least three months in advance of the Constituting Convention, and may take action thereon and may bring the Council into formal existence on the basis of such amended Constitution. It is assumed that the advance notice of the Planning Committee regarding the proposed amendments fulfills for this Constituting Convention the requirements for advance notice set forth in Article XVII on Amendments.

It is further assumed that, in order to meet any technical legal objection, it would be wise to have the proposed amendments acted upon according to the provisions of Article XVII of the revised document.

It is also assumed that any additional amendments to the Constitution presented on the floor of the Convention by any member or representative may be received but may not be acted upon at this time since advance notice has not been given. Any such amendments will be dealt with thereafter under the provisions of the article on amendments.

The procedure recommended, on the basis of the foregoing, is as follows:

a. That at the Wednesday morning session, the Planning Committee present the Constitution with amendments approved prior to July 27, 1950 and recommend its approval and adoption as the Constitution of the National Council of the Churches of Christ in the United States of America and that action on this recommendation be taken under a special rule requiring an affirmative vote by two-thirds of the representatives present and voting, followed by a majority vote of the denominational delegations, each voting separately.

b. That the parliamentary ruling be that any of the proposed amendments may be acted on separately, if requested, but that each proposed amendment must be either accepted or rejected as presented, any proposal to modify any proposed amendment or to amend the original Constitution in any additional particulars being out of order; that any proposed amendment on which action is taken separately by the General Assembly shall, if it receives the requisite two-thirds vote, likewise be acted on separately by the denominational delegations, but otherwise the action by the denominational delegations shall be on the Constitution and amendments as a whole. That request be made of the denominational delegations to appoint a convener or chairman for these meetings.

c. That on the basis of a two-thirds vote of the General Assembly and a majority vote of the denominational delegations, voting separately, the Constitution shall be declared to be in effect.

It was

A-50-114   VOTED to approve the recommendation of the Planning Committee.

GENERAL BY-LAWS   Dr. Morse then read the following statement prepared by the Planning Committee regarding the General By-Laws:

The original document submitted to the agencies and denominations did not include a draft of By-Laws but did indicate certain matters which would ultimately be included in By-Laws.

The Planning Committee has drafted proposed By-Laws as set forth in the Convention Work Book and unanimously recommends their adoption.

Following the adoption of the Constitution and the declaration that the Council is now formally in existence, the General Assembly may proceed, under the authorization of Article VII, 1g of the Constitution, to adopt General By-Laws. Action may be taken in any manner and under any rule that the General Assembly itself may approve. However, once the By-Laws are approved any subsequent revision must be in accordance with the provision of the By-Laws, as adopted, for amendment.

The procedure recommended is as follows:

a. That as the next order of business following the completion of action on the Constitution the Planning Committee present the proposed General By-Laws and recommend their approval and adoption as the General By-Laws of the Council.

b. That the motion be for the approval and adoption of the General By-Laws as a whole, subject to a ruling that a separate motion may be presented and acted on, as an amendment, for the alteration or rejection of any particular By-Law or portion thereof, affirmative action on the original motion or on any amendment to be by a two-thirds vote of the representatives present and voting, to adopt or to reject.

229

It was

A-50-115   VOTED to adopt the recommendation of the
                Planning Committee.

On recommendation of the Planning Committee, it was also

A-50-116   VOTED to authorize the General Board to appoint
                a special committee on Constitution and By-Laws
with the understanding that this committee will:

COMMITTEE ON   a. Study all suggestions or proposals which may be
CONSTITUTION   forthcoming concerning amendments to the Con-
AND BY-LAWS   stitution, the General By-Laws, and the By-Laws
                       of the various units of the Council.

    b. Make a careful study of the Constitution and all By-Laws in order
       to discover any errors, discrepancies, contradictions or shortcom-
       ings which in their judgment warrant the consideration of further
       amendments by the Council or its various units.

    c. Submit to the General Board any recommendations which they
       may have concerning amendments to the Constitution or General
       By-Laws.

    d. Give due notice as provided in the Constitution concerning any
       amendments which, in their judgment, ought to be considered by
       the General Assembly at its next meeting.

On recommendation of the Planning Committee regarding a proposed
Joint Department of Benevolence Promotion, it was

A-50-117   VOTED to refer to the General Board with power
                    the matter of constituting, at its discretion, a pro-
JOINT DEPARTMENT   posed Joint Department of Benevolence Promotion
OF BENEVOLENCE   with the understanding that the General Board
PROMOTION   will have authority to act on behalf of the Council
                    in constituting this Joint Department and in ap-
proving By-Laws under which it shall operate if and when constituted.

CONSTITUTION   Dr. Morse then presented the proposed Constitu-
                    tion for the National Council of Churches, prefacing
the presentation with remarks concerning editorial changes to be made
on the following pages:

    Page 33, Article VIII, Section 2 should state "Vice-Presidents-at-
       large" rather than the singular form.

    Page 34, Article IX, Section 3 should refer to General Departments,
       "Commissions," Joint Commissions. . . . The word "Com-
       missions" was inadvertently omitted from the printed copy.

230

Page 38, Article XIII, Section 2, line 4 should read "correlate its field work with the national denominational field programs" eliminating the word "and" between "national" and "denominational."

Dr. Morse also presented the following proposed amendments upon which action was taken:

A-50-118

LAY REPRESENTATION
ON GENERAL BOARD

VOTED that the amendment of the Constitution to provide for representation of the General Departments of United Church Men and United Church Women on the General Board by the Chairman and two representatives of each General Department instead of by the Chairman only be referred to the proposed Committee on Constitution and By-Laws for their favorable consideration and that the Committee be asked to consider the matter of more adequate lay representation through other avenues of appointment to the General Board.

AMENDMENT AS
PROPOSED BY
INTERNATIONAL
COUNCIL OF
RELIGIOUS
EDUCATION

A-50-119

VOTED that the following recommendations of the International Council of Religious Education be referred to the proposed Committee on Constitution and By-Laws for their favorable consideration:

Article II: That a statement be added to the objects outlined in this Article similar to the statement in the present charter of the International Council of Religious Education, "to encourage study of the Bible and to assist in the spread of the Christian religion."

Article VI,
Section 2: That a phrase be added to the first sentence to read: "and may retain and continue such operations as may be used, owned or controlled by any of the agencies above-named for the purposes within the scope of the Division as set forth in the General By-Laws of the Council or the By-Laws of a Division."

Article X,
Section 4: That a phrase be inserted after the words "Division Assembly" in the second line to read: "which shall be the governing body of a Division, such assignment to be made" etc.

231

The Chairman called the attention of the delegates to the beautiful edition of the Bible which was presented to the National Council by the American Bible Society and expressed the deep appreciation of the Council for this lovely and lasting gift.

RADIO ADDRESS BY SECRETARY OF STATE   Dr. Cavert announced that, due to the world crisis, Secretary of State Dean Acheson could not be present as scheduled but would address the delegates by radio at the time originally planned for his address.

The morning worship was led by Mrs. Howard G. Colwell, former President of the American Baptist Convention.

GENERAL SESSION

Wednesday, November 29, 1950—2:15 p.m.

Music Hall, Cleveland Public Auditorium

MRS. CLIFFORD HEINZ was the Chairman for this general session.

Dr. Desmond W. Bittinger, President of McPherson College, led the opening devotional service.

The theme of this first general session was "This Nation Under God— Our Educational Task." Professor Nevin C. Harner, of the Theological Seminary of the Evangelical and Reformed Church, Lancaster, Pennsylvania, addressed the meeting on "Religious Education—Foundation of the National Life." He discussed the present confused world situation and the necessity of taking seriously our task of religious teaching.

President Howard F. Lowry of Wooster College, Ohio spoke on "The Christian College and the National Life." He pointed out that "Christian education extends the area of human inquiry to its legitimate height and depth. It may turn out to be the most far-thinking liberal education there is . . . because it does put first things first . . . it may well be the only free education." Dr. Lowry stated, too, that "if the churches are to remain in any important way in the field of higher learning they must stand up and pay for their colleges and not hand them over by default to the State. They must lay upon their members capable of coming to the support of church colleges their obligation and opportunity to do so." He concluded by saying that "Any great church movement such as this depends, as does the life of our nation, on the kind of mind and the kind of faith America possesses. The contribution of the Church colleges to such a mind and such a faith has been and will be, if they survive, all out of proportion to their size."

Following Dr. Lowry's address, the Oberlin College a cappella choir sang the following selections:

Hodie Christus Natus Est........................Palestrina
Rejoice and Sing, Christmas Oratoria...................Bach
Salvation Is Created..........................Tschesnokov
O Be Joyful in the Lord........................Gretchaninov
Alleluia ....Thompson

The choir, directed by Professor Robert Fountain, added much to the enjoyment of the afternoon with the beauty of their rendition of this devotional music.

Mr. F. William Barrick, President of the United Christian Youth Movement reported on the work of the Movement and called the youth of America to act in cooperation with other Christian forces at work in the world. UCYM wants to enlist a million Christian young people during 1951 in a special project of the United Youth Movement and the Department of Young People's Work of the National Council. The call to youth will be issued during Youth Week, January 28 to February 3, 1951 and come to a climax during the 1952 Youth Week. Major emphasis will be put on a new commitment to service in projects of evangelism, etc. on the local, state, national and world levels. Those answering the call will contribute $1.00 each toward these projects and give volunteer time toward them.

Mr. John Deschner, Executive Secretary, United Student Christian Council, spoke on "Christian Youth and the Nation." He described the unsettled condition of the young people of this generation and their desire for some kind of real service to humanity; of their eagerness for a truly ecumenical church and the hope that they can be reassured of worthwhile tasks for them to do.

Dr. Edwin T. Dahlberg, minister of Delmar Baptist Church, St. Louis, Missouri, gave an address on "The Nation's Dependence on the Local Church." He stressed the fact that the Convention was organizing a National *Council* of Churches and not a National Church and said that "the best guarantee of a free faith in a free society is a strong local church, completely sovereign and close to the mind and heart of the people. National religious and educational agencies may prepare the study curriculum for the churches; but it is in the local congregation and the local Sunday School that young people are introduced to Christ and secure a warmhearted commitment to the Christian way of life."

Mrs. Rosa Page Welch, Chicago concert artist, song leader of the Convention, led the meeting in the hymns of the afternoon and sang one spiritual as a solo.

At the end of the closing hymn, "Thine is the Glory," Dr. Dahlberg pronounced the benediction.

EVENING SESSION

Wednesday, November 29, 1950—8:00 p.m.

Cleveland Public Auditorium

THE EVENING SESSION of the Constituting Convention of the National
Council of the Churches of Christ in the United States of America was
held in the Arena of the Cleveland Public Auditorium at 8:00 p.m. The
theme of the meeting was "This Nation Under God."

Dr. Edward H. Pruden, President of the American Baptist Convention, presided.

After the organ prelude, the Cleveland Philharmonic Orchestra, under
the leadership of F. Karl Grossman, rendered the overture "Freischmetz"
by Weber.

The congregation then joined in the singing of the hymn "O God
Beneath Thy Guiding Hand" and the Rev. J. McDowell Richards, President of the Columbia Theological Seminary, gave the Invocation.

Then followed two musical numbers by the orchestra:

Symphony No. 1—Allegro con brio...................Brahms
A Mighty Fortress is our God.................Bach-Damrosch

Mrs. Frank C. Brooks of the Methodist Church read the Scripture
and Bishop Ivan Lee Holt of the Methodist Church led in the "Prayer of
the Nation."

Miss Gretchen Garnett sang the aria, "Hear Ye Israel" from Mendelssohn's "Elijah."

The Assembly stood at attention while the following message from
President Truman was read by the presiding officer:

"I extend heartiest congratulations to the National Council of the
Churches of Christ in the United States of America as it begins its
task of drawing twenty-nine great communions into united action on
a still greater scale than in the past. I have followed with warm appreciation the work which has been done in recent years by the interdenominational agencies which now combine their forces into a new
Council. I hope and believe that this step will enable the American
churches to exert a greater influence in the strengthening of the
spiritual foundation of our national life at a time when a materialistic philosophy is rampant.

"I am grateful for the contributions which the churches of the National Council are making to the faith of our people, to the maintenance of freedom throughout the world, to social welfare and to interracial and international good will. I hope the coming years will bring
still greater unity of purpose and effort among the religious forces of
America."

The Honorable Dean Acheson, Secretary of State, was scheduled to give the address of the evening. However, because of the critical world situation, he was obliged to remain in Washington and his address was broadcast direct from his office.

After the singing of the closing hymn "God of our Fathers," Bishop C. H. Stauffacher of the Evangelical and Reformed Church led the closing prayer and pronounced the benediction.

The orchestra then played "Dream Pantomime" from "Hansel and Gretel" which was followed by the Organ Postlude "Festival Toccata" by Percy Fletcher.

PLENARY BUSINESS SESSION OF THE GENERAL ASSEMBLY

Thursday, November 30, 1950—9:30 a.m.

Cleveland Public Auditorium

BISHOP G. BROMLEY OXNAM, Secretary of the Council of Bishops of the Methodist Church, presided at this session.

The meeting was opened with a period of meditation and prayer led by Errol T. Elliott, Clerk of the Religious Society of Friends—Five Years Meeting.

GREETINGS TO CONVENTION

Dr. Hermann H. Morse, reporting for the Business Committee, read greetings sent to the Convention by:

Doc. Rec. A-102   Dr. Adolph Keller of Zurich, Switzerland

Doc. Rec. A-103   The British Council of Churches

Doc. Rec. A-104   The Synagogue Council of America.

The Secretary was authorized to send a suitable reply to each of these greetings expressing the appreciation of the General Assembly.

BUSINESS COMMITTEE

Continuing the report of the Business Committee, Dr. Morse stated that the Committee had felt it unwise to recommend the appointment of a special committee to draft a statement on the present critical world situation but that the committee had conferred with the Committee on Message concerning the inclusion of a suitable expression of the concern of the churches.

The Business Committee recommended and it was

A-50-120   VOTED that the following message be sent to the President of the United States in the name of the Constituting Convention of the National Council of the Churches of Christ in the United States of America:

235

"In this hour of crisis for the peace of the world, the National Council of the Churches of Christ in the United States of America, in session in Cleveland, is keeping you in its prayerful remembrance. May the God who holds the nations in the palm of His hand and from whom, in times past, our fathers sought wisdom and understanding, guide you and your advisers to the end that peace may be vouchsafed to the peoples of the earth. The delegates here assembled, representing twenty-nine communions whose combined membership exceeds thirty-one millions, express the fervent hope that the United Nations, assured of the full participation of our country, may act under God, to secure with justice, the enduring welfare of mankind. The responsibilities which are yours can be borne only with the aid that comes from God and to Him we commend you in our prayers."

On recommendation of the Committee, it was also

A-50-121   VOTED that the following message be sent to Hon. Trygvie Lie, Secretary General of the United Nations, in the name of the Constituting Convention of the National Council of the Churches of Christ in the United States of America:

"The National Council of the Churches of Christ in the United States of America, in convention at Cleveland, Ohio, has offered special prayer to Almighty God that the United Nations, in face of serious threats, may find just and effective procedures for containing and resolving the conflict in Korea. The National Council is composed of twenty-nine churches with a combined membership exceeding thirty-one million people in this country and the activities of its component bodies extend to virtually every country throughout the world. Christians have expressed the conviction that the goals of peace and order must be sought through international action, and that support of the United Nations and its decisions will at this time provide the best safeguard against the selfish interests of any nation or group of nations. Fully aware of the dangers in the immediate situation, we reaffirm our conviction that war is not inevitable. To avert the catastrophe of war is the responsibility of every nation and every people and, particularly, the responsibility of States Members of the United Nations, both large and small. We pray that the representatives of all governments will manifest wisdom, unity and strength in seeking peace based on justice and good will."

It was

A-50-122   VOTED to approve the report of the Business Committee.

COMMUNICATIONS FROM: FRIENDS—PHILA. ILLINOIS COUNCIL Resuming the presentation of Constitution and General By-Laws, Dr. Morse presented the recommendations of the Planning Committee regarding two communications, one from the Religious Society of Friends of Philadelphia and Vicinity and the other from the Illinois Council of Churches. As recommended, it was

A-50-123 VOTED to refer to the proposed special committee on Constitution and By-Laws for study the communication from the Religious Society of Friends of Philadelphia and Vicinity regarding a revision of the Preamble of the Constitution, with the understanding that if the General Board is in agreement with the suggestion, it will be submitted to the next meeting of the General Assembly for consideration.

A-50-124 VOTED to refer to the proposed special committee on Constitution and By-Laws the communication from the Illinois Council of Churches regarding denominational approval for those chosen to represent the cooperative work of the churches in the various states, with the understanding that if the General Board approves of this recommendation it will be submitted to the next meeting of the General Assembly for consideration.

FRATERNAL DELEGATES The following fraternal delegates to the Convention were introduced and welcomed by the Chairman:

Canadian Council of Churches:	Dr. William Barclay
	Rev. W. J. Gallagher
	Rev. Fred Poulton
World Council of Churches:	Miss Eleanor Kent Browne
	Dr. William Keys
	Dr. Henry Smith Leiper
American Bible Society:	Dr. Daniel Burke
	Rev. Gilbert Darlington
Salvation Army:	Lt. Colonel Edward Carey
International Missionary Council:	Rev. John W. Decker
	Rev. Charles W. Ranson
	Miss Gloria M. Wysner
National Board, YWCA:	Mrs. Harrison S. Elliott
National Council, YMCA:	Mr. Fred W. Ramsey
	Mr. E. V. Rasmussen
	Mr. J. Edward Sproul
International YMCA:	Mr. Tracy Strong

International Council of
Community Churches: Dr. J. Ruskin Howe

CONSTITUTION   Dr. Morse continued the report of the Planning
Committee with the reading of the revised Constitution, beginning with Article IV. It was thereupon

A-50-125   VOTED that the Constitution as submitted by the
Planning Committee with the amendments approved prior to July 27 and of which three months' notice had been
given be approved and adopted as the Constitution of the National
Council subject to its approval by a majority vote of denominational
delegations voting separately.

Vote by member churches:

For adoption—
African Methodist Episcopal, *unanimous*
African Methodist Episcopal Zion, *unanimous*
American Baptist Convention, *unanimous*
Augustana Lutheran Church, *unanimous*
Church of the Brethren, *unanimous*
Colored Methodist Episcopal, *unanimous*
Congregational Christian, *unanimous*
Disciples of Christ, *unanimous*
Danish Evangelical Lutheran, *unanimous*
Evangelical and Reformed, *unanimous*
Evangelical United Brethren, *unanimous*
Evangelical Unity of Czech Moravian Brethren, *unanimous*
Friends, Five Years Meeting, *unanimous*
Friends of Philadelphia and Vicinity, *unanimous*
Methodist, *unanimous*
Moravian Church (Northern and Southern Provinces) *unanimous*
National Baptist Convention, USA, Inc., *unanimous*
Presbyterian Church in the U.S., *unanimous*
Presbyterian Church in the USA, *unanimous*
Protestant Episcopal, *unanimous*
Reformed Church in America, *unanimous*
Russian Orthodox Church in America, *unanimous*
Seventh Day Baptists, General Conference, *unanimous*
United Lutheran Church in America, *unanimous*
United Presbyterian Church of North America, *unanimous*

Not voting due to absence—
National Baptist Convention of America
Roumanian Orthodox Episcopate of America

Syrian Antiochian Orthodox Church
Ukrainian Orthodox Church of America
Since a majority of the member churches voted in the affirmative, the
Constitution was declared to be in effect as the Constitution of the National Council of the Churches of Christ in the United States of America.

GENERAL
BY-LAWS

Dr. Morse then presented the General By-Laws, calling attention to the following editorial changes:

Page 57, Line 8 should read: "Administrative Secretaries and Associate Administrative Secretaries"
Line 12 should read: "Executive Directors and Associate Executive Directors"
Line 17 should read: "Administrative Secretaries and Associate Administrative Secretaries"
A line should be added following Line 17, to read: "General Directors of Commissions"
Line 24 should read: "Joint Commissions and Joint Departments"

After some discussion regarding Headquarters Location and the power of the General Board in this respect, it was

A-50-126

VOTED that the General By-Laws as submitted by the Planning Committee be approved and adopted as the General By-Laws of the National Council.

HEADQUARTERS
LOCATION

The report of the Planning Committee was then continued with its recommendation concerning Headquarters Location. After lengthy discussion, it was

A-50-127

VOTED that the General Assembly request the General Board in its consideration and determination of Headquarters Location, to appoint a special committee which shall be widely representative both denominationally and geographically to study the question of Headquarters Location, and that the General Assembly request the General Board to weigh carefully in that study the advantage and possibility of establishing such headquarters in an area reasonably adjacent to the population center of the United States.

CHAPLAIN
STANTON W.
SALISBURY

The Chairman introduced Chaplain Stanton W. Salisbury (U.S.N.), Chairman of the Board of Chaplains, who addressed the Assembly on "Our Christian Responsibility for Men and Women in the Armed Forces."

239

ANNOUNCEMENT   Announcement was made that since Sir Oliver Franks, the British Ambassador to the United States, would not be able to speak as scheduled, due to the international crisis, Dr. O. Frederick Nolde, Director of the Commission of the Churches on International Affairs of the World Council of Churches and the International Missionary Council, would speak in his place on Thursday evening, November 30.

General announcements were made by Dr. Samuel McCrea Cavert and the assignments for organizational meetings were approved by consent.

Doc. Rec. A-105   Closing worship was led by Dr. Benjamin E. Mays, President of Morehouse College.

GENERAL SESSION

Thursday, November 30, 1950—2:15 p.m.

Music Hall, Cleveland Public Auditorium

THE CHAIRMAN for this session was Mrs. Hugh D. Taylor.

The meeting was opened with a devotional service led by Dr. J. Lowrie Anderson, Moderator of the General Assembly of the United Presbyterian Church of North America.

The theme of the afternoon was "This Nation Under God—Our Missionary Responsibility" and the first speaker was Dr. Hermann N. Morse, General Secretary of the Board of National Missions of the Presbyterian Church in the U.S.A. He cautioned against depending on "organizational mechanics" to accomplish the aims of the new National Council. "What we do here must finally be judged on its contribution to the spiritual life of our time. In that effort the missionary enterprise must have a central place," stated Dr. Morse. He concluded by saying that "We dare to believe that a Christian and a Protestant America can be the strongest force in the world against the new and the old paganisms that are contending for the mastery of the world."

In an address on "The Church in the World," Dr. Sarah Chakko, President of Isabella Thoburn College, Lucknow, India, and Secretary of the World Council's Commission on the Life and Work of Women in the Church, stated that the world Christian community is "the great new fact of our time" but asked whether it is strong enough to save world civilization. She felt that the church should try in every possible way to influence the nations into right public policies and yet not let the church be captured by the national interests. Dr. Chakko stated that the important thing is not for a civilization to be saved, but for God's scheme of redemption to be worked through us, if we can fulfill our obligations,

240

but in spite of us if that is necessary. "Whatever the case, the Christian hope is always there."

Mrs. Rosa Page Welch sang two spirituals, "The Amen Chorus" and "Down by the River." Because of the weather, the Baldwin-Wallace College Choir was unable to be present as scheduled.

Dr. A. D. Stauffacher, Executive Secretary of the Missions Council of the Congregational Christian Churches, spoke on "Our Missionary Responsibility in the Nation and the World." He stated that our missionary responsibility will be successful only when we have brought the many millions outside the church into it and have helped them to assume their responsibilities within the church. Our responsibility is not over until we reach every church in every nation—our responsibility is to the whole church and to the whole nation, said Dr. Stauffacher.

Mrs. Rosa Page Welch then led the audience in singing the hymn, "God grant us peace on earth."

Toyohiko Kagawa of Japan then addressed the meeting on the subject, "God and the Nations." This was an inspirational and moving address closing with Kagawa's statement that "Universal consciousness of Christ —the redemptive love of Christ is the only way to redeem and save the world. Are you Americans willing to bear the cross of Jesus in order to unite all nations into one?"

Dr. Kagawa pronounced the benediction.

EVENING SESSION

Thursday, November 30, 1950—8:00 p.m.

Cleveland Public Auditorium

THE THEME of the Thursday evening session of the Constituting Convention of the National Council of the Churches of Christ in the United States of America held in the Arena of the Cleveland Public Auditorium was "The Church and the Nations."

Dr. Hugh I. Evans, Moderator of the General Assembly of the Presbyterian Church in the U. S. A., presided.

After the reading of the scripture and the singing of the hymn "God of the Spirit Wind," Mrs. James D. Wyker, Chairman of the Ohio Council of Church Women, led in the "Prayer for the Nations."

Mrs. Rosa Page Welch sang two solos: "One World" and "There is a Balm in Gilead."

In the absence of Sir Oliver S. Franks, Ambassador of Great Britain to the United States of America, Dr. O. Frederick Nolde, Director of the Commission of the Churches on International Affairs of the World Council of Churches and the International Missionary Council, delivered an address on "A Christian View of the International Crisis."

The Assembly sang the hymn "A Mighty Fortress Is Our God," after which Dr. W. A. Visser 't Hooft, General Secretary of the World Council of Churches, spoke on the subject, "The Church in the World of Nations."

Dr. Luther Wesley Smith made an appeal in behalf of the new National Council of Churches. The delegates were urged to fill out personal pledge cards and thereby become founding donors of the National Council. These, together with the offering, were collected by the ushers.

The Singers Club of Cleveland, under the direction of Robert M. Stofer, rendered the following numbers:

Onward Ye People .... Sibelius
Thanks Be To Thee, from "Samson" .... Handel
Sheep May Safely Graze .... Bach
Let Their Celestial Concerts All Unite, from "Samson" .... Handel

As part of a "We, The People" broadcast over the National Broadcasting Company shortwave network, messages were heard from His Grace, the Archbishop of York, speaking from London and Dr. Gonzalo Baez Camargo, Secretary of the National Evangelical Council of Mexico and Dr. W. A. Visser 't Hooft participated from Cleveland.

The meeting closed with prayer and benediction by Bishop D. Ward Nichols of the African Methodist Episcopal Church.

PLENARY BUSINESS SESSION OF THE
GENERAL ASSEMBLY

Friday, December 1, 1950—9:30 a.m.
Cleveland Public Auditorium

DR. L. W. GOEBEL, President of Evangelical and Reformed Church, presided at this session.

Bishop J. Arthur Hamlett of the Colored Methodist Episcopal Church led the Convention in a brief devotional service.

CHANGE IN PROGRAM Dr. Hermann N. Morse, reporting for the Business Committee asked that the order of the morning program be changed as follows:

Report of Planning Committee
Report of other committees
Report of General Board on nominations and other recommendations
concerning election of officers
Election of officers

242

Report of General Board on election of staff
Statement concerning other units of the Council

The General Assembly agreed to this change and the meeting proceeded accordingly.

RESOLUTION RE: Dr. Morse then presented on behalf of the committee a resolution concerning Displaced Persons
DISPLACED
PERSONS   and the Committee's recommendation that, because of the urgency of this situation, it be referred to the General Board with the request that the General Board give this matter immediate consideration and take appropriate action. It was, therefore,

A-50-128   VOTED that the following resolution be referred to the General Board for immediate consideration and appropriate action:

WHEREAS the plight of Displaced Persons in Europe, including many of our fellow-believers, is still desperate more than five years after the termination of hostilities and calls for the practical demonstration of Christian sympathy in order to take advantage of the opportunity provided by law and by the resources of international agencies for their resettlement in the United States; and

WHEREAS the representatives of the churches in the Executive Committee of the Federal Council of Churches urged Congress to adopt the legislation which provided for a greatly increased number of Displaced Persons to escape from their misery in Europe to a place in American life; and

WHEREAS the necessary assurances of work and residence for some 35,000 Displaced Persons still in Europe have already been underwritten by the communions working through the Department of Church World Service of this Council and similar assurances for more have been secured by other related agencies; and

WHEREAS the coming to America of these thousands of our fellow believers requires sufficient funds to be provided through the Department of Church World Service and through other related agencies to meet the costs of completing the process of selection, expediting sailings, welcoming them to America and arranging for their transportation to the homes and work assured by their sponsors; therefore be it

RESOLVED that the National Council endorse the program of its constituent communions in cooperation with the Department

243

of Church World Service and with other related agencies to bring to this country the Displaced Persons for whose coming they are under obligation, and urge the people of these several communions to give adequate financial support to their agencies responsible for the resettlement of these Displaced Persons so that through the Department of Church World Service and other related agencies every Protestant and Eastern Orthodox Displaced Person for whom opportunity is provided under the expanded legislation shall be brought to our shores and welcomed into our communities and churches.

Also, on recommendation of the Business Committee, it was

A-50-129

OHIO COUNCIL
OF CHURCHES

VOTED to refer a communication from the Ohio Council of Churches regarding the Headquarters Location of the National Council to the General Board for reference to the Committee it is to appoint for the study of this matter.

On motion of Bishop Henry W. Hobson of the Protestant Episcopal Church, it was

A-50-130

PRINTING OF
NOLDE ADDRESS

VOTED that the staff of the National Council be instructed to print Dr. O. Frederick Nolde's address given at the Assembly session on the evening of November 30, 1950 and make it available to all who may desire copies; and to send copies to the President, the Secretary of State and the members of the Foreign Relations Committees of the Senate and House of Representatives.

On recommendation of the Planning Committee it was

A-50-131

WASHINGTON
OFFICE

VOTED to continue the present Washington Office of the Federal Council of Churches and associated agencies on the same basis and with the same function and purposes now prevailing with the understanding that the Washington Office Committee will function as a Standing Committee of the National Council, under the supervision of the General Board and the General Secretary.

On recommendation of the Planning Committee it was

A-50-132

MINISTRY TO MEN
& WOMEN IN
ARMED FORCES

VOTED to request the General Board to appoint a committee to study the matter of the responsibility of the National Council in connection with the ministry of the churches to men and women in uniform and to defense industry workers, this committee to include representatives from the following units:

244

Division of Christian Education, especially the *Commission on General Christian Education*
Division of Christian Life and Work
Division of Home Missions
General Department of United Church Men
General Department of United Church Women
Central Department of Field Administration
Joint Department of American Communities Overseas
United Christian Youth Movement
Central Department of Publication and Distribution

To request the above committee to prepare preliminary memoranda with regard to the services which the churches ought to render in the light of past experience and a survey of present needs.

ADDITIONAL
UNITING AGENCIES

Dr. Morse presented the following resolution concerning additional uniting agencies:

We rejoice at the enlarging number of common interests of cooperative Protestantism which desire to continue their services within the framework of the National Council of the Churches of Christ in the United States of America. These agencies include:

1. *Church World Service Inc.*, whose ministry of healing and relief will be continued and extended through the Central Department of Church World Service of the National Council.

2. *The Interseminary Movement*, whose ecumenical student ministry will be continued and extended through the Interseminary Committee, a Department of the Commission on General Christian Education of the Division of Christian Education of the National Council.

3. *The Protestant Radio Commission*, whose cooperative religious radio and television ministry together with the film ministry of the Protestant Film Commission following their unification, will be continued and extended within the Central Department of Broadcasting and Films as the unit within the National Council for the promulgation of the Christian Gospel through these mass media of communication.

This Constituting Convention welcomes these agencies into an ever widening fellowship and within the provisions of the Constitution and By-Laws of this Council recognizes them as integral parts of its enlarging service.

It was

A-50-133   VOTED to adopt the above resolution.

The following recommendation concerning the Protestant Film Commission was also presented:

WHEREAS the Protestant Film Commission has certified its approval of the By-Laws of the Central Department of Broadcasting and Films of the National Council of the Churches of Christ in the United States of America, listed on pages 168-174 of the Work Book, as the basis for the merging of all its interests and the continuation and extension of its functions; and

WHEREAS this action was not consummated in time to complete the necessary procedural, legal and budgetary steps required by the Planning Committee for uniting within the Central Department of Broadcasting and Films the work of the Protestant Radio Commission and the Protestant Film Commission; it is

RECOMMENDED: 1. That the Constituting Convention of the National Council approve the application of the Protestant Film Commission to become an integral part of the National Council's Central Department of Broadcasting and Films;

2. That the National Council refer to the General Board with power all matters necessary to the completion of the unification of the Protestant Film Commission within the Central Department of Broadcasting and Films of the National Council.

It was

A-50-134   VOTED to adopt the above recommendation.

Upon recommendation of the Planning Committee, it was also

A-50-135   VOTED to invite the following agencies to become consultative members of the National Council of Churches and to refer to the General Board the decision as to the number of non-voting representatives in the General Assembly and the General Board to be accorded to each of these agencies:

The American Bible Society
The National Council of the Young Men's Christian Association
The National Board of the Young Women's Christian Association

REPORT OF
COMMITTEE ON
REGISTRATION AND
CREDENTIALS

Doc. Rec. 107

Dr. James E. Hoffman presented the report of the Committee on Registration and Credentials which is made a Document of Record. It was voted to accept the report of the Committee including the adoption of a resolution of appreciation for the fine services rendered to this committee by persons representing the following agencies:

The Cleveland Convention Bureau
The Cleveland Church Federation
Members of the clerical staffs of the merging agencies and a large number of friends and interested persons who, seeing the press of the work, volunteered their services.

INTRODUCTION OF
LAY LEADERSHIP

The Chairman introduced Mr. J. Howard Pew and expressed the appreciation of the Assembly for the work of the National Lay Sponsors Committee of which Mr. Pew is Chairman. Mr. Lem T. Jones and Mr. Ray Nichols, newly elected Chairman and Vice-Chairman respectively, of the General Department of United Church Men were also introduced.

DR. HAROLD
E. STASSEN

Dr. Goebel then introduced Dr. Harold E. Stassen who addressed the Assembly on "The Laity and the National Council."

MR. J. HOWARD Pew

At the close of his address, Dr. Stassen presented Mr. J. Howard Pew, former President of Sun Oil Company, who spoke briefly on the work of the National Lay Sponsors Committee.

REPORT OF
COMMITTEE ON
RESOLUTIONS OF
COURTESY

The report of the Committee on Resolutions of Courtesy which was given by Dr. P. O. Bersell is attached hereto and made a Document of Record.

It was

Doc. Rec. 108
A-50-136

VOTED to adopt the resolutions in the report of the Committee on Resolutions of Courtesy.

REPORTS OF
ORGANIZATIONAL
MEETINGS

Reports of the organization of the four Divisions were given by the following:
Dr. Roswell P. Barnes for Division of Christian Life & Work
Mrs. Margaret Sherman for Division of Foreign Missions

247

Dr. Truman Douglass for Division of Home Missions
Dr. Arlo Brown for Division of Christian Education

It was agreed by consent that the above reports as well as reports for all other units would be filed with the Secretary and made part of the record.

NOMINATIONS   The report of the General Board on Nominations was presented by Dr. Hermann N. Morse. He stated that the Board had designated the Nominating Committee of the Planning Committee to act in its behalf in the presentation of the slate as follows:

Standing Committees:

BUSINESS AND FINANCE—Mr. Harvey Firestone, Jr., *Chairman*
CONSTITUENT MEMBERSHIP—Dr. Luther A. Weigle, *Chairman*
LEGAL—Hon. Charles H. Tuttle, *Chairman*
NOMINATING—Dr. J. Earl Moreland, *Chairman*
PERSONNEL—Dr. Hermann N. Morse, *Chairman*

Committees reporting to Committee on Business and Finance:

BUDGET—Dr. Luther Wesley Smith, *Chairman*
PENSIONS—Dr. F. Eppling Reinartz, *Chairman*

Standing Committees to be provisionally constituted as follows:

BUSINESS AND FINANCE

Representing Denominations

Mr. Harvey Firestone, Jr., *Chairman* (Episcopal)
Dr. Torrey Walker, *Vice Chairman* (United Lutheran)
Dr. Reuben E. Nelson (American Baptist)
Dr. P. O. Bersell (Augustana Lutheran)
Mr. Lem T. Jones (Presbyterian USA)
Dr. Truman B. Douglass (Congregational)
Dr. Alfred Jensen (Danish Lutheran)
Dr. H. B. McCormick (Disciples)
Dr. James E. Wagner (Evangelical and Reformed)
Bishop D. T. Gregory (Evangelical United Brethren)
Bishop W. C. Martin (Methodist)
Rev. J. G. Patton, Jr. (Presbyterian US)
Dr. Bernard J. Mulder (Reformed)
Pres. C. C. Ellis (Brethren)
Bishop D. Ward Nichols (African M. E.)
Bishop C. C. Alleyne (African M. E. Zion)
Rev. T. Donald Black (United Presbyterian)
Dr. Henry A. Boyd (National Baptist, American)

248

Rev. O. C. Maxwell (National Baptist, USA)
Rev. A. Arthur Hamlett (Colored M.E.)
Dr. F. P. Stocker (Moravian)
Dr. Errol T. Elliott (Friends—Five Years)
Dr. Howard G. Taylor (Friends—Philadelphia)
Dr. Elmo F. Randolph (Seventh Day Baptist)
Rev. Josef A. Barton (Czech-Moravian)
Mr. Ralph M. Arkush (Russian Orthodox)
Very Rev. John Trutza (Roumanian)
Bishop Bohdan (Ukrainian)
Very Rev. Elias Meena (Syrian)

Representing Cooperative Work in States, Cities and Counties

Mr. Grove Patterson, Toledo, Ohio
Dr. Glenn W. Moore, Los Angeles, California
Miss Gertrude L. Apel, Seattle, Washington
Dr. Frank Jennings, Boston, Massachusetts
Dr. John K. Benton, Nashville, Tennessee
Dr. Henry Reed Bowen, Newark, New Jersey

CONSTITUENT MEMBERSHIP COMMITTEE

Dr. Luther A. Weigle, *Chairman*
Dr. Riley B. Montgomery
Bishop Ivan Lee Holt
Dr. Ralph Waldo Lloyd
Dr. Franklin C. Fry

LEGAL COMMITTEE

Hon. Charles H. Tuttle, *Chairman*
Mr. Charles C. Parlin
Mrs. Sadie Alexander
Mr. Rush Taggart
Mr. Thomas B. K. Ringe
Mr. C. O. Loucks

NOMINATING COMMITTEE

Dr. J. Earl Moreland, *Chairman*
The Chairmen of the Assemblies of the four Divisions
The Chairmen (or other representatives) of the Nominating Committees of the four Divisions
One representative each of the General Department of United Church Men and the General Department of United Church Women

PERSONNEL COMMITTEE

Dr. Hermann N. Morse, *Chairman*

The Chairmen of the Executive Boards of the four Divisions
The Chairmen of the Boards of Managers of the General Department of United Church Men and the General Department of United Church Women and of the Joint Commission on Missionary Education

BUDGET COMMITTEE

Dr. Luther Wesley Smith, *Chairman*
Mr. Francis S. Harmon, *Vice Chairman*
Dr. Hermann N. Morse
Dr. F. M. Potter
Mrs. James D. Wyker
Mr. Charles H. Seaver
Dr. Leon M. Adkins
Bishop D. Ormand Walker
Bishop G. Bromley Oxnam
Dr. S. E. Engstrom
Dr. L. W. Goebel
Mr. Charles P. Taft
Dr. C. Franklin Koch
The Chairmen of the Committees on Budget and Finance in the four Divisions and the Joint Commission on Missionary Education
Three persons to be named by the General Board on nomination of the National Lay Committee

PENSIONS COMMITTEE

Dr. F. Eppling Reinartz, *Chairman*
Mr. Donald L. Hibbard
Dr. M. Forrest Ashbrook
Dr. Frank Scribner
Dr. T. A. Stafford
Dr. Paul Preston
Dr. Gerard Gnade
The Chairmen of the Committees on Budget and on Business and Finance

It is recommended that the following be appointed as officers of Central and Joint Departments in accordance with the provisions of their By-Laws:

Central Department of Finance:

Chairman—Dr. Luther Wesley Smith
Vice Chairman—Mr. Francis S. Harmon

Central Department of Field Administration:
  Chairman—Dr. Hugh C. Burr
  Vice Chairman—Mrs. William Sale Terrell
  Recording Secretary—Dr. Raymond R. Peters

Central Department of Public Relations:
  Chairman—Mr. Joseph E. Boyle
  Vice Chairman—Dr. Ralph W. Stoody

Central Department of Research and Survey:
  Chairman—Mr. Shelby M. Harrison

Central Department of Ecumenical Relations:
  Chairman—Mrs. Leslie E. Swain
  Vice Chairman—Rt. Rev. Angus Dun

Joint Department of Evangelism:
  Chairman—Prof. E. G. Homrighausen
  Vice Chairman—Dr. Edwin T. Dahlberg
  Vice Chairman—Bishop Richard Raines
  Recording Secretary—Hugh D. Darsie

Joint Department of Religious Liberty:
  Chairman—Rt. Rev. Malcolm E. Peabody

It was

A-50-137   VOTED to adopt the above recommendations of the General Board.

It was

A-50-138   VOTED to adopt the recommendation of the General Board that the General Assembly authorize the General Board to elect a woman Associate General Secretary. Separate actions were taken on the following nominations:

A-50-139   VOTED to elect as President—Rt. Rev. Henry Knox Sherrill.

A-50-140   VOTED to elect as Vice Presidents-at-large:
Mrs. Douglas Horton of New York
Mrs. Abbie Clement Jackson of Louisville
Dr. M. E. Sadler of Fort Worth
Dr. Harold E. Stassen of Philadelphia

A-50-141   VOTED to elect as Treasurer—Mr. Charles E. Wilson of New York
to elect as Associate Treasurer—Mr. James L. Kraft of Chicago.

251

A-50-142	VOTED to elect Chairmen of Standing Committees of the Council as listed above.
A-50-143	VOTED to elect as General Secretary—Dr. Samuel McCrea Cavert.
A-50-144	VOTED to elect as Associate General Secretary— Dr. Roy G. Ross.

Dr. Morse reported to the Assembly regarding the Executive Staff elected by the General Board at their meeting on November 29 as follows:

GENERAL ADMINISTRATION

To be Nominated for election by General Assembly:
Samuel McCrea Cavert, General Secretary
Roy G. Ross, Associate General Secretary

To be Elected by General Board:
(to be filled) Associate General Secretary
Earl F. Adams, Administrative Secretary
Philip C. Landers, Administrative Secretary
J. Quinter Miller, Administrative Secretary
Wilbur C. Parry (one-third time), Associate Administrative Secretary
Aenid A. Sanborn, Assistant to the General Secretary

DIVISION OF FOREIGN MISSIONS

Sue Weddell, Executive Secretary (for General Administration)
Fred Field Goodsell, Executive Secretary (for General Administration)
Rowland M. Cross, Executive Secretary of Far Eastern Joint Office
Royal H. Fisher, Assistant Secretary of Far Eastern Joint Office
Emory Ross, Executive Secretary of Africa Committee
Clara L. Bentley, Associate Secretary of Africa Committee
A. Russell Stevenson, Executive Secretary of Western Asia and Near East Joint Office
Douglas H. Forman, Executive Secretary of Christian Medical Council for Overseas Work
J. Horton Daniels, Director of Associated Missions Medical Office
Frank S. Beck, Staff Physician of Associated Missions Medical Office
Eve J. Weddigen, Staff Physician, Associated Missions Medical Office
John H. Reisner, Executive Secretary of Rural Missions Cooperating Committee
Ira W. Moomaw, Educational Secretary of Rural Missions Cooperating Committee
Alfred D. Moore, Executive Secretary of Committee on World Literacy and Christian Literature

252

Arnold Vaught, Executive Secretary of Committee on Relief and Reconstruction Services

Helen M. Eklund, Associate Secretary of Committee on Cooperation in Latin America

Alberto Rembao, Editor of *La Nueva Democracia*, Committee on Cooperation in Latin America

Josephine C. Lawney, Staff Physician of Associated Missions Medical Office

Joint Department of American Overseas Communities
(Administratively Related to Division of Foreign Missions)
(to be filled) Executive Director

DIVISION OF HOME MISSIONS

Edith E. Lowry, Executive Secretary

I. George Nace, Executive Secretary

Louisa R. Shotwell, Associate Secretary

Benson Y. Landis (Half-time) Secretary of Department of Town and Country

Don F. Pielstick (Half-time) Secretary of Department of Town and Country

Ross W. Sanderson (quarter-time) Secretary of Department of the Urban Church

Mrs. F. E. Shotwell, Western Supervisor for Migrant Work

Ellis Marshburn, Midwestern Supervisor for Migrant Work

Merle Gripman, Assistant Treasurer

Rev. G. E. E. Lindquist, Field Representative for Indian Work

Rev. Harry V. Davidson (Part-time) Director of Sharecroppers' Committee

DIVISION OF CHRISTIAN LIFE AND WORK

Roswell P. Barnes, Executive Secretary

C. Arild Olsen, Associate Executive Secretary

Walter W. Van Kirk, Executive Director of Department of International Justice and Goodwill

Richard M. Fagley, Director of Department of International Justice and Goodwill

Cameron P. Hall, Executive Director of Department of the Church and Economic Life

Dudley Ward, Director of Study of Department of Church and Economic Life

Elma Greenwood, Assistant Executive Director of Department of the Church and Economic Life

J. Oscar Lee, Executive Director of Department of Race Relations
Thomas C. Allen, Director of Department of Race Relations
Otis R. Rice (part-time) Executive Director of Department of Pastoral
Services
Paul J. Tilden, Associate Director of Department of Pastoral Services
Beverley M. Boyd, Executive Director of Department of Social Welfare
Deane Edwards, Executive Director of Commission on Worship

Joint Departments
(Administratively Related to Division of Christian Life and Work)

Joint Department of Evangelism
Jesse M. Bader, Executive Director
H. H. McConnell, Field Secretary
Harry H. Kalas, Director of Educational Evangelism
James L. Stoner, Director of University Christian Missions
Edward Gebhard, Assistant Director of Educational Evangelism

Joint Department of Stewardship
(to be filled) Executive Director

Joint Department of Religious Liberty
Armond D. Willis, Executive Director

DIVISION OF CHRISTIAN EDUCATION

Central Administration and Operations
Roy G. Ross (half-time) Executive Secretary
Wilbur C. Parry (two-thirds time) Associate Executive Secretary
(to be filled), Director of Department of Educational Promotion
Mrs. Orville Smith, Administrative Assistant
Helen F. Kindt (one-third time) Business Assistant
Virgil Foster, Editor of *International Journal of Religious Education*
Lillian Williams, Managing Editor of *International Journal of Religious
Education*

Commission on General Christian Education
Gerald E. Knoff, General Director of Commission and Associate Executive
Secretary of Division
Alice L. Goddard, Executive Director of Department of Children's Work
and Vacation Religious Education
Ruth Elizabeth Murphy, Associate Executive Director of Department of
Children's Work and Vacation Religious Education
A. Wilson Cheek, Executive Director of Department of Young People's
Work

254

Dennis Savage, Associate Executive Director of Department of Young People's Work

Richard E. Lentz (half-time) Executive Director of Department of Adult Work

Lee J. Gable, Executive Director of Department of Leadership Education and Department of Church School Administration

Paul King, Associate Executive Director of Department of Leadership Education and Department of Church School Administration

Mildred A. Magnuson, Executive Director of Department of Curriculum Development

Erwin L. Shaver, Executive Director of Department of Weekday Religious Education

John C. Trever, Executive Director of Department of the English Bible

Pearl Rosser, Executive Director of Department of Audio-Visual and Radio Education

Helen F. Spaulding (one-third time) Associate Executive Director of Department of Educational Program

Luther A. Weigle, Executive Chairman of Standard Bible Committee

Fleming James, Executive Secretary of Old Testament Section of Standard Bible Committee

(to be filled) Director of Department of Intergroup Relations

Commission on Christian Higher Education

Dr. E. Fay Campbell (part-time) General Director of Commission and Associate Executive Secretary of Division

Arch Tolbert, Executive Director of Interseminary Committee

(to be filled) Executive Director of Department of Campus Christian Life

Joint Departments
(Administratively Related to Division of Christian Education)

Joint Commission on Missionary Education

Franklin D. Cogswell, General Director of Joint Commission and Associate Executive Secretary of Division

Gilbert Q. LeSourd, Associate Director

T. H. P. Sailer, Honorary Secretary

Nina Millen, Director and Editor of Department of Children's Work

Lucy M. Eldredge, Director and Editor of Department of Youth Work

Leslie C. Sayre, Director and Editor of Department of Adult Work and Assistant Treasurer

Hazel V. Orton, Director of Production and Acting Director of Sales and Promotion

Priscilla Chase, Director of Order Department

255

Joint Department of Family Life
Richard E. Lentz (half-time) Executive Director

Joint Department of Christian Life Service
(to be filled), Executive Director

GENERAL DEPARTMENT OF UNITED CHURCH WOMEN

Mrs. W. Murdoch MacLeod, General Director
Miss Edith L. Groner, Associate General Director
Miss Esther C. Stamats, Director Christian Social Relations
Miss Luella Reckmeyer, Director of Christian World Relations
Mrs. Emory Ross, Director of Promotion and Education
Mrs. James M. Evans, Director of World Missions of the Church
Mrs. Abram LeGrand (half-time) Editor, *The Church Woman*

GENERAL DEPARTMENT OF UNITED CHURCH MEN

(to be filled), Executive Director

CENTRAL DEPARTMENTS

N.B. In cases where uniting agencies are making funds and staff available for the work of Central Departments of the National Council of Churches, the program units carrying forward the work of those uniting agencies are permitted to list such personnel in their staff roster, with the understanding that the primary relationship of such staff personnel is to the Central Departments involved.

Broadcasting and Films
Ronald Bridges, Executive Director
Everett C. Parker, Director of Program
Albert Crews, Director of Broadcasting and Television
Arthur B. Rhinow, Business Manager and Assistant Treasurer
Wesley Goodman, Director of Special Programs
Paul F. Beard, Director of Films
Orrin W. Evans, Assistant Director of Films
(N.B. List of other personnel in the section dealing with films will be completed when integration of Protestant Film Commission and National Council is completed)

Field Administration
J. Quinter Miller, Executive Director
John B. Ketcham, Associate Executive Director
George D. Kelsey, Associate Executive Director

Don F. Pielstick (half-time) Director of Church Planning and Adjustment
(to be filled), Director of Field Program Coordination and Counseling
Dr. Ernest J. Arnold, Director of Southeastern Office
Harry C. Munro (part-time) Director of Southwestern Office
Miss Theresa Capell, Assistant to Executive Director

Business and Treasury

Earl F. Adams, Acting Executive Director
John M. Johansen, Assistant Treasurer
Mrs. B. Margaret Rieber, Office Manager
Miss Betty Drury (part-time), Personnel Manager
Helen F. Kindt (two-thirds time), Associate Personnel Manager (Midwest Office)

Finance

Richard B. Smith, Executive Director
Miss Josephine Little, Associate Director
Milo J. Vondracek, Director of Mid-west Office
Clark L. Snyder, Associate Director of Mid-west Office
Mrs. Myra Ammerman, Assistant to the Executive Director
Miss Edith Groner (one-quarter time), Staff Member

Research and Survey

F. Ernest Johnson, Executive Director
Benson Y. Landis (half-time) Associate Executive Director
David Barry, Director of Field Research
Helen F. Spaulding (two-thirds time) Director of Research in Christian
Education
R. Pierce Beaver (half-time), Director of Research in Foreign Missions
Inez M. Cavert, Research Associate
Agnes Campbell, Librarian
Marion Nelson, Assistant to the Executive Director

Public Relations

Don Bolles, Executive Director
Lemuel Petersen, Associate Director
William W. Clemes, Associate Director
Beata Mueller, Editorial Assistant
(to be filled), Editor of National Council's magazine

Publication and Distribution

Norman E. Tompkins, Executive Director
Donald F. Heldt, Production Manager
George Franklin Ketcham, Assistant to the Executive Director
Mrs. Elizabeth Dunn, Administrative Assistant

Ecumenical Relations

Robbins W. Barstow, Executive Director

Church World Service

Wynn C. Fairfield, Executive Director
Wayland Zwayer, Assistant Executive Director
Stanley I. Stuber, Director of Information and Promotion

Church Building and Architecture

Elbert M. Conover, Executive Director

Washington Office

Miss Nadine Blair, Assistant Secretary

It was reported that greetings had come to the Assembly from:

Doc. Rec. A-109	*The American Friends Service Committee*
Doc. Rec. A-110	*Rabbi Barnett R. Brickner, Euclid Avenue Temple, Cleveland, Ohio*
Doc. Rec. A-111	*The Council of Churches, Lewisburg, Pennsylvania*
Doc. Rec. A-112	*The Conference of Missionary Societies of Great Britain and Ireland*

It was

A-50-145   VOTED that the Secretary be authorized to send grateful acknowledgment.

BUDGET   Bishop G. Bromley Oxnam presented the following recommendation on behalf of the General Board:

RECOMMENDED that this Board request the General Assembly to empower the Chairman of the Council after consultation with the General Secretary and the Chairmen of the four Divisions to appoint a Committee of approximately twenty-one persons to make a thorough study and appraisal of the program and budgets of the Council, including its several units, it being understood

1. That the Committee will not include any executive personnel.

2. That the four Divisions and the two Central Departments will nominate one person each to the membership of the Committee.

3. That the Committee will report to the next General Assembly and will make such earlier reports of progress as are possible to the General Board.

It was

A-50-146   VOTED to adopt the above recommendation.

Doc. Rec. A-113   Dr. Ross then presented the Summary and Analysis of the Budget for information to the General Assembly. This is attached to the record as a Document of Record.

OFFERING   Dr. Cavert reported that the offering received on Thursday evening, November 30, 1950, amounted to $25,030.15 and expressed appreciation for the generous support given by those who participated in this special offering.

Morning worship was led by the Very Rev. Georges Florovsky, Dean of St. Vladimir's Orthodox Seminary.

GENERAL SESSION

Friday, December 1, 1950—2:00 p.m.

Music Hall, Cleveland Public Auditorium

Dr. Charles J. Turck, President of Macalester College, was the Chairman of this session which considered the theme "This Nation Under God— Our Christian Witness."

Rev. Elmo F. Randolph, minister of the Seventh Day Baptist Church, Milton, Wisconsin, led the opening devotional service.

"The Christian's Witness in Our National Life" was discussed by Hon. Francis B. Sayre, Delegate of the United States to the Trusteeship Council of the United Nations. After a searching presentation, Dr. Sayre stated, "Here at Cleveland we have the inestimable advantage of a common religious faith. Christianity, if we have the faith to see it, lights the way forward. There is danger that we Americans will try to generate spiritual power through organization and outward form which cannot be done. If Jesus were physically present today, His way would not lead through organizations, but rather through individual lives, their influence upon community and nation, working in His Spirit. God waits upon us for the doing of His work. Are we in dead earnest? Are we prepared to take the hand of Christ and go forward?"

Mrs. Douglas Horton, former President of Wellesley College and former Commander of the WAVES, addressed the meeting on "The Wit-

259

ness of the Church in Public Affairs." She opened her talk by saying, "The Church makes a witness in public affairs because it is, itself, a public institution." Mrs. Horton pointed out the importance of all persons in authority in all fields taking their religion seriously and considering God's will in their daily occupations. In closing Mrs. Horton said, "If the church is to be a 'herald of a better day,' it must forever call attention to the shortcomings of the present day. Churchmen who look at life as though they saw it from God's point of view could be expected to be ever-critical of society's inadequacies. Some churchmen will see ills others will not see. None see them from God's total point of view. The interpretation of God's will for the individual is not the same for all individuals. We all, as seekers of God's will, should ever be respectful of each other's final interpretation as to what they should or should not do." Mrs. Horton then read the concluding paragraphs of the report of the Federal Council Commission on "The Christian Conscience and Weapons of Mass Destruction" ending, "Before Him we dare to believe that we have a citizenship which no human weapons can destroy. From Him who would 'fold both heaven and earth in a single peace' there comes even in our darkness that strange word, 'Be not anxious.' "

Dr. Randolph closed the session with a benediction.

PLENARY BUSINESS SESSION OF THE
GENERAL ASSEMBLY

Friday, December 1, 1950 at 4:00 p.m.

Cleveland Public Auditorium

DR. MARVIN O. SANSBURY, President of the International Convention of Disciples of Christ, presided at this session.

Dr. Alfred Jensen, President of the Danish Evangelical Lutheran Church of America, led the Assembly in a brief devotional service.

SIMULTANEOUS DENOMINATIONAL EMPHASES

Dr. Hermann N. Morse presented a recommendation of the Planning Committee concerning a proposed program of simultaneous Denominational Emphases and it was

A-50-147

VOTED to approve in principle the development of simultaneous denominational emphases.

To request the General Board to create a Committee on Simultaneous Denominational Emphases to be composed of persons designated by the member communions.

To invite each of the constituent communions to authorize through its appropriate official body participation in this study and to designate its representatives to serve on the Committee on Simultaneous Denominational Emphases.

To authorize the General Secretary, or someone whom he will designate, to convene the committee when a sufficient number of the communions have designated representatives.

To request the present Committee on Simultaneous Denominational Emphases to transmit to the new committee the results of the study.

CLOSING REMARKS BY DR. HERMANN N. MORSE   Dr. Morse expressed appreciation on behalf of the Planning Committee and himself to the delegates for their part in making the Convention a success and discussed briefly the ultimate goals of the National Council.

COMMITTEE ON MESSAGE   Dr. Douglas Horton then presented the report of the Committee on Message. During the discussion of part of the phraseology of this message, the following action was taken:

A-50-148   VOTED to request the General Board to study the desirability of changing the phrase "Divine Lord" in the Preamble of the Constitution to "God" or of making such other changes in the wording as might express more explicitly the testimony that Jesus Christ is God.

Dr. John O. Gross pointed out that no statement covering the ministry of institutions of higher learning had been included in the message and it was thereafter

A-50-149   VOTED to approve the draft of the message to the churches with the addition of a sentence regarding higher education.

Doc. Rec. A-114   A copy of the corrected Message is attached hereto and made a Document of Record.

DR. NOLDE'S ADDRESS   Dr. Cavert announced that Dr. Nolde's address on "A Christian View of the International Crisis" would be available within the next two weeks from the Department of International Justice and Good Will, 297 Fourth Avenue, New York at a price to be announced.

It was

A-50-150   VOTED to adjourn at the close of the evening session, Friday, December 1, 1950, subject to the call of the officers of the National Council.

The closing prayer and benediction were given by Dr. Douglas Horton.

EVENING SESSION

Friday, December 1, 1950—8:00 p.m.

Cleveland Public Auditorium

A SERVICE of Installation and Consecration held in the Arena of the Cleveland Public Auditorium brought to a close the Constituting Convention of the National Council of the Churches of Christ in the United States of America.

During the processional hymn, the new officers, general board members and executive staff of the National Council of Churches took their places at the tables in front of the auditorium.

Dr. Vere Y. Loper, Moderator of the General Council of the Congregational-Christian Churches, led in the Act of Adoration, after which the Rev. F. P. Stocker, President of Provincial Elders Conference of the Moravian Church, offered the Invocation.

The scripture, Romans 12:1-21, was read by Mrs. Harper Sibley, former President of the United Council of Church Women.

Following the "Prayer for the Church" by the Very Reverend John Trutza, President of the Episcopate's Council, Roumanian Orthodox Church of America, the Messiah Chorus of Cleveland, conducted by T. R. Evans, sang two anthems from Handel's "Messiah"—"And the Glory of the Lord" and "Worthy the Lamb."

The sermon on "The Cost of Discipleship" was preached by Rev. Eugene C. Blake, pastor of the First Presbyterian Church, Pasadena, California.

After the singing of the hymn, "I Love Thy Kingdom, Lord," the Service of Installation was conducted by Dr. Hermann N. Morse, Chairman of the Planning Committee of the National Council.

Bishop William J. Walls of the African Methodist Episcopal Zion Church offered the Prayer of Consecration.

The closing statement was made by the Rt. Rev. Henry Knox Sherrill of the Protestant Episcopal Church, First President of the National Council of Churches.

The Assembly rose as the Messiah Chorus sang "The Halleluia Chorus" from Handel's "Messiah."

The service was closed with prayer and benediction by Bishop Sherrill.

"The Church's One Foundation" was sung as the recessional hymn.

SECTION VIII

Details of Organization

Constitution OF THE

NATIONAL COUNCIL OF THE CHURCHES OF CHRIST

IN THE UNITED STATES OF AMERICA

Preamble

IN THE Providence of God, the time has come when it seems fitting more fully to manifest oneness in Jesus Christ as Divine Lord and Saviour, by the creation of an inclusive co-operative agency of the Christian churches of the United States of America to continue and extend the following general agencies of the churches and to combine all their interests and functions:

Federal Council of the Churches of Christ in America
Foreign Missions Conference of North America
Home Missions Council of North America
International Council of Religious Education
Missionary Education Movement of the United States and Canada
National Protestant Council on Higher Education
United Council of Church Women
United Stewardship Council

ARTICLE I—*Organization and Name*

There shall be an organization which shall be called NATIONAL COUNCIL OF THE CHURCHES OF CHRIST IN THE UNITED STATES OF AMERICA, hereinafter referred to as "the Council."

ARTICLE II—*Objects*

The objects of the Council are:

1. To manifest the common spirit and purpose of the cooperating churches in carrying out their mission in the world.
2. To do for the churches such cooperative work as they authorize the Council to carry on in their behalf.
3. To continue and extend the work of the interdenominational agencies named in the Preamble of the Constitution, together with such additional objects and purposes as the churches through their representatives in the Council from time to time agree upon.
4. To encourage fellowship and mutual counsel concerning the spiritual life and religious activities of the churches.
5. To foster and encourage cooperation among the churches for the purposes set forth in this Constitution.

6. To promote cooperation among local churches and to further in communities, states or larger territorial units the development of councils of churches and councils of church women, in agreement with the Preamble of this Constitution.

7. To establish consultative relationships with National Councils of Churches in other countries of North America.

8. To maintain fellowship and cooperation with similar councils in other areas of the world.

9. To maintain fellowship and cooperation with the World Council of Churches and with other international Christian organizations.

Article III—*Membership*

1. Communions which accept the objects and purposes of this Council, as set forth in this preamble and Constitution, are eligible to membership in the Council as a whole and in its various Divisions, General Departments, Joint Commissions and Joint Departments; or boards and agencies of the churches may have membership in any one or more of the Divisions, General Departments, Joint Commissions and Joint Departments of the Council.

2. a) Communions which are now members or the boards or agencies of which are now members of any four or more of the general agencies named in the Preamble of this Constitution, shall be charter members of the Council upon their acceptance of this Preamble and Constitution, provided that such action is taken not later than the organizing convention of the Council.

   b) Each board or agency which is now a member of one or more of the general agencies named in the Preamble of this Constitution, shall be a charter member of the appropriate Divisions, General Departments, Joint Commissions or Joint Departments of the Council, provided that it accepts such charter membership not later than the organizing convention of the Council.

3. a) Communions which declare their acceptance of this Preamble and constitution may become members of the Council upon their request, if approved by a two-thirds vote of the communions represented and voting at any regular meeting of the General Assembly; the delegations of each communion voting separately, and by a two-thirds vote of the representatives present and voting at any regular meeting of the General Assembly.

   b) Denominational boards or agencies which accept the basis of membership as defined by each Division, General Department, Joint Commission or Joint Department of the Council, may, upon their request, become members of any one or more of these units if approved by a two-thirds vote of the members present and voting at any regular meeting of the Division, General Department, Joint Commission or Joint Department concerned. No board or agency, except as provided in Article III, Section 2b, of this Constitution, shall be eligible to membership in Divisions, General Departments, Joint Commissions or Joint Departments of the Council unless its communion is in agreement with the Preamble of this Constitution.

4. The Council may name as consultative members such boards or agencies not constituted by the churches as it may determine. The representatives of these boards or agencies in the General Assembly in such number as the Council shall determine shall be advisory members of the Council without vote.

Article IV—*Representation*

1. The governing body of the Council shall be a General Assembly. Each communion which has membership in the Council as a whole shall be entitled to representation in the General Assembly as follows:

   a) Five representatives, and one additional representative for every 100,000 of its communicants or major fraction thereof, having regard to adequate representation of ministers, lay men, lay women, and young people.

266

b) Additional representatives, not exceeding one-third of the number provided for in a) above, equally divided as far as possible among lay men, lay women, and young people.

c) All representatives of a communion shall be elected by that communion in such manner as it shall determine. Of the total number of representatives at least one-half shall be nominated by the boards and agencies of that communion cooperating in the work of the Divisions of the Council, on such basis as the communion shall determine; having regard to the interests of the several age groups and the various functions of the Council.

2. The cooperative work of the churches in the various states, cities and counties shall have representation in the General Assembly in the following manner:

a) One representative for each state council of churches which is in agreement with the Preamble of this Constitution and which is constituted by the communions in its area.

b) Ten additional representatives, at least three of whom shall be women, elected by the Council from nominations submitted by the city and county councils which are in agreement with the Preamble of this Constitution and which are constituted by the communions in their areas.

c) Each such representative shall be a member in good and regular standing of a communion included in the membership of the Council, and shall serve only when approved by action of his communion. Whenever voting in the General Assembly is by communions, these representatives shall vote with the communions of which they are members.

3. A church board or agency of a communion not holding membership in the Council may have membership in one or more of the Divisions of the Council.

Article V—*Functions*

The functions of the Council shall include the following:

1. The general oversight and coordination of the whole field or work of the Council and of its Divisions and other units.

2. All actions and utterances of the Council in representation of the cooperating churches.

3. Basic studies in fields of common interest to the churches.

4. The safe-guarding for each Division of the fullest measure of autonomy consistent with presenting a united front and a mutually-supporting program.

5. The fostering among the Divisions and other units of united fellowship, planning and action.

6. The relations of the Council to other cooperative bodies, either directly or through one or more of the Divisions.

7. General relations with the public and with governments, either directly or through one or more of the Divisions.

8. Fostering the formation and development of effective local agencies of interdenominational cooperation in agreement with the Preamble of this Constitution.

9. General control of the finances of the Council including the preparation and authorization of its annual financial budget.

Article VI—Incorporation

1. The Council shall be incorporated under a state or the national government as the Council shall determine.

2. Each Division may be incorporated under a state or the national government as it shall determine. Subject to the provisions hereinafter specified, each incorporated Division shall be subject to the supervision of the Council and responsible to it.

3. Subject to the approval of the General Board, other units of the Council may be incorporated with the understanding that each such incorporated unit shall be subject to the supervision of the Council and responsible to it.

ARTICLE VII—AUTHORITY

1. The Council shall have authority:
   a) To regulate its own proceedings in accordance with its Constitution and Charter.
   b) To elect the necessary officers and members of its staff, remove them for cause and fill vacancies.
   c) To buy, acquire, or receive, by gift, devise, or bequest, property, real, personal, and mixed.
   d) To hold, sell, and dispose of property.
   e) To secure, appropriate, and administer funds for its work.
   f) To sue and be sued.
   g) To make General By-Laws in harmony with its Charter and Constitution.
2. The Council shall have no authority or administrative control over the churches which constitute its membership. It shall have no authority to prescribe a common creed, or form of church government, or form of worship, or to limit the autonomy of the churches cooperating in it.

ARTICLE VIII—*Officers*

1. The Officers of the Council shall be a President, a Vice-President for each of the administrative Divisions to be nominated by the Division, additional Vice-Presidents at large in such number as to provide an equal number of clerical and lay Vice-Presidents, a Treasurer, a Recording Secretary, a General Secretary and such other Officers as it may need. They shall be elected by the General Assembly at its Biennial Meeting for a term of two years. They shall serve as Officers of the General Assembly and perform such other duties as are customarily performed by such Officers. The President and the Vice-Presidents at large shall be so chosen that at least one shall be a lay woman. Each Officer must be a member in good standing of a communion which is a constituent member of the Council.
2. The President and the Vice-Presidents at large shall not be eligible for immediate re-election.

ARTICLE IX—*General Board*

1. The Council shall have a General Board, to be named as hereinafter provided, which Board shall have the full powers of the Council ad interim, except the power to determine the membership of the Council and the power to revise its Constitution and General By-Laws.
2. Either the Council or the General Board may appoint such standing or special committees as may be necessary or convenient for the discharge of the work of the Council.
3. Each constituent communion of the Council shall name to the General Board one-seventh of its representatives in the General Assembly, to be selected in harmony with the principles of representation stated in Article IV, Section 1, of this Constitution for the Council itself. The representatives of state and local councils of churches appointed to the General Assembly as authorized in Article IV, Section 2, of this Constitution, shall name to the General Board one-seventh of their number, but not less than five, of whom one-third, or not less than two, shall be women. Each Division shall name to the General Board one lay man, one lay woman, and one youth from among the voting representatives in the General Assembly assigned to the Division. The President, Vice-Presidents, Treasurer and Recording Secretary of the Council, the Chairman, or if for any reason the Chairman is unable to serve a Vice-Chairman, of the General Departments, commissions, Joint Commissions and

Joint Departments, Department of Field Administration, Department of Publication and Distribution and Department of Finance shall be members of the General Board. The Chairmen of other units in the Council may be invited to meet with the General Board as consultants. Each member of the General Board must be a member in good standing of a communion which is a constituent member of the Council.

ARTICLE X—*Divisions*

1. The Council shall constitute four Divisions, the distinctions between which are broadly functional, as follows:

   a) Division of Christian Education
   b) Division of Christian Life and Work
   c) Division of Foreign Missions
   d) Division of Home Missions

   The Division of Christian Education and the Division of Christian Life and Work shall continue and extend the work of certain departments of the Federal Council of the Churches of Christ in America, the International Council of Religious Education, the Missionary Education Movement of the United States and Canada, the National Protestant Council on Higher Education, the United Council of Church Women, and the United Stewardship Council, except as otherwise provided for in this Constitution, with such allocation between the two Divisions as the Council may find to be desirable and effective.

   The Division of Foreign Missions shall continue and extend the work of the Foreign Missions Conference of North America.

   The Division of Home Missions shall continue and extend the work of the Home Missions Council of North America.

   Each Division shall help to carry forward the work of those General Departments, Joint Commissions and Joint Departments, Central Departments and Commissions in which it is represented.

2. Each Division shall have the primary responsibility, subject to the provisions of Article V, Section 1, of this Constitution, for developing the basic philosophy and the requisite programs and procedures within its assigned field, it being understood that there will be interdivisional cooperation and exchange of ideas.

3. Each Division may establish and maintain direct relations with the church boards and agencies corresponding to its field of operation, and with other organizations carrying closely related interests.

4. Each representative on the Council shall be assigned to membership in a Division Assembly in a manner which the Council shall determine, seeking in so far as possible to assign each representative to the Division of his special interest, each Division Assembly to have as nearly as possible one-fourth of the total number, provided that any communion which so desires may designate those of its representatives who are to serve as members of the several Division Assemblies. Each Division in its By-Laws may provide for additional representation from member churches of the Council and from its corresponding church agencies, including the agencies of communions which are not constituent members of the Council but which are in agreement with the Preamble of this Constitution, and also from state and local councils of churches, and councils of church women which are in agreement with the Preamble of this Constitution. The membership in the Division Assembly of any persons from communions which are not constituent members of the Council shall be subject to confirmation by the General Board of the Council unless they represent organizations which are members of the Division in accordance with Article III of the Constitution of the Council.

5. Each Division shall endeavor to secure a full measure of participation in its work on the part of lay representatives, both men and women, and of young people.

6. Within the limitations of the Constitution of the Council and of such general actions as may be taken by it, each Division will have substantial autonomy. This autonomy will be exercised within the following general understandings:

   a) No Division, without specific authorization, shall take actions which impinge upon functions of the Council itself.

   b) No Division shall make financial commitments which involve the Council or any other Division or Commission.

   c) The work of each Division shall be reported to the Council which shall be responsible for its coordination with the work of other Divisions.

7. Each Division shall elect its own Officers. The person chosen as Chairman of the Division shall ordinarily be nominated by the Division for election by the Council as a Vice-President of the Council, in accordance with Article VIII, Section 1, of the Constitution of the Council.

8. Each Division may create such Commissions, Departments and Committees as it may deem necessary or desirable.

9. Each Division may sponsor such professional or lay advisory groups within the field of its interest as the Division may deem desirable.

10. Each Division may make By-Laws in harmony with the Constitution and General By-Laws of the Council.

ARTICLE XI—*General Departments*

1. The Council shall constitute a General Department of United Church Women which shall continue and extend the work of the United Council of Church Women.

2. The Council shall constitute a General Department of United Church Men which shall interpret the work of the Council to church men and serve those agencies of the denominations and state and local councils which are concerned with the special interests and needs of men.

3. Each Department shall be related administratively to the General Board of the Council.

4. Each General Department may draw additional members from member churches of the Council and from its corresponding church agencies, including the agencies of communions which are not constituent members of the Council, but which are in agreement with the Preamble of this Constitution, and also from state and local councils of churches, and councils of church women, which are in agreement with the Preamble of this Constitution. The membership in a General Department of any persons from communions which are not constituent members of the Council shall be subject to confirmation by the General Board of the Council.

5. Each General Department shall have responsibility, subject to the provisions of Article V, Section 1, of this Constitution, for interpreting the program of the Council as a whole, for serving the special needs of its constituency and for determining its organizational procedures and relationships.

6. The basic philosophy and program of a General Department shall be developed as an integral part of the total philosophy and program of the Council.

ARTICLE XII—*Joint Commissions and Joint Departments*

1. The Council shall constitute such Joint Commissions and Joint Departments as may be necessary or desirable in the interest of two or more Divisions. Each Joint Commission and Joint Department shall be functionally responsible to the Divisions which are represented in it but shall be related administratively to one of the Divisions, as the Council may direct.

2. A Joint Commission on Missionary Education shall be constituted which shall continue and extend the work of the Missionary Education Movement of the United States and Canada, including publication.

3. A Joint Department of Stewardship shall be constituted which shall continue and extend the work of the United Stewardship Council.

4. A Joint Department of Evangelism shall be constituted with representatives from all the Divisions.

5. Each Joint Commission and Joint Department may draw additional members from member churches of the Council and from its corresponding church agencies, including the agencies of communions which are not constituent members of the Council but which are in agreement with the Preamble of this Constitution, and also from state and local councils of churches, and councils of church women, which are in agreement with the Preamble of this Constitution. The membership in the Joint Commission or Joint Department of any persons from communions which are not constituent members of the Council shall be subject to confirmation by the General Board of the Council.

6. Each Joint Commission and Joint Department shall have the primary responsibility, subject to the provisions of Article V, Section 1, of this Constitution, for developing the basic philosophy and the requisite programs and procedures within its assigned field, it being understood that there will be inderdepartmental cooperation and exchange of ideas.

ARTICLE XIII—*Central Departments and Services*

1. The Council shall establish and maintain such Central Departments and Service Bureaus as may be necessary or desirable. These Central Departments or Service Bureaus shall serve the Council as a whole, the Divisions, the local and territorial cooperative organizations, and the agencies constituent to the Council.

2. There shall be a Central Department of Field Administration through which the field activities of the Council and of its various units shall be coordinated, and through which the Council shall correlate its field work with the national denominational field programs and with the field programs of state and local councils of churches.
This Department shall include representatives of the Council, of the territorial councils, of the four Divisions and of the General Departments and Joint Commissions and Joint Departments as the General By-Laws may provide. The various Joint Commissions and Joint Departments and Coordinating Committees shall be related to the Field Department through the Divisions to which they are administratively related.

3. There shall be a Central Department of Publication and Distribution constituted by the Council from the membership of the constituent communions of the Council. Not fewer than one-half of the members of the Board of Managers of the Department shall be Executives of the publication houses established by and responsible for publishing activities within the several communions which are members of the Council. In this Department there shall be centered:

   a) All the publication and distribution activities of the Council and all its Divisions, General Departments, Joint Commissions and Joint Departments (other than the Joint Commission on Missionary Education), Central Departments and Bureaus and other units of the Council. Such activities shall include production, distribution, cost accounting and business management but not any control of content or editorial policy or the determination of the use to which surplus from any publication shall be put.

   b) All cooperative publication and distribution activities, other than those on behalf of the Council, which the denominational publishing houses wish to undertake under general policies and procedures which they recommend and which are approved by the General Board. The Department shall be administratively responsible to the Council.

4. There shall be a Central Department of Finance which shall coordinate and carry on the solicitation of financial support for the Council and its several units. The Department may also render service when requested to constituent bodies and to the co-

operating local and territorial councils. The Department shall consist of representatives of all the interests of the Council concerned.

5. Provision shall be made through Central Departments or other appropriate agencies for such interests as:
   a) Architectural Services
   b) Broadcasting and Films
   c) Church World Service
   d) Ecumenical Relations
   e) Public Relations
   f) Research and Survey
   g) Treasury and Business Management

ARTICLE XIV—*Coordinating Committees*

1. The Council shall constitute Coordinating Committees as the media through which the various Divisions and other units will study together the interest, needs and service of the various age groups.
2. The following Coordinating Committees shall be constituted:
   a) Coordinating Committee on Children's Work
   b) Coordinating Committee on Young People's Work
   c) Coordinating Committee on Adult Work
3. The function of these Coordinating Committees shall be primarily that of program consultation and the coordination of field promotion.
4. Each Coordinating Committee may draw additional members from member churches of the Council and from its corresponding church agencies, including the agencies of communions which are not constituent members of the Council but which are in agreement with the Preamble of this Constitution, and also from state and local councils of churches, and councils of church women which are in agreement with the Preamble of this Constitution. The membership in the Coordinating Committee of any persons from communions which are not constituent members of the Council shall be subject to confirmation by the General Board of the Council.
5. Each Coordinating Committee shall be related administratively to one of the Divisions, as the Council may direct.

ARTICLE XV—*Financial Support*

The financial support of the Council, and of its Divisions, shall be primarily the responsibility of the bodies which are members of the Council and of the Divisions.

ARTICLE XVI—*Staff*

The Council shall have a General Secretary, Executive Secretaries of Divisions and such other staff personnel as may be required.

ARTICLE XVII—*Amendments*

Amendments to this Constitution may be proposed at any regular meeting of the General Assembly or at any regular meeting of the General Board. Three months' notice, in writing, of any proposed amendment must be given representatives before action is taken. Subject to this provision, action may be taken by the General Assembly at its next Biennial Meeting. A two-thirds vote of the representatives present and voting is required for adoption, followed by a majority vote of the denominational delegations, each voting separately.

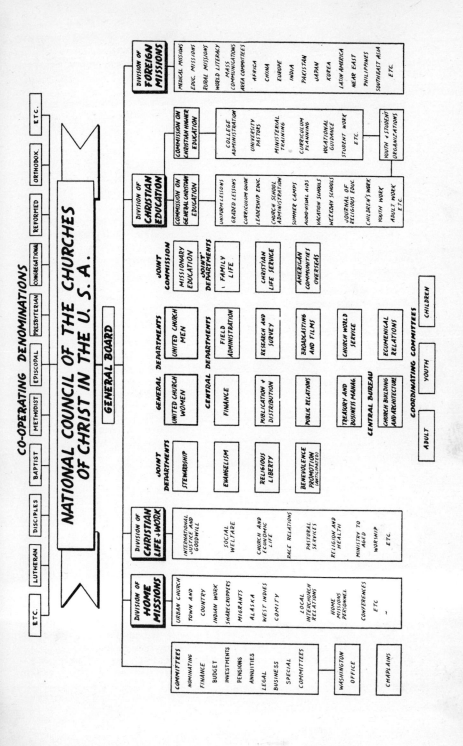

CO-OPERATING DENOMINATIONS

ETC. | LUTHERAN | DISCIPLES | BAPTIST | METHODIST | EPISCOPAL | PRESBYTERIAN | CONGREGATIONAL | REFORMED | ORTHODOX | ETC.

NATIONAL COUNCIL OF THE CHURCHES
OF CHRIST IN THE U. S. A.

GENERAL BOARD

DIVISION OF HOME MISSIONS
- URBAN CHURCH
- TOWN AND COUNTRY
- INDIAN WORK
- SHARECROPPERS
- MIGRANTS
- ALASKA
- WEST INDIES
- COMITY
- RACE RELATIONS
- LOCAL INTERCHURCH RELATIONS
- HOME MISSIONS PERSONNEL
- CONFERENCES
- ETC.

COMMITTEES
- NOMINATING
- FINANCE
- BUDGET
- INVESTMENTS
- PENSIONS
- ANNUITIES
- LEGAL
- BUSINESS
- SPECIAL COMMITTEES

WASHINGTON OFFICE

CHAPLAINS

DIVISION OF CHRISTIAN LIFE & WORK
- INTERNATIONAL JUSTICE AND GOODWILL
- SOCIAL WELFARE
- CHURCH AND ECONOMIC LIFE
- RACE RELATIONS
- PASTORAL SERVICES
- RELIGION AND HEALTH
- MINISTRY TO AGED
- WORSHIP
- ETC.

JOINT DEPARTMENTS
- STEWARDSHIP
- EVANGELISM
- RELIGIOUS LIBERTY
- BENEVOLENCE PROMOTION (ANTICIPATED)

GENERAL DEPARTMENTS
- UNITED CHURCH WOMEN
- UNITED CHURCH MEN

CENTRAL DEPARTMENTS
- FINANCE
- FIELD ADMINISTRATION
- PUBLICATION & DISTRIBUTION
- RESEARCH AND SURVEY
- PUBLIC RELATIONS
- BROADCASTING AND FILMS

CENTRAL BUREAU
- TREASURY AND BUSINESS MANAG.
- CHURCH WORLD SERVICE
- CHURCH BUILDING AND ARCHITECTURE
- ECUMENICAL RELATIONS

JOINT COMMISSION
- MISSIONARY EDUCATION

JOINT DEPARTMENTS
- FAMILY LIFE
- CHRISTIAN LIFE SERVICE
- AMERICAN COMMUNITIES OVERSEAS

DIVISION OF CHRISTIAN EDUCATION
- COMMISSION ON GENERAL CHRISTIAN EDUCATION
  - UNIFORM LESSONS
  - GRADED LESSONS
  - CURRICULUM GUIDE
  - LEADERSHIP EDUC.
  - CHURCH SCHOOL ADMINISTRATION
  - SUMMER CAMPS
  - AUDIO-VISUAL AIDS
  - VACATION SCHOOLS
  - WEEKDAY SCHOOLS
  - JOURNAL OF RELIGIOUS EDUC.
  - CHILDREN'S WORK
  - YOUTH WORK
  - ADULT WORK
  - ETC.
- COMMISSION ON CHRISTIAN HIGHER EDUCATION
  - COLLEGE ADMINISTRATION
  - UNIVERSITY PASTORS
  - MINISTERIAL TRAINING
  - CURRICULUM PLANNING
  - VOCATIONAL GUIDANCE
  - STUDENT WORK
  - ETC.
- YOUTH & STUDENT ORGANIZATIONS

DIVISION OF FOREIGN MISSIONS
- MEDICAL MISSIONS
- EDUC. MISSIONS
- RURAL MISSIONS
- WORLD LITERACY
- MASS COMMUNICATIONS
- AREA COMMITTEES
  - AFRICA
  - CHINA
  - EUROPE
  - INDIA
  - PAKISTAN
  - JAPAN
  - KOREA
  - LATIN AMERICA
  - NEAR EAST
  - PHILIPPINES
  - SOUTHEAST ASIA
  - ETC.

COORDINATING COMMITTEES

ADULT | YOUTH | CHILDREN